Dreaming and Self-Cultivation in China

300 BCE – 800 CE

Harvard-Yenching Institute Monograph Series 138

Dreaming and Self-Cultivation in China

300 BCE – 800 CE

Robert Ford Campany

Published by the Harvard University Asia Center
Distributed by Harvard University Press
Cambridge (Massachusetts) and London 2023

Printed in the United States of America

The Harvard University Asia Center publishes a monograph series and, in coordination with the Fairbank Center for Chinese Studies, the Korea Institute, the Reischauer Institute of Japanese Studies, and other faculties and institutes, administers research projects designed to further scholarly understanding of China, Japan, Vietnam, Korea, and other Asian countries. The Center also sponsors projects addressing multidisciplinary and regional issues in Asia.

The Harvard-Yenching Institute, founded in 1928, is an independent foundation dedicated to the advancement of higher education in the humanities and social sciences in Asia. Headquartered on the campus of Harvard University, the Institute provides fellowships for advanced research, training, and graduate studies at Harvard by competitively selected faculty and graduate students from Asia. The Institute also supports a range of academic activities at its fifty partner universities and research institutes across Asia. At Harvard, the Institute promotes East Asian studies through annual contributions to the Harvard-Yenching Library and publication of the *Harvard Journal of Asiatic Studies* and the Harvard-Yenching Institute Monograph Series.

Cataloging-in-Publication data is on file at the Library of Congress.

ISBN-13: 9780674293724 (hardcover)
ISBN-13: 9780674293731 (paperback)

Index by Mary Mortensen
♾ Printed on acid-free paper
Last figure below indicates year of this printing
32 31 30 29 28 27 26 25 24 23

for Steve Bokenkamp
colleague, teacher, friend

Dreaming is a longer and more lucid wakefulness. Dreaming is knowing. In addition to diurnal learning arises another, necessarily rebellious form of learning, beyond the law.

—Octavio Paz,
The Siren and the Seashell

夢無自性.
Dreams lack any intrinsic nature.

—Kumārajīva,
Mahāprajñāpāramitā sūtra
摩訶般若波羅蜜經

Contents

Preface xi

Acknowledgments xiii

Note to the Reader xv

Introduction: Approaching Dreaming and Self-Cultivation 1

1. Purifying 31
2. Diagnosing 81
3. Spilling Over 122
4. Not Dreaming, Waking Up, and Not Minding the Difference 169

Epilogue: Fish Traps and Rabbit Snares 183

Appendix A: Dream Signs in *Explication of Dreams for Bodhisattvas* 187

Appendix B: Comparing Versions of the Chapter on Diagnostic Dreams in Perfection of Wisdom Texts 194

Appendix C: Incubatory Spells in *Three Dongshen Registers of Red Writs of the Most High* 199

Notes 203

Bibliography 253

Index 297

Preface

This book began its life as a planned part of another book. When I was working on the manuscript that became *The Chinese Dreamscape, 300 BCE–800 CE*, I intended to include a chapter on the relationships between dreaming and self-cultivation. But I soon realized that the topic was too complex and the amount of relevant material too great to be dealt with adequately in such brief compass. So *The Chinese Dreamscape* was published without the planned chapter, certainly for the better. Optimistically, though, I promised at several points in the book's pages to discuss this or that topic in a future work to be titled *Dreaming and Self-Cultivation in China, 300 BCE–800 CE*. This is that book.

All along I hoped, and still hope, that some few intrepid souls might read the two works together. (Should you wish to undertake this ordeal, I recommend starting with *The Chinese Dreamscape*.) While writing this book I had fresh in mind—perhaps too fresh—the approaches and stances I'd taken in the earlier one, and that has surely shaped this one in ways I can't yet see. But I believe that each volume can stand on its own as the report of an investigation into what remains, to me, a fascinating, intrinsically strange, ultimately elusive chapter in the history of human cultures.

Acknowledgments

I am profoundly grateful to the John Simon Guggenheim Memorial Foundation for a year-long fellowship that, supplemented by the dean's office of the College of Arts and Science at Vanderbilt University, afforded me the time to complete this book. It is only by the grace of such support that humanistic scholarship remains possible.

I thank the patient souls who turned out to hear me speak on this topic over the past decade and more, offering their reactions and productive questions. In addition to those listed in the acknowledgments to *The Chinese Dreamscape*, I would here like to express my appreciation to the following institutions and individuals for the chance to share my in-progress work: Arizona State University and Wong Pui See; Brown University, Yang Baoli, and the Department of East Asian Studies; Florida State University, Jimmy Yu, and the Sheng Yen lecture series; the Needham Research Institute of Cambridge University and Avital Rom; Rutgers University and Tao Jiang; and the Southeast Early China Roundtable, whose 2022 meeting was hosted by Steve Kory at the University of Florida.

Beyond the individuals mentioned in the acknowledgments to *The Chinese Dreamscape*, I would here like to offer a further word of thanks to Chris Jensen, a fellow laborer in the vineyard of dreams, who read and commented with great care on a partial draft of this manuscript, as well as to two anonymous readers. All made thoughtful and useful suggestions.

Bob Graham and Kristen Wanner at the Publications Program of Harvard University Asia Center once more proved fantastic to work with. This is certainly a better book because of Kristen's efforts. Special thanks to Linda Campany, Chris Campany, Peter Haskins, Maggie Higgins, Michael Higgins, Sadie the four-legged assistant, and especially

Sue Higgins. Their love, support, and good cheer have sustained me through the writing process.

I count it as one of my greatest good fortunes to have had Stephen R. Bokenkamp as a close colleague and steadfast friend for more than thirty years. It's because of all that I've learned from him that I was able to contemplate attempting a project such as this. This book is dedicated to him with gratitude and affection.

RFC

Note to the Reader

When quoting Western-language publications, I silently convert romanizations of Chinese to the Hanyu Pinyin system (except for the publications' titles). All chronological dates fall in the Common Era (CE) unless noted. Translations are my own except where indicated.

In the notes, when citing particular passages from Chinese texts, I have not supplied the Chinese characters for titles of works listed in the bibliography. Readers may find the characters there.

When referring to specific passages in Chinese texts, I follow these conventions:

- a colon (:) separates a physical volume in a set from a page number in that volume
- a period (.) separates a chapter or scroll number from a page number, even when the volume in question is continuously paginated
- a slash (/) separates a chapter or scroll number from the ordinal position of the item in question in the chapter or scroll in question
- lowercase letters following page numbers indicate recto (a) and verso (b) pages or horizontal registers
- the > sign indicates that instead of accepting the character appearing just before the sign, I am following the alternate reading given just after it.

Asterisks denote reconstructed early pronunciations or presumptive but unattested Sanskrit equivalents. I have consulted several printed and online dictionaries, but most definitions of terms are based on Kroll, *A*

Student's Dictionary of Classical and Medieval Chinese, or (in the case of Buddhist terminology) on A. Charles Muller's Digital Dictionary of Buddhism 電子佛教辭典, available at www.buddhism-dict.net.

INTRODUCTION

Approaching Dreaming and Self-Cultivation

This is a book about the roles dreams and dreaming played in disciplines of self-cultivation in China from roughly 300 BCE to 800 CE. To begin, let's consider a tension already suggested by the juxtaposition of *dreams* and *disciplines*.

A moment's reflection will show that dreams have anomalousness built into them. While dreaming, we interact with familiar people and animals long since deceased, we encounter people now old as young, and we see and do all sorts of things improbable or impossible in waking life. We move through spaces built of oddly reassembled bits of the familiar waking world. The emotions we experience are powerful. Everything is unexpected; everything seems so *real*. Then comes the jolt of waking to discover we were "only" dreaming. At once the dream starts to flee our grasp, the emotions start to thin out, and when recounting our experience we know our words don't come close to conveying what the dream was like. In these and many other ways, from the perspective of our waking lives dreams are incongruous, unpredictable, uncontrollable[1]—in short, quite strange, even if it's a strangeness we recurrently experience throughout our lives.[2]

Yet practitioners of any of the paths of self-cultivation available in the Chinese cultural repertoire during these centuries engaged daily in practices meant to bring most aspects of their experience and comportment under control. They took on regimens designed to discipline their bodies, minds, diet, speech, their senses and feelings, their appetites and desires, their sexuality, their relationships with humans and other creatures, and in some cases even their breathing. Close your eyes, open almost any text to any page, put your finger down, open your eyes, and you'll probably have landed on a passage mandating some practice, stipulating some rule, revealing some method, relaying some cautionary tale, or recommending some attitude to those who sought to transform themselves.

The passage might emphasize the key role such discipline plays in maintaining social order:

> After things are investigated, knowledge is brought about; after knowledge is brought about, one's intentions are sincere; after one's intentions are sincere, one's mind is rectified; after one's mind is rectified, one cultivates oneself; after one has cultivated oneself, one's family is regulated; after one's family is regulated, the state is ordered; after the state is ordered, the world is at peace.[3]
>
> 物格而後知至，知至而後意誠，意誠而後心正，心正而後身修，身修而後家齊，家齊而後國治，國治而後天下平.

It might speak quite specifically about the correct and incorrect ways of carrying out some vital practice:

> When writing a petition, do not mix the brush or inkstone [with those used for other purposes]. Grind the ink, turning to the left forty-nine times; do the same when regrinding. When writing "for your consideration," write it an inch below the phrase "I bow twice." . . . If the writing of the petition is completed and you are interrupted by a minor matter, you cannot send up the petition for an entire year. . . . When writing a petition, leave eight-tenths of an inch margin at the top; on the bottom, there should be room for a column of ants. When writing a petition, spread a kerchief on the table; do not let the petition come into contact with the table. Do not let your robe rest on top of the petition or let it fall to the ground. When you enter the oratory to write a petition, do not let common people make a ruckus, discuss other matters, or use profane language. When writing a petition, do not let the brush touch the water or your mouth. You should close your mouth; you must not eat anything or breathe on [the petition]. When writing a petition, wash your hands first, and write it facing north. If your person has been polluted by exposure to a dead body, you must not write a petition. You must not write incorrect or incomplete characters; the paper must not be ripped or torn; and you must not drink wine, eat meat, or smell of onions. You should straighten your robes and cap.[4]

書章筆硯勿雜用. 研墨左轉四十九, 重磨亦然. 以聞去再拜下一寸.... 若書章已成而有小事, 經年不可上 .... 書章上讓八分, 下通蟻走. 書章以巾敷案上, 不得令著床. 勿以衣著章上及落地. 書章入靜不得常人亂鬧, 論及他事, 臭穢之言.書章不得以筆點水中及口. 當閉口, 不得有所食及氣衝. 書章淨洗手, 向北. 書身經殗穢不得書章. 書不得敗字不成, 紙不得破裂, 不得飲酒食肉薰穢. 當整理衣冠.

It might describe in minute detail the masterful conduct of a past exemplar:

When entering the gate of his lord, he would draw himself in, as if the gate were not large enough to admit him. He would not come to a halt at the center of the doorway and when walking would not tread upon the threshold. When passing by his appointed place, his countenance would become alert and serious. He would hasten his steps, his words falling to a whisper as if he could barely get them out. When he ascended to the lord's dais with the hem of his gown gathered in his hands, he would draw himself in, slowing his breath to the point that it seemed as if he were not breathing at all. Upon leaving the lord's dais, his expression would relax as he descended the top stair and he would seem at ease. On reaching the bottom of the stairs he would hasten forward smoothly, as though gliding upon wings. When returning to his own place he would resume his attitude of cautious respect.[5]

入公門鞠躬如也如不容, 立不中門, 行不履閾. 過位色勃如也. 足躩如也, 其言似不足者. 攝齊升堂鞠躬如也屏氣似不息者, 出降一等逞顏色怡怡如也. 沒階趨進翼如也, 復其位踧踖如也.

It might vividly portray the consequences of violating moral codes or social norms:

During the Song there lived one Zhou Zong, a native of Feiru in Guangling commandery. In the seventh year of the Yuanjia period he followed Dao Yanzhi on a northern campaign. The force was defeated. Along with six others from his city, Zong fled and traveled furtively. North of Pengcheng they came to an empty monastery with no monks residing in it. Within it was an icon bearing bodily marks made from crystals. These they stole and took into town to exchange for food. One of the men was weakened by illness, and the others, slighting him, did

> not share any of the food with him. Three or four years after they'd returned home, Zong and each of the other five by turn contracted leprosy and died. Only the man who had received none of the food escaped this fate and survived.[6]
>
> 宋周宗者, 廣陵肥如人也. 元嘉七年隨劉彥之北伐王師失利. 與同邑六人逃竄間行. 於彭城北遇一空寺, 無有僧徒, 中有形像, 以水精為相. 因共竊取, 出村貿食. 其一人羸病, 等輩輕之, 獨不得分. 既各還家. 三四年中宗等五人相係病癩而死. 不得分者獨獲全免.

Or it might depict someone evaluating someone else's character, their fitness for carrying out a cultivational practice, or their performance of a culturally prized role, as in the following two passages:

> Secretariat Director Pei Kai evaluated Xiahou Xuan: "Solemn and stern, like entering the imperial palace and temple; he does not seek respect yet others naturally respect him." . . .
>
> "When I see Zhong Hui, it is like gazing at an armory; all one sees are spears and polearms in thick profusion."
>
> "When I look at Fu Gu: a vastness in which nothing is not contained."
>
> "When I look at Shan Tao, it is like climbing a mountain and looking out: a remoteness that is deep and faraway."[7]
>
> 裴令公目夏侯太初: 肅肅如入廊廟中, 不修敬而人自敬.... 見鍾士季, 如觀武庫, 但覩矛戟. 見傅蘭碩, 江廧靡所不有. 見山巨源, 如登山臨下, 幽然深遠.

> Cai Jing had a neighbor whose family name was Chen. . . . Hearing that there was a divine personage at Cai's house, he appeared at the gate, knocking his head on the ground and seeking an audience. So Wang Yuan directed for him to be brought forward. This man requested to be made a Supporting Express Courier like Cai Jing. Wang told him to stand facing the sun for a moment; while he did so, Wang regarded him from behind. Then Wang pronounced: "Whew! Your heart is perverse and not correct. You will never be able to be taught the Way of transcendence."[8]
>
> 經比舍有姓陳者, 失其名.... 聞經家有神人. 乃詣門叩頭. 求乞拜見. 於是遠使引前與語. 此人便欲從驅使. 比於蔡經. 遠曰: 君且向日而立. 遠從後觀之曰. 噫, 君心邪不正. 終未可教以仙道.

Whatever the case, dreaming was a type of experience that lay athwart these carefully constructed programs for self-fashioning. It might wreck them, it might be used to further them, it might even reveal new ways to do them, but this much is clear: given how frequently and how freely human beings dream, any discipline of self-cultivational practice had to address dreaming in some way.[9] This book considers some of the evidence for how this was done. But before taking up that evidence, I must explain how I've approached it.

Paradigms and the Dreamscape

Some might expect a book on this topic to proceed differently than this one does. They might look for a survey showing diachronic changes in how dreams were viewed. Alternatively, they might anticipate seeing each tradition or "ism" taken up separately, assuming that "Daoism," say, must have had a single official doctrine about dreams. It would then be a relatively simple matter of seeing how that doctrine or belief was "expressed" in various texts.[10] They might hope such a treatment would attend as well to borrowings across the isms, with the implicit supposition that each must originally have espoused a single stance toward dreaming, only to see it altered by external "influences" over time.

A diachronic survey of even a fraction of the relevant texts would run to several volumes and would amount to an anthology of sources rather than a critical reflection on them. (An anthology of sources would be useful but isn't what I attempt here.) A treatment that organized textual material in terms of traditions would face several additional challenges, not least of which are common but flawed assumptions about what religious and cultural traditions *are*, the metaphors by which they're construed as essentialized entities, and how people and artifacts relate to them. I've treated these methodological quagmires elsewhere, so let me here refer the reader to those studies and move on.[11]

The fundamental question this book asks is not when certain ideas or practices originated, how they changed through time, which tradition they belonged to, or how they expressed the essence or doctrines of this or that ism, but *how they worked*—what we might call their *practical logic*. What I mean is this: Given any particular notion of what sort of event a dream is, only certain responses to it make sense. Conversely, any textually depicted or scripturally recommended attitude or action involving a dream presupposes some view of what the dream is and excludes other views (including other views that might be found in the same text, even in the same passage). And here is the crucial point: when we read through the body of extant texts (let's call it *the archive*) attuned to this practical logic rather than to sectarian affiliation, we find important differences, to be sure, but the most telling are differences at the level of how the ideas and practices worked and the work they did, *not* at the level of tradition-specific nomenclature. (More will be said on practical logic later in this introduction.)

The situation resembles Jonathan Z. Smith's characterization of the study of the religions of the Late Antique Mediterranean:

> The traditional vague terminology of "Early Christianity," "Jewish," "Gentile," "Pagan," "Greco-Oriental," etc. will not suffice. Each of these generic terms denote[s] complex plural phenomena. For purposes of comparison, they must be disaggregated and *each component compared with respect to some larger topic of scholarly interest*. That is to say, *with respect to this or that feature, modes of Christianity may differ more significantly between themselves than between some mode of one or another Late Antique religion*. The presupposition of "holism" is not "phenomenological," it is a major, conservative, theoretical presupposition which has done much mischief in the study of religious materials, nowhere more so than in the question of Christian "origins."[12]

To borrow Smith's wording, my approach has been to select a "larger topic of scholarly interest"—the ways in which dreaming intersected discourses and practices of self-cultivation—and to develop questions that get at "this or that feature" by pinpointing differences and similarities not immediately obvious. This takes us beneath the surfaces of what texts say to disclose how ideas and practices *worked* and *what work they allowed to be done* with dreams. With respect to this or that feature, two passages in texts designated "Daoist" may—and, as we'll see, in fact do—differ more significantly between themselves than from passages in texts conventionally designated "Buddhist," "Confucian," or what have you. In other words, the fact that a passage appears in a text associated with this or that tradition is not the only thing to note about it; it might even be the least important thing, depending on what our question is.

By proceeding in this way I do not intend to suggest that there were no important differences between, say, Daoist and Buddhist and Confucian repertoires of practices and goals; that there wasn't intense competition among distinct lineages of ordination and regimens of practice; or that practitioners participating in these repertoires placed no importance on which lineage they'd been ordained into.[13] What I do suggest is that these traditions didn't constitute organic wholes[14] and that focusing on practical logic allows us to see other important differences as well as sometimes surprising commonalities across lineages, traditions, and communities. To borrow Smith's terminology again, I here practice an "analytical approach" where the "scholar's tools" are foregrounded and

> the result can no longer be thought of as "natural" but rather stands . . . marked as a construction. Whether this fabrication be judged as informative . . . depends not on presumptions of congruence but on the exercise of a critical intelligence that assesses the cognitive gain or loss made possible by the constructive difference and distance from [the data per se]. The fabrication is, necessarily, a representation rather than a claimed presence . . . . The cognitive power of any translation, model, map, generalization or redescription . . . is, by this understanding, a result of its *difference* from the subject matter in question.[15]

How, then, to proceed in a way that will disclose the practical logic at work in texts and practices?

In *The Chinese Dreamscape* I developed the metaphor of *dreamscape* to characterize the range of ways in which dreams were thought about, talked and written about, and responded to in a given culture and era—in short, a culture's *imaginaire* of dreaming. I think of the Chinese dreamscape as populated by a handful of distinct *paradigms*, each a cluster of answers to basic questions about what dreams are and how dreamers should react to them, each therefore resulting in a coherent, interlocking set of ideas and patterns of action. In the case of intersections between dreaming and self-cultivation, the list of questions looks something like this:

For any given text, what sort of thing should the practitioner imagine the dream to be? (Is it a mental event, a demonic assault, a divine visit, a soul journey, a sign of *qi* 氣 imbalance, an index of karmic status, an instructive example of the transformation of things?)

How is the "self" under cultivation imagined or metaphorically constructed? (Is it a walled city with gates, a federation of agents with their own agendas, a bundle of causes and conditions with an opaque multi-lifetime karmic history, a human being gradually transforming into a god or Buddha?)

How should, or how did, the practitioner respond to the dream? (Ignore it, exorcise it, interpret it, follow its directives, record it, tell of it, keep it secret, look up its meaning in a manual?)

How does the dream impinge on, disturb, reflect, or further the practitioner's disciplines of self-cultivation during waking hours? (Is it an unwelcome interruption of cultivational pursuits? Does it result from and extend those pursuits? Does it indicate progress in those pursuits, or, conversely, reveal obstacles?)

Three features of the dreamscape and its paradigms should be borne in mind. First, discerning any given text's answers to these questions is usually a matter of inference; we must often delve beneath what a text says to grasp what it implies on the topic of dreams. Second, rather than being thought up independently and then imposed on the texts, these paradigms emerged from the process of pondering the above questions in relation to them. And third, the paradigms are heuristic tools for making sense of textual materials. They offer a way of redescribing what disparate texts depict or recommend in a way that foregrounds the underlying practical logic involved. There are surely passages that combine or blur these paradigms or that seem to fit none of them, but I wager that the paradigms are nevertheless useful for understanding both the large number of passages they do fit and any possible passages they do not.

In *The Chinese Dreamscape* I identified five paradigms that can be observed at work in the late classical and medieval Chinese archive. Two were investigated in that book and are only occasionally mentioned here:

The PROSPECTIVE PARADIGM: What appears in dreams is a code, a message couched in symbols that must be interpreted by someone. The interpretation yields a prediction of future events. Dream interpretation is a type of divination.

The VISITATION PARADIGM: Dreams are face-to-face encounters with other beings. The encounter is direct, not in code; the dream is a real event in the world, not a meta-statement about events in the world. Something in waking life changes as a result of the dream encounter.

The three paradigms that take up most of *this* book, focused as it is on the relationships between dreaming and self-cultivation, are these:

The PURIFICATION PARADIGM: The dream is an incursion by an exogenous, sometimes malevolent, being, or else its content is something foul, disgusting, or improper. Either way, it poses a threat to self-cultivational practice because, at a minimum, it leaves the dreamer in a state of pollution, while in the worst cases it might even threaten the dreamer's health. The response takes the form of an exorcistic, prophylactic, or cleansing ritual whose function is to restore the dreamer to a state of purity. (In *The Chinese Dreamscape* I referred to this as the "exorcistic paradigm" because I had in mind the many cases where contact by an exogenous demonic agent triggers the dream. I now think that cases of demonic assault should be seen as a subcategory of a larger set whose crux is that the dream is a polluting contact. Sometimes no exogenous agent is directly responsible for bringing this about.)

The DIAGNOSTIC PARADIGM: The dream is a coded message requiring interpretation. The message concerns the self-cultivator's progress on the path, sometimes pointing to obstacles otherwise opaque. The text provides keys for correctly unlocking the diagnosis expressed in the dream signs. It might or might not also recommend practices to surmount the indicated obstacle.

The SPILLOVER PARADIGM: The dream is a continuation of the dreamer's waking self-cultivational activity. It is almost always a direct encounter, not a coded message. The dreamer continues to perform the role being cultivated in waking-life practice. The dreamer is not a passive witness to the dream but an agent interacting with the other beings encountered within its frame. Dreams are here an extension of waking practice and a portal to wider possibilities for practice. (This paradigm can be seen as a subset of the VISITATION PARADIGM.)

This book moves across centuries, traditions, and textual genres to elucidate each of these three paradigms by turn. My goal is to map and better understand these zones of the late classical and medieval Chinese dreamscape, not to amass as many textual instances of them as possible.

With two main exceptions in which I treat whole texts at some length—*Sutra on the Explication of Dreams for Bodhisattvas* in chapter 2 and *Records of Master Zhou's Communications with the Unseen World* in chapter 3—I will mostly take up one passage at a time, looking at it independently of the text in which it's now embedded and setting it alongside other passages from the same or other texts. This is an important aspect of the analytical approach I've taken here. There are three main reasons for it. First, I am primarily interested in the practical logic or cognitive schemas that shape the various approaches to dreams and self-cultivation that we find documented in texts. Crucially, this logic and these schemas become visible at the level of the passage, not of the whole text.[16] Second, any given text of any length typically contains several such schemas, not just one. Indeed, a single passage may incorporate multiple schemas; later in this introduction and again in chapter 1 we'll look at an example built on no fewer than five. Third, many texts from the period considered here—at least texts of the sort relevant to self-cultivation—were *assemblages* of discrete sections and passages in the first place. Few texts as they have come down to us were written in their entirety *ab initio* as unitary wholes by single authors. Rather, bits of text (as well as units of self-cultivational practice) often had a modular character, allowing them to circulate independently and be incorporated into diverse textual and ritual frameworks by multiple fashioners of texts and practices in the service of diverse rhetorical and praxeological needs.[17]

I have also, to some extent, extracted texts from their specific institutional, sectarian, and lineage—but not their practical—contexts. This is because I prefer to treat each text as, in the words of Antonello

Palumbo, "the product of historical actors, three-dimensional human beings engaging their own world, rather than the putative witness to some ill-defined sectarian tradition that it is usually taken to be or not be."[18] I view the people who fashioned the texts, read them, copied them, and followed their prescriptions as agents striving, under material and social constraints, to improve their soteriological fortunes however they understood these, not as avatars of isms.[19]

Approaching the Texts

Before we turn to particular texts, it will be helpful to consider at a general level what sorts of things they were, how they came to be produced and preserved, and how they were related to the people who made them, read them, and sometimes followed their directives. This is necessary because the advent first of printing, and then of digital and electronic media, fundamentally changed what texts are. Standing in the wake of these momentous technological shifts, we must exert considerable effort to mentally place ourselves in the manuscript culture that preceded them. It is only by doing so that we can understand what sorts of things texts should and shouldn't be taken as evidence of, and how to approach them.

Let me begin by starkly posing a problem. Many of the texts considered below are prescriptive or normative in nature. They largely consist of directives about what to do or avoid doing, or they depict people who have internalized such directives and who exemplify the norms they want to inculcate. Take any such text at random. How can we know that it wasn't simply written at one go by a lone author in a studio, deposited somewhere, and then ignored until the printing of whatever canon or edition it now appears in? How are we justified in thinking that anyone ever paid it any mind at all? To put it differently, we have a large number of texts that were written in Chinese[20] between 300 BCE and 800 CE and that are stuffed with all sorts of regulations, recommendations, mandates, warnings, prohibitions, and specifications about what readers should and should not do. Why assume that anyone other than their respective authors ever even saw these texts, much less put any of their many prescriptions into practice? How can we claim to go beyond what texts say to what people actually thought, said, cared about, and did—assuming that it's those people and their activities that we most want to understand?

Granted, we should never facilely read a prescriptive text as descriptive, taking guidelines about what people should do as a prima facie description of what they did. Rules for life in Daoist or Buddhist monasteries, for instance, should not be taken as straightforward accounts of actual practice, at least not without considered justification. This is a perennial historiographical problem. But the questions in the previous paragraph presuppose a certain model of what texts were that has become so familiar we often forget there were ever alternatives. It is a model of texts that sees them as mostly detached from readers and from life as it was lived. And that model is severely anachronistic when it comes to a manuscript culture.

One still finds mentions of when this or that ancient or medieval Chinese text was "published." The locution conjures an image of a solitary "author" who emerges from a studio to mail off a typescript from the local post office (or to email digital files from the local internet server) to a publisher who converts the material into physical objects (or electronic bits) that could be limitlessly disseminated to a potentially worldwide faceless mass of readers. But this image is misleading. In a manuscript culture, considerable investment of materials and labor was required every time a copy of a text was produced. Additionally, each individual who newly acquired a copy had to do so through a connection with some other individual. The transmission of each copy was therefore a laborious physical process unfolding within a network of persons in the same place and at (or near) the same time. All these people invested heavily in what the text had to say and expended considerable effort in preserving it against oblivion.

This matters not just as an aspect of the history of textual production and consumption in China, as important as that topic is, but also for what it tells us about the social embeddedness of the texts that have survived. Each bears witness not just to what one "author" had to say but also to what many other readers and scribes thought important enough to transmit and preserve. In fact, the default modern notion of authorship breaks down entirely. Many recent studies have shown that copying amounted to coauthoring.[21] Unless we are talking about an autograph manuscript buried in a tomb or sealed in a cave, unattested in the archive and only recently recovered by archeologists, every now-extant text from the pre-printing era is the product of many hands. Given the hazards confronting bamboo, paper, and silk artifacts in premodern times, there was simply no other way for a text to have perdured. Although we often take it for granted, the sheer survival of any text down to today is something of a marvel.

Texts from the manuscript era must, then, be seen primarily in relation to the readers, copyists, collectors, and transmitters who invested in their production. We misapprehend them if we see them as immaterial containers of words and ideas directed to any conceivable audience or to no audience at all. It would be a mistake to separate the contents of what texts had to say from either the material conditions under which they were produced, transmitted, and preserved, or from the people who did the producing, transmitting, and preserving. The demographic range of involved parties has recently been shown to be much wider than previously assumed.[22] And when it comes to texts about self-cultivational matters, many of those involved in their production were practitioners themselves, and practitioners were treading paths that in this period were taught, in part, through texts. Texts and practitioners must therefore be seen as inseparable.[23] Even when it's impossible to prove from extant sources that there was ever any individual who put a particular text's directives into practice—as in the case of a Buddhist guide to dream interpretation discussed in chapter 2—the text's very circulation was itself an important aspect of social practice. Moreover, the issuing of prescriptions was itself a practice.

Creating, compiling, copying, and disseminating prescriptions were not, then, exercises occurring in a separate realm from the lived world of practice. They formed part of that world. Producing and engaging with texts about self-cultivation were themselves modalities of self-cultivation. That is, making, copying, collating, reciting, memorizing, transmitting, and even correctly handling copies of texts about self-cultivation were all practices held to be conducive to advancement on one or another self-cultivational path. The texts themselves often mandated these treatments, to the extent that these texts became self-ritualizing artifacts. Their production and transmission cannot be separated from the people who made and copied them and from the body of practices on which they offered instruction. Although we sometimes can't prove that anyone actually carried out a given text's prescriptions, we can at least posit that there must have been many people invested in perpetuating the text and its prescriptions. Texts needed readers, copyists, transmitters, and expounders to perdure; people needed guidance, instruction, and frameworks for practice to advance on their cultivational paths.[24]

If our modern, print-era notion of authorship is anachronistic, so is our print-era-based image of the reader and of reading. For one thing, "moderns tend to read texts silently and alone. We often take for granted that one's relationship to a text is a matter of eye and mind, forgetting the long history of reading aloud alone or in groups that was often central to devotional textuality."[25] Engagement with texts was communal, vocal, sonic, somatic, and ritualized. People usually came to the sorts of texts discussed in this book through these matrices of embodiment and relationship. Further, these weren't just any texts. Most of them were canonical in one sense or another—uniquely invested with authority by the communities in which they were transmitted. And finally, the stakes for readers could not have been higher. Successful practice might result in becoming an exemplary human being, a Buddha, or an exalted deity, while failure meant being dragged before underworld magistrates to answer for one's sins, suffering torture, or being condemned to ceaseless rebirth in a world of suffering.

Still, we may wonder what it was about the sorts of texts examined in these pages—features of the texts themselves, not just of their extra-textual framing and staging—that helped inspire the considerable effort of transmitting them. After all, many texts ended up not being preserved. Bibliographic catalogs list the titles of many once-extant texts that were subsequently lost; many more surely once existed of which not even a trace remains. Can we identify any characteristics of surviving texts that may have contributed to their successful preservation? To return to the topic at hand, how is dreaming addressed in texts in ways that might have spurred readers to take up the practices prescribed or at least to continue propagating copies? "Let us assume that one of the tasks to which a poem must offer a solution is that of its own perpetuation," Haun Saussy writes—and the same task confronted texts (whether in prose or verse) relating dreaming to self-cultivation.[26]

What is needed to answer this question is a *rhetorical reading*. Texts concerning self-cultivation were made to do things to readers—to persuade, move, motivate, reorient, or change them.[27] In short, they are rhetorical artifacts, not disinterested descriptions of states of affairs, meta-level artifacts bearing no relationship to actual practice, or reports of things a community already entirely agreed on (no need of a text for that). Such artifacts had many devices for persuading readers, foremost among them the framing of their messages as the direct speech of gods, Buddhas, sages, or worthies from the past, as well as the promise of extraordinary benefits for anyone who promulgated copies of them. But there is one less obvious persuasive strategy we'll often encounter: texts portray dire problems, depict ideal outcomes that would result if the problems were eliminated, and prescribe specific ways to solve the problems and realize the outcomes.[28] If a text could convince readers of the existence and seriousness of a problem—or, in the case of obvious and ubiquitous predicaments (such as death and illness), if it could convince them of its particular characterization of their cause—and also persuade them of the efficacy of its recommended solutions, then it upped the likelihood of its perpetuation through time. This is why, I think, we find many a text claiming that it alone conveys the knowledge or techniques needed to solve a problem it depicts in harrowing terms. The more serious the problem, the more potent the prescribed techniques, and the more glorious the promised outcome, the more urgent the call for readers to invest in transmitting the text and following its guidelines. And the more numerous the texts and practices jostling for sponsorship by practitioners, the greater the role these textual features needed to play in order for any one text to secure a following and strengthen its odds of survival.

There were, of course, no guarantees when it came to readers' and hearers' reception.[29] Readers might be so persuaded by the text's message that they enacted its recommendations and helped to perpetuate it, especially if others in their lineage or community were doing so. (Again, here we must discard the model of individual readers as consumers with an abundance of texts readily available to them. Most readers of texts on self-cultivation would have come to them through interactions with teachers or fellow practitioners and would have had access only to a limited number of manuscripts.) Or they might never have come into contact with any given text or might have rejected it once having done so. Between these poles were numerous other possibilities: commenting on the text, criticizing it, supplementing it, only selectively following its dictates, borrowing from it, recontextualizing, reworking, reframing, emending, or repurposing it, using it as a protective talisman or devotional object, or destroying as many copies of it as possible.[30]

It's also because of texts' need to persuade audiences that we may infer from them some things about those audiences. Ancient and medieval text-fashioners knew much about the people they hoped would be reading their texts. The makers of texts on self-cultivation would have needed to understand their readers in order to move them to take up some new practice, which would in turn perpetuate the text urging them to do so. When read carefully, the texts can be seen to imply some things their makers expected their audiences to know, prefer, or be concerned about. That is, they reveal some things about their *implied readers*.[31] We can glean much by noticing the things texts do and don't explain. Allusions and other intertextual features presuppose readers competent to recognize them. In the case of things texts insist on strongly or topics they explain at length, we can reasonably assume these aren't matters the implied readers already agreed with or knew about. Then there are things mentioned but not explained. Absent textual corruption (always a possibility), these are probably things the text's makers assumed their readers to be familiar with. Texts met readers on familiar territory, then led them to new places.

Much of this book's source material, then, is a body of communally produced and transmitted textual artifacts designed by their makers to shape people's experiences and steer their efforts at self-cultivation as these related to dreaming. These artifacts' very survival constitutes evidence that they fulfilled this purpose to some extent.

Self-Cultivation

For the purposes of this study, what I mean by self-cultivation is simply any communally sanctioned practice, program, or prescription for advancing oneself toward some soteriological goal. By soteriological I mean some improvement of status or condition that texts promise will result (or depict as resulting) from the practices in question. In a book of this size, it is impossible to discuss at length any of the self-cultivational paths that will be referred to throughout, and I must presume that my readers are at least broadly familiar with them. We'll glimpse them only where they intersect with dreaming. But I would like to explain some ways in which I approach the topic of self-cultivation. And before doing so, it is necessary to mention one way in which I do *not* approach it: through individuals' experiences.

Dreams are, of course, a type of experience. One thing that becomes abundantly clear from the texts studied here and in *The Chinese Dreamscape* is that, with a few interesting exceptions,[32] dreams were not seen as events of a psychological nature happening solely inside dreamers' heads. Even so, dreams were presumably still experienced privately, in this sense: if we could travel back in time and sit beside someone who was asleep, we might detect from their motions and muffled sounds that they were dreaming, but we wouldn't know what they'd dreamt until they'd woken and told us. Even when the dream was seen as a real encounter with other beings, as it often was, it was an encounter unknowable by others until the dreamer woke and spoke of it.[33] We might wonder, then, how a book on dreaming and self-cultivation in a past era is even possible.

The idea that the fundamental datum of religion or of the study of religion is some sort of special experience is of relatively recent inception. Its roots lie in the Protestant Reformation; it was developed and furthered by the writings of Friedrich Schleiermacher (d. 1834) and others; and William James famously built an entire approach to religion on it in *Varieties of Religious Experience* (1902).[34] These efforts succeeded insofar as many people today would be hard pressed to identify anything about a religion that matters besides its participants' personal experiences. This privileging of experience is a modern trope that we must bracket if we want to understand a culture such as that of medieval China. There, what counted seems to have been forming selves and building lineages through instruction, self-examination, and ritual practice. When practitioners did report putatively significant experiences, their reports were subject to evaluation by teachers and communities. It was these other parties who determined what meaning, if any, the experience might have.[35] The experience-based model of religion thus has it backward: what mattered most wasn't individuals' experiences per se but their interpretation and reception by others in a community of practice.

Historians have no access to other people's dream experiences except through texts, which isn't to deny that people have had and still have uncanny, "special" experiences of many sorts.[36] In this I concur with Robert Sharf, who has written cogently on the topic.[37] Robert Orsi, a historian and ethnographer of modern American Catholicism, urges us to "approach history and religion through a matrix of presence,"[38] writing of one example: "Bernadette's experience . . . arose within a particular context. But it does not follow from this that the context accounts for or explains the experience or what becomes of the many lives touched by it in the . . . afterlife of the experience. Such narratives of the social origins and consequences of experiences of the gods really present can never be exhaustive for many reasons, beginning with what those on the scene say, which is that the gods *came to them*."[39] In this book I don't try to explain accounts of experience, whether by reducing them to their social contexts, invoking a psychological theory, or otherwise. Nor do I attempt to give an exhaustive account of dreams (or of anything else). I try to see what was and could be done with dream experiences, to learn what projects those experiences were subordinated to and what projects they disrupted, and to examine the practical logic, communal expectations, and affordances of discourse and action in terms of which dreams mattered. Dreams were putatively experienced by people, who together with others *made something of* the dream, and it's the written traces of this making that constitute the material we have to work with. Arguing about whether this or that dream "really happened" is not a viable historiographic agendum. This isn't an ontological claim but rather an assertion about what's knowable from past records. But those records bear witness to the labors of those who made and circulated them, and they, too, are presences, if one chooses to speak of them thus.

What's studied in this book, then, is not individuals' experiences (or their "beliefs"[40]) per se but the latticework of ideas and practices within which their experiences could acquire meaning, as well as the matrices of norms and social patterns through which their experiences were brought into alignment with collectively defined self-cultivational paths. My approach to that latticework and those matrices is informed by three main clusters of ideas: the canonicity of practice, practical logic, and the performance of roles.

Canonicity of Practice

The rules, rituals, and procedures structuring practitioners' efforts at self-cultivation can be seen as so many canons of practice. I intend "canon" in the etymological sense of a rule or set of rules. Out of the totality of possible ways of acting, speaking, and being, each path of self-cultivation was formed around a selection of ways deemed soteriologically advantageous—ways of acting that were seen as moving the practitioner toward a collectively defined goal. Practitioners were individuals who had voluntarily submitted to the constraint of tradition.[41] The practices they undertook constituted not an orthodoxy but an orthopraxy, a gradual process of self-transformation under the guidance of teachers and the authority of norms handed down from an authoritative past. Such training, to borrow Mary Carruthers's language, is perhaps best understood in terms of "an apprenticeship model, more like masonry or carpentry than anything in the modern academy." Despite our frequent "over-concentration on the individual and personal," in ancient and medieval contexts of self-cultivation as I intend it here "the individual always had his or her being within a larger community, within which a single life was 'perfected,' 'made complete,' by acquiring a civic being and identity."[42] Individuals were fashioned into new subjects with new identities.[43]

To understand these disciplines of practice we must consider the ideas that informed them. But this isn't the same thing as investigating individual practitioners' "belief in" or assent to doctrines. The ideas relevant here are those implied or entailed by what was done in the practices themselves (or what was recommended to be done in prescriptions for practice), that is, those ideas in terms of which the practices made sense, not those that might or might not happen to have been in individuals' heads. It was a matter of the logic inherent to the practices (a notion further explored below), not of the thoughts or beliefs of practitioners. (Note that this doesn't require us to slight the role of faith, if by faith we mean the considering of something or someone as trustworthy.[44]) Sometimes texts explicitly articulate those ideas; sometimes we must infer them. But to say that understanding a practice means considering the ideas that structured it is not to say that the practice merely "expresses" the ideas. Lamenting the influence of post-Reformation Protestantism on the study of religion and culture, Caroline Humphrey and James Laidlaw observe that "the efficacy of ritual has been terminally undermined by understanding ritualization as a modality for communicating or expressing the religious beliefs and moral ideas of the participants. . . . So pervasive is this idea that ritual on its own, without subjective convictions, comes, for many, to seem mere mumbo-jumbo."[45] Sarah Coakley makes the point this way: practice "is no optional frill attendant on metaphysical theories acquired somewhere else; rather it is the very medium of such belief, ultimately transcending the thought/action divide. Or to put it conversely, in Talal Asad's acute observation, the inability 'to enter into communion with God' may well be 'a function of untaught bodies.'"[46]

One fruitful way to think about any discipline meant to instill new dispositions and shape the bodies and minds of practitioners—insofar (and only insofar) as it can be said to have succeeded in this—has been developed first by Marcel Mauss and then by Pierre Bourdieu under the name *habitus*. As both use this term, it

> refers to an ensemble of schemata of perception, thinking, feeling, evaluating, speaking, and acting that structures all the expressive, verbal, and practical manifestations and utterances of a person. . . . It is "embodied history, internalized as a second nature," as Bourdieu says, "the active presence of the whole past of which it is the product." By contrast with the familiar sociological concept of role [on which more shortly], habitus refers to something *incorporated*, *not* to a set of norms or expectations existing independently of and externally to the agent. Likewise, as it is thought to be part of the living organism, . . . habitus refers to a generative principle, not to a set of fixed and finite rules.[47]

Seen in this way, the canons of practice relevant here were not ways of expressing personhoods or beliefs already formed by other means but instead were ways of producing personhoods, beliefs, and dispositions of specific sorts.

Modern scholars have often viewed certain texts—particularly those deemed "philosophical" and generated during the late Warring States and Han periods—through the categories of moral philosophy, thought, or doctrine. If one wishes to do so one can, of course, excise ideas from their cultural settings of practice, render them into propositional form, and set them onto a sort of culture-free, universal game board populated by disembodied concepts moved about detachedly as though they were pieces in a chess match. I fear that this sort of still-prevalent approach risks losing sight of everything else at stake in that chess match, as if the ideas in question hadn't emerged from—and carried no profound implications for—the patterns of living, styles of ritual and social practice, and communities of practitioners that had produced the texts in the first place. My point is not that the texts don't talk about matters we tend to isolate as moral or philosophical. It's that they talk about—or assume the reader's prior understanding of—much else besides, and in ways that connect the moral (understood narrowly) with other areas of action and concern that don't usually factor into modern philosophical discourse at all. Even works that at first glance seem engaged in abstract thought or technical niceties for their own sake—such as the discourse of "names and reality" (*ming shi* 名實)—upon closer inspection turn out to bear directly on projects of self-cultivation.[48] This isn't to deny texts' sophistication as products and vehicles of reflection. It's rather to recall the contexts and projects of practice in which they were produced, read, discussed, and transmitted. My own approach has been informed by the work of Pierre Hadot on ancient Mediterranean philosophies as "ways of life," Michel Foucault's work on the same texts as "technologies of the self" and "hermeneutics of the subject," and Wiebke Denecke's monograph on "masters literature" in early China, with its close attention to textual genre and rhetorical form.[49]

Practical Logic and Metaphoric Coherence

Much of this book's subject matter involves the practical logic operating at the interface of dreaming and self-cultivation. What I mean by practical logic is as follows. In textual passages mentioning dreaming in relation to self-cultivation of whatever sort, we find dreaming framed (explicitly or implicitly) as an event of a certain kind. This way of framing it both enables and constrains how it should be responded to. It creates certain affordances[50]—that is, it makes possible certain responsive actions—while also closing off other possible avenues of response. Or, if we start with texts and move back toward dreams, the particular action prescribed by a text in response to a dream entails that the dream is a particular kind of event at the same time that it rules out (or is incompatible with) other views. It's this *fit* or *compatibility* (or coherence, systematicity, or entailment) between the sorts of things dreams were framed as being, on the one hand, and the responses to them prescribed or described in texts, on the other, that I mean by practical logic.[51] Neil Schmid writes of

> how cultures use cognitive models to structure understanding and experience—models that are instantiated through cultural practice and given material form for transmission and retention. Such *gestalt* representations are intersubjective constructs that schematize knowledge and experience into "chunks" such as scripts, scenarios, and referential frames. They provide efficient mental strategies for individuals to gain access to complex sets of knowledge rapidly, simultaneously, and without sequential restraints, such as having to go through a checklist of semantic features. Cognitive models constrain but do not determine thought and action.[52]

In short, objects, images, architectural spaces, and texts "instantiate cultural models that schematize" and stabilize elements of a culture's *imaginaire*, enabling verbal representation and structuring ritual performance.[53]

This practical logic has the following features:

- It is not just a characteristic of texts. Practical logic is instantiated in structures or scripts of understanding, experience, knowledge, action (including but not limited to ritual action), and narrative. It spans the divides among thought, action, and narrative.
- It is shared, not private; it "knits with social life all along" since it both arises from and gives shape to "our conduct in primarily shared worlds."[54]
- Its units—call them cognitive models, cultural schemas, or scenarios—are often found to have been propagated widely,

in many types of texts and settings and across the various "isms" that (as noted above) are often viewed (mistakenly in my view) as all-determinative.

- These units are *modular* in nature. Once circulating in the larger cultural repertoire, they could be, and were, plugged into multiple contexts for diverse purposes.
- Every culture is populated with such schemas, models, or gestalts. They are certainly not unique to China.[55]
- Practical logic (of the sort I intend here) usually becomes visible at the level of particular practices within larger sequences of action or in particular passages within larger texts. Only rarely does it operate at the level of an entire ritual or text; it's usually more finely grained than that.
- Closely related to the previous point is that multiple models are often found in the same text or practice, sometimes even in the same passage.

As an example of practical logic in action and of the multiplicity of cognitive models often found in a single passage, let me here preview a text translated and discussed in chapter 1. The problem being addressed is that a practitioner has had a series of undesirable dreams. No fewer than five models are deployed in rapid succession (table 1). The passage doesn't suggest that any model is better than the others, but simply piles them up in a kind of praxeological overkill. Each model presupposes a specific notion of what the dreams in question are; each notion of what dreams are entails a specific sort of action to be undertaken in response; and the fit in each case is neat:

Table 1. An Example of Practical Logic and the Multiplicity of Cognitive Models

If the dream was. . .	*the recommended response is:*
a wandering of one's whitesouls 魄 into mischief	to command one's cloudsouls 魂 to restrain them
a mental test 心試	to recognize the dream as undesirable
a corpse depredation 尸賊	to expel the corpses and seal up the portals of ingress so that they can't re-enter
the result of entanglements with deceased relatives	to minimize family ties
a contact with befouling *qi* 氣	to seal up that *qi* below the three barriers 三關

This example happens to be drawn from a text participating in the PURIFICATION PARADIGM, but the same sort of practical logic operates across all the other paradigms as well. In a text built on the SPILLOVER PARADIGM, for instance, where dreams are framed as instructive interactions with divine beings, fitting responses might include making a record of what one heard in the dream, or evaluating what was heard in relation to knowledge acquired during waking practice. Under the DIAGNOSTIC PARADIGM, where dreams are treated as coded indications of self-cultivational progress, fitting responses would involve consulting a teacher, a manual, or an oral body of precedent to ascertain the dream's meaning and then adjusting one's practice as needed.

An important building block of cognitive models is metaphor—"understanding and experiencing one kind of thing," typically less concrete, "in terms of another," typically more concrete.[56] Metaphor has been shown to be fundamental not just to language but also to human thought and action.[57] In this book, metaphor figures in three ways: in generic terms for self-cultivation as a type of human activity; in the ways in which ensembles of techniques and goals of self-cultivational practice were conceptualized; and as an element of the practical logic structuring both practice itself (that is, sequences of actions) and discourse about practice (that is, what texts say about the problems addressed and outcomes realized through practice).

Although I use the term "self-cultivation" etically to refer to the areas of human concern and the repertoire of pursuits looked at here as pertaining to dreaming, it has several close emic analogs. For "cultivation" itself as a type of activity, the two most commonly attested are *xiu* 修 and *yang* 養. To *xiu* is to adorn, embellish, beautify, improve, amend, or correct. In early texts it's often glossed with *shi* 飾, meaning to polish, wipe, make bright, enhance, decorate, or adorn.[58] To *yang* 養 is to nurture, rear, raise, foster, tend, train, or groom. Both words frequently appear in reflexive forms such as *zi xiu* 自修, *xiu shen* 修身, *xiu ji* 修己, *yang shen* 養身, *yang ji* 養己, and *yang sheng* 養生, all of which connote the performance of some sort of ameliorative or soteriologically relevant activity on oneself.

This list includes only generic metaphors for self-cultivation, and only the most frequently attested of those (we could add others, such as *zheng shen* 正身, to rectify oneself); it does not descend into the total body of more specific metaphors for such activities.[59] But in these generic expressions we already see what Lakoff and Johnson term the subject-self metaphor system.[60] This system is

> based on a fundamental distinction between . . . the Subject and one or more Selves. The Subject is the locus of consciousness, subjective experience, reason, will, and our "essence," everything that makes us who we uniquely are. There is at least one Self and possibly more. The Selves consist of everything else about us—our bodies, our social roles, our histories, and so on. . . . Each such metaphor conceptualizes the Subject as being personlike, with an existence independent of the Self.[61]

To mention just one example, we often speak of losing ourselves in some activity—an expression with exact analogs (e.g., "I have lost myself" 吾喪我) in texts such as *Zhuangzi*.[62] Here the structuring metaphor might be summarized as *self-control is object possession.*

The most common way in which ensembles of self-cultivational practices and goals were conceptualized was as so many paths or roads (*dao* 道).[63] A *dao* was a path charted by authoritative past sages, and it was up to the individual practitioner to walk it. To traverse the path to its end meant that one became a new sort of being, and the same word, *xing* 行, denoted both this "walking" and the "practices" that moved the practitioner along toward the goal. Self-cultivators could "go along with" (*shun* 順) or "go in reverse against" (*ni* 逆), "advance" (*jin* 進) or "retrogress" (*tui* 退) on the path. They could "lose" (*shi* 失) or "mistake" (*mi* 迷) the correct path or veer off onto a deviant (*xie* 邪) one. So richly developed is the metaphor of *mārga*, or path, in Buddhist discourse that two modern scholars of East Asian Buddhism have called for its adoption as a cross-cultural way of characterizing religions.[64]

Finally, when it comes to metaphoric idioms structuring the logic of practice and of discourse about practice, we find an even richer array. While not a complete list even of the idioms glimpsed in these pages, the following ones can serve as a preliminary sketch (with the proviso that these idioms could sometimes function less metaphorically than literally[65]):

- the practitioner's self or body as *a configuration of flowing vital energy* or *qi* 氣, with many aspects of this system subject to pollution, corruption, decay, and loss. The self was sometimes imagined as a system of energy coursing in liquid fashion between depots (*fu* 府) and storehouses (*zang* 藏/臟) via channels of flow, and the body as a network of canals or roads connecting the depots. Characteristic dangers involved blockage, leakage, excess, and depletion.[66]
- the practitioner's self or body as *a container* or inner territory (often a walled city) with an outer surface and points of ingress and egress (gates, doors, or passageways) that must be monitored, defended, and (when necessary) sealed off. Sensory faculties and organs were construed as ingress points, with sensation configured as being entered, touched, or tugged at by outer entities or forces (as we'll see in chapter 1).
- a *bureaucratic idiom* in which the practitioner both hosted elements of a hostile or at least unsympathetic bureaucracy and was answerable to one located outside the self. One's very lifespan depended not only on the health of one's bio-spiritual organism but also on the ledger of sins maintained and regularly adjusted by otherworld bureaucrats. It's they who consulted the ledgers to determine when to send armed subordinates to arrest one's soul and bring it before them for interrogation and punishment. Additionally, in ritual settings the practitioner in this idiom assumed the persona and style of a high official authorized to command spirit beings. Practitioners as subjects also controlled or managed (*zhi* 制 or 治) aspects of themselves.
- a *metallurgical and alchemical idiom* often used for processes of transformation. Practitioners refined (*lian* 煉) components of themselves or dissolved (*xiao* 消) unwanted or impure aspects. Relatedly, agricultural processes of purification, fermentation, and distillation were metaphorically appropriated, starting with the ubiquitous "essence" (*jing* 精), a component of the self that the practitioner as subject often worked to purify, retain, and amass.
- an *embryological idiom* in which the practitioner harbored (or could be made to harbor) an embryo constituting his new,

divine self. (I use the gendered pronoun advisedly, as this metaphor mostly appears in discussions of male practitioners.[67])

- a *financial, economic, and accounting idiom* involving "the assimilation of sin with debt or mortgage, and of deliverance with pawn redemption. . . . The monetization of redemption . . . was amplified in China by the Buddhist doctrine of merit transfer that permitted supplicants to intercede in the realm of the dead, or on behalf of otherwise inaccessible beneficiaries, by means of offerings to religious institutions."[68]
- a *microcosmic* idiom in which the practitioner was a miniature version of the entire cosmos.[69]

These idioms were often blended, such as when all human beings were said to be inhabited from conception by "corpses" who hastened their hosts' demise by reporting their sins to outlying bureaucratic officials who kept ledgers for this purpose. Until expelled from the practitioner's body, the corpses were thus at once congenital biospiritual components of the subject's own self and bureaucratic functionaries working for an otherworld administration. And besides metaphors in the strict sense, we also see self-cultivation discussed in terms of a number of cross-domain similes and analogies.[70]

Roles and Performance

The Chinese cultural repertoire in early and medieval times can be usefully pictured as comprising, among many other things, a variety of roles. People learned to enact them, observed others playing them, and evaluated their own and others' performances of them. An often-discussed example is the role of mourner: we have many passages in which this or that individual's performance of mourning is sized up by others as revealing his character. In many such passages it's the appropriate criteria for evaluation that are the real topic being debated.[71] The array of cultural roles was not fixed or static. Over time, older roles might fade in significance, while newer ones were sometimes collectively created. Two examples of newly emergent socio-religious roles that have been studied in some detail are, first, the fashioning (in the late Warring

States and Han periods) of the transcendent-in-training, and, second, the fifth-century rise of the meditation master.[72] Other roles included but were certainly not limited to bodhisattva (future Buddha), member of the Buddha's clan lineage,[73] monk, nun, Daoist citizen,[74] Perfected person (which is how I render the *Zhuangzi* and Shangqing term *zhenren* 真人 throughout), spirit-medium, performer of sacrifice, diviner, virtuous woman, and filial son or daughter.[75] Over the course of their lifetimes—and indeed beyond, if we recall such roles as ancestor, local temple god, or transcendent—individuals were called upon to perform distinct, often overlapping roles, and their performances were continually evaluated by many other parties, some of them visible, others normally invisible to mortal eyes.[76] Their performances were evaluated not simply on their adherence to rules but also on subtler qualities such as sincerity and style.

Combining these notions of roles and performance with that of habitus (mentioned above), we might say that to perform each role well in the estimation of audiences was to have effectively taken on (or to have been thoroughly shaped by) the habitus associated with the role in the cultural repertoire. No longer simply a follower of the rules and restrictions, one could then improvise in novel situations yet still not transgress the boundaries set by the discipline one had been practicing—precisely as Confucius is represented as saying of himself at age seventy, that he could finally then "give free rein to my passions without once stepping over the line" 從心所欲不踰矩.[77]

Ritual performance of one sort or another was often viewed as an essential matrix for self-cultivation. This is well established.[78] It has been less often observed that many aspects of self-cultivation can be seen first as the taking on of roles and second as the increasingly skillful performance of roles. Practitioners learned to play their roles under the constraints of the canonicity of practice as well as the evaluative gaze of teachers and fellow disciples. Once having voluntarily entered a particular path of practice, they were not at liberty to perform just any sort of self in just any sort of way: this is what it meant to tread that path.

A word on the social scope of this book. The people who made, transmitted, and read the texts and carried out the practices discussed here should not be thought of as a separate class of individuals. Instead, they comprise all who were consciously trying to better themselves in any way that could be impacted by textually conveyed or recorded practices *and* by dreaming. Additionally, picturing the monk absorbed in meditative trance or the seeker of transcendence alone in his mountain hut, we might be tempted to imagine self-cultivation in China (and perhaps everywhere) as an essentially solitary pursuit. This is an illusion. For one thing, most of the practitioners glimpsed here participated in the life of monasteries, abbeys, and less formally organized networks and lineages. For another, even if there were seemingly solitary meditators and transcendence seekers, they were after all practicing teachings and methods that had been collectively fashioned and transmitted. And they, too, were performing these roles under the gaze of audiences.[79] If they sometimes isolated themselves—think of "the recluse" as a social type—this was part of the repertoire of behaviors expected of someone performing the role. If we take the idea of canonicity of practice seriously, the utterly solitary practitioner is a fiction.

The book's structure is straightforward. Chapter 1 treats the PURIFICATION PARADIGM, chapter 2 the DIAGNOSTIC PARADIGM, and chapter 3 the SPILLOVER PARADIGM. Chapter 4 briefly takes up passages in which the general phenomenon of dreaming is put to work analogically in service to some persuasive agenda. An epilogue offers some closing thoughts, and three appendices delve into particular texts at greater depth than was possible in the main body.

Among this book's contributions, I hope, are to explore the relationships between individuals' experiences and some of the exuberantly imaginative collective attempts to discipline, channel, interpret, or deploy them; to illuminate aspects of Chinese religious practice and thought that have scarcely been studied; and to reveal a common landscape of dream-related practices underlying traditions often treated in mutual isolation.

CHAPTER ONE

Purifying

This chapter investigates what I call the PURIFICATION PARADIGM of dreaming as it relates to self-cultivation. In passages constructed on this paradigm, the practitioner of some path of self-cultivation has had (or is taking steps to prevent) a dream that is deemed dangerous in one or both of these ways: it is a vector of demonic contact, often resulting in illness, or it includes disgusting or improper content. Either way, given that practitioners were meant to maintain tight control over their comportment, the dream impedes their practice because it puts them in direct contact with beings or situations beyond the canon of discipline structuring their self-cultivational path. In sum, the dream leaves practitioners in a state of ritual impurity. The prescribed response has the character of an exorcistic, apotropaic, or cleansing ritual that closes the breach of boundaries opened by the dream (or preemptively works to prevent such a breach) and restores the dreamer to a state of purity.

E meng 惡夢 and "Nightmares"

First we must deal with a question of terminology. The sorts of dreams taken up here were most often termed *e meng* 惡夢.[1] Nowadays this expression is usually rendered as "nightmare" and used in more or less the same ways as that English term, simply connoting any frightening dream. To call a dream a nightmare is to characterize the content, imagery, or affective tone of a psychological experience transpiring in the sleeper's brain; it is to imply that the dream's predominant affective tone was fear. If we were to simply translate *e meng* as "nightmare" at every occurrence, we would be projecting this modern psychologistic notion of dreaming[2] onto our textual sources. And we would fail to understand what was so troubling about the dreams dealt with in those texts.

Early in its history, the English word "nightmare" denoted not a scary dream but "a female spirit or monster supposed to beset people and animals by night, setting upon them when they are asleep and producing a feeling of suffocation by its weight." Old English *mare* was a word for such spirits and the nocturnal experiences they induced.[3] This chapter will show that if *e* dreams were "nightmares," it was in something much closer to the ca. 1300 Old English sense than to contemporary usage.

What about the term *e* 惡 itself? Scholars often render it as "evil." Might we then simply call *e meng* "evil dreams"? This linguistic overlay would again obscure key aspects of the world of practice we seek to understand. It assumes that our texts presupposed a moral *dichotomy* between two sets of cosmic agents, whereas many did no such thing. (The nature and agendas of these dream-causing agents are explored below in the section "Dream Agents and Idioms of Practice.") More precisely, it assumes that what made *e* dreams problematic was something about the *moral* nature of the dream-causing agent or of its impact on the dreamer. This was surely true in some instances, as we'll see, but not in all, so that to automatically render *e* as "evil" is to occlude the logic involved. Although in certain contexts *e* does mean "evil" or "wicked(ness)," that's not all it can mean, so automatically translating it thus obscures the specific ways in which beings or situations can acquire this designation. Etymology again proves useful: the root meaning of Old English *yfel*, ancestor of the modern "evil," seems to have been "exceeding due limits"—in a word, transgressive.[4]

While this isn't the place for a full-scale investigation, *e* 惡 seems to have worked in parallel fashion. We find Xu Shen 許慎 in his *Script Explained and Graphs Explicated* (*Shuowen jiezi* 說文解字, completed in 121), the earliest complete Chinese dictionary, defining *e* as *guo* 過, "transgressive."[5] Du Yu 杜預 (222–284), in his *Zuo Tradition* (*Zuo zhuan* 左傳) commentary, similarly glosses it at one point as *guo* 過 and at another as *gouhui* 垢穢, "adulterated, foul, polluted, unclean."[6] At the end of the second century, Kang Mengxiang 康孟詳, a monk born in China of Sogdian parents and translator of the earliest extant narratives of the Buddha's life, *Middle[-Length] Scripture on Former Events* (*Zhong benqi jing* 中本起經),[7] rendered the Prakrit *bhikṣu* ("monk") with "one who destroys *e*" (*po'e* 破惡), and since "exorcist" is clearly not the intended meaning in this context, we should understand it as "one who eliminates defilement." The *Treatise on the Great Perfection of Wisdom* (*Da zhidu lun* 大智度論, translated by Kumārajīva and his team between 402 and 406—a text to which we'll return in chapter 2) treats *e* and *fannao* 煩惱 ("defilements") as synonymous.[8] The *Sutra on Achieving the Bright Light Concentration* (*Chengju guangming sanmeijing* 成具光明三昧經, ca. 300) renders *bhikṣu* as *chu e* 除惡, "one who eliminates *e*," where the sense of *e* is clearly "defilements."[9] Commenting on Jean Lévi's rendition of *Analects* 4.4 (子曰: 苟志於仁矣, 無惡也) as "Qui aspire de toutes ses forces au bien sera sans défaut," Christoph Harbsmeier writes: "Lévi frees us from the implications of 'evil' with his 'défaut,' as does, by the way, Yang Bojun [in his modern Chinese translation] with his *huaichu* 壞處."[10] I would have to agree.

What I am getting at is that with *e* and related terms (*wu* 污, *wu* 汙, *xie* 邪, *liu* 流, *yin* 淫, and the like) we are in the domain, most fundamentally, not of good and evil but of purity and pollution—as much aesthetic as moral, involving things like disgust, revulsion, and horror. Without elaborating on his rationale, Donald Harper has translated *e meng* felicitously, I think, as "foul dreams," and that is how I will render this term.[11] Such dreams were deemed "foul" not necessarily because they were induced by an evil being (although some were) or because they were frightening (although some were)—some may well have been experienced as pleasurable while they were occurring—but because they were *polluting*. The next section begins to unpack what this meant for practitioners.

Ritual Purity and Oneiric Danger

This section sketches the notions of pollution that informed ancient or medieval Chinese approaches to dreams analyzed in the rest of this chapter. I will show three things: that pollution was seen as spreading through physical proximity and contact; that sensation was often construed as physical contact; and that, on the model of dreaming implied in texts of this paradigm, to dream was to be contacted by exogenous agents or by the people, objects, or situations appearing in one's dream.

Let's begin by considering the advice offered sometime between 362 and 364 through the medium Yang Xi 楊羲 to Sima Yu 司馬昱, the future Jin emperor Jianwen 簡文 (r. 371–372), by a goddess whose title in the Upper Purity or Shangqing 上清 Daoist pantheon was Lady Right Blossom of the Cloudy Copse Palace 雲林宮右英夫人:

> Place some deer-musk incense in your pillow at the neck. This will block any watery infusions from coming and will prevent foul dreams. Frequently actualizing the three barriers is [also] fitting [for this].[12]
>
> 枕麝香一具於頸間, 辟水注之來, 絕惡夢矣. 常存三關佳也.

If he ever received this advice,[13] Sima Yu was unlikely to have understood the reference to "actualizing the three barriers," a procedure I will explain later in this chapter. That the goddess mentioned it without further explanation was likely a rhetorical gambit I've termed the esotericizing dynamic: powerful secret knowledge is alluded to, but only opaquely, with the aim of enticing the prince to inquire further.[14] But Sima Yu was probably already well acquainted with deer-musk incense (*shexiang* 麝香) and with the notion of "watery infusions" (*shuizhu* 水注) as agents responsible for inducing foul dreams.

The Han-period pharmacopoeia *Divine Farmer's Classic of Materia Medica* (*Shennong bencao jing*) recommends deer-musk incense for "warding off befouling *qi*" (*bi e qi* 辟惡氣), "killing demons and specters" (*sha gui jingwu* 殺鬼精物), protecting against charmed potions, expelling the three worms (*san chong* 三蟲), eradicating pathogens (*chu xie* 除邪), and thus staving off dreams caused by demonic incursion, that is, *yan* 魘, a graph incorporating the term for the agents responsible for them, *gui* 鬼(demons, ghosts, or shades).[15] Likewise, deer-musk incense ranks high among the many medicinal substances Ge Hong 葛洪 (writing around 317) suggests for repelling predatory mountain-dwelling animals and demons.[16] That this scent would be prescribed in a pharmacopoeia for warding off foul dreams indicates how far we are from any psychologistic notion of dreaming.[17] It worked not because of its effect on dreamers' psyches but because it was an apotropaic agent: it kept unwelcome Others away, thus preventing dreams that might otherwise be triggered by contact with them.

The notion of "watery infusions" as a source of misery, illness, and foul dreams was likewise ubiquitous at the time. The words *zhu* 注 and *zhu* 疰, often used interchangeably, denoted not a single malady but a complex of disorders caused by contact with impure substances or environments, whether or not a demonic agent (a *gui* 鬼, *jing* 精, *mei* 魅, *sha* 煞, or the like) was involved.[18] When such agents were involved, other, related terms such as *sui* 祟 might be used.[19] Extant sources reveal a spectrum of etiologies, from agentive beings with agendas to *qi* coursing through the world.[20] Regardless of the particular agent deemed responsible, many diseases, disorders, and misfortunes were explained in terms of hazardous contact with other entities.

The *Divine Farmer's Classic* prescribes over fifty treatments for infusion disorders.[21] In Chao Yuanfang's 巢元方 *Origins and Symptoms of Medical Disorders* (*Zhubing yuanhou lun* 諸病源候論, 610) we find passages such as these:

> When we say that *zhu* 注 means "to stay" 住, we mean that noxious *qi* takes up residence in the patient's body. That is why these disorders are called *zhu*. . . . When one unwittingly provokes the *qi* of life and death,[22] or disturbs demonic beings, these disorders may be the outcome. They transform into multiple shapes, appearing in as many as thirty-six or even ninety-nine different forms, but they never reveal their names.[23]
>
> 凡注之言住也，謂邪氣居住人身內，故名為注. . . . 或乍感生死之氣；或卒犯鬼物之精，皆能成此病. 其變狀多端，乃至三十六種，九十九種，而方不皆顯其名也.
>
> People with no prior illness may suddenly be struck by demons and immediately experience piercing pains in their heart and abdomen, or they may suffocate and faint, as happens in cases of *zhongwu* 中惡 [literally "being hit by a pollutant"]. After such patients recover, the remaining *qi* is not exhausted, and it stagnates and accumulates. Every now and then it breaks out, persistently remaining in the patients until it eventually kills them. After death the infusion is transmitted to others nearby. This is why it's called demonic infusion.[24]
>
> 人有先無他病，忽被鬼排擊，當時或心腹刺痛，或悶絕倒地，如中惡之類，其得差之後，餘氣不歇，停住積久，有時發動，連滯停住，乃至於死. 死後注易傍人，故謂之鬼注.

The line "After death the infusion is transmitted to others nearby" 死後注易傍人 alerts us to the fact that people acquired such pollution by proximity and contact. This notion is widely attested in texts produced by many communities of practice. For example, if someone used the wood from a broken coffin to fashion carriages, they risked suffering "infusion-caused disasters" (*zhulian xionghuo* 注連凶禍) from the death pollution thus incurred.[25] In some regions, when someone had just died relatives fled the house, writing talismans on tiles (*huawa shufu* 畫瓦書符),[26] and on the day of the burial they lit a fire in the doorway, spread the ashes outside, and sent up petitions (*zhang* 章) to the heavens to "cut off the infusions" (*duan zhulian* 斷注連).[27] An early alchemical scripture warns that in the week prior to commencing the elixir process adepts must purify themselves by bathing in perfumed water and "must not pass by filthy [i.e., polluted] places or homes where mourning is being observed or where there are marriageable women" 勿經穢汙喪死嫁女之家.[28] A text by Shandao 善導 (613–681) similarly cautions that when those aiming for rebirth in Amitābha's pure land are on the verge of death, they must not be approached by anyone ritually impure on account of having broken the dietary regulations. Otherwise the patient will suffer grave consequences despite not having personally violated the prohibitions.[29] The *Scripture on Great Peace* (*Taiping jing* 太平經) describes practitioners who were preparing to be inducted into the teachings of the Dao as "nurturing themselves inside a grass hut, conducting a purificatory fast and observing the regulations, not looking upon anything deviant or polluting but daily refining their form until nothing grabs onto their desires" 故當養置茅室中，使其齋戒，不睹邪惡，日練其形，毋奪其欲.[30]

We find the Upper Purity gods recommending precautions against such dangers in specific terms: "The beds people lie on should be set up high. If they are high then the *qi* from the ground will not reach them and they will not be encroached upon when demons blow. Violations of people by demonic *qi* often happen when the *qi* runs along the ground and then rises" 人臥床當令高，高則地氣不及鬼吹不干，鬼氣之侵人常依地而逆上.[31] Tao Hongjing 陶弘景 (452–536) elaborates on this advice as follows:

> Demons are Yin beings. They often use clutter to spread their *qi*.[32] Sometimes the *qi* attaches itself to people or domestic animals; sometimes it sticks to vessels and objects; sometimes it lodges in food and

> drink. Only then is it able to fully deploy its malignant poison. Once there was someone who fell ill and was lying on the ground. Because he was in the throes of sickness he saw a demon bore a hole through [the base of] the wall.[33] It then used its hand as a tube to blow through it. This is precisely an instance of "demonic blowing."[34]
>
> 鬼者陰物, 多因藉以宣其氣, 或附人畜, 或依器物, 或託飲食, 然後得肆其凶毒耳. 昔有人病在地臥, 於病中乃見鬼於壁穿下, 以手為管而吹之. 此即是鬼吹之事也.

By the same cultural logic, purification was also accomplished by proximity and contact. To mention just one example, objects could be ritually impregnated with sacred power—pillars consecrated by Buddhist spells or *dhāraṇīs*, say—and positioned so as to purify all who drew near. As Paul Copp writes, "The pillars were placed where . . . their beneficence . . . could reach the most people: at crossroads, at entrances to temples, or within or beside tombs, where their blessings would seep into the bones of the beloved dead."[35]

Sensation itself was often construed—again in texts produced in a wide range of communities of practice—as the influx of subtle substances through the portals of the sense organs. Already in the Guodian bamboo-strip text known as "Human Nature Comes via Mandate" ("Xing zi ming chu" 性自命出), written no later than 300 BCE, we find people's emotions (*qing* 情), vital energies (*qi* 氣), and even their natures (*xing* 性) and heart-minds (*xin* 心) described as things that are "taken hold of" (*qu* 取) and brought forth by elements of their environment, just as bells and chimes sound only when struck.[36] We find the same basic model of sensation across a wide range of other early texts. "The office of the ears and eyes lies not in thinking but in being occluded by things. It's simply a matter of things contacting things and pulling them" 耳目之官不思而蔽於物. 物交物則引之而已矣 (*Mencius*, ca. 300 BCE).[37] "The capacities of the ears, eyes, nose, mouth, bodily form: each has its own contact" 耳目鼻口形能各有接, whereas "the heart dwells in the central vacuity and controls the five [sensory] offices" 心居中虛以治五官 (*Xunzi*, 3rd century BCE).[38] Some early translations of Buddhist texts, done in the second and third centuries, similarly speak of the sense organs as "entrances" (*ru* 入) and as "grasping" (*shou* 受) their objects.[39] Across multiple traditions, then, sensory contact was often metaphorically or literally constructed as a touching.[40] For this reason, to look upon, hear, touch, or even smell[41] the wrong thing was to expose oneself to contact pollution.

It is against this cultural background that we must understand the cautions about sensory exposure that we find scattered profusely through the archive. For instance, Sun Simo's 孫思邈 *Essential Prescriptions for Urgent Ills* (*Beiji qianjin yaofang* 備急千金要方), written between 650 and 659, cautions that "although a parturient woman is [already] in a state of pollution,[42] when she is on the verge of suffering [i.e., of childbirth], whether she has already delivered or not, do not let members of households polluted by death and mourning come to look at her, for if they do, the birth will be difficult, and if she has already delivered, the child will be harmed" 產婦雖是穢惡然，將痛之時，及未產已產，並不得令死喪污穢家人來視之，則生難，若已產者則傷兒.[43] Elsewhere he warns, "Do not let the mother examine the polluting fluids" 勿令母看視穢汙耳.[44] What a pregnant woman laid eyes on could even adversely affect the fetus. A text recovered at Mawangdui (pre-168 BCE) warns that in the third month of gestation the fetus "does not yet have a fixed configuration, and if exposed to things it will transform accordingly. For this reason lords, sires, and great men must not employ dwarves and must not observe bathing monkeys" 未有定儀, 見物而化, 是故君公大人毋使侏儒, 不觀沐猴.[45]

Sight was not the only sensory contact that could trigger pollution. Confucian texts[46] express concern that music be of the right sort, as considered by their authors, for "musical sound," as Jane Geaney observes, "has the dangerous potential to leak and penetrate boundaries."[47] *Xunzi* insists that the ancient sage kings "prevented corrupt and impure *qi* from making contact" 使夫邪汙之氣無由得接焉 with the people through music,[48] and the music of Qin draws praise because, unlike some other regional modes, "it does not cause a flow of impurity" (*bu liu wu* 不流汙).[49] Sound itself was often seen as a vehicle of cosmic resonance, of transformations in *qi*, and of access to the distant normative past.[50] Music and that large body of customs and protocols summarily known as "the rites" therefore formed the bedrock upon which the Ruist program of cultural formation was built.[51]

The impact of cultural programs of self-formation was often framed in terms of purity and pollution. Practicing the wrong thing exposed the practitioner to pollution, as glimpsed in this passage from the *Annals of Master Lü* (*Lüshi chunqiu* 呂氏春秋, ca. 239 BCE): "In an age of perfect order, people dislike empty words and vacuous phrases, learning that pollutes, and theories that corrupt" 至治之世，其民不好空言虛辭，不好淫學流說.[52] Even discussions of law and administration often frame matters in terms of pollution and purity, as in this line from *Xunzi*: "To repress the unprincipled, restrain the overbearing, dike against pollution, and exorcise the noxious, executing them according to the five punishments, so that oppressive and overbearing [persons] are transformed and polluting and noxious [deeds] are not carried out: such are the duties of the Minister of Crimes" 抃急禁悍，防淫除邪，戮之以五刑，使暴悍以變，姦邪不作，司寇之事也.[53] In *Records of Rites* (*Li ji* 禮記) and *Records of Rites of the Elder Dai* (*Da Dai liji* 大戴禮記), the metaphor of the embankment dam or dike (*fang* 防/坊) is repeatedly used to characterize the rites' function of restraining human behavior from overflowing proper bounds. In fact, *Records of Rites* has a chapter titled "Records concerning the Embankment Dams" ("Fang ji" 坊記). It does not discuss hydraulic engineering.[54]

Examples could easily be multiplied. Particularly when it comes to late classical texts often approached as "philosophy," scholars have attended to notions of pollution and purification much less than is warranted by their actual importance in Chinese culture.[55] Scholars have often focused on moral aspects of self-cultivation at the expense of noticing those rooted in purity/pollution practices. Rules of purity and rules of morality are not unrelated, but they are not the same thing. If we could map a society's entire moral code and also its pollution practices, we would find that the two maps overlap here and there but are by no means completely congruent.[56] Our view has been obscured by under-translations of telling passages that, if rendered more literally, would spotlight rather than hide this aspect of culture.[57] Contact or proximity with the dead, menstrual blood and childbirth,[58] amputees and convicts, slaves and ethnic others,[59] members of the opposite sex, demons and ghosts, and dirt and excrement were all deemed polluting in many situations and so were hedged about with rituals and restrictions. As Mary Douglas recognized, such understandings are produced by the boundaries that figure importantly in a culture. "Dirt [i.e., pollution] . . . is never a unique, isolated event. Where there is dirt there is system. Dirt is the byproduct of a systematic ordering and classification of matter, in so far as ordering involves rejecting inappropriate elements."[60] In other words, "Where there is no differentiation there is no defilement."[61] Seen in this light, the demonic is dirt mobilized, as recognized by Jonathan Z. Smith: "The demonic is a relational or labeling term which occurs only in certain culturally stipulated situations and is part of a complex system of boundaries and limits. . . . Demons serve as classificatory markers which signal what is strong and weak, controlled and exaggerated in a given society at a given moment."[62]

The points where pollution and dreaming practice intersected form what I call the PURIFICATION PARADIGM of dreaming. In a foul dream the dreamer has been contacted, attacked, or invaded by an exogenous agent or has dreamed of a polluting situation, putting the dreamer in a dangerous, liminal state. The paradigm's logic can be reduced to something like this: Pollution is acquired through contact with an impure being, substance, or situation. To dream is to contact or be contacted. Therefore, to dream of impure beings, substances, or situations is to enter a state of pollution. *To dream is to be contacted*: this notion, often implicit, occasionally emerges into clear view, as in a passage in the *Qiwu lun* 齊物論 chapter of the *Zhuangzi* 莊子 (ca. 300–150 BCE).[63] The text's lack of further elaboration suggests the notion was already commonplace:

While it [the heart-mind (*xin* 心)] sleeps, the cloudsouls *contact* [things]	其寐也魂交
When it wakes, the bodily form opens up [to sensory contact]	其覺也形開
Whatever we *come in contact with* entangles it	與接為構
Each day we use that heart-mind of ours for strife	日以心鬭.[64]

The view of dreaming implied here is that dreams occur when one of our multiple souls—cloudsouls (*hun* 魂), whitesouls (*po* 魄), or simply the dreamer's "spirit" (*shen* 神)—wanders outside the body during sleep. But it is specifically the souls' *contacts* with other beings or things that constitute dreaming, and therein lies the risk. Note the language: *jiao* 交 and *jie* 接 are the key verbs for oneiric touching, precisely as they were in the *Xunzi* and *Mencius* passages (quoted above) portraying sensation as contact through the portals of the sense organs. And although I have translated *jiao* 交 rather neutrally (and perhaps too weakly) as "contact," this is a graph with rich associations, from "intertwine" to "intercourse." We might be justified, then, in seeing in these sorts of passages an implied erotics of sensory and oneiric entanglement.[65]

One way to glimpse the polluting power of some dreams is to observe the process from the viewpoint of the being contacting the sleeper. I close this section by discussing two cases.

In the first case, it's a matter of a deity who is too pure to appear in the dreams of a particular human individual, lest this contact pollute the god. The dreamer is the recalcitrant Xu Lian 許聯 (328–404), second son of the paterfamilias and Yang Xi's patron, Xu Mi 謐 (303–?). Earlier Xu Lian had been sent a dream in which the figure of his more assiduous brother, Xu Hui 翽, appeared to him, instructing on a matter of some urgency to him and his family. But Xu Lian still failed to heed the instructions. So we find the youngest of the three divine Lords Mao, Mao Zhong 茅衷,[66] revealing that it had actually been he himself who'd appeared in the dream *in the form of* Xu Hui. His rationale is telling:

> The reason this was presented in a dream through Xu Hui's form is that Xu Lian's cloudsouls and whitesouls are not such that he can communicate with the Perfected. Xu Hui is pure and cleansed. He has purified his whitesouls and his heart for a long time and is close to transcendence. Thus, I borrowed his image to appear in the dream.[67]
>
> 所以夢假於玉斧之形者，虎牙魂魄未得通接仙真故也．玉斧清淨藻潔，久齋濯魄心，近於仙，故假象以通夢也．

Observe the language used. For Xu Lian to dream of someone is for him to be communicated with (*tong* 通) and touched or contacted (*jie* 接) by the other party. His multiple souls, which (on the view of dreaming presupposed here) are involved in such contact, are not pure enough: there's the strong implication not just that Lian isn't able to see the god in a dream in the god's own form, but also that *the god would risk pollution* by the contact.[68] Xu Hui, by contrast, is described as *qingjing* 清淨, "purified, cleansed"; *zaojie* 藻潔 (*zao*: polished, adorned; *jie*: cleansed, purified); and *zhuo* 濯, washed clean, purified (contrasting with its homophonic antonym 濁). (Note the water radicals, prevalent in the vocabulary of purity and of pollution.[69]) How has he achieved this? By years of practicing *zhai* 齋, a term that for centuries had denoted rites of self-purification before presenting offerings to spirits.[70] So the god had to *jia xiang* 假象—to borrow the simulacrum (*xiang* 象) or form (*xing* 形) of Lian's purified brother Hui as a prophylactic against Lian's impurity.[71] Nothing in this passage is unique to the Upper Purity Daoist context except that here it's the figure appearing to a human in a dream who risks pollution. Usually it's the dreaming human who is polluted through contact with an Other (at least an Other of the sorts considered here). That background is what lends this passage its contrastive force.

The second example affords us a look at dream pollution from the point of view of the polluter—although this polluter works on behalf of the Buddha. The passage occurs in the *Vaipulya Dhāraṇī Sutra* (*Da fangdeng tuoluoni jing* 大方等陀羅尼經, translated between 402 and 411 by Fazhong 法衆).[72] The Buddha is in the process of preaching the sutra in which the event of its own preaching is recorded when a member of the audience, the celestial king Pishamen 毘沙門天王 [Vaiśravaṇa[73]], vows to protect all future upholders of it—a type of scene common in Mahāyāna sutras. The divine king

> rose from his seat, bared his right shoulder, and knelt with his right knee to the ground. Joining his palms facing the Buddha, he said to him, "World-Honored One, I am a general among ghosts and spirits. I direct them just as you direct us. Will you allow us to protect and uphold this *dhāraṇī* scripture?" The Buddha said to him, "Excellent, great king of ghosts and spirits! He who desires to protect this *dhāraṇī* sutra is the son of all the Buddhas of the triple cosmos, repaying the favor of all the Buddhas." The celestial king Pishamen then stood before the Buddha and made this vow: "World-Honored One, if there is a good man or a good woman who upholds this *dhāraṇī* sutra yet is harassed and troubled by wicked people, causing that practitioner to be of scattered thought and troubled mind, so that he or she is unable to read, recite, and practice this *dhāraṇī* sutra, at that time we will go to where that man or woman is and will cause the wicked people to weaken and waste away. We will beset them relentlessly with floods and fires, or robbers, or false charges from local officials.[74] Some of them will die as a result; others will be near to death. If those wicked people are officials, we will see to it that they fail to advance in rank. Or we will cause them to have foul dreams in which their body is smeared with hemp oil and they roll around in the dirt, or to have dreams in which they remove their clothes and walk about naked, or

> their teeth fall out and their hair goes white, or their face grows wrinkled and they go blind. World-Honored One, we will cause them to have dreams such as these. I will send ghosts and spirits to disturb their households and cause those wicked persons to fall seriously ill, and some will die as a result. Will you permit me to protect this sutra in these ways?" The World-Honored One remained silent and did not answer [thus consenting].[75]
>
> 爾時毘沙門天王即從座起. 偏袒右肩右膝著地. 合掌向佛而白佛言. 世尊我為鬼神將軍攝諸鬼神. 猶如世尊盡攝我等. 世尊今聽我等護持陀羅尼經典不耶. 爾時佛告毘沙門天王. 快哉鬼神大王. 欲護陀羅尼經者. 即是三世諸佛之子. 即報三世諸佛之恩. 爾時毘沙門天王. 即於佛前而自立願. 世尊若有善男子善女人. 持陀羅尼經者. 有諸惡人為起衰患. 令其行人意散心亂. 不得讀誦修行陀羅尼經. 我於爾時往彼人所. 令彼惡人復得衰耗. 或令水火盜賊縣官枉橫不隱之事來逼其身. 或時致死若近於死. 如是惡人若仕官者不得高遷. 或令惡夢麻油塗身宛轉土中. 或時於其夢中. 脫衣裸走. 牙齒墮落. 頭白面皺眼目瞎. 世尊我令其夢中見如是事. 世尊我於爾時. 遣諸鬼神惱其舍宅. 令彼惡人得大重病. 或時致死. 世尊聽我如是護此經不. 爾時世尊默然不答.

Here, it's not just that the "gods and spirits" pollute the dreamer by contact (though that might be true, depending on which specific sorts of agents the celestial king sends to carry out his order); it's also noteworthy that what happens in the dream is itself impurifying. Both in dreams and in waking life the harasser of sutra-upholders will undergo a relentless sequence of illness, disaster, and death, just as do persons afflicted by infusions.

But what if, at least in some texts, this language of pollution is only metaphorical? My answer is twofold. First, even if some passages can be read metaphorically rather than literally, we still fail to grasp the metaphor if we ignore the background of pollution discourse and practice. By failing to grasp the metaphor we miss the rhetorical force these sorts of passages would have carried for contemporary readers. And by missing the rhetorical force, we strip these texts from their contemporary contexts and trim away much of what they were actually saying so that we can fit them more neatly into our denatured discourse of "philosophy." Second, we can gauge how contemporaries viewed these matters by observing their responses. And when it comes to polluting dreams, the prescribed responses went beyond metaphor to take ritual form, as we'll see next.

Expunging Dream Pollution

Reading through the archive, we discover two basic options for dealing with foul dreams. One is restorative—to be performed the morning after the dream's occurrence—and the other is prophylactic, meant to prevent such dreams from occurring in the first place. In this section I take up the former type, and in the next section the latter.

Some restorative methods involve summoning deities to expel the polluting agents. In others, the practitioner performs the exorcism on his own authority. Some texts combine both approaches. I will discuss examples of each type in turn.

Summoning Divine Aid to Expunge Oneiric Pollution

I begin by comparing two sets of instructions for how to deal with polluting dreams preserved in manuscripts separated by perhaps as much as a thousand years. The first appears near the end of an illustrated demonography, *White Marsh Diagrams of Spectral Prodigies* (*Baize jingguai tu* 白澤精怪圖), recovered in incomplete form in a Dunhuang manuscript (thus probably dating to the late Tang).[76] Extant references to texts with titles linking them to White Marsh (Baize 白澤), a creature supposed to have revealed the secrets of demonology to the Yellow Thearch 黄帝 in hoary antiquity, date at least from Ge Hong's *Master Who Embraces the Unhewn* (*Baopuzi neipian* 抱朴子內篇, 317),[77] and similar lists of demons' names and descriptions stretch back to ancient times, a notable example found among the bamboo strips at Shuihudi.[78] The text's title is written on the last column. In the penultimate column the scribe identifies himself as the monk Daoxin 道昕 (natal surname Fan 范), saying that he has copied the text "for the benefit of Daoists and [Buddhist] monks alike."

> When a person has had a polluting dream during the night: Rise at dawn, and in the northeast part of the house unbind the hair and chant this incantation: "Boqi. Boqi. He does not drink ale or eat meat, but regularly dines in exalted realms on high. May this polluting dream return to Boqi. Crushing dreams cease, give rise to great blessings." Chant the invocation like this seven times and there will be no odium.[79]

> 人夜得惡夢, 旦起, 於舍東北被髮呪曰: 伯奇伯奇, 不飲酒食肉, 常食高興地. 其惡夢歸於伯奇, 厭夢息, 興大福. 如此七呪無咎也.

A similar procedure is prescribed in two daybooks (*ri shu* 日書) written on bamboo strips that were buried in 217 BCE and recovered at Shuihudi 睡虎地 in Hubei province in 1975.[80] The Shuihudi A passage reads:

> When a person has had a polluting dream: Upon waking, unbind the hair, sit facing the northwest, and incant this prayer: "Heigh![81] I dare to report you to Qinqi. So-and-so[82] has had a polluting dream. Flee back home to the place of Qinqi. Qinqi, drink heartily, eat heartily. Grant so-and-so great broadcloth.[83] If not coins, then cloth. If not cocoons, then silkstuff." Then it will stop.[84]
>
> 人有惡夢, 覺乃繹髮, 西北面坐, 禱之曰: 皋, 敢告爾Qinqi,[85] 某有惡夢, 走歸 Qinqi 之所. Qinqi 强飲强食, 賜某大幅, 非錢乃布, 非繭乃絮. 則止矣.

The Shuihudi B passage is worded slightly differently, and the being who is asked for help is named Wanqi 宛奇, but the process—with one exception discussed below[86]—outlined in both the Dunhuang and Shuihudi texts is the same, including the direction to face and the incantation to be chanted.[87]

Donald Harper has emphasized the similarities among all three of these texts. They indeed bear witness to a remarkably stable exorcistic tradition coursing below the threshold of most received literature over many centuries. Here I want to explore both the similarities and the differences, which go beyond the names of the deities invoked (Boqi/Wanqi/Qinqi) and the directions in which the performer is to face (northeast/northwest).

I begin at the end, with what performers of these rituals could expect from their actions. The Dunhuang text's *wujiu* 無咎 could simply mean that dreamers will suffer no further misfortune. But it might also mean that there will be no odium—that is, that the dreamers, having purified themselves with the incantatory ritual, will not be faulted (by whatever divine powers were imagined to oversee such matters) for any pollution incurred. If this is the meaning, then the text implies the hovering presence of a spirit-world bureaucracy that can hold dreamers accountable for whatever pollution they acquired, or whatever transgression they committed, in the dream. No such superstructure is implied in Shuihudi A's "then it will stop," a phrase presumably meaning that the dream-causing agent will move on and not repeat its action.[88]

All three texts direct practitioners to unbind their hair when beginning the action. As in most societies, hairstyles, hair ornaments, and head coverings were important markers of social status and role—perhaps even more so in ancient and medieval China since they (along with the face and sometimes the hands) were the only publicly visible parts of the body.[89] Hair was to be kept clean as a matter of ritual purity. Unbound and fully exposed hair was strongly associated with ethnic others and with demons. "Han men only exposed their hair when they moved into liminal states, such as when mourning a close relative."[90] So, by unbinding their hair the ritual performers were stepping onto the threshold between civilization and Otherness.

The texts use different verbs to denote the ritual actions prescribed. In Shuihudi A it's *dao* 禱, "a type of prayer in which offerings are promised to a spirit if it performs the requested deed (after which the offerings must be delivered in sacrifice)."[91] Shuihudi B has *zhu* 祝, while P2682 has *zhou* 呪, both meaning to utter an incantation or spell. In all three cases the dreamer addresses other beings in performative speech, speech that (claims to) bring about the results it names.[92] Shuihudi B adds one other action: just before starting the incantation, performers are to exhale (*xi* 呬) to the northwest, thus adding the power of their own breath to that of the words. "Like spitting and spouting, utterances concentrate the vapor which is the breath as it is ejected from the mouth."[93] The performer launches a stream of breath and then sets an armada of incantatory words afloat on it.

In the Shuihudi strips the dreamer addresses both the distant overseer of dream-causing spirits (Qinqi or Wanqi) and those proximate spirits themselves.[94] The latter are not named, whether by a general designation (such as *gui* 鬼) or by specific types, but the second-person pronoun *er* 爾 is used when speaking to them. We should pause to ponder the implications of this. Despite being non-human, these beings are addressed as persons in a properly formatted verbal utterance. One tries to *persuade* them to go back home. As Marshall Sahlins observes,

"The 'magical' power of words and ritual performances may seem less mystical or at least less mystifying when it is realized that they are addressed to persons. As such they are intended to influence these other-than-human persons by rhetorical effects, in the same way as interpersonal dialogue among people moves them to thought and action. For this purpose, a full semiotic repertoire of associations is brought to bear. . . . Praxis becomes poetics, since it is itself persuasive."[95] Despite their alien nature, it seems, the unnamed spirits participate alongside us in the same set of cultural forms. It's this shared trans-species culture that allows them to be addressed, and it's their being addressed that allows them to be sent away. Yet their not being named is also significant, for it was by knowing and calling out spirits' names that one usually exorcised them, as succinctly stated in our Dunhuang manuscript just after the polluting-dream method: "These are all the demons' names. So if you first call out their names, this will cause people not to dread them and will render them unable to cause harm" 此皆是其鬼名,故先呼其名,即使人不畏之,鬼之不傷者也.[96]

In the Dunhuang method, by contrast, one goes over the proximate dream polluters' heads to address their distant superior. All three texts construe the polluting being(s) who contacted the dreamer during the night as based in a distant locale and under the sway of a being residing there. That locale is unnamed, though its direction on the compass is surely what's indicated by the direction in which the performer is to face. The Dunhuang text suggests it's distant both horizontally and vertically. So far as I know, the beings named in the two Shuihudi texts are otherwise unattested. But all three names seem interrelated phonetically, and Boqi 伯奇, addressed in the Dunhuang version, is attested as early as the Han-era end-of-year *danuo* 大儺 exorcism as one of twelve spirits summoned to drive off demons. Each of the twelve specializes in devouring a particular category of demons or calamities. Dreams are what Boqi devours: 伯奇食夢.[97]

Another difference in the procedures is that the Shuihudi strips recommend accompanying the incantation with food offerings, while the Dunhuang method does not. As if anticipating readers' surprise at this, the Dunhuang incantation supplies a rationale: "He does not drink ale or eat meat, but regularly dines in exalted realms on high." Harper translates 常食高興地 as "regularly eats the earth of High Elevation" (or "regularly eats from the land of High Elation"),[98] speculating: "Perhaps it refers to an ultimate land of bliss in popular belief. Apparently Boqi's divine power derives from his association with this land."[99] I think "high elevation" isn't a specific place on the cosmic map and isn't the object of "regularly eats" but is rather a modifier. The phrase signals Boqi's august status by characterizing the elevated and refined realms in which he dines, which render it unnecessary for him to consume mortals' food and drink. The sense is that Boqi, like a transcendent (*xianren* 仙人), frequents lofty locales and does not depend on ordinary foodstuffs for sustenance, instead dining on *qi* and celestial rarities[100] (perhaps including dreams, as mentioned in the account of Han-period new year exorcism). Hence, there is no need for the practitioner to present food offerings. In effect, then, the Dunhuang method bespeaks a more exalted view of the distant dream-controlling spirit. One risked insulting him by offering food, just as one wouldn't add a request (as in the Shuihudi strips) for coins, cloth, silkworms, or silk. One's relationship with him is not structured in terms of the reciprocity model governing relations with most spirits, because Boqi is not the sort of being who needs or wants the gifts people have to offer.[101]

We see the same structure of events and response—demonic incursion in the form of a dream, followed by the practitioner's invocation of a superior being—in some sutra passages. *Dhāraṇī Sutra in Which the Bodhisattva Akāśagarbha Questions Seven Buddhas* (*Xukongzang pusa wen qi fo tuoluoni zhou jing* 虛空藏菩薩問七佛陀羅尼呪經), apparently translated in the first half of the sixth century,[102] recommends to those who have "seen a foul dream in the night" (*ye jian e meng* 夜見惡夢) that they avoid eating for fourteen days.[103] Without leaving their place of practice (*daochang* 道場), each evening they are to bathe in scented water, don a new robe, and intone a *dhāraṇī* before a Buddha icon as many times as they are able before falling asleep. On the morning of the fifteenth day, they are to rise and heat pure water with fragrant herbs in a clean cauldron, then strain out the plant material, form a powder of incense and purple and white sandalwood, and add this to the water. They should then fill a bowl with this water, place it before the icon, enchant it with a spell spoken 108 times, and bathe with it. Afterward they may eat again.[104] A method prescribed in the Indian monk Atikūṭa's *Compendium of Dhāraṇīs* (*Tuoluoni jijing* 陀羅尼集經, 654) has practitioners "who have been frightened by seeing in a dream any sorts of animals or other defiling objects of the senses" 夢中驚怖見諸畜生惡境界等 prepare a pure ritual space with a basin of clean, heated, scented water (adding flower petals if available), pronounce a *dhāraṇī* 108 times with accompanying *mudrās*,[105] and then put their minds at ease.[106] They may also employ this method if they've seen such things as a result of Māra's actions (*mo shi* 魔事) while awake. (For more on Māra see the section "Dream Agents and Idioms of Practice" below.)

Expunging Oneiric Pollution on One's Own Authority

In the methods seen so far, the practitioner performs a ritual that appeals to a divine authority to (re)take control of dream-causing agents. But there is a subgenre of practices in which the ritualist, rather than calling for assistance, declares his or her *own* power to expel those agents and proceeds to do so by means of an incantation accompanied by ritual gestures and assistive technologies such as talismans. Wang Yanshou's 王延壽 second-century "Rhapsody on Dreams" ("Meng fu" 夢賦), both a poem about a nightmare and an incantation to expel the demons that caused it, is a rich example of this less petitionary, more self-performative model. The speaker twice claims to be a Perfected person 真人 "harboring the pure harmony of heaven and earth" 含天地之淳和. (Note this assertion of one's own purity in contrast to the demons' pollution.) At no point does the speaker/author ask for help. Instead, the text is at once a narrative and an incantation consisting of a string of commands issued on the speaker's own authority.[107]

In at least three texts (two of them dating from the Tang) we find these instructions:

> If in the night you have had a foul dream, do not tell of it. In the morning, take some water in your mouth,[108] face eastward, and spurt the water out, then say this incantation: "Let this foul dream be covered over with plants and trees [木 **muwk*]. Let good dreams become pearls and jade [玉 **ngjowk*]." Then there will be no odium.[109]
>
> 夜惡夢, 不須說, 平旦以水向東方噀之, 咒曰: 惡夢著草木, 好夢成珠玉. 即無咎.

The wording differs slightly across the three versions, but the key component—the rhyming incantation itself—is identical. As in the Dunhuang text's "crushing dreams cease, give rise to great blessings," we see in these texts the command to convert inauspicious to auspicious. The polluting dream is also to be covered over with grass and wood, neutralizing the pollution.[110]

In such passages, the admonition not to speak of the dream is commonplace. Here is another example, drawn from the Tang-period *Records concerning Cultivating One's Nature and Lengthening Life* (*Yangxing yanming lu* 養性延命錄): "Beneficial dreams may be told, but keep silent about polluting dreams. In this way you will cultivate your nature and live long" 善夢可說，惡夢默之，則養性延年也.[111] Such passages don't explain why they counsel silence, probably because they didn't need to. Pollution could be spread through speech, as through any other sound; speaking of the wrong topic on the wrong occasion could be polluting. *Records of Rites* cordons off speaking of certain topics in specified ritual contexts: "When in mourning, one does not speak of music; when sacrificing, one does not speak of the inauspicious; when at court, one does not speak of wives or daughters" 居喪不言樂，祭事不言凶，公庭不言婦女.[112] To give voice to such matters was to activate a stream of foul *qi* that, entering listeners' ears, might corrupt them too. Xunzi had written in his disquisition on music, "As for the gentleman: his ears do not listen to corrupting sounds, his eyes do not look upon seductive forms, his mouth does not emit polluting speech. Regarding these three things the gentleman takes special care" 君子耳不聽淫聲，目不視女色，口不出惡言. 此三者，君子慎之.[113] In social circles made up of people engaged in self-improvement and self-cultivation of whatever sort, such matters must not be spoken of. To tell of one's dreams is to move them out from the private to the social, from the nocturnal to the diurnal spheres, making them a "party to the unfolding of reality."[114] Dream accounts are performative: they do things, and they change things.[115] So foul dreams were to be quarantined from social discourse.

We find a more elaborate way of expunging dream pollution on one's own authority in the final section of *New Collection of the Duke of Zhou's Book for Interpreting Dreams* (*Xinji Zhougong jiemeng shu* 新集周公解夢書, P3908), a Dunhuang manuscript mostly comprising a key to dream interpretation but ending with the following apotropaic advice:[116]

Exorcising demonic dreams. Section 23

If someone in the night has had a polluting dream, they should rise early and tell no one of it. Having reverently purified their mind, let them write these talismans in ink [three talismans appear here on a separate line] and place them at the foot of their bed without letting anyone know. Then let them say this incantation:

> Red! Red! Yang! Yang!
> The sun rises in the east.
> These talismans cut off dreams
> And expel all that is inauspicious.

Say it thrice. [Then say:]

> Hundred demons, hide yourselves away!
> Do this speedily in accordance with the statutes and commands!
> Polluting dreams, your surname is Yun, your given name Xinggui.
> Polluting thoughts, your surname is Jia, your given name Zizhi.
> I know your names, I know your bynames!
> Depart a thousand *li* away from me!
> Do this speedily in accordance with the statutes, commands, and edicts!
> Your surname is Zi, your given name Shihu.
> I know your names, I know your bynames![117]

厭禳惡夢章第二十三

凡人夜得惡夢, 早起且莫向人說, 虔淨其心, 以黑 [> 墨] 書此符安卧床脚下, 勿令人知. 乃可呪曰: 赤赤陽陽,[118] [three small talismans are written here] 日出東方. 此符断夢, 辟除不祥. 讀之三遍, 百鬼潛藏. 急急如律令. 夫惡夢姓雲名行鬼, 惡想姓賈名自直. 吾知汝名, 識汝字, 遠吾千里, 急急如律令敕. 又姓子字世瓠, 吾知汝名, 識汝字.

The topical heading incorporates two ancient terms. *Yan* 厭 is often used interchangeably with *yan* 魇, which contains the "demon" classifier 鬼; both connote a loathsome exogenous entity pressing down on the dreamer—paralleling Old English *mare*, as noted above. *Rang* 禳, attested in early texts such as *Shuowen* and *Lüshi chunqiu*, was a sacrificial exorcism ritual, perhaps performed (if the "Jichun ji" 季春紀 chapter of *Lüshi chunqiu* is any guide[119]) in the third month of spring, when sacrificial animals were to be split open (*zhe* 磔) and laid at the city or palace gates to, as *Shuowen* puts it, drive off pestilence- and calamity-causing demons (*chu liyang* 除癘殃). The procedure outlined here, however, requires no sacrifice. The feeding of invisible guests is replaced by other ritual modalities.

Because the dream was polluting, the dreamer's mind was to be purified (*jingxin* 淨心). The Protestant model of religion would see this mental component as the centerpiece of the practice and write off the rest as outward rote, just as the predominant psychological view of dreaming would see the dream as a merely mental event. But this inward purification, the correlate of the *zhai* 齋 carried out before ancestral and other sacrifices, only prepares for the actual ritual work.[120]

I am intrigued by the mantle of solemn authority the dreamer puts on here. In speaking the incantation and writing the talismans, the practitioner performs the role of one duly authorized to command spirits. The repeated injunction to "do this speedily, in accordance with the statutes and commands!" only reinforces this performance. These aspects of the ritual serve to remind the demons that the performer is backed by both a long tradition of sacred knowledge and a spiritual army. The content of the rhyming incantation is heavily Yang 陽 (the sun, the east, the color red) to dispel the demonic Yin 陰. The ritualist's insistence that he knows the names of the offending beings partakes of the ancient notion that it is by invoking demons' and sprites' names that one drives them off, just as it is by their names that humans are administratively kept track of in this world and the next. Perhaps most tellingly, the foul dreams and thoughts are themselves addressed by name, as if the demon were the dream or the dream the demon.[121] The whole performance is a rhetorically complex attempt to persuade the dream-triggering Others to depart. To quote Sahlins again, "The 'magical' power of words and ritual performances may seem less mystical or at least less mystifying when it is realized that they are addressed to persons. As such they are intended to influence these other-than-human persons by rhetorical effects."[122]

Another text, "Method for Ridding Oneself of the Three Corpses Using Talismans" ("Qu sanshi fufa" 去三尸符法), similarly warns that the three corpses and nine worms can cause all manner of illnesses. One can detect their activity by a specific sort of dream: "In all cases when persons with such maladies dream at night of fighting, it is caused by these worms" 夜夢戰鬬皆此蟲也. Here, too, the method combines the writing of talismans with an oral incantation. The reader is instructed to write three talismans on peachwood boards, and then to bury them beneath the doorway lintel. Further copies are to be written on thin paper or bamboo slips and worn from the sash on *gengshen* 庚申 days as well as ingested on *gengzi* 庚子 days of the calendar. These are times when the corpses were imagined to report one's transgressions to the celestial ledger-keepers, resulting in lifespan reduction.[123] While doing this, the adept is to pronounce a tetrasyllabic, rhymed incantation. The first two four-character phrases are reminiscent of the opening of the incantation seen in the Dunhuang manuscript just discussed:[124]

The sun rises in the east	日出東方
Fiery red, massive and magnificent.	赫赫堂堂
I ingest the divine talismans	某服神符
And the talismans protect me on all sides.	符衞四方
The divine talismans upon entering my belly	神符入腹
Clear out my stomach and wash my intestines.	換胃蕩腸
All illnesses are expunged and cured,	百病除愈
My bones and frame are vigorous and strong.	骨體康強
The thousand demons and myriad perverse wraiths	千鬼萬邪
Do not dare confront me!	無有敢當
One who knows the talismans is a spirit,	知符為神
One who knows the Dao is a Perfected [person].	知道為真
When I ingest these talismans	吾服此符
The nine worms quit my body	九蟲離身
And all things harmful [in me] are rounded up	攝錄萬毒
That I may ascend to become a Perfected person.	上昇真人
Do this speedily in accordance with the statutes and commands!	急急如律令

In "clear out my stomach and wash my intestines," we see again that purification involves a washing. But here the ablution occurs inside the practitioner's body.[125]

Other methods for expunging the three corpses similarly call upon practitioners to use their dreams diagnostically.[126] One of them is recommended in the third-century *Array of the Five Talismans* (*Taishang lingbao wufu xu* 太上靈寶五符序): "On *gengshen* nights, if you dream of fighting with someone, this is due to the struggle going on between your whitesouls and the corpses" 庚申夕. . . 人夢與他人爭鬪者是魄與尸鬪也; or, in the *Cloudy Bookcase with Seven Labels* (*Yunji qiqian* 雲笈七籤, ca. 1025) version of this passage, the dream betokens an inner struggle between your cloudsouls (*hun* 魂), on the one hand, and the corpses (*shi* 尸), shades (*gui* 鬼), and your whitesouls (*po* 魄, who are here imagined, as in many other passages, to be playing for the opposing team: 庚申夕人夢與他諍鬪者是魂與尸魄鬼鬪).[127] Here, however, the method for expunging the corpses (and thus also the polluting dreams they cause) involves neither an incantation nor a talisman but simply the scheduled ingestion of a medicinal preparation, the recipe for which is provided.[128] (We'll see another example of this below.) This procedure, the texts promise, will "rot out" 爛出the corpses.[129]

Combinatory Methods

Many texts build on both of the above models: dreamers can pronounce their own authority and invoke the might of a divine imperium in order to cast out the demons. I begin with three relatively simple examples.

First, in *Essentials of the Practice of Perfection: Protocols of Right Unity* (*Zhengyi fawen xiuzhen zhiyao* 正一法文修真旨要), a Sui or early Tang miscellany of instructions, within a discussion of the use of seals (*yin* 印) in healing rituals[130] we find the following stipulation:

> If when asleep you should suddenly be frightened by a dream or unusually shaken by a sound, arise at once and call out in a loud voice: "Ye seven spirits of the house, Overseer of Lifespans, Lord of the Hearth! How have you permitted uncouth demons to strike at the descendant of the Yellow Thearch? Apprehend them, and remand them to the prison officers to be punished for their crime!" When you have said this, take the seal and hang it over the door. Return to bed. A moment later you will hear the sounds of whipping and torture.[131]

若卒有夜夢驚怖, 音聲震響動不如常者, 即起大呼曰: 宅中七神 竈君, 何以令非常之鬼干犯黃帝子孫, 收捕之付獄吏治罪, 言訖, 將印掛戶上, 還, 外須臾自聞鞭罰之聲.

It's on his authority as the Thearch's descendant that the ritual performer chastises and issues commands to the common gods of the household.

Second, *Protocols of the Twelve Hundred Officers* (*Qian er bai guan yi* 千二百官儀), an early Celestial Master schedule of gods to be invoked in various situations,[132] mandates that the dreamer call upon a powerful lord for help:

> Those enwrapped and troubled by foul dreams should invite the Lord of Heavenly Glory with his 100,000 yellow-clad soldiers, [saying]: "You are primarily responsible for apprehending the 120 sorts of harmful oddities within [my] home, powerful perversities within and without, and the twelve types of killer demons. As for the ones that render [my] dreams perverse,[133] you are to expunge and destroy them all. My faith offering will be clothing, as stipulated."[134]
>
> 惡夢錯亂者, 當請天昌君, 黃衣兵士十萬人: 主為某家收 [冢 >] 家中百二十殃怪, 中外強殃, 十二刑殺鬼, 令某夢忤者, 皆使絕滅. 餽儀衣物.

Third, writing around 317, Ge Hong recommended appealing to a particular astral deity for assistance:

> If you have a demonic dream while sleeping, go outdoors at once and, gazing up at the Auxiliary star, make a fist with your thumb inside and "hold to the One." The demon will immediately depart. If it is cloudy or rainy, remain in your room and simply face north while visualizing the Auxiliary star.[135]
>
> 或臥而魘者, 即出中庭視輔星, 握固守一, 鬼即去矣. 若夫陰雨者, 但止室中向北思見輔星而已.

For Ge Hong, "holding to the One" (*shou yi* 守一) seems to have entailed a visualization-style meditation on the One as a divine entity equivalent to the Dao itself.[136] But his goal was not the mystical gnosis associated with the term in earlier texts such as *Guanzi* 管子, *Zhuangzi* 莊子, *Huainanzi* 淮南子 (139 BCE), and for that matter *Taiping jing* 太平經.[137] Rather, the meditation functioned to secure protection from various proximate harms, including diseases and assaults by animals, ghosts, and dream-triggering demons.[138] "If someone is able to hold to the One, the One will hold him in turn" 人能守一, 一亦守人, advises Ge, and that, for him, is the point of doing so.[139]

The three examples discussed to this point involve relatively uncomplicated procedures by which practitioners were to call for celestial help in the wake of a foul dream. We find the same celestially assisted exorcistic structure, but now greatly elaborated (as well as supplemented with a protocol for responding to auspicious dreams), in a set of instructions issued by the Perfected to Yang Xi and the Xu clan in the mid-fourth century and incorporated into several[140] later Daoist texts:

> When you encounter a series of foul dreams, [this can have any one of three causes]: first, whitesoul seductions; second, tests of the mind; third, depredations by the corpses. As for the method of dispelling them, once you have awakened from the dream, trace lightly with your left hand over the abdomen twice seven times, grind the teeth twice seven times, and softly incant:
>
> 數遇惡夢者, 一曰魄妖, 二曰心試, 三曰尸賊. 厭消之方也, 若夢覺以左手躡人中二七過, 琢齒二七遍, 微祝曰:

Perfected and Mysterious[141] of the Grand Cavern,	大洞眞玄
Extend and refine my three cloudsouls [so that]:	張鍊三魂
The first cloudsoul quickly guards my seven whitesouls;	第一魂速守七魄
The second cloudsoul quickly guards my muddy pellet;[142]	第二魂速守泥丸
And the third cloudsoul guards[143] the heart within bounds and measures.	第三魂受心節度
Quickly inform the Most High Lord of the Three Primes [as follows]:	速啓太上三元君
"I have encountered an unpropitious dream	向遇不祥之夢
Due to my seven whitesouls having roamed	是七魄遊尸
Together with corpses' having come in, bringing myriad perversities.	來協萬邪之源
Summon Peach Vigor at once to protect my allotted lifespan.	急召桃康護命
Inform the Thearchical Lord above	上告帝君
And the Five Elders and Nine Perfected	五老九眞
That they should all guard the gates to the body.	皆守體門

Let the spirit-masters of the Yellow
Gatetowers　黄閣 > 闕[144] 神師
And the generals of the Purple Doors,　紫戶將軍
Holding halberds and waving bells,　把鉞搖鈴
Annihilate all the fords of pollution　消滅惡津
And turn inauspicious into auspicious,　反凶成吉
So that there is no connection between living
and dead."　生死無緣

Then it is complete. If you lie back down, you are sure to obtain an auspicious response,[145] and the *qi* that fashioned the foul dreams will be sealed up below the three barriers. After three years, your dreams will be only those in which gods have been stimulated to respond [to you] with instructions. Your dreams henceforth will be ones that clarify the future. You will for the most part no longer have foul dreams or unpropitious imagery.

畢. 若又臥必獲吉應, 而造爲惡夢之氣則受閉於三關之下也. 三年之後, 唯神感旨應乃有夢也. 夢皆如見將來之明審也. 略無復惡占不祥之想矣.

The ensuing passage outlines the appropriate response when the practitioner, having requested divine aid, has duly received an auspicious response in the form of another dream:

If you do [that same[146]] night meet with a good dream, and good fortune responds to the dream and in your heart you consider it fitting, then it is a fortunate response.[147] When you wake from sleep you should massage your eyes twice seven times, knock the teeth together twice seven times, and softly incant:

若夜遇善夢, 吉應好夢而心中自以為佳, 則吉感也. 臥覺當摩目二七叩齒二七遍而微呪曰:

Highest essences of the Most High,　太上高精
Cinnabar numina of the Three Thearchs,　三帝丹靈
Brightly suffuse the scarlet palace [of my heart]　絳宮明徹
And announce the circumstances of this auspicious
response.　吉感告情
In the three primes, pacify the whitesouls.[148]　三元柔魄
May the Celestial august ones bestow scriptures
on me,　天皇授經

Agreeably harmonious whichever way I turn.	所向諧合
I will fly as a transcendent to Upper Purity,	飛仙上清
Ever to join with the Jade Perfected	常與玉真
And assembling with them in the Purple Halls.	俱會紫庭

Then it is complete. These are secret instructions issued from the Grand Cavern, to be transmitted to those who have only just begun to wade across the ford.[149]

畢. 此太洞祕訣, 以傳於始涉津流者矣.

The last line makes clear that these directives were aimed at beginners. This is surely because advanced practitioners were not supposed to have unclean dreams at all, as the text implies. Disciplines of self-cultivation could be so exacting, touching on so many aspects of life, that even one's dreams were to be regulated. Xu Mi, we know, was especially prone to foul dreams. He had related two of them to Yang Xi, so the practice outlined above may have been revealed with him in mind.[150] The *Declarations of the Perfected* (*Zhen'gao* 真誥) entries on those two dreams of Xu Mi's are as follows: "On the twelfth of the eleventh month I dreamed that liquid was leaking from the grave goods in the coffin" 十一月十二日夢棺器露有水. "On about the eighteenth of the twelfth month I dreamed that the Dark Warrior had been pierced by iron tridents" 十二月十八日左右夢以鐵釵刺玄武. Tao Hongjing comments that this latter dream must have involved the image of this god that had been placed on the north wall of the tomb of Xu Mi's deceased wife, Tao Kedou 陶科斗.[151] Characteristically, both dreams constituted polluting contact with her tomb and its contents.

Several models of foul dreams, and of dreaming more generally, structure this passage. (As discussed in the introduction, it's not unusual to find this sort of multivocality in discussions of dreaming, a notoriously uncanny and elusive experience. What is unusual is to find *this many* models of dreaming packed into a single passage.[152]) Each entails its own fix for the problem, though these aren't all made explicit. Initially we find a trio of models. First, the whitesouls have wandered into mischief. The fix: command the three cloudsouls to restrain them. (We'll see shortly why the whitesouls posed particular danger.) Second, the dream was a mental test (*xin shi* 心試). No fix seems to proceed directly from this theory, unless it's to see whether the dreamer will recognize the dream as polluting and undertake the prescribed practice to restore purity. Third, the dream was a corpse depredation (*shi zei* 尸賊). (For more on the corpses see "Dream Agents and Idioms of Practice" below.) The fix: alert the celestial authorities of the breach. After expelling the corpses, seal up the portals of ingress into the cultivated self. From this passage alone it's not clear what the corpses are and what they do. But the notion that they were a typical inflictor of pollution and suffering was common at the time, not at all distinctive to Shangqing teaching, and their baleful habits were elaborated in other texts to which we will turn shortly. Readers of this passage were surely familiar in general terms with that lore.

Then come further implicit theories. The clause "so that there is no connection between living and dead" (*si sheng wuyuan* 生死無緣) evokes an archaic etiology for foul dreams and must refer to Xu's entanglement with several aggrieved relatives' souls. The fix: sever family ties to minimize such hazardous entanglements with the dead.[153] Last: "The *qi* that fashioned the polluting dreams. . ." 造為惡夢之氣. The fix: ". . . will be sealed below the three barriers" 受閉於三關之下. In one brief passage, then, we see five models of dreaming, each entailing a distinctive response. This etiological overkill, reflective of dreams' indeterminacy, testifies to the rich cultural repertoire available by the fourth century for thinking about dreams.[154]

Here we finally learn more about the goddess's oblique advice to Sima Yu to "frequently actualize the three barriers" (*chang cun sanguan* 常存三關), discussed at the outset of this chapter. In the various Daoist mappings of the inner landscape of the human person, the three barriers were often—particularly in contexts of inner alchemy practice—understood as points along the spine, with the lowest situated at the coccyx, the middle at chest level, and the highest at the level of the occipital bone.[155] They came into play when *qi* was being moved upward or downward in the torso, the spine functioning as a sort of freight elevator. Because of the "below" (*xia* 下) in the line "the *qi* that fashioned the polluting dreams will be sealed up below the three barriers" 造爲惡夢之氣則受閉於三關之下也, it's tempting to understand the passage as referring to these vertically arrayed checkpoints. But Yang Xi and his interlocutors likely had in mind the three barriers mentioned in the

Scripture of the Yellow Court, "probably the earliest extant work describing the human body as animated by inner gods."[156] They are mentioned in both extant versions of that text, the "outer" (and briefer) of which predated the Shangqing revelations and the "inner," *Precious Scripture of the Interior Landscape of the Yellow Court* (*Huangting neijing yujing* 黃庭內景玉經), perhaps composed by Yang Xi himself. (We have a fragment of it written in Yang's own hand.[157]) There, in the section on the spleen, we read of how, by "sealing and stopping up the three barriers" and "making fists with the thumbs inside and stopping" 閉塞三關握固停, swallowing only saliva as it forms in the mouth, the adept can reach the point of no longer craving food, thus causing the death of the three worms (*san chong* 三蟲, on which see more in the section "Dream Agents and Idioms of Practice" below).[158] And a subsequent section on the three barriers identifies them as the mouth (the celestial barrier, *tianguan* 天關), the feet (the terrestrial, *diguan* 地關), and the hands (the barrier of humanity, *renguan* 人關).[159]

If we picture a gateway in an early medieval city wall, with its two doors each hinged on a tower also serving as a defensive bulwark,[160] we can easily see why these three points of human physiology formed barriers and passageways between the inside of the person and the outer environment: two lips, feet, and hands. And it's these towers *below* which "the *qi* that fashioned the polluting dreams will be sealed" 造為惡夢之氣則受閉. The Shangqing invocation, after all, mentions the "gates to the body" (*ti men* 體門) and the "yellow gatetowers" (*huang que* 黃闕).[161] It seems the speaker is envisioning looking down from a fortified tower upon the foul *qi* flowing away outside the gate. Described more simply, then, the process is one of expelling the exogenous substance or force that caused the dream, whether demon, ghost, corpse, or *qi*, and then shutting the portals behind it. Again we see the command to convert inauspicious to auspicious (*fanxiong chengji* 返凶成吉). Here, confirmation of this conversion arrives in a follow-up dream, this time an auspicious one.

All of this presumes an elaborate inner structure. The human being is a system of zones (three primes [*sanyuan* 三元] and an array of storehouses [*zang* 臟] and depots [*fu* 腑]) interlinked by circulatory paths, equipped with portals mediating interaction with the outside. Enlivened by *qi*, this system is also populated by two sets of volatile spirits (*hun* and *po*) and harbors various gods, some of whom must be installed according to instructions provided in other texts. This federation of discrete entities is the compound being who, by dint of gradual purification, is being cultivated to ascend to the heaven of Upper Purity, there to join a divine assembly of similarly self-cultivated companions in the Purple Halls.

Despite the complex add-ons, however, the practitioner is here still expunging a foul dream by petitioning divine powers for help. As is characteristic of Shangqing methods, the underlying platform is ancient, but on it has been built an innovative edifice of language, imagery, and practice.

Expunging Others' Dream Pollution and Obtaining Purification through Dreams

Although this chapter is primarily concerned with recommendations for removing or preventing one's own dream pollution, I pause here to note that practitioners were sometimes called upon to rescue others from oneiric danger, and that practitioners could sometimes be cleansed of pollution through dreams. A single example of each will suffice.

The first concerns the monk Guṇabhadra 求那跋陀羅 (394–468), an important reciter and translator of Buddhist sutras who arrived in China in 435 and was a guest of Song emperor Wen 文 (r. 424–453).[162] He was setting up a temple in or near the southern capital of Jiankang when disturbances broke out:

> Every evening around midnight, doors would be pushed open and voices would call out, but when someone went to look, no one was there. Many people nearby repeatedly suffered demonic dreams. Guṇabhadra lit incense and pronounced an incantation, saying: "You who are here because of karma from past lives: I am now founding a temple here, where I will constantly practice the path and perform rituals and confessions for your sake. If you remain here [you must] act as spirits of goodness who protect the temple. If you cannot remain, may you each move on to where you can be at peace." Right away, more than ten monastics and laypersons dreamed on the same night that they saw a thousand or more ghosts and spirits carrying [their belongings] on their backs and moving off. The temple community was thenceforth at peace.[163]

每至夜半, 輒有推戶而喚, 視之無人, 眾屢厭夢. 跋陀燒香呪願曰: 汝宿緣在此, 我今起寺, 行道禮懺, 常為汝等. 若住者, 為護寺善神; 若不能住, 各隨所安. 既而道俗十餘人, 同夕夢見鬼神千數, 皆荷擔移去, 寺眾遂安.

Here, as above, a practitioner dispels dream-causing agents, once again by addressing them directly. But in this case the dreamers are multiple members of the local community.

The second example, in which pollution wasn't incurred but cleansed through a dream, occurs in a story about the monk Zhu Fayi 竺法義 (307–380), who specialized in reciting the *Lotus Sutra*. Having fallen ill, Fayi tried various cures, none of which was effective. He then

> gave up trying to effect a cure himself but instead entrusted himself with utmost sincerity to [the bodhisattva] Sound Observer. He kept it up for several days. One day he fell asleep and dreamed he saw a monk arrive to see about his illness, then set out to cure it. The monk cut him open and pulled out his bowels and liver, then washed them clean of filth. Fayi saw that many impure things had collected and concentrated in them. Once the washing was complete, the monk returned the organs to Fayi's body and said to him, "Your illness is now cured." When he awoke, his ailments had dissipated, and soon he had recovered fully. Considering that the *Lotus Sutra* says that "sometimes [the bodhisattva Sound Observer] appears in the image of a monk or brahman,"[164] one suspects that the monk Fayi dreamed of may have been such an instance.[165]
>
> 不復自治, 唯歸誠觀世音. 如此數日. 晝眠夢見一道人來候其病, 因為治之. 刳出腸胃湔洗腑臟, 見有結聚不淨物甚多. 洗濯畢還內之, 語義曰: 汝病已除. 眠覺眾患豁然. 尋得復常. 案其經云: 或現沙門梵志之像, 意者義公所夢其是乎.

Rather than being a vector for pollution, here the dream becomes a vehicle for its elimination. The being contacting the dreamer is an agent of purification, not of pollution. The impurity is pictured graphically and—literally—viscerally, a trope already seen above. Pollution can take concrete, somatic form, as can its removal.

Preventing Foul Dreams

In the previous section we looked at ways of responding to polluting dreams shortly after they'd occurred. A less often attested approach was to prevent them from happening in the first place. (Unsurprisingly, we sometimes find both methods side by side. For example, in one short passage in *Dili sanmeiye budong zunshengzhe niansong bimi fa* 底哩三昧耶不動尊聖者念誦祕密法 by Amoghavajra 不空金剛 [704–774] we see a method to use when lying down to sleep to ward off polluting dreams [*ling wu e meng* 令無惡夢]; a ritual for purifying oneself in the wake of a polluting dream—interestingly, after chanting the mantra 108 times the practitioner is also directed to "purify and cleanse the space where you have slept, according to the [standard] methods" 於所眠處如法辟除結界; and a way of discerning which among one's dreams are auspicious marks, and which are polluting. The methods all involve chanting mantras and deploying seals.[166])

Ultimately, we might imagine the texts discussed in this section arranged along a continuum. At one end, a method for preventing foul dreams is described in sufficient detail to allow us to see how it was thought to work. At the other end are directives to undertake this or that practice, backed by the bare assertion that doing so prevents foul dreams.

I begin at the bare-assertion end of the continuum. Many Mahāyāna Buddhist scriptures promise that engaging in some specified practice will ensure various benefits, usually without explaining exactly how the practice achieves them.[167] And quite often, one of the benefits claimed is the prevention of foul dreams. In such cases, warding off unclean dreams is not the main benefit of the recommended practice, but it is a salutary side effect.

For example, sutras translated from the second century onward—including ones commonly read more for their "philosophical" content than as evidence of practice, such as the Perfection of Wisdom sutras—insist that their upholders and reciters will suffer no unclean dreams. Rather, in their dreams they will exclusively see Buddhas, hear Dharma, and enjoy other sights and sounds conducive to progress on the path.[168] If a person practices compassion and teaches others to do so, he or she will not experience foul dreams.[169] If one deploys the *dhāraṇīs* provided in the sutra, any further unclean dreams will be destroyed.[170] If one wears the talismans and seals provided in the scripture, one will avoid illness, injury in combat, drowning, burning, and foul dreams.[171] If one chants the *dhāraṇīs* provided, upholding them in one's mind, one will be freed of all sorts of troubles, including befouling dreams.[172] If one refrains from killing living beings, one will no longer have foul dreams.[173] To receive, uphold, and chant the sutra in question is to free oneself from unclean dreams so that one will instead dream only of things conducive to progress.[174] To hear and uphold the sutra in question protects against all demonic assaults and anomalies, including unwanted dreams.[175]

All such passages leverage people's dread of pollution to encourage the practices recommended in the texts, not least of which was the recitation, copying, veneration, and dissemination of the very texts recommending them. From the frequency of these promises we may infer that unclean dreams were seen as misfortunes on a par with falling ill, sustaining an injury, or running afoul of a government official. Another is that, in the view of dreaming presupposed by such passages, polluting encounters could occur in dreams just as well as as in waking life.

Moving toward the methodological end of the continuum, we find other passages, some of them found in sutras indigenously composed in China, that afford a better glimpse of how the recommended practices stopped foul dreams. The *Sutra on the Four Celestial Kings* (*Si tianwang jing* 四天王經, fourth or early fifth century), for example, explains that there are twenty-five spirits of goodness (*shanshen* 善神) invisibly surrounding and protecting the practitioner who upholds all the precepts. It's these spirits who repel illness, demons, polluting dreams, overweening local officials, thieves, floods, and fires.[176] The *Consecration Sutra* (*Guanding jing* 灌頂經, fifth century) promises that those who wear the names of the spirits of goodness, or (in another passage) those who wear the names of seven divine kings, or (in yet another passage) those who venerate the Master of Pharmaka Beryl Radiance Buddha 藥師琉璃佛 (Bhaiṣajyaguru) will receive protection from weapons, demons, poisoning by nefarious sorcerers (*gudao jia* 蠱道家), entanglements with local officials, sprites and anomalies, ominous bird calls, wild beasts, corpse-pathogens' depredations, and unclean dreams.[177]

At the methodological end of the continuum we have texts like the Shangqing *Supreme Scripture of Purple Texts Inscribed by the Spirits* (*Huangtian shangqing jingque dijun lingshu ziwen* 皇天上清金闕帝君靈

書紫文上經),[178] which weaves the method across the warp threads of a specific theory of dreams. That theory's articulation leaves no doubt that practitioners faced a potentially catastrophic problem to which the scripture offered a solution. (As discussed in the introduction, many a text works in this manner, persuading readers that there exists a malady to which it furnishes the cure.) The problem lies within: our cloudsouls and whitesouls expose us to pollution by exiting our bodies and roaming about during sleep. The whitesouls in particular spell trouble. Although they are components of our multipartite selves from conception forward, they are also revealed here and in many other texts to have malevolent aspects. They are of-us and yet not-us, an inner Other, or, as the text puts it, "polluting demons within the body" 身中之濁鬼也 (10b1):

> The nights when the moon is beginning its cycle, when the moon is full, and when the moon is darkened are the times when the seven whitesouls ramble free,[179] roaming into all sorts of corruption and filth. Sometimes they have intercourse with blood-eating[180] demons and sprites who roam to and fro. Sometimes they enter into sexual orgies with corpses. Sometimes they defile and delude the Ruddy Infant, joining together in lasciviousness to attack their own residence. Sometimes they visit the Three Offices or the River Sire to tell of your transgressions.[181] Sometimes they transform into *wangliang* demons to bewitch you. Sometimes they lead demons into the body or summon perverse wraiths[182] to destroy you. All manner of injuries and illnesses owe to the transgressions of the whitesouls. Their nature is to delight in your death; their priority is to destroy you. Daoists should control them with discipline, transform them by refining them, rectify them by ruling over them, and overawe them with firm regulation.[183]
>
> 月朔月望月晦夕是此時也七魄流蕩, 遊走穢濁. 或交通血食往鬼來魅; 或與死尸共相關入; 或淫惑赤子, 聚姦伐宅; 或言人之罪,詣三官河伯; 或變為魍魎使人厭魅; 或將鬼入身, 呼邪殺質. 諸殘病生人皆魄之罪. 樂人之死皆魄之性.欲人之敗皆魄之疾.道士當制而勵之, 鍊而變之, 御而正之, 攝而威之.

Further on, the scripture explains:

> The human body contains the spirits of the Palaces of the Three Primes, and within the Gate of Allotted Lifespan are the Grand Sovereign of the

> Mystic Pass as well as the three cloudsouls. Altogether, then, there are seven spirits within the body who want to help the person live long. These are greatly propitious lords of kindness and benevolence. Although the seven whitesouls are also born within the same body, they are thieves who combat and attack the body. This is why they must be controlled. If Daoists know only methods for seeking transcendence but not the way to control the whitesouls, they can only labor in vain.[184]
>
> 人一身有三元宮神, 命門有玄關大君及三魂之神. 合七神皆在形中, 欲令人長生仁慈大吉之君也. 其七魄亦受生於一身, 而與身為攻伐之賊. 故當制之. 道士徒知求仙之方而不知制魄之道, 亦不免於徒勞.

What to do, then? The practitioner must "restrain" (*ju* 拘) and "control" (*zhi* 制) both sets of souls[185] to prevent their unregulated motion during sleep. Having divulged their secret names, the text lays out procedures for anchoring them in the body. To restrain the whitesouls

> you should lie down flat with your head away from the pillow, feet extended, with the centers of your palms over your ears. Your fingertips should just cross in the middle of the nape of your neck. Stop breathing for the space of seven normal breaths and clack your teeth seven times. Actualize white *qi* the size of a small bean on the tip of your nose. After a while, it will gradually enlarge to cover your body in nine layers, from above your head to below your feet. Once this is complete, the white *qi* will suddenly change into the celestial beasts. Position the two green dragons in your eyes and place the two white tigers inside your nostrils. They should all face outward. The vermilion sparrow should be above your heart, facing your mouth. The gray-green tortoise should be below your left foot and the numinous snake beneath your right foot.[186] Inside your ears are jade maidens, dressed in dark brocade and blocking the ear canals, holding torches in both their hands. After a long time, when all these are in place, swallow saliva seven times, clack the teeth seven times, and call out the names of the seven whitesouls.
>
> 當正臥去枕, 伸足, 兩手掌心掩兩耳,令指端相接交於項中. 閉息七過,叩齒七通,存鼻端有白氣如小豆. 須臾漸大以冠身九重,下至兩足,上至頭上. 既畢, 於是白氣忽又變成天獸. 使兩青龍在兩目中, 兩白虎在兩鼻孔中, 皆向外. 朱雀在心上向人口, 蒼龜在左足下, 靈蛇在右足下. 兩耳中有玉女, 著玄錦衣當耳門, 兩手各杞火光.良久都畢, 又咽液七過,叩齒七通,呼七魄名.

Having completed these preparations, the practitioner softly incants:

> With elemental *qi* nine times wound 素氣九回
> I control the perverse malignance of the whitesouls. 制魄邪凶
> Celestial beasts guard the gates, 天獸守門
> Enchanting maidens hold the passes. 嬌女執關
> They refine the whitesouls to passive compliance, 鍊魄和柔
> Granting me peace and calm. 與我相安
> You [whitesouls] are not to engage in reckless movement! 不得妄動
> They are keeping watch over the source of your [multiple] shapes. 看察形源
> If you hunger or thirst, 若汝饑渴
> You may ingest [only] Lunar Yellow and Solar Cinnabar. 聽飲月黃日丹

> Once the preceding incantation is finished, the seven whitesouls will be shut inside. They will be kept under guard and will accept your control. If you regularly practice this, the whitesouls' corruption will be dissolved away, replaced by goodness. Your whole body will then match the Three Palaces above, and you will join in holiness with the Three Primes.[187]
>
> 右祝誦都畢, 於是七魄內閉, 相守受制. 若常行之則魄濁下消反善,合形上和三[官 > 宮] 與元合靈.

As there are seven whitesouls, so the seven orifices are placed under guard,[188] the teeth clacked seven times, the breath held for seven beats, saliva swallowed seven times. The whitesouls' names are spoken aloud since knowing the names of demons and other anomalous agents—and showing them that you know—is the way to control them. In brief compass we see several metaphoric idioms at work: ceasing motion, guarding passages, refining base substances, surveilling unruly subjects, restricting dietary consumption, and draining off turbid waters.

Finally, one way to avoid polluting dreams was to remain awake on the nights when the corpses and worms were scheduled to exit practitioners' bodies and report their transgressions to celestial authorities. To sleep was to relax one's vigilance and allow these volatile components to sneak out, opening the door to dreams. By staying awake on *gengshen* nights one could keep oneself sealed.[189]

Dream Agents and Idioms of Practice

We've seen that dreaming sometimes resulted from contact with harmful exogenous entities. But who or what were these entities? My purpose in this section is not to give an exhaustive account—that would require another book[190]—but to sketch the range of Others who might contact dreamers, as well as to explore some of the operative metaphoric idioms of discourse and practice. All these beings were by nature indeterminate. They often metamorphosed, disguising their true identities. Many had hybrid forms—a somatic expression of their role as polluters.

We might imagine these entities arrayed along a spectrum from non-personified to personified. At the non-personified extreme we find *qi* 氣. *Qi* was a living force but was not an agent with volition, an agenda, or a proper name. It simply flowed through and constituted everything, its movements and stasis, clarity or turbidity, metaphorically characterized as if it were vapor or water—unsurprisingly, since water formed the metaphoric basis for both the graph and the concept.[191] If it had flowed through a ritually unclean entity or area—a rotting corpse, say, or a demon's mouth—or if it had been ritually charged with a curse, or if it was simply stale and lifeless (what Daoist texts termed *guqi* 故氣), it could trigger a foul dream. The state and flow or stagnation of *qi* in the body was sometimes understood to cause certain dream contents, and those could be used diagnostically to ascertain a patient's medical condition (as discussed in chapter 2).[192]

Then we have *xie qi* 邪氣, as well as *xie* 邪 used nominally. *Xie* is often flatly translated as "evil," but, as in the case of *e* 惡, this obscures its root meaning: deviant, off-perpendicular, twisted, or slanted—the antonym of *zheng* 正, "upright" or "straight." A couple of passages in the *Scripture on Great Peace* illustrate its basic meaning of declivity from a norm, worsening over time. In the section "Service of the Dead Should Not Exceed That for the Living" 事死不得過生, for example, the text describes the correct, modest funerary practices of upper antiquity. Then, in middle antiquity, bereaved family members "deviated slightly from the proper model and measure" (*xiao shi fadu* 小失法度), expanding offerings to the dead while putting less thought into these observances, so that the spirits of only half the invited dead actually arrived to partake 死人鬼半來食. The degree of deviation increased as, meanwhile, "who knows what sorts of ghosts and spirit beings arrived to feast on the offerings, lingering at the site to haunt living persons and causing people to fall ill more often" 不知何鬼神物來共食其祭, 因留止祟人, 故人小小多病也. (Here is *sui* 祟 used verbally; more on it in a moment.) Now, "in lower antiquity, people have inherited and passed on the small deviations of middle antiquity, augmenting them and adding larger deviations" 下古復承負中古小失, 增劇大失之, "so that the degree of deviance increases by the day" 故邪日甚劇.[193] Similarly, in the section "Explaining 'Inheriting and Passing On' with Five Analogies" 五事解承負法, several scenarios are sketched in which initially upright teachings give way to small declivities (*xiaoxiao shizheng* 小小失正) so that eventually everything ends up deviant (*xie* 邪), with no evident way back.[194]

When used nominally, *xie* often abbreviates *xie qi* 邪氣, because it is often as a harmful sort of *qi* that *xie* operates. In the earliest Daoist commentary on the *Daode jing* 道德經, the *Xiang'er zhu* 想爾注, we find this passage:[195]

> The heart is a regulator. It may hold fortune or misfortune, good or evil.[196] The belly is a sack for the Dao. Its [i.e., the Dao's] *qi* constantly wants to fill it. When the heart produces ill-omened and evil [conduct][197] the Dao departs, leaving the sack empty. Once it is empty, *xie* enters, killing the person. If one expels the ill-omened and evil, emptying them from the heart, the Dao will return and the belly will be filled.[198]
>
> 心者, 規也, 中有吉凶善惡. 腹者, 道囊, 氣常欲實. 心為凶惡, 道去, 囊空. 空者邪入, 便煞人. 虛去心中凶惡, 道來歸之, 腹則實矣.

This is a good example of the blending of moral and physiological registers: *xie* is both moral property and gaseous pathogen. *Sha* 煞, here used as a verb, often functions nominally in ways similar to "infusions" or "miasmas" (*zhu* 注) and with the same basic meaning of an exogenous pathogen bringing illness or death for humans contacted by it—thus Verellen's "death bringers" is apt.[199] It's mostly synonymous with *sui* 祟, often translated as "haunting."[200] Later in the commentary *xie* is used in a different but related sense to condemn much of the written word in China as polluting—an astonishing claim. On the *Daode jing* line "When 'wisdom' emerged, fabrications came into being" 智慧出, 有大偽, the text says:

> When the true Dao is hidden away, deviant writings emerge. Those who commonly practice false arts proclaim them as the teachings of the Dao, but they are all fraudulent and should not be employed. What are these deviant writings? Of the five scriptures,[201] a good half are deviant. Beyond the five scriptures, all of the writings, traditions, and records are but the productions of corpses—they are all deviant.[202]
>
> 真道藏, 邪文出. 世間常偽伎稱道教, 皆為大偽不可用. 何謂邪文? 其五經半入邪, 其五經以外, 衆書傳記, 尸人所作, 悉邪文.

Close to the non-personified end of the spectrum we have "infusions" or "miasmas" (*zhu* 注/疰), which we met at the outset of this chapter. Because they were held to cause a variety of physical and mental illnesses, they were the targets of innumerable therapeutic and ritual practices of purification. Of all the agents surveyed here, they were perhaps the most contagious by contact.[203]

Toward the personified end of the spectrum of exogenous entities we have the ubiquitous *gui* 鬼, designating a range of beings from ghosts or shades (spirit elements of deceased persons, still active in the human world) to demons or sprites of many forms. Ghosts of relatives now suffering in the unseen world posed particular danger to their surviving kin, which is why so much of Daoist practice involved severing or minimizing familial relations.[204] With Buddhism's advent *gui* came additionally to designate one of the five (or six) paths of rebirth and its unfortunate inhabitants. Related to *gui*, though not commonly used to designate spirits of deceased human beings but instead meaning something like "sprites" or "goblins," are terms such as *mei* 魅,[205] *jing* 精, *yaojing* 妖精, and *wangliang* 罔兩. All of these are agents—they do things—and non-human *persons* of a sort. They want things; they have agendas. As we've seen, they are often directly addressed in ritual speech. Thanks to their skill at changing form and concealing their true nature, they could lure unsuspecting human beings into intimate relationships, sometimes with dire consequences.[206]

The polluting agents that live within the practitioner's body (until expelled) are the three corpses (*san shi* 三尸) and the three or nine worms (*chong* 蟲). Because they've been mentioned several times, I want to pause here to consider them in a bit more detail. They are quintessential pollution agents, not only by their actions but in their very names, synonymous with death and corruption, and in their hybrid bodily forms—for if pollution is a boundary breach, hybrid beings instantiate pollution in their very bodies.[207] In a culture in which death pollution was an extremely serious matter, these were built-in pollutants, hideous of form and deadly in effect. They were an Other within, an *abject* in the sense developed by Julia Kristeva and Judith Butler.[208] Their motive was to trigger the death of their human host so that they might roam freely about, pilfering sacrificial offerings intended for gods and ancestors.

The corpses and worms, which come pre-installed in all human beings, must be expelled before one undertakes any "nurturing life" (*yangsheng* 養生) work. Texts implicate them in dreams in at least four ways, some of which we saw above. They trigger counterproductive dreams by sending out their hosts' cloudsouls and whitesouls during sleep. The middle of the three corpses, in particular, is guilty of this.[209] They cause illness, and when a practitioner dreams of fighting it's because his own souls are struggling against the corpses within. (More on this in chapter 2.) They bewitch practitioners while they sleep, prompting unguarded responses to their many transformations.[210] Finally, not only do they trigger certain dream content: they themselves may appear as the subjects of dreams, especially when the rituals for expelling them begin to take effect.[211]

"Discourse on a Dream of the Three Corpses" ("Meng sanshi shuo" 夢三尸說), a bizarre anecdote about a certain Song Yanhua 宋彥華 who sees the three corpses in human form in a dream, affords us a rare opportunity to hear from the corpses directly. They politely introduce themselves as the Three Pengs 三彭 (this was their standard surname). Dressed in archaic caps and gowns, they come to bid their host a polite farewell just as he is learning techniques for expelling them. He threatens to carry out the methods, but the corpses plead their case, explaining their useful functions and asserting that he will be disoriented if they depart.[212] At the dream's conclusion "they leapt back into him through the nostrils, and he woke with a start" 三彭倏然躍入其鼻，怳而驚乃寤. Afterward he stops learning methods for expelling them and devotes his energies to amassing wealth. The passage closes with: "I've written this story of a dream to be passed down, so that people may laugh at this degree of delusion."[213]

Daoist texts are replete with methods for expelling the corpses.[214] Some involved ingesting medicinal compounds. (Incidentally, this is a good example of how the spirit/matter dichotomy often unconsciously assumed by modern scholars obscures what the texts say: these pathogens are both "spiritual" and "material," and practitioners would not have been surprised that ingesting medicinal substances could expunge them.) Consider, for example, the "Method for Expelling the Three Corpses and Nine Worms, including a Medicinal Formula" ("Chuqu sanshi jiuchong fa bing yaoshu" 除去三尸九蟲法并藥術).[215] The passage explains that the indwelling corpses assume various forms and inflict all sorts of troubles. Going by what people regard as frightening or loathsome, they transform into these very things. While practitioners are sleeping, the corpses call their names, or pretend to be officials come to arrest and bind them, or take the form of their parents or siblings, scolding and accusing them. Or they cause their hosts to dream that their spouses and children have died of illness, leaving them terrified and wailing sorrowfully, or to dream of tombs that have been broken open, their occupants' remains strewn about 或夢妻子困病死喪, 使人憧惶, 悲哀哭泣.或夢塚墓, 狼籍尸骸. They might even knock the dreamer's cap off his head.

The text proceeds to prescribe a medicinal means of expulsion. (Here is another example of how prescriptive texts often present the reader with a dire problem, then offer a way to solve it. The seriousness of the problem is meant to deepen the reader's investment in the methods prescribed by the text—and thus in the text itself.) The practitioner is to make a powder of three ingredients: *fuzi* 附子, or "appended offspring," processed offshoots of the main tuber of wolfsbane; *wuyi* 蕪荑, or processed fruit of elm; and *ganqi* 乾漆, or the dried sap of lacquer trees.[216] After ingesting one spoonful with wine on an empty stomach each day for one lunar cycle, all three corpses will be expelled. At that point the practitioner should void his runny stool[217] into a basin. In it he will see the wormlike forms of the three corpses 即見三尸蟲狀. He should enclose them in a cloth and submerge them into an eastward-flowing stream while softly wailing for them (as one would mourn a newly deceased relative) and incanting, "While *you* are now dead, and belong to earth, *I* will attain celestial ascension" 汝死屬地, 我得升天. He must then return by a different route, taking care not to look back. After three days he may have spells of wailing loudly during the day or feeling troubled or dazed 或自於日中

大哭, 煩惱恍惚, but he should not be alarmed by this. Afterward such troubles will resolve, and he will have become a person of the Dao.[218]

Finally, at the extreme personified end of the spectrum we have *mo* 魔, a term created as an equivalent for the Buddhist Māra, the being who reigns over this realm of ceaseless birth-and-death, or *saṃsāra*, and interferes with ascetics' attempts to escape it. *Mo* often designated both this being and marauding demons generally[219]—especially demons who were conceived of as launching coordinated attacks. They are ubiquitous wreakers of havoc in apocalyptic narratives and prophecies.[220] We will meet Māra again in the next chapter.

A Closing Example

The following passage will do several jobs for us: illustrate the extent to which practitioners' daily lives were supposed to be guided by innumerable rules; exemplify the overlaying of distinct metaphoric registers in the same text; and show how dreams might factor into all this. It appears in the Shangqing *Prohibitions for Transcendents Recorded by the Perfected, from the Purple Texts Inscribed by Spirits* (*Taiwei lingshu ziwen xianji zhenji shangqing* 太微靈書紫文仙忌真記上經). This text warns that although readers may have the bodily marks (*xiang* 相) of a future transcendent, if they violate any of a list of prohibitions those marks will be removed and their quest for divine ascension will fail. The prohibitions mostly concern sex and diet and warn against killing living things, stealing, acting violently, and becoming ritually impure. More specifically, they forbid numerous specific actions on particular days of the calendar or when one is facing in a particular direction. Practitioners are not to face north when relieving themselves or arranging their hair or clothing, or when spitting or cursing; not to administer corporal punishments on the solstices, equinoxes, or the first days of the four seasons; not to eat the flesh of shelled creatures on *jia* days, or of fowl on *bingwu* days, or of black-colored animals on *bingzi* days; not to cut plants or trees on the eighth day of the fourth month, look at blood on the fifth day of the fifth month, buy or sell shoes on the fourth day of the eighth month; and so on. These prohibitions were by no means the only rules known even to Shangqing practitioners; they're simply the ones this text happens to insist on. Reading such lists, we see that almost every aspect of the practitioner's life was to be regulated. It is against this background that the danger of dream pollution should be understood. The seemingly countless regulations formed boundaries that diked against pollution but also created the conditions for it. And the ongoing creation of pollution necessitated the creation and prescription of ways of dispelling it.

The passage is built on two distinct metaphoric registers for purity and danger. First, its warning of the consequences of violations is framed in the bureaucratic idiom, where it's a matter of investigations and reports by the Three Offices (*san guan* 三官) resulting in the removal of transcendent marks. But a visceral idiom of pollution and bodily corruption, rot, and filth comes to predominate. The two great modes of pollution, then, transgression pollution and contact pollution, are deployed side by side as we move from an administrative language of investigations and reports to a somatic and *qi*-based discourse of disorder, boundary-breaching, and corruption.[221] The imagery is shot through with the vile and the disgusting, and the consequences for the practitioner-victim are rendered in a vivid vocabulary of pollution and decay. If you engage in sexual debauchery (*yin* 淫), "your cloudsouls and bodily fluids leak away, your glowing essences wither and dry up. Your spirits are scorched, your whitesouls scatter. Your bones become thin, your marrow sullied" 魂液外漏，精光枯竭，神燋魄散，骨薄髓穢. If you steal or act viciously, your yellow court will be thrown into contention, the three corpses will delight in killing you, and "your cloudsouls and corporeal spirits will observe the lasciviousness as your whitesouls have intercourse with demons, blocking your inner chambers" 魂神鬭姦，魄鬼干室. "Your eyesight will lose focus and harmful *qi* will issue from your mouth." If you get drunk, "your physical form deteriorates and your internal spirits grow confused. Your cloudsouls forget their proper chambers and your whitesouls roam off to perverse dwellings" 形質淪壞，神真交錯，魂忘本室，魄遊邪宅. If you become "sullied and impure" 穢慢不盛, your pure spirits will lose their state of perfection 清靈失真; your essence and cloudsouls will not remain in place, and worms will arise in your three palaces 精魂不居，三宮生蟲. Your blood will thicken and your marrow will rot 血濁髓臭. Then:

> On account of this, foul dreams will encroach on the crimson heart, and demons and sprites will scale its scarlet towers. Your essences and fluids

will become contaminated[222] . . . . When this happens, your spirits become confused and you begin transgressing the interdictions without regard to the prohibitions.[223]

是以惡夢交於丹心，妖魅乘其朱闕，精液觸犯，神真恍惚流變多禁莫識忌.

The imagery of polluting dreams and demons joining forces in an assault on the towers of the heart is quite vivid. In light of all we've seen, it should not surprise us.

Conclusion

Presenting oneself at a temple or at court or before a magistrate; offering sacrifice; handling, transmitting, reciting, or copying a scripture; appearing before an altar; submitting a petition to the celestial gods; performing confession and repentance; observing mourning: these and countless other situations were governed by manifold boundaries and norms, even for individuals who hadn't taken monastic vows and were not full-time religious practitioners. Maintaining ritual purity was a ubiquitous aspect of culture, society, and daily life in ancient and medieval China, despite the scant attention paid it by modern scholars. Dreams were just one of many areas of life in which pollution might figure and in which actions undertaken to maintain or restore ritual purity were seen as essential.

Given that religious practitioners were meant to self-regulate almost every aspect of their lives, some dreams had the potential to wreck this control, befoul practitioners' carefully maintained purity, and thus block their progress. The PURIFICATION PARADIGM treated dreams not as psychological events happening inside the dreamer's mind but as assaults or contagions by other beings or forces, whether originating without or (in the case of corpses, worms, and whitesouls) within, or else as real contacts with polluting substances and scenarios, resulting in a state of pollution that brought other dire consequences. This is why the response most often took the form of exorcistic or apotropaic ritual. This is practical logic at work: *the model of what dreaming is dictates the form the response to it can take*. Although the same word, *meng* 夢, might be used to denote all cases, not all dreams were understood to be of the same type, to be caused by the same processes, or to trigger the same results.

Foul dreams may be compared to the many extant narratives of amorous encounters with spirits (*jing* 精, etc.) of various sorts. Both involved physical contact between a human subject and some other being. Both might be experienced as pleasurable while occurring. Only afterward did the human party come to realize that the situation carried grave risk.[224] Even more danger lurked in this situation for the human subject *qua* practitioner, for the encounter threatened to spoil his or her carefully cultivated persona and undo progress on the path of self-cultivation. This is one reason accomplished practitioners were often depicted calmly exorcising demons (something few ordinary persons would dare attempt), impervious to their threat precisely because of the distance they'd already traveled on their path.[225]

If we were to inventory the repertoire of techniques we have seen to this point, the list might look like this:

- placing deer-musk incense in one's pillow
- mentally actualizing sequences of scenes or inner components of oneself
- positioning one's bed at least thirty inches above the floor
- pronouncing an incantation or a *dhāraṇī*
- pronouncing an invocation of a deity or spirit
- unbinding one's hair
- exhaling a stream of breath or spurting water out of one's mouth (and facing a particular direction while doing so)
- offering food or clothing to a divine being
- donning clean clothes and washing oneself
- sleeping in one's place of practice before an icon
- refraining from putting a polluting dream into social circulation by speaking of it
- writing and deploying talismans
- making and deploying a seal
- voicing demons' names (and knowing their names)
- purifying one's mind
- sending a prayer request to spirits

- issuing commands to spirits
- preparing and ingesting a medicinal compound
- visualizing a star in the sky
- commanding inner components of oneself to restrain other components
- minimizing or severing family ties
- sealing off the somatic passages connecting one to one's surroundings
- upholding, reciting, copying, or hearing a scripture
- wearing a talisman, seal, or list of spirits' names
- keeping the precepts and purity rules
- staying awake on particular nights of the calendar

This inventory attests to the creative work of culture across traditions and communities of practice. Note that relatively few items in this list are actions completed by thought alone. Dreaming wasn't usually seen as a mental event at all.[226]

What are the predominant metaphoric idioms that structure the discourse and practices we've seen so far? Pollution, of course, is foremost—but, as in medieval Japan (where this topic has been explored by Jayne Sun Kim), pollution came in at least two distinct metaphoric registers: contact pollution, generally transmittable, and transgression pollution, usually not in itself transmittable, though its consequences might be. As Kim explains in the case of Japan, "Concern for transmittable defilement, which was rooted in the standardization of ritual protocol, helped to delimit the physical and cosmological boundaries of the medieval world. Efforts to check the transmission of defilement influenced both the way in which physical spaces such as buildings were created and the manner in which individual persons navigated them."[227] In Chinese culture, similar systems of boundaries and protocols were developed. However, as we've seen, in modern scholarship much discourse around ritual distinctions, separations, and pollution tends to get transposed into the key of morality. Another important pair of metaphoric registers in China is *qi*-based versus administrative, or what I previously termed pneumatic versus bureaucratic.[228] *Qi*-based notions and practices tended to be paired with contact pollution (in part because *qi* was spread by contact and proximity), while practices and narratives structured in terms of the administrative register tended to be paired with transgression pollution (in part because transgressions were observed, recorded, and adjudicated by a complex bureaucratic system). But there are exceptions, and it is not unusual, as we've just seen, to find these registers deployed side by side in the same text, even in the same passage.

What models of the dreaming self tend to predominate in this PURIFICATION PARADIGM? There was, of course, no singular view of the human person underlying the many practices and prescriptions I have outlined in this chapter. But there are commonalities. The practices imply a self that is multipartite, fissiparous, volatile, easily prone to disintegration; a self that is an enclosed, bounded system, but with ports of ingress and egress through which pollution was liable to enter or components of oneself were liable to escape; and, often, a self that harbors components that could spell their host's demise—whether they take the form of biospiritual parasites or of the impure karmic legacy of one's previous rebirths. Cultivating such a self was like trying to tie down multiple sails on a leaky sailboat in a typhoon while keeping an eye on the horizon for marauding pirates. Things were liable to fly away from you, or to enter without your awareness, potentially with grave consequences. In the same way that meditators, alchemists, petitioners, scripture reciters, or copyists were supposed to maintain purity in their enclosed ritual space dedicated to practice—their "chamber of stillness" (*jing shi* 靜室) or "abstinence hall" (*zhaitang* 齋堂) or oratory—so practitioners of all sorts were also to maintain purity in their own person. The points of ingress and egress had to be carefully controlled. Buddhist monks were served by "purifiers" (*jingren* 淨人) to mediate their interactions with laypersons when accepting meals and donations, they were instructed to carefully separate "pure" (*jing* 淨) from "soiled" (*zhuo* 濁) implements and articles of clothing, and they lived inside an inter-nested series of purified precincts carefully demarcated through the ritual of "fixing the boundary" (*jie jie* 結界).[229] But they had no such buffers when it came to dreams.

To close this chapter, let's broaden our gaze from individual dreamers to the larger contexts in which they were embedded. The Protestant model of religion has conditioned many of us to take individuals' experiences as the primary data for the study of religion—doubly so in the case of dreaming, often seen as the private, solipsistic experience *par excellence*. On this model it's hard to see what was so dangerous about foul dreams. To do so, we must set the Protestant model aside and pan out from the dreamer as an individual.

It wasn't just the dreamer who was put at risk by polluting dreams, for practitioners always operated within communities both visible and invisible. They lived and practiced in carefully curated circles of teachers, masters, fellow disciples, the "wholesome friends" (*shan you* 善友), the "older/younger siblings under the same teacher" (*shi xiongdi* 師兄弟), and the "fellow practitioners" (*tong xue* 同學) so often mentioned in texts. Many had joined extended families distinct from their natal ones. They operated in temporo-spatial networks under rules and rhythms established by divine beings and revered founders, within the bounds of a hard-won order not of their own making. They saw themselves as positioned in lineages that stretched backward and forward in generational and cosmic time, knit together in networks extending outwards into terrestrial and cosmic space, their activities keyed to the cycles of the sun and moon and the motions of the stars and planets. Their daily thoughts, words, and deeds were subject to disciplines ordained by divine beings and sages. Their knowing was a process of connecting with things commonly held, shared subject matters and texts and practices (that is, with *res* in the sense illuminated by Mary Carruthers),[230] and it was this activity of learning, remembering, acting, thinking, speaking, that was their labor of self-cultivation. Even when working in apparent solitude, they were never alone, always overseen by and tied to a normally invisible cloud of beings and their lineage forebears. All this was endangered by dreams that exposed practitioners to beings or forces outside the boundaries, outside the canon, and thus threatened to loosen their ties to the community as they fell into a merely private world, making them a peril to others within that circle—making them an Other. The measures taken to restore purity would knit the practitioner back into the circle.

I find instructive Peter Brown's way of capturing what was problematic about sexual dreams and nocturnal emissions in medieval European monasteries:

> The continuance of sexual dreams and emissions served to warn the monk, in a mercifully concrete manner, of the presence within his heart of a more faceless, lingering desire—the wish to possess experiences of his own. The sexuality of the emission created a disjunction between his public, daylight self and a last oasis of incommunicable, privatized experience. When such dreams ceased, the last fissure between the private person and his fellows could be assumed to have closed.[231]

I think that the most fearsome thing about the sorts of dreams discussed in this chapter was not their emotional valence. It was that practitioners had been touched by beings, forces, or situations from beyond the canon, a situation which if left unremedied threatened to tug them loose from the connective web of community and tradition, throw them off their self-cultivational path, and cast them out into idiosyncrasy. *That* was the nightmare.

CHAPTER TWO

Diagnosing

Consider this bit of instruction preserved in *Cloudy Bookcase with Seven Labels* (*Yunji qiqian*), an anthology by Zhang Junfang 張君房 completed around 1025 of mostly much earlier texts:[1]

> Method for interpreting indications concerning the three corpses: If you suddenly[2] dream of building a house or erecting a fence, this means that the corpses and worms are taking up residence together in your abdomen. If you dream of having intercourse with a woman, this means the corpses and worms are having a meeting. In serious instances you will become ill. If you are ingesting powdered cinnabar [to expel the corpses and worms] and it is taking effect, you will dream that a great fire is burning up your house. If you are consuming other medicines [for the same purpose],[3] when they start to work you will dream that your father and mother have died, or that your wife and child have been killed, or else the victims will be your sisters or brothers or [other] women. Or [you will dream that] a grave has been destroyed and the coffin has vanished, or that you are undergoing the five types of mutilating punishment[4] and dying. All these are indications that the corpses and worms are being destroyed.[5]
>
> 候三尸法: 若忽夢起屋舍籬障者, 是腹中尸蟲共相依止. 若夢與女人交通者, 其尸蟲會也. 重者皆成病. 若服丹砂有功者, 當夢大火燒其屋宇. 服諸藥有應者, 當夢父母喪亡, 妻子被殺, 或是姊妹兄弟之屬或女人, 或塚墓破壞失去棺槨, 及被五刑死者. 此是尸蟲皆將消滅候也.

We met the corpses and worms in chapter 1. Here I want to focus for a moment on the rhetorical features of such a passage, for they structure all of the texts examined in this chapter. To begin, we should ask what sort of implied readers the passage seems to aim at. I would say that the text assumes readers who are practitioners of methods of self-cultivation and not just people interested in theories about corpses and worms (or dreams). These readers apparently need no introduction to the idea that we all have such pathogens lurking within us—an idea that seems to have enjoyed wide distribution, as we saw in chapter 1. But the details of the expulsion methods glancingly referred to here would normally have been transmitted from master to disciple in rituals requiring the disciple's pledge of secrecy and would have been accompanied by oral instructions.[6] Many passages anthologized in *Cloudy Bookcase* had been selected from scriptures normally transmitted in this way. The anthology thus rhetorically positions itself as looking over the shoulder of an initiate who had gained access to such texts. Through it, we glimpse privileged information.

Observe, next, the divinatory conceit on which the passage is constructed. For centuries, the verb *hou* 候 had meant to observe phenomena for signs or portents, notably in the practice of *hou qi* 候氣, or observing weather and cloud patterns, and in using pitchpipes for divinatory signals. As a noun, *hou* named those signs themselves.[7] Again, a particular sort of audience is assumed. It isn't just anyone, but rather an informed specialist, who is implied to be scanning some field of phenomena for subtle alterations that, by virtue of some technique not universally available, *can be read to mean* something.

Here, that field is dreams and, specifically, what they were about—not, say, the day or hour of their occurrence. (Some dream keys were hemerological, considering only dreams' timing while ignoring their content.[8]) The key consists in a correspondence between a small group of dream themes and a set of corpse activities. This correspondence is all the text supplies. The reader finds no explanation of *why* a certain kind of dream content indicates a certain action by the corpses—or, for that matter, of what dreams even are. X *simply is* Y: the copula *shi* 是 is repeated three times.[9]

Notice one other aspect of the passage's rhetorical workings: the inner states indicated by certain dreams are things practitioners would (it's implied) have no other way of knowing. The corpses and their activities are normally opaque in the extreme. But for practitioners now equipped with these semiotic correlations, their dreams afford access to some of these inward goings on. This view of dreams as revealing aspects of dreamers' inner states was not uncommon across the ancient world. It was often employed diagnostically in medical contexts, for example.[10] And it is, of course, fundamental to a dominant modern view of dreams as psychological, as products of our anxieties. But this apparent similarity is deceptive. One point I will make again in this chapter is that, even in texts such as those we'll investigate next, dreaming was usually not seen as a merely psychological phenomenon.

This brief passage exemplifies all the key aspects of what I term the DIAGNOSTIC PARADIGM of dreaming. In this paradigm, first, dreams are seen as pertaining to aspects of dreamers themselves—specifically, their progress (or lack of progress) in self-cultivation. Second, the dream often serves to disclose some problem or blockage impeding their practice. (I regard uses of dreams in medical diagnoses as a subset of this much larger group.) Third, dreams are approached as constituting a code, made up of symbolic signs. In the semiotics of Charles Peirce, a sign is "something which stands to somebody for something in some respect or capacity."[11] Signs fall into three classes. Icons are likenesses of their objects (e.g., photographs). Indexes, rather than resembling the objects they represent, point to them (e.g., weathervanes as indices of wind direction). Symbols refer to their objects indirectly as a function of their systemic and conventional relationship to other symbols (e.g., words in a human language—or specific dream components in relation to others).[12] In the DIAGNOSTIC PARADIGM, dreams are treated as containing symbols relevant to the dreamer's self-cultivational process. In other words, dreams are like utterances in a strange language. What they mean is never evident on the surface; they must undergo interpretation. What texts do in this paradigm is provide a key or glossary for deciphering dreams' cryptic messages.

In approaching dreams as utterances in a strange language, the texts investigated here resemble those of the PROSPECTIVE PARADIGM,[13] with one key exception: rather than yielding predictions of future *events* (as in the PROSPECTIVE PARADIGM), here the decoded signs disclose otherwise opaque aspects of the dreamer's present state. To say it differently, the PROSPECTIVE and DIAGNOSTIC PARADIGMS are similar in that they both adopt a hermeneutic stance toward dreams, treating them as coded messages whose meanings are cryptic and must be unlocked by some method of interpretation. Where they differ is in the application of the method. In the PROSPECTIVE PARADIGM dreams are taken to indicate coming events and are therefore used to navigate the uncertainties of the future. In the DIAGNOSTIC PARADIGM dreams are used as indications of the dreamer's own present state of progress *qua* self-cultivator, as well (sometimes) as signs of the specific obstacles or lapses preventing the practitioner from advancing toward the goal. There are, then, two vectors of difference: the PROSPECTIVE PARADIGM focuses on future time, the DIAGNOSTIC PARADIGM on present (and in some cases also past) time; and the PROSPECTIVE PARADIGM focuses on the shape of events, whereas the DIAGNOSTIC PARADIGM addresses dreamers themselves *qua* self-cultivators, as individuals treading some particular path of self-cultivation.

A literary genre characteristic of texts constructed on both the PROSPECTIVE and DIAGNOSTIC PARADIGMS is what I've elsewhere termed the dreambook: a list of dream elements and their meanings.[14] In dreambooks the meanings assigned to dream signs are usually so non-intuitive as to appear arbitrary, and this apparent arbitrariness positions the dreambook as an indispensable repository of arcane knowledge, whether about future events or about the dreamer's present condition.[15] In *The Chinese Dreamscape* I focused on dreambooks that are lists of dream signs keyed to predictions of future events, but, as we are about to see, other dreambooks, while similarly treating dream components semiotically, peg their meanings to diagnoses of present problems confronting the dreamer.

This chapter investigates texts structured around the DIAGNOSTIC PARADIGM, asking questions such as these: How does the dream key work? Which aspects of practitioners' selves or of their progress are diagnosed? What is the nature of the "self" presupposed in the texts? What sorts of information does the dream interpretation yield? What broader views of dreaming and of self-cultivational practice can be gleaned from the rhetorical structuring of such texts?

A Diagnostic Dream Manual for Bodhisattvas

Although it has been little studied, *Sutra on the Explication of Dreams for Bodhisattvas* (*Pusa shuomeng jing* 菩薩說夢經) is one of the most extensive dreambooks produced anywhere in the medieval world. As its title indicates, it is a dream key for those who saw themselves as treading the bodhisattva path toward eventual Buddhahood. Although I am aware of no extant depiction of someone using this text to interpret a dream, we do know that it existed in enough copies and over enough years to gain the attention of successive scriptural catalogers, that it addresses a pressing concern of practitioners (a concern attested in many other texts circulating in China), that it is referenced in at least one Dunhuang manuscript (Pelliot 3017) containing a list of corrections to the compilation in which it sometimes circulated,[16] and that prior to this compilation it had circulated independently, probably for several centuries.

Textual History

As it has come down to us, the *Pusa shuomeng jing* occupies rolls 15 and 16 of the 120-roll *Ratnakūṭa*, or *Heap of Jewels* (*Da baoji jing* 大寶積經),[17] a compilation of sutras dealing with the bodhisattva path and other aspects of Mahāyāna teaching.[18] Although no Sanskrit version has survived, *Svapnanirdeśa* is a putative Sanskrit equivalent of the Chinese title.[19] In the *Da baoji jing* it is called *Deva who Dwells in Purity* (*Jingju tianzi* 淨居天子), presumably for the first deity to be mentioned by name in the audience to whom Śākyamuni preaches the sutra.

A complete *Ratnakūṭa* had been brought from India by the celebrated monk, pilgrim, and translator Xuanzang 玄奘. In 664 he was asked to translate it, but on account of his age and illness he declined.[20] In 713 the southern Indian monk Bodhiruci 菩提流支 (d. 727), who had arrived in Chang'an and Luoyang in 693, finished compiling (and in some cases translating or editing)[21] forty-nine separate sutras into a *Ratnakūṭa* that is the source of modern textual versions. His work was patronized by the Tang emperor Zhongzong 中宗 (d. 710), as well as his brother and successor Ruizong 睿宗, who personally served as scribe in some sessions. The finished work was presented to the court in July of 713. But not all of the forty-nine sutras had been newly translated by Bodhiruci. For twenty-three of them he adopted translations that had been circulating for decades or more.[22] As Zhisheng 智昇 wrote in his scripture catalog, *Record of Buddhist Teachings from the Kaiyuan Era*

(*Kaiyuan shijiao lu* 開元釋教錄, 730): "This sutra [i.e., the *Da baoji jing*] consists of forty-nine *pariṣad*. Translators of previous eras had chosen some of the *pariṣads* and translated them separately, so it was not complete" 此經都有四十九會. 上代譯者摘會別翻而不終部帙.[23] The text on dreams was one of these twenty-three, as Zhisheng indicated when characterizing it as "an older translation, a stand-alone text" (*jiuyi danben* 舊譯單本).[24]

Modern editions list Dharmarakṣa 竺法護 (fl. ca. 266–308) as the sutra's translator. This attribution may or may not have begun with Fei Changfang's 費長房 expansive catalog of 598, *Record of the Three Treasures through the Generations* (*Lidai sanbao ji* 歷代三寶紀). In any case, it is certainly false, as already recognized by Zhisheng.[25] But Zhisheng does group the sutra among translations thought to have been done in the Wu and Jin eras, that is, the third and fourth centuries. Regardless of who produced it, we know that it must have existed by 598 CE, when Fei's catalog was completed.[26]

The Nature of the Text

Explication of Dreams lays out an extensive system for dream-based self-diagnosis. After the standard sort of sutra introduction, the text opens by simply listing 108 dream signs, which it terms *xiang* 相. Then follows the main body, where each sign is decoded to yield the point(s) on the bodhisattva path the dreamer has reached. Following the diagnosis in many cases comes a prescription of practices to remove whatever blockage is evidenced by the dream. The text, then, answers three basic questions for its implied reader: What stage of the path have I reached? What are the karmic roots of the blockage that triggered my dream? From the available repertoire of devotional and cultivational activities, which ones should I now undertake to remove this blockage?[27]

Over the course of several centuries, Mahāyāna sutras circulating in China had mapped the bodhisattva path in a confusing variety of ways. A letter written by the monk Dao'an 道安 (312–385) reveals the difficulty even a learned monastic practitioner faced in navigating the many conflicting descriptions known to him.[28] Texts centering on this topic, all produced between the mid-second and early fourth centuries, include An Shigao's 安世高 (fl. 148–180) *Daodi jing* 道地經 (an abridged version of the *Yogācārabhūmi*),[29] Lokakṣema's (fl. 178–189) 支婁迦讖 *Dousha jing* 兜沙經,[30] Zhi Qian's 支謙 (fl. 220–252) influential *Pusa benye jing* 菩薩本業經,[31] Nie Daozhen's 聶道真 *Zhu pusa qiufo benye jing* 諸菩薩求佛本業經, and Dharmarakṣa's 竺法護 (fl. 266–308) *Pusa shizhu xingdao pin* 菩薩十住行道品, *Xiuxing daoji jing* 修行道地經, and *Jianbei yiqie zhide jing* 漸備一切智德經.[32] The path implied in *Explication of Dreams* is the basic ten-stage one seen (for example) in Zhi Qian's *Pusa benye jing*, except that in *Explication* the stages are not even assigned names or descriptions, only numbers. There are no "abodes" or substations within the distinct stages. Regardless of how low or high the stages are in the ten-stage ranking, *Explication of Dreams* variously terms them *di* 地 (the most commonly used one), *zhu* 住 (used both nominally and verbally, to "dwell in" this or that stage), the compound *zhudi* 住地 (compare Zhi Qian's use of 地住), or *chu* 處 (often modifying *di* in the phrase 處處地, "[any of] the various stages"). Furthermore, the text measures progress in two additional ways: whether one has received a prediction (*shou ji* 受記) from a Buddha of one's future Buddhahood, guaranteeing eventual success, and whether one is "irreversible" (*bu tuizhuan* 不退轉) in one's quest. (More below on irreversibility.) From these features we may infer that the text's makers assumed an audience already quite familiar with the notion of bodhisattvas and their gradual progression over many rebirths toward Buddhahood, with the assurance of irreversibility and a former-life prediction of Buddhahood as key signposts.[33] *Explication*'s mission is not to describe the bodhisattva path but to satisfy practitioners' desire to know precisely where they stood on it.

The text as reproduced in two major modern movable-type canons, *Taishō shinshu daizōkyō* 大正新修大藏經 (prepared in Tokyo 1922–1933) and *Zhonghua dazang jing* 中華大藏經 (Beijing 1984–1996), is in some disarray.[34] The phrasing is often difficult. Some dream signs given in the initial list lack interpretations in the main section. Conversely, some interpretations in the main section concern dream content not found in the opening list. The ordering of signs is occasionally jumbled. Contradictory statements are sometimes made in the same entry.[35] The wording in the list of signs often fails to match the interpretations in the main section, as if these two sections had been translated by different persons or from distinct source texts or stemmed from a text that had resulted from the merging of independent sources. When we bear in mind that translation was typically done by a team of individuals with varying competencies, and that no one person commanded both the source and the target languages, it's hardly surprising that the text reads roughly.

Explication of Dreams naturally breaks into four parts: (1) the setting of the scene; (2) the initial list of dream signs; (3) the detailed unpacking of the meanings of each sign; and (4) the conclusion and send-off. Like most sutras, this one is rhetorically structured as the report of what the Buddha said on a particular occasion to an audience, with certain auditors posing questions. Before turning to the heart of the sutra (that is, part 3), I will first discuss parts 1 and 4, then (in the next section) part 2. Part 2 is also translated in appendix A.

Part 1 opens with one among an assembly of celestial beings, Vajra Obliterator (Jingangcui 金剛摧), asking the Buddha for instruction on the "signs" (*xiangmao* 相貌) pertaining to the practice of the bodhisattva path (*pusa suo xing* 菩薩所行 or *daoxing* 道行). *Xiangmao* was often used to translate the Sanskrit *mukha*, meaning the features, look, form, shape, or character of something. Outside the opening and closing sections, the term used throughout the text to indicate the signs forming its main topic is simply *xiang* 相. *Xiang* was often chosen to translate the Sanskrit *lakṣana*, meaning an attribute, mark, or distinctive feature. Both terms had had a long indigenous history prior to this translation, notably in texts on the art of physiognomy, where it was similarly a matter of interpreting surface-level signs to discern non-obvious characteristics within.[36]

After agreeing to Vajra Obliterator's request, the Buddha proceeds to his discourse. Oddly, the notion that the signs discussed will involve things seen in dreams is not yet so much as hinted at. Other than the work's title, it is only in part 2 that the sutra mentions dreams.

In the brief closing in part 4, the Buddha begins by saying that he has provided the signs to quell doubt on the part of bodhisattvas, recognizing the immense difficulty of the path they are on. He briefly mentions the immediate benefits to the audience of having heard the sutra: their karmic and demonic obstructions are at once removed. Then he insists on the benefits to subsequent generations of hearing, upholding, and reciting this sutra—a feature typical of Mahāyāna sutras. Such practitioners, having expunged twenty kalpas' worth of karma and demonic obstructions, will attain Buddhahood alongside Maitreya or else be reborn in another world.

The Initial List of Signs

In part 2, the Buddha lists in quick succession 108 signs without yet divulging their meanings. Each item opens with one of two formulations: "If you see in a dream" (*meng jian* 夢見) some phenomenon, or "if you dream of yourself" (*zi meng* 自夢) doing some activity. Only in part 3 of the sutra, where many of the initial signs are further ramified into as many as ten sub-indices, does it become clear that these 108 signs actually function as headings. Around 676 distinct signifiers are introduced in the text overall.[37] This makes *Explication of Dreams* one of the largest medieval dreambooks to have survived into modern times. To find another example of so many dream signs treated in a single work, one would have to turn to Artemidorus' *Oneirocritica* (mid-second or early third century)[38] or, in China, to one of the massive compendia assembled a thousand years later, such as Chen Shiyuan's *Mengzhan yizhi* 夢占逸旨 (ca. 1562), Zhang Fengyi's 張鳳翼 *Mengzhan leikao* 夢占類考 (1585), or He Dongru's 何棟如 and Huang Tang's 黃堂 *Menglin xuanjie* 夢林玄解 (1636).[39]

Appendix A contains my translation of the list of 108 signs along with speculation about its numerological significance. Here I want to comment on the nature of this list. As "perhaps the most archaic and pervasive of genres,"[40] lists have information retrieval as their prime function. Ancient and medieval cultures developed forms of *Listenwissenschaft*, "a science which takes as its prime intellectual activity the production and reflection on lists, catalogs, and classifications, which progresses by establishing precedents, by observing patterns, similarities, and conjunctions, by noting repetitions. Such a science is particularly noticeable in omen and legal materials."[41] Probably every culture has at some point developed standard lists of oneiric signs. Dreambooks are *Listenwissenschaft* applied to dreams.[42]

Lists of many sorts have played a prominent role in the Buddhist tradition. Scholars have noted the mnemonic function of its many *mātikā*s (Pāli) or *mātṛkā*s—this latter Sanskrit term etymologically related to *matrix*. Rupert Gethin and several other writers have emphasized the generative function of such lists—the ways in which they have acted as matrices for the ongoing development of thought and discourse. Gethin writes, "The indefinite expansions based on the *mātikā*s continually remind those using them that it is of the nature of things that no single way of breaking up and analyzing the world can ever be final."[43] Each list could be used as "a veritable matrix for a whole series of further lists," not so much a summary as "the seed from which something else grows."[44] Following this suggestion, we might see the subsequent expansion in part 3 of *Explication of Dreams* as resulting from the sort of unfolding process *mātṛkā*s are known for. But if we take seriously a key phrase in part 1—where the Buddha tells his audience, "I will explicate for you *all of the signs*" 當為汝說 所有相貌 —we might regard the text's entire list of around 676 primary and secondary signs not as a matrix meant to remain open to "indefinite expansion" but as something meant to be closed and comprehensive—a canon of dream signifiers.[45] That the primary signs total 108 supports this conjecture, as I explain in appendix A.

Fifty-one of the signs are not specific to Buddhist contexts; they could be dreamt by anyone. Of the five senses, the one most involved, not surprisingly, is vision, but hearing also figures importantly. Fifty-seven of the primary signs involve seeing a Buddha doing something or witnessing or joining some unmistakably Buddhist practice. Twenty-three of those involve seeing or hearing the Buddha himself; nine have to do with relics and stupas; six concern hearing or expounding Dharma; five involve hearing *dhāraṇīs* or sutras. Furthermore, five involve ritual acts of presenting offerings and ornamentations; two mention icons, and two consist of seeing ritual spaces. Three involve other worlds.[46] The text is explicitly addressed to practitioners who have taken the bodhisattva vow, but the list of signs in part 2 mostly mentions aspects of practice that would have been familiar to any Buddhist, monastic or lay. At least in early medieval China, practitioners who understood themselves to be on the bodhisattva path included both monastery- and household-dwelling individuals, up to and including emperors.[47] At the same time, like other texts in the *Ratnakūṭa* much of part 3 seems to assume readers living a renunciant life, that is, ones ordained as monks or nuns, whether or not they currently reside in a monastery.[48]

The sequence of signs has no evident shape. The first forty signs are specific to Buddhism, but afterward Buddhism-specific and non-Buddhism-specific signs are intermixed. Some contiguous items are related, such as ones relating to things heard (items 57–65) or to the cult of stupas and relics (items 12–16), but overall the list seems not to work its way up or down to anything. The movement from 106 (hearing a prediction of one's own eventual Buddhahood) to 107 (attaining enlightenment) seems significant, but the final sign (obtaining a full pitcher) is rather anticlimactic.

The Interpretive Key

Anatomy of an Entry

We now turn to part 3, which is the heart of *Explication of Dreams*. I will first present a typical entry as an example, chosen because (unlike some entries) it contains all seven of the components found throughout this part of the text. I mark these components with bracketed numerals. Sign 89 happens to be one of the sutra's most unfavorable.

> [89] Next, Vajra Obliterator, [1] if he[49] dreams of smearing feces[50] on himself, [2] this bodhisattva is at any of the first three stages. [3] In a previous life[51] he slandered worthies and sages and cultivated transgressive actions. [4] This bodhisattva should assiduously perform confession every day and night for three years. After having done so, he should not acquire the mental state of disdain toward others, instead greatly cultivating faith and understanding. [5] He will thus render himself cleansed and purified. [6] If [in the dream] he is [entirely] covered in filth, this indicates the first stage. If he is half-covered, this is the second stage. If he has filth here and there on himself, this is the third to the sixth stage. [7] He should be aware of Māra's activity.
>
> 復次金剛摧. [1] 夢中見不淨塗身. [2] 是菩薩見初地三地. [3] 於前身毀罵賢聖. 修惡行菩薩.[52] [4] 此菩薩應三年中. 晝夜三時勤修懺悔. 自後更不於餘人生輕慢心. 應多修信解. [5] 如是清淨. [6] 以青淤泥自塗身者是初地. 若塗半身是二地. 若處處被塗 是三地. 乃至六地. [7] 應覺魔業 [88c–89a/537c–538a].[53]

I will first comment summarily on each of these components, then discuss some of them in more detail.

1. *Main dream sign*. After the phrase "Next, Vajra Obliterator" 復次金剛摧, which throughout part 3 (as in part 2) marks the beginning of almost every new entry (and which I omit in the following discussion),[54] each item opens with a phrase indicating the main dream sign. The wording often repeats that in the initial list, but not always. The ordering of items mostly matches that in the initial list, but not entirely.[55]
2. *Summary diagnosis*. Here is delivered the primary message: to tell at which stage or stages of the ten-stage path the practitioner has arrived. Sometimes only one stage is indicated. More often, as here, the main sign indicates a range of possibilities. In such cases, the text usually[56] goes on to list secondary signs correlated with specific stages (see item 6 below).
3. *Etiology of karmic obstacle*. Here practitioners learn why they haven't progressed farther. Invariably the problem lies with some past transgression or unfortunate tendency. In a few cases, such as the fifteenth sign (translated below), the practitioner is so advanced that no blockage is mentioned and thus no etiology is supplied.
4. *Prescription*. The dreamer is advised to perform certain actions to remove the obstacle signaled by the dream. The more serious the obstacle, the more arduous the prescribed actions. In a few cases no such prescription is made.
5. *Prognosis*. The reader is told what effect the prescribed practices will have. In most cases (as here) it's "in this way he will render himself cleansed and purified" (*ru shi qingjing* 如是清淨). A variant phrasing is "by this means he will purify away his karmic obstructions" (*yi ci jing yezhang* 以此淨業障). One other phrase recurring in these passages is based on a different metaphor, that of the bodhisattva vocation as a path leading to a goal: having carried out the prescribed practices, one can *qu xiang* 趣向, "proceed onward toward [Buddhahood]."
6. *Fine-tuning the diagnosis*. Some dream signs indicate only a single stage of the path. More often, as here, a sign may mean that the dreamer is currently at any of several stages, from

two to ten. The primary sign is then ramified into an array of secondary indices.

7. *Warning of Māra's activity*. In slightly more than half the entries (57 out of the 108) the reader is warned to watch out for interference by Māra.

The Range of Diagnoses

With some exceptions, the most favorable diagnoses tend to be the briefest.[57] For example:

> [15] If a bodhisattva sees in a dream an ornamented stupa to a Tathāgata, it will not be long until he realizes enlightenment, and he is being kept in mind by the *devas*. This indicates that he resides in the eighth stage of the bodhisattva [path] [82c/527a–b].
>
> 菩薩夢中見如來莊嚴塔, 不久覺菩提道, 為諸天憶念. 此是菩薩第八住.
>
> [33] If a bodhisattva in a dream simply sees a Tathāgata, he should assiduously practice the *samādhi* of emptiness in a quiet place. This bodhisattva is at the eighth stage but faces various karmic obstacles. He should assiduously cultivate a purified mind [84a/529b].
>
> 菩薩夢中見一如來, 應靜處勤修空三昧. 此菩薩是八地雜業障, 應勤修淨心.

For comparison, here are a couple of unfavorable diagnoses:

> [10] If a bodhisattva sees in a dream a Tathāgata attaining *parinirvāṇa*, this person has previously vilified the Dharma. He deceitfully left the household only in order to seek profit. He should assiduously make offerings to the three treasures and should support and give to those who are expounding Dharma. He should single-mindedly exert himself at all times. In this way he may purify away this blockage. This is a sign of being at any one of the first five stages [82b/526c].
>
> 菩薩夢見如來般涅槃者. 此人前謗法. 出家諂曲求利. 應勤供養三寶奉施說法之人. 一心三時精進. 如是以淨除業障. 見前五地處處相.
>
> [11] If in a dream the bodhisattva sees a Tathāgata cremated, this person has maligned the wise and delighted in defaming Dharma. This bodhisattva is

at the first stage, having conceived the thought of enlightenment not long ago. He should hold a lamp for seven days and nights before those who are expounding Dharma or before a Tathāgata's stupa, and with a unified mind confess and repent. At all times of day he should exhort others to listen to Dharma. He may thus purify away this blockage [82b/526c].

菩薩夢見闍維如來. 是人口惡知識. 見毀法隨喜. 此菩薩初地. 此人發菩提心不久. 是人應於七日七夜中持燈, 若說法人前, 若如來塔前.一心懺悔. 於日中晝三時. 勸眾人聽法. 以此淨除業障.

Some signs admit of an unusually large range of diagnoses. For example, this one begins very auspiciously but then expands:

[13] If in a dream a bodhisattva obtains an intact[58] hair of a Tathāgata, this indicates that this bodhisattva dwells in the ninth stage. If he dreams of being before a Buddha and receiving a prediction of his own future Buddhahood, he has removed all *saṃsāric* obstructions. [But] if he dreams of obtaining the hair while still a householder, this indicates the first stage. If he dreams of obtaining it while a monk, this is the second stage. If he dreams of obtaining it while in a market, this is the third stage. If he obtains it while in a city, this is the fourth stage. If he obtains it while in the city gate, this is the fifth stage. If he obtains it while outside, this is the sixth stage. If he obtains it while in a garden pavilion, this is the seventh stage. If he obtains it while on a chariot, this is the eighth stage. If he obtains it while in midair, this is the ninth stage. If he obtains it while in *samādhi*, this is the tenth stage [82b–c/527a].[59]

菩薩夢見得如來髮不散. 此是菩薩第九住地. 夢佛前授菩提記. 除生死業障. 夢得在家時髮是初地. 夢得出家時髮第二地. 夢市中得髮說第三住. 於城中得髮第四住. 於城門中得說第五住. 於外得第六地. 於園觀中得第七地. 於乘上得第八地. 於虛空中得第九地. 於三昧中得第十地.

Some diagnoses are decidedly mixed:

[9] If the bodhisattva sees in a dream a Tathāgata exercising his divine powers by walking in midair, this is a sign of [any one of] seven stages. If [in addition?] he hears a prediction of [his own] future Buddhahood, this bodhisattva should cultivate himself in deep silence, cultivating his

> accomplishments with deep forbearance. He will thus quickly attain enlightenment. If he sees the Tathāgata in midair, this is a sign of the first stage. If he sees the Tathāgata eating, this is the second stage. If he sees [the Tathāgata emitting] radiance, this is the third stage. If he sees [the Buddha] expounding Dharma, this is the fourth stage. If he sees him displaying his divine powers, this is the fifth stage. If he sees him entering *samādhi*, this is the sixth stage. If he sees the Tathāgata emitting light while walking in midair, this is the seventh stage [82b/526b–c].
>
> 菩薩夢中見如來虛空中神通行者. 此是七地相. 聞受道記. 此人常應修尊重默然. 修習成就甚深忍. 如是疾成正覺. 見如來在虛空中. 是初地相. 見如來食是第二地. 見光是第三地. 見說法是第四地. 見現神通是第五住地. 見入三昧是第六住地. 見放光見如來虛空中行去. 是第七住地.

In a very few cases the correspondence between dream sign and diagnosis seems somewhat non-arbitrary—an exception to the norm for dreambooks. For example:

> [5] If in a dream he sees an icon of a Tathāgata made of mud, this is a sign of the first bodhisattva stage. It is caused by this person's having once slandered teachers of Dharma. This person should go before sutras, icons, or a Tathāgata's stupa and with an unobstructed mind prostrate himself, light lamps, and make offerings. He will thereby purify away the obstruction [82a/526a].
>
> 若夢見如來泥像. 是菩薩初地相. 是人曾毀呰說法師故. 此人應於經像前若如來塔前.以無礙心. 頂戴燈供養. 如是用淨業障.

The slander of Buddhist teachers seems aptly symbolized by dreaming of an icon made of mud. This sign is reminiscent of scriptural passages such as those in the *Oceanic Samādhi Sutra on Visualizing the Buddha* (*Guanfo sanmei hai jing* 觀佛三昧海經) in which, if one's thoughts are polluted or one has not repented of transgressions, one sees only a figure of charcoal or red clay or ink when gazing upon a Buddha's body.[60] Here is another example:

> [8] If a bodhisattva in a dream realizes he is expounding Dharma for an assembly but doesn't know what he is saying, this is a sign of the second

stage. This person, after the Tathāgata had obtained *parinirvāṇa*, has slandered teachers of Dharma and has not recognized his fault. This person should seek good friends, make offerings, and listen to the good Dharma, without pursuing this fault.[61] This person will thus purify away [this] karmic hindrance.

菩薩夢中自知為衆生說法不知所說. 是第二地相. 是人於如來般涅槃後. 毀呰說法師.不自知過. 此人當求善知識. 供養聽聞善法. 不求其過. 如是淨除業障.

However, this entry then shifts perspective: rather than dreaming of oneself expounding Dharma, it now speaks of hearing the Buddha do so, an example of the text's occasional inconsistency:

If he hears the Buddha explaining giving, this is a sign of the first stage. If he hears him speaking of the precepts, this is a sign of the second stage. If he hears him speaking of forbearance, this is a sign of the third stage. If he hears him speaking of exertion, this is a sign of the fourth stage. If he hears him speaking of meditative absorption, this is a sign of the fifth stage. If he hears him speaking of wisdom, this is a sign of the sixth stage.[62] If he hears him speaking of compassion, this is a sign of the seventh stage. If he hears him speaking of being without hindrance, this is a sign of the eighth stage. If he hears him speaking of *samādhi*, this is a sign of the ninth stage. If he hears him speaking of accomplishment, this is a sign of the tenth stage [82a–b/526b].

聞佛說施. 是初地相. 聞說戒是二地相. 聞說忍是三地相. 聞說精進是四地相. 聞說禪是五地相. 聞說般若慧是六地相. 聞說大悲是七地相. 聞說無礙是八地相. 聞說三昧是九地相. 聞說成就力是十地相.

No diagnosis issued in the text addresses actions taken during a former extra-human rebirth, for the simple reason that it was normally only as a human being that one could generate karma in the first place. But it's of some interest that the non-human paths of rebirth (god, animal, hungry ghost, and purgatory-dweller) are nowhere mentioned in the text.[63]

Prescriptions

Not every entry in part 3 recommends specific actions to the reader/hearer in response to the dream. (The fifteenth sign, translated above, is an example of one that does not.) But most do. Each prescription is introduced by *ying* 應 or *dang* 當, "[the dreamer] should." As an example of the generic nature and the multiplicity of the prescriptions for even a single dream sign, consider this passage:

> If the bodhisattva in a dream sees a Tathāgata walking, this person should practice more vigorously. He should assiduously receive, study, and chant [sutras]. This is a sign of the third bodhisattva stage. This person should regularly make donations. He should also sweep a Tathāgata stupa and eliminate arrogance. He will thereby purify away this obstruction [82a/526a–b].[64]
>
> 菩薩若夢中見如來行者. 此人應勤修精進. 當勤修受學讀誦. 此是菩薩三地見相. 此人常應法施. 又應掃如來塔. 破除憍慢以此淨業障.

But the passage continues in a question-and-response format that is different from the rest of the text, fine-tuning the diagnosis as it goes:

> "Suppose the bodhisattva [in a dream] visits the place where a Tathāgata is. What does this signify?" "If he sees the Tathāgata facing a place where there is food, this is a sign of the first stage. If he sees the Tathāgata facing a walking-corridor,[65] this is a sign of the second stage. If he sees a Tathāgata facing a place where Dharma is expounded, this is a sign of the third stage. If he sees the Tathāgata sitting silently,[66] this is a sign of the fourth stage. If he sees the Tathāgata sitting in a quiet place, this is a sign of the fifth stage. If he sees the Tathāgata walking and singing, this is a sign of the sixth stage. If he sees the Tathāgata walking quickly, this is a sign of the seventh stage. If he sees the Tathāgata displaying divine powers, this is a sign of the eighth stage. If he sees the Tathāgata undergo transformation and depart,[67] this is a sign of the ninth stage. If he sees the Tathāgata walk away but turn back to speak with him, discoursing on emptiness, this is a sign of the tenth stage" [82a/526b].
>
> 見餘菩薩詣如來所. 是何相. 見如來向食之處. 此是初地相. 見如來向經行處. 是第二地相. 見如來向說法處. 是第三地相. 見如來默然坐. 是第四地相. 見如來靜處坐. 此是五地相. 見如來行唄者. 是六地相. 見如來疾走.

是七地相. 若見如來作神通. 是八地相. 見如來變化. 變化去者. 是九地相. 見如來行去迴顧共語說空. 是十地相.

By an implied but unexplained practical logic, specific actions are recommended for removing the particular blockages revealed by the dream. Sign 73 (87b24/535c), for example, in which one has dreamed of mounting a dragon or elephant,[68] specifies that the bodhisattva should cultivate reverence and generosity and avoid delusion and falsehood. The listing under sign 99 (89c15/539a–b), in which the dream is of seeing lightning issuing from a thundercloud, recommends cultivating thoughts of goodness, relinquishing things one is attached to, and gathering more *dhāraṇīs*. All of the recommended practices were already standard bits of the bodhisattva's repertoire, but the advice varies across the 108 signs, implying that particular practices are especially good for removing particular obstructions. And some of the prescribed practices are especially rigorous, such as confessing daily and nightly for three years after dreaming of being smeared in filth (sign 89),[69] or purifying the mind every day at all times of day for seven years (sign 41).

Unsurprisingly for a text aimed at bodhisattvas, cultivating one of the standard six perfections (*pāramitās*) is often prescribed. The most frequently mentioned is *vīrya* (usually rendered as *jingjin* 精進 except for the transliteration *piliye* 毘梨耶 in item 100), signifying exertion, vigor, or effort and mandated in thirteen dream signs.[70] Next is *dāna* (*shi* 施), or giving, recommended in the case of ten signs.[71] In addition to cultivating giving as a perfection, the text also often prescribes making donations (*gongyang* 供養 or *gongji* 供給) to certain recipients—to stupas, teachers, the three treasures, icons, or other practitioners.[72] Cultivation of forbearance (*ren* 忍, *kṣānti*) is prescribed eight times; of behavioral discipline (*jie* 戒, *śīla*) four times; of skill in means (*fangbian* 方便, *upāya*) three times; and of contemplation (*chan* 禪, *dhyāna*) only once.[73] Occasionally the text simply urges the practice of "the six perfections" without specification, as in the entry for the ninety-eighth sign (translated in the next section). Other recommendations include cultivating certain mental qualities (faith [*xin* 信], compassion [*dabei/ci* 大悲/慈], an unobstructed mind [*wu ai xin* 無礙心], fearlessness [*wu wei* 無畏]), holding a lamp before those expounding Dharma or before a stupa, keeping silence, eliminating arrogance, and bearing the Buddha in mind (*nian fo* 念佛).[74]

Fine-tuning Diagnoses

One of the text's most remarkable features is the degree to which it unfolds its initial matrix of dream signs into an exuberant array of secondary indices. This allows for the fine-tuning of diagnoses. Here are three examples of such secondary indices:

> [108] If in a dream he obtains a full pitcher, this bodhisattva is seeing any one of the ten stages. Which one may be known as follows: If he obtains it in a village, this indicates the first stage. If he obtains it in a doorway, this indicates the second stage. If he obtains it on a road, this is the third stage. If he obtains it beneath a tree, this is the fourth stage. If he obtains it while standing, this is the fifth stage. If he obtains it while seated, this is the sixth stage. If he obtains it on a mountain peak, this is the seventh stage. If he obtains it in midair, this is the eighth stage. If he obtains it during a meal, this is the ninth stage. If he obtains it while riding an ornamented mount and sightseeing in a garden, this is the tenth stage. Māra's activity and karmic hindrances may be in effect at any of the stages. He should be aware of them, and thus he will purify himself and proceed onward toward [the goal] [90b/540a–b].
>
> 若夢中得滿瓶. 此菩薩見一切十地. 當如是知. 若村中得是初地. 若門中得是二地. 若道中得是三地. 若樹下得是四地. 若住得是五地. 若坐得是六地. 若山頂頭得是七地.若空中得是八地. 若食時得是九地. 若莊嚴乘騎. 若園觀是十地. 此地地魔業業障. 應覺如是清淨趣向.
>
> [12] If in a dream the bodhisattva obtains a relic of a Tathāgata's body, this indicates he is at one of [the first] three stages of the bodhisattva path. [But] if in the dream he approaches near to the Tathāgata, hears a prediction of his future Buddhahood, or obtains a relic of the Tathāgata, then the dream indicates he resides in more advanced stages, as follows: If in the dream he obtains a hair of the Tathāgata, this indicates the first stage. If in the dream he obtains a fingernail of the Tathāgata, this indicates the second stage. If in the dream he obtains a *śarīra*,[75] this indicates the third stage. If in the dream he obtains an incisor, this indicates the fourth stage. If in the dream he obtains a molar, this indicates the fifth stage. If in the dream he obtains a white tuft, this indicates the sixth stage. If in the dream he obtains a finger,[76] this indicates the seventh stage. If in the dream he obtains the crown, this indicates the eighth stage. If in the dream he sees the Tathāgata cremated but with his entire body still intact, this indicates the ninth stage. If he sees the Tathāgata's entire body, this indicates the tenth stage [82b–c/526c–527a].

菩薩夢中得如來舍利. 此說菩薩三地. 夢中親近如來. 聞受記得度. 夢住餘地. 得如來舍利. 如是相: 得如來髮是初地. 夢得如來爪是第二地. 夢得舍利是第三地. 夢得齒第四地. 夢得牙第五地. 夢得白毫第六地. 夢得手第七地. 夢得冠第八地. 夢見闍維如來全身不散第九地. 夢見如來全身第十地.

[98] If you dream of riding on a boat, this can indicate any of six bodhisattva stages. If you are steadily practicing the six perfections but are suffering and having difficulties, you should practice them without support.[77] In this way you will cleanse and purify away [your obstruction]. If you dream of riding on a boat but do not reach a destination, this indicates the first stage. If you are riding and reach the destination, this is the second stage. If you dream of two boats traveling together, this indicates the third stage. If the two boats are tied together, this is the fourth stage. If you see a big crowd boarding a boat, this indicates the fifth stage. If you see them boarding the boat and it sets off, this indicates the sixth stage [89c/539a].

若自夢 [集 > 乘] 船. 此菩薩是六地. 若平等行六波羅蜜有艱難. 當行無依六波羅蜜. 如是清淨. 若夢作船未竟是初地. 作船竟是二地. 若夢二船並是三地. 若並縛二船是四地. 見大眾上船是五地. 見入船去是六地.

Etiologies

The text supplies not only diagnoses and prescriptions but also (sometimes) etiologies of whatever obstacle is correlated with the relevant dream sign (or, in a few cases, etiologies of the advantageous state revealed by the dream). It does so by pointing to specific types of failings (or meritorious acts) in the past. Although the explicit term for previous lifetimes, *qianshen* 前身, occurs only four times, it's implied throughout. The idea is that the practitioner once did something that has caused the hindrance indicated by the dream; exactly when is irrelevant. To dream of sitting atop Mount Sumeru, for example (sign 68, 87a22/535b), indicates an insufficiency of merit due to having befriended evil persons, cultivated wickedness, and ignored the advice of wholesome friends in past lives. To see oneself at the top of some other mountain (sign 69, 87a29/535b) indicates one has disrespected preachers of Dharma. As seen above, to dream of being smeared with filth (number 89, 88c25/537c–538a) indicates that one has maligned the Buddha and habitually practiced evil deeds. Here's another example:

[4] If in a dream he sees a Tathāgata sitting with his back toward him, this person previously created obstacles for monastics or for those listening to the Dharma. He should now and often donate a Dharma seat[78] and encourage living beings to listen to the Dharma. He will thus remove the blockage. This is a sign of having commenced the seventh stage. It may also indicate any stage from the first to the seventh [82a/526a].

夢中見如來背坐者. 前為出家人作留難. 為聽法人作留難. 此人今[79] 常當敷施法座. 勸多衆生. 聽法如是. 得除業障. 是七地初相. 亦是從初地至七地 處處地相.

Three sorts of obstacles figure repeatedly. The first are *yezhang* 業障, a term which often translates *karmāvaraṇa* and means "karmic hindrances." (In many contexts these are one of four types of hindrances or obstructions [*zhang* 障], the others being afflictive and cognitive hindrances [*huo zhang* 惑障], hindrances accompanying karmic retribution [*bao zhang* 報障],[80] and hindrances of views [*jian zhang* 見障].[81]) In part 3, karmic hindrances or obstructions are mentioned at least sixty-nine times, usually as the factor triggering a particular dream but sometimes when being ruled out as the relevant trigger.

The second are *fannao* 煩惱 (*kleśa*), "torments, defilements of the mind, by virtue of which actions (*karman*) 'accumulate' . . . , that is, they gather force and fruitfulness and necessarily produce a retribution, notably a new existence in the world of painful rebirth."[82] These are mentioned nine times in part 3, again sometimes when being ruled out. For example, in the entry on the sixty-fifth sign ("hearing the voice of some bodhisattva in some world or other" 聞某世界某菩薩聲) we find: "This bodhisattva is at any stage from the fifth down to the first. He is being borne in mind by bodhisattvas [or perhaps by the bodhisattva whose voice he heard in the dream] and has but few defilements, [but] he should distance himself from arrogance, encourage many others to cultivate wisdom, and procure *dhāraṇīs*" 此菩薩是五地初地. 此菩薩為菩薩所憶念, 少煩惱, 應離憍慢, 勸多人修智, 如是相應得陀羅尼 [87a/535a].[83]

But it's not only bodhisattvas' karmic pasts that create their present obstacles. They are also subject to interference by Māra 魔, gatekeeper of *saṃsāra*. The scripture uses two terms for the traces of his interference in practitioners' progress: "residual difficulty" or *liunan* 留難,

which appears only twice (in entries 3 and 4), and *moye* 魔業, sometimes translated as "evil karma" but here, it seems, meaning something closer to "Māra's activity" or "demonic action." *Moye* is mentioned in fifty-seven entries, often in passages warning the practitioner at a particular stage to "be aware of [the potential for] Māra's activity" 覺魔業.[84] Some scholars have understood Māra as only an aspect of practitioners' own mentation,[85] but such is not the case in *Explication of Dreams*. There, as in much Perfection of Wisdom literature[86] as well as in teachings given by the monk Zhiyi to his fellow monks, Māra is said to create objects of the senses—external, physical disturbances—to distract, delude, or tempt the practitioner, much as China's indigenous demons were said to do.[87] In one of his early works based on lectures he gave between 568 and 575, Zhiyi taught that "as practice progresses, Māra flourishes" 道高則魔盛,[88] meaning that as a practitioner advances on the path Māra's attempts at interference gain intensity. Later Zhiyi gave extended discussions of Māra's depradations and how practitioners should combat them.[89] In *Explication*, however, it's not only advanced practitioners who are liable:

> [3] If in a dream he sees a Tathāgata with his head covered, seated: This person is seeing the results of his having had good and wise friends, cultivated good deeds, and expounded the Dharma being hindered [by Māra]. He should with an unobstructed mind practice the expounding of Dharma. This sign indicates the first stage [81c–82a/526a].
>
> 若見如來覆頭坐者. 是人見善知識修善說法因緣. 為作留難. 應以無礙心修集說法所須. 此是說初相.

The admixture of demonic interference with one's labyrinthine (and otherwise unknowable) karmic history makes for an extraordinarily complex diagnostic system. At any given point on the path one might be hindered by the effects of one's own forgotten deeds, by Māra's interference, or both at once. And although this manual incorporates both sorts of factors, its unpacking of the meanings of particular dream signs often fails to offer potential users any definitive way of untangling them to determine which is which.

Diagnosis across the Boundary between Dreaming and Waking Life

One item offers its diagnosis in a way unusual for this scripture:

> [20] If a bodhisattva in a dream sees himself offering flower garlands, incense powder, and sandalwood to a Tathāgata stupa,[90] he is at any of the first five stages. In the past he has practiced only slightly the perfection of giving. Upon waking, as he recollects this [dream] sign, if the thought of giving[91] arises in him, this is a sign of the first stage. If the thought of following the precepts arises, this indicates the second stage. If forbearance, the third stage. If vigor, the fourth stage. If meditative absorption, the fifth stage. And if an unobstructed mind arises in him, this means he will rapidly attain the stage of irreversibility [83a/527c].
>
> 菩薩若夢中自見以花鬘香末栴檀供養如來塔, 此是菩薩見初地五地處處地, 是前少行檀波羅蜜. 覺已憶念此相, 生長施心此說是初地相, 生長戒心說是二地, 生長忍說是三地, 生長精進是見四地, 生長禪是見五地, 生長無礙心疾遍一切不退轉地.

Rather than simply providing the dream's meanings, the text here advises doing something a bit more involved. After having dreamed of ornamenting a stupa, upon awakening the bodhisattva is to notice the quality of mind that arises when he recalls and thinks about the dream. In this case, then, it's the combination of dreaming of something and having certain thoughts upon later recalling it that indicates one's current path stage. In this respect the passage resembles certain ones in Perfection of Wisdom sutras, to which we now turn.

Perfection of Wisdom Texts

A more complex diagnostic use of dreams is prescribed in a cluster of passages in early Perfection of Wisdom, or *prajñāpāramitā*, sutras translated between 179 and 404.[92] These passages are found both in translations of the *Perfection of Wisdom in 8,000 Lines* (*Aṣṭasāhasrikā prajñāpāramitā*), which happens to be the Mahāyāna sutra for which we have the earliest datable evidence (in the form of a manuscript written with Kharoṣṭhī script on birchbark in Gāndhārī language, carbon dated to around 75

CE),[93] and in translations of expanded versions of Prajñāpāramitā material. (These are conventionally referred to as the smaller, or 8,000-line, and larger Prajñāpāramitā sutras respectively. But current scholarship holds that these larger versions were in part based on expansions of the smaller ones, so the distinction is fluid.[94]) I'm interested not in reconstructing the Indic "original(s)" but in pondering what these texts were saying to their contemporary Chinese readership. Whatever might have been the specific differences in the underlying Indic-language texts, we essentially have to deal with the same basic textual content rendered in subtly—but for our purposes interestingly—different ways by successive teams of translators and redactors of both the smaller and larger sutras over about twenty-two decades. Let's consider parallel passages in seven texts:

1. *Daoxing banruo jing* 道行般若經 (T 224) by Lokakṣema's 支婁迦讖 team, the earliest propagators of Mahāyāna texts in China. A translation of a Gāndhārī version of the *Perfection of Wisdom in Eight Thousand Lines*, completed in 179.[95]
2. *Da mingdu jing* 大明度經 (T 225), Zhi Qian's 支謙 version of the *Perfection of Wisdom in Eight Thousand Lines* or *Aṣṭasāhasrikā prajñāpāramitā sutra*—a revision of Lokakṣema's earlier rendition. Completed between 220 and 252.[96]
3. *Fangguang banruo jing* 放光般若經 (T 221), Mokṣala's 無羅叉 translation of some version of the larger sutra, completed in 291.[97]
4. *Mohe banruo chao jing* 摩訶般若鈔經 (T 226), a revision of parts of Lokakṣema's translation. Attributed to Dharmapriya 曇摩蜱 and the prolific Zhu Fonian 竺佛念 (and thus completed ca. 382 if this attribution is correct), but its authorship remains uncertain.[98]
5. *Mohe banruo poluomi jing* 摩訶般若波羅蜜經 (T 223), Kumārajīva's 鳩摩羅什 translation of the larger sutra, which quickly superseded Mokṣala's version and was completed in 403 or 404.[99]
6. *Xiaopin banruo poluomi jing* 小品般若波羅蜜經 (T 227), Kumārajīva's team's translation of the smaller sutra.[100]
7. *Da zhidu lun* 大智度論 (T 1509), a commentary on the larger sutra, translated by Kumārajīva's team between 402 and 406.[101]

In these passages, consistently clustered in the same chapter and arranged in the same order,[102] the question on the table—answered by the Buddha at the prompting of his disciple Subhūti 須菩提—is the same as the one addressed in *Explication of Dreams*: How can practitioners of the bodhisattva path assess their own progress? And here, as there, dreams are enlisted as diagnostic indicators. In these texts, however, there aren't yet ten stages on the path. There is only one distinction: whether one has passed the point where progress is irreversible and future Buddhahood assured, or whether the practitioner might still retrogress or exit the path prematurely into *nirvāṇa*, thus failing in the quest.[103] And this question of irreversibility (*avinivartanīya*, "not liable to turn back," translated as *bu tuizhuan* 不退轉 or *bu tui* 不退 or transliterated as *aweiyuezhi/*a-ywij-hjwot-trij* 阿惟越致), was often linked to whether one had received a prediction (*vyākaraṇa/shou ji* 授記 or 受記) from a Buddha of one's future Buddhahood. Since this would have happened in a past lifetime inaccessible to ordinary memory, how were practitioners to know? Perhaps their dreams might yield up the answer if they knew how to read the signs dreams contained.[104]

The section of interest here moves through the same sequence of seven signs in all seven versions. Here I will summarize and then discuss their common content. Appendix B points out interesting ways in which these versions diverge from one another.

> [1] If, even when dreaming, a bodhisattva does not enter the state of *arhat* or that of *pratyekabuddha*, and does not teach others to enter those states, but rather stays fixed on the goal of Buddhahood, this is a sign of irreversibility on the path.
>
> [2] If in a dream a bodhisattva sees himself surrounded by hundreds of disciples, seated at the center of the group, or as the foremost disciple in an audience of thousands listening from a front-row position as the Buddha expounds Dharma,[105] this is a sign of irreversibility.
>
> [3] If in a dream a bodhisattva is seated high in the air expounding Dharma for monks, sees his own halo a span wide, and he transforms himself at will, acting as a Buddha,[106] this is a sign of irreversibility.
>
> [4] If a bodhisattva experiences no fear, shock, or dread when dreaming of a city sacked by soldiers, or a raging fire, or tigers, wolves, lions, and other beasts, or someone having their head severed, or when experiencing hunger or thirst; but rather, having seen these things in a dream,

upon rising thinks, "Like a dream is all this which belongs to the triple world. When I become a Buddha, I will expound the Dharma for all beings so that they may be taught," this is a sign of irreversibility.

[5] If in a dream a bodhisattva sees animals devouring each other and people falling ill, and if he or she produces this thought and vow—"When I am a Buddha, I will cause there to be no ills [or unfortunate rebirth paths] in my realm"[107]—this is a sign of irreversibility.

[6] If the bodhisattva wakes from a dream and, seeing that his city is on fire, forms this thought—"According to what I have seen in my dreams, using it as a comparison and a sign, I was not frightened. To possess this attribute is a sign of being a non-retrogressing bodhisattva. Because of this attribute of mine, let this fire now be completely extinguished"—and if the flames die out, this bodhisattva has received a prediction of future Buddhahood. If the fires continue to burn, he has not yet obtained such a prediction. If the fire gods burn only a house here and a district there, this has been brought about by the members of those households having rejected sutras (or Dharma) in previous lifetimes, and they will realize this karmic connection. Because of this realization their karma will be burned away.[108]

[7] If someone is seized by a ghost or demon, let the bodhisattva say: "If it is true that I have been predicted to achieve Buddhahood and am irreversibly on the path toward that goal, then let this ghost depart!" If it does, this indicates that the bodhisattva has received a prediction of future Buddhahood. If it does not, this indicates no such prediction has yet been received.

The sequence of signs forms a progression. The first through the third are in the performative mode, in that dreamers stick firmly to their role in waking-life cultivation—the role of Buddha-in-training—even when dreaming. In this respect these passages are also examples of what I term the SPILLOVER PARADIGM (the topic of chapter 3), in that dreaming practitioners continue to think and act as they have been training to do while awake. This performative mode continues in the fourth and fifth signs as well. But the roles performed gradually climb upward, and this is another sort of progression in the sequence. That is, in the first sign the bodhisattva dreams of sticking to the ultimate goal of Buddhahood and not diverting onto lesser paths. In the second, he dreams of listening to a Buddha as his foremost disciple. In the third, the dreamer is himself a Buddha, preaching to others.

Surveying the whole chapter, we notice a third progression: from dreaming, to the interface between dreaming and waking, to actions taken while awake. The sixth and seventh signs involve "truth acts": *saccakiriyā* (Pāli), *satyakriyā* (Sanskrit), usually rendered as "vow" (*yuan* 願) or "oath" (*shi* 誓), terms whose range and connotations in Chinese discourse deserve closer examination than I can render here.[109] A truth act is "a formal declaration of fact, accompanied by a command or resolution or prayer that the purpose of the agent shall be accomplished,"[110] or "something between an oath and a magical charm."[111] It is ritualized speech in which speakers call upon the universe to issue a sign confirming the truth of what they're declaring. At first blush, truth acts might seem to be an example of what philosophers of language have termed "speech acts" or "performative utterances": utterances that lack the property of being true or false and instead perform an action, to the extent that "to issue such an utterance *is* to perform the action."[112] But in the truth act, speakers call on other beings or powers to ratify what they've just said. It's not, then, that saying the words makes something true that wasn't true moments before ("The court finds you guilty"). Rather, something is already the case, and the speaker calls upon unseen cosmic witnesses to confirm it for the witnesses present.[113] Their response, if it comes, is the confirmation (*yan* 驗) or verification (*zheng* 證). The very nature of the utterance presupposes the possibility that the confirmation will fail to arrive. The truth act, then, is a particular type of speech act that depends for its efficacy on its having a certain effect or outcome. Without this response it is ineffective. The presence of witnesses is always implied: the speaker demonstrates for an audience (and himself) that what was asserted is in fact true.

Other Dream-Based Diagnoses

Dreams were sometimes used alongside somatic symptoms to arrive at medical diagnoses. I've elsewhere discussed two examples. One, a section in *The Yellow Thearch's Classic on the Numinous Pivot* (*Huangdi neijing lingshu* 黃帝內經靈樞), correlates specific states of *qi* in the body with an array of about thirty dream signs. Another, in *Origins and*

Symptoms of Medical Disorders (*Zhubing yuanhou lun* 諸病源候論) by Chao Yuanfang 巢元方 (fl. 605–616), correlates dreaming of intercourse with ghosts and demons (as well as some behavioral and affective symptoms) with depletion of *qi* in the organs.[114] A further brief example is preserved in a sixth-century discourse by Zhiyi to fellow monks:

> If the diseases of the five organs are hidden and difficult to know, they can be divined through sitting in meditation or in dreams. If during meditation or in a dream you see many instances of the color blue-green, [such as] blue-green people or animals such as lions, tigers, or wolves, and you are fearful, this indicates a disease of the liver. If during meditation or in a dream you see many instances of the color red, [such as] fires burning, red people, red animals, red swords and weapons, or red-colored young men and women embracing intimately, or fathers and mothers or siblings giving rise now to joy, now to fear, this indicates a disease of the heart. And so on down the line: by following the colors you can corroborate [the causes of a disease].[115]
>
> 若五藏病隱密難知. 坐禪及夢占之. 若禪及夢多見青色青人獸師子虎狼, 而生怖畏, 則是肝病. 若禪及夢多見赤色火起, 赤人獸赤刀仗, 赤少男女親附抱持, 或父母兄弟等生喜生畏者, 即是心病. 下去例隨色驗之.

Here again we see a straddling of the waking/dreaming boundary: you can employ meditative visions and dreams to divine (*zhan* 占) the hidden cause of a condition. In this case the sign/cause correlations are based straightforwardly on the five phases. And the passage implies but doesn't articulate a theory of why we dream of certain things at certain times, having to do with the workings of *qi* in the patient.[116]

Many other texts occasionally approach dreams as containing soteriologically relevant signs, but on a much smaller scale and in less comprehensive fashion. To give just one example, *Compendium of Dhāraṇīs* (*Tuoluoni jijing* 陀羅尼集經), a collection of spell texts completed by the Indian monk Atikūṭa 阿地瞿多 in 654,[117] instructs on how to perform a series of hand seals (*mudrās*) to secure the space around a ritual area, purifying oneself of sins in the process. After completing the series, the practitioner is to watch for any of ten auspicious signs (*shizhong ruixiang* 十種瑞相) to see if the ritual has been effective. The signs are these: an icon emits light; the pennants in your place of practice move despite the absence of wind; you hear thunder in the sky despite the absence of clouds; your lamps suddenly flare up several feet; smoke issues from your incense burner despite your not having lit any incense; you hear music in the air; blessings and long life pile up and you remain free from illness and attacks by dangerous animals; your mind remains unsullied by the five desires; demons and spirits are unable to disturb you; and in visions or dreams you see Buddhas and bodhisattvas, or you dream of climbing mountains or tall trees, crossing to the farther shore on a boat, riding elephants or horses; or you see your teachers, fellow monks, parents, or wholesome friends. "If in a dream you see these sorts of signs, you may know that your sins have been dissolved. These are all favorable responses and auspicious signs" 若於夢中見是相類, 即知罪滅皆是好應靈瑞之相.[118] Further on we find the promise that if, while doing the prescribed practice, you see in a dream the bodhisattva Guanyin adorned with ornaments, you will obtain your every wish, and if you dream of ornamented Buddhas or other bodhisattvas, "this is an advance sign by which you may know that you will be reborn in a pure land" 此是先相, 即知當生淨土.[119]

Seeking Diagnostic Dreams

Some texts counseled readers not simply to treat dreams as soteriologically relevant signs but also to take active measures to elicit such dreams. In other words, they prescribed dream incubation practices for diagnostic purposes. These instructions don't always clearly entail all three aspects classically associated with the "sought" dream—intentionality (the practitioner deliberately acts to elicit a dream), locality (the practitioner sleeps in a purified ritual space conducive to this purpose), and epiphany (a deity visits the practitioner through a dream)—but they sometimes do.[120] Not many passages of this sort appear to have survived,[121] but here I will adduce a few examples.

In a sixth-century text in the Three Sovereigns, or Sanhuang 三皇, Daoist tradition, *Scripture of the Wondrous Essence of the Eight Thearchs* (*Dongshen badi miaojing jing* 洞神八帝妙精經), we find guidance for neophytes who are "having difficulty receiving communications from the gods" (*bu neng tong shen* 不能通神). They are urged to first correct their faults. Afterward, "if they wish to test themselves for readiness to advance" 欲驗法自試, thus qualifying to receive the scriptures and teachings of the Sovereigns and to summon gods, they are to "first quiet and settle their minds in solitude" 先靜寂定心, fast and maintain ritual purity, ingest three talismans designed to "summon the Perfected" (that is, the three Sovereigns) to descend, and "lie down quietly, seeking a dream" (*an wo qiu meng* 安卧求夢). Having "ascertained whether one's dream was auspicious or not" (*juepan jixiong* 訣判吉凶)—which would probably have involved consulting a teacher[122]—one might proceed to "ascend the altar and enter the chamber" (a formula for advancing by stages to receive teachings). But should any doubt remain, one must not proceed.[123] The practitioner is to "wait as long as necessary for an indication" (*jiujiu you wei* 久久有徵) rather than rushing ahead despite doubts, for doing so would lead to disaster.

We have here a basic framework for incubation. Adepts would probably have undertaken it with guidance from a teacher who would interpret any resulting dream and assess the disciple's fitness.

A passage preserved in the pre-Tang *Scripture of the Forty-Four Methods on Yellow Silk* (*Shangqing taishang huangsu sishisi fang jing* 上清太上黃素四十四方經) and collected under the rubric "Assorted methods" in *Cloudy Bookcase* is even less detailed. A Daoist, it says, who wishes to "ascend the altar and enter the chamber" should have had a numinous response from the gods indicating their approval. If not, the candidate "must secure an auspicious dream" (*dang you jixiang zhi meng* 當有吉祥之夢), applying himself diligently until "visited in sleep by numinous spirits or jade maidens." Upon waking from such a dream, he should straighten himself, look upward, grind his teeth twenty-one times, shut his eyes, and softly pronounce the invocation provided. If one continues this practice for three years, the text promises, various celestial deities will descend into one's body and provide protection.[124]

In the eighth roll of *Compendium of Dhāraṇīs* (*Tuoluoni jijing*), diagnostic dreams unexpectedly come into play when a master of Buddhist esoterica is called upon to cure illness. "If a member of the household of an ailing patient comes seeking the master's help, he is first to perform the indicated *mudrā* and spell when lying down to sleep" 若病人家遣使問師, 師作此印誦呪臥時. If in his resultant dreams he sees

Buddhas, bodhisattvas, or *vajradevas*, this indicates the patient will recover (or is treatable), and so he should make the house call. But if he dreams of donkeys, horses, and other animals, or of naked persons like practitioners of "other paths" (a reference to non-Buddhist ascetic practitioners in India), and so on, it means the patient will soon die and the master shouldn't go. And if he sees copper or iron bowls or the like, it means the illness is untreatable and he should likewise stay away.[125] Another incubation method involves a master leading a group of disciples through a ritual series before an altar on which the eleven-faced Guanyin is seated. He instructs them to wash their heads with perfumed water, then lie down and sleep. The next morning, if any of them have had dreams, they are to relate them to the master.[126]

Elsewhere we find similar lists of dream signs indicating the success or failure of the practitioner's performance of a recommended rite. For example, Yijing's early eighth-century translation of a version of the *Sutra of Spells of the Great Peacock Queen* (*Da kongque zhou wang jing* 大孔雀呪王經)[127] explains that, after carrying out a particular rite, practitioners will know its success or failure by the sorts of dreams they have while sleeping in the ritual space before the icon. If one sees fine carriages or dreams of riding on a cow or elephant, or sees mountains and fruit-bearing trees, or if one dreams of soaring upward or of climbing steps into a hall or palace, or if one sees one's parents or distinguished persons or youths of either sex, or sees ritual ornaments, flowers and fruits, celestial spirits, choice foods, or fine horses or peacocks, these are all auspicious signs of the rite's success. But to dream of things other than these—including donkeys and mules, camels, monkeys, dogs, pigs, snakes, scorpions, cats, rodents, owls, kites, and other birds of prey, or of ugly vessels, trees being felled, empty houses, corpses, or dried-up rivers—is inauspicious and indicates the rite has failed.[128]

Finally, the *Vaipulya Dhāraṇī Sutra* (*Da fangdeng tuoluoni jing* 大方等陀羅尼經), subject of much recent scholarly attention, briefly prescribes what seems to be a basic incubation scenario.[129] The Buddha instructs Mañjuśrī that "if there are good sons or daughters who come to you seeking this *dhāraṇī* sutra, you should teach them to seek the twelve dream kings, and if they are able to see one of the kings, you should confer on them the teaching of the seven-day practice" 來詣汝所欲求陀羅尼經者，汝當教求十二夢王，若得見一王者，汝當教授七日行法.[130] As explained earlier in the sutra, the twelve dream kings are converted demons. Each has a proper name and is correlated with a specific dream image by which he may be recognized. For example, "if one in a dream sees a figure riding an elephant across a great river" 於其夢中若見乘象渡於大江, this is the dream king Ganjiluo 乾基羅; "if a *bhikṣu* dreams of seeing a figure entering a *dhyāna samādhi* beneath a tree bearing flowers and fruit" 若有比丘於其夢中 見有一樹華果茂盛, 於其樹下入禪三昧, this is Qiongjialinluo 窮伽林羅; and so on. If supplicants pass this oneiric test, they are then qualified to undertake the seven-day practice. That practice involves constructing on each of the seven days a ritual space ornamented with incense, banners, and parasols, and presenting offerings to a copy of the sutra. According to their karma, some practitioners as they undertake this devotion will be visited in visions by one or more former Buddhas.[131]

Appendix C considers a Daoist scriptural passage likely dating to the tenth century conveying spells to be used as incubation devices—that is, mantras said to induce dreams of particular sorts.

The Hermeneutic Habit

Diagnostic uses of dreams are a subset of situations in which practitioners were taught to interpret certain experiences, events, or bodily markings as signs of progress (or of problems) or of soteriological potential (or lack thereof). Here I briefly pan out to this broader set of practices. My purpose in doing so is to show that the approaches taken to dreams in texts of the DIAGNOSTIC PARADIGM were part of a much larger and variegated repertoire of semiotic practices aimed at assessing one's own or another practitioner's soteriological condition by means of specified sets of signs. As in all texts operating under the DIAGNOSTIC PARADIGM, the focus was on the practitioner *qua* practitioner rather than the prediction of future events.

As an entryway into the topic, consider a passage translated by Xuanzang 玄奘 and his team (656–659) from a commentary on the most important of the seven Sarvāstivādin Abhidharma treatises.[132]

Question: The marks (*xiang* 相) of the wholesome roots conducive to liberation in sentient beings are subtle. How can one know whether their seeds have already been planted?

Answer: One knows by signs (*xiang* 相).[133] What are these signs? If while listening to a wholesome friend expound the right Dharma one's body hairs stand erect and tears flow, if one turns away from *saṃsāra* and delights in *nirvāṇa*, if one forms deep love and respect for that Dharma teacher, then one should know that one has definitely already planted the wholesome seeds of liberation. If not,[134] one should know that one has not yet planted them.

There is a simile for this. It's like a man who has already long ago planted seeds in a field but begins to have doubts, [wondering]: "Have I already planted seeds in this field or not?" Being undecided, he becomes halting and hesitant. Someone might say to him, "Why be like this? You need only water the field and fertilize it. If sprouts come up, you will know it was already planted, and if they don't, then it wasn't." The man follows the suggestion and obtains a determination. Similarly, if a practitioner doubts whether he has already planted the seeds of liberation in himself, a wholesome friend might tell him, "Go to a place where Dharma is being spoken. If while listening to Dharma your body hairs stand erect and tears flow, and if you form love and respect for that Dharma teacher, you should know that you've already planted the seeds of liberation, and if not, then you haven't. From these signs you can know."[135]

問: 順解脱分善根在有情身其相微細. 已種未種云何可知. 答: 以相故知. 彼有何相. 謂若聞善友說正法時. 身毛為竪悲泣流淚. 厭離生死欣樂涅槃. 於法法師深生愛敬. 當知決定已種順解脱分善根. 若不能如是當知未種. 此中有喻. 如人於田畦中下種子已經久生疑. 我此畦中曾下種不. 躊躇未決. 傍人語言. 何足猶豫. 汝今但可以水灌漬以糞覆之. 彼若生芽則知已種. 不然則不. 彼如其言便得決定. 如是行者. 自疑身中曾種解脱種子已不. 時彼善友而語之言. 汝今可往至說法所. 若聽法時身毛為竪悲泣流淚. 乃至於法法師生愛敬者. 當知已種解脱種子. 不然則不. 故由此相可得了知.

The passage's opening vividly captures an existential problem confronting Buddhist practitioners: How can I know whether I have planted the seeds of liberation?[136] Less specifically: How can I know where I stand on the path and whether my karmic history holds serious hindrances? Recalling one's deeds in this present lifetime won't suffice, because a long series of *previous* lifetimes is relevant yet inaccessible to all but the most advanced practitioners. The anxiety inherent in this set of ideas is poignantly captured in the simile's wording: the seeds were planted "already long ago"—but the farmer forgets and "begins to have doubts." "Being undecided, he becomes halting and hesitant." At long last he "obtains a determination" (*de jueding* 得決定) thanks to his watering and fertilizing. (Note the agricultural metaphor that structures much of Buddhist soteriological discourse: merit is seeds that over time develop into good fruit.[137]) As a way of obtaining this vital determination, practitioners are advised to place themselves where Dharma is being taught and observe their own responses. Their physiology and feelings become a semiotic field yielding the answer to their question.

Early medieval Buddhist and Daoist texts issue many such directives on how to scan events or experiences for *signs* indicating—if one knows how to read them—where one presently stands soteriologically or, in some cases, whether one qualifies for advancement on a path of self-cultivation. Such texts often provide keys for interpreting the signs correctly. To set the above dream-related materials into this broader context, I will here note a few examples.

Watching for and collecting signs in deathbed practice. Sick and dying practitioners were instructed to watch for indications in the form of perceptual objects (often termed *jingjie* 境界)—that is, waking visions, dreams, or other intimations of their impending rebirth in Amitābha's (or another) pure land, or else of their unconfessed transgressions. Those in attendance were to record these signs.[138]

Watching for signs of the effectiveness of repentance and confession or of self-ordination. Numerous texts instruct practitioners that they must receive auspicious signs confirming that their performance of confession and repentance rites (*chanhui* 懺悔) has effectively purified them of transgressions. Otherwise, they are not yet qualified to receive the bodhisattva precepts. In the fifth century, bodhisattva precepts were "a new and eventually widely popular form of Buddhist empowerment available to both monastics and laypersons,"[139] and they made self-ordination possible for those lacking a master to ordain them.

The indigenously composed and widely influential *Brahmā Net Sutra* (*Fanwang jing* 梵網經), for example, specifies that one wishing to ordain himself should first practice repentance for seven days before icons of Buddhas and bodhisattvas. Then, "once having been able to see auspicious signs, he will have obtained the precepts" 得見好相便得戒, otherwise not. " 'Auspicious signs' are such things as seeing the Buddha come to rub his head, seeing a radiance, seeing flowers, or other similar unusual signs. [Only after seeing them] will his transgressions have been dissolved. Without auspicious signs, his repentance will have been of no benefit" 好相者, 佛來摩頂, 見光見華種種異相, 便得滅罪. 若無好相, 雖懺無益.[140] Eric Greene has written extensively of ways in which visions experienced by Buddhist practitioners were understood diagnostically as signs of the success or failure of their performance of meditation or of repentance rituals.[141] I'll return to elements of his argument in the conclusion to this chapter. There are many other Buddhist examples. To mention only three: (1) In the Gāndhāran monk Guṇavarman's 求那跋摩 translation (completed at Jianye in 431) of *Upāli Asks about the Method of Bodhisattva Ordination* (*Youboli wen pusa shoujie fa* 優波離問菩薩受戒法), we find another ritual procedure for self-ordination in which the practitioner is instructed to watch for signs of having successfully received the precepts from the invisible beings who were thought to confer it.[142] (2) Zhiyi instructed his disciples on how to watch for indications of their success in eliminating karmic burdens from past offenses.[143] (3) An illustrative episode occurs in the biography of Dharmakṣema 曇無讖 (385–433).[144] Some Daoist texts and practices participated in a similar configuration of ideas. For example, texts on the Celestial Master penitential healing rite specify that recovery itself functions as a sign of an otherwise opaque soteriological status. If the illness abates, one's sins have been expunged and penitence has been successful. If not, one must continue the practice.[145]

Watching for signs of divine approval before conferring esoteric scriptures. Several alchemical scriptures contain instructions for their transmittal from master to disciple, and the instructions often provide a method for diagnosing the fitness of the intended recipient. These typically specify that before transmitting the text along with the oral instructions meant to accompany it, the master must wait a spell, watching for signs of divine disapproval. This, the texts often explain, is a final failsafe to prevent transmission to anyone unqualified.[146]

Assessing candidates' bodily signs for fitness to receive esoterica. Many passages in Daoist texts assert that only those with "the bones and marks of a transcendent" are fit to receive transmission of esoteric methods and texts. Here, the signs allowing for the diagnosis of soteriological potential are carried on the body of the would-be disciple. Hagiographies depict masters of esoterica visually evaluating people to see if they have these "bones and marks" (*gu xiang* 骨相).[147] These narrative portrayals match up with scriptural prescriptions such as this one: "One must have the bones and marks of a transcendent and must have his name written in the Thearch's ledger to qualify for transmission."[148] We often see this idea applied retrospectively, in statements to the effect that if someone already enjoys access to a scripture, method, or master, he or she must be prequalified. In other words, access is a de facto sign of election or an index of soteriological potential. For example, "This scripture should be transmitted only to those with the bones and marks of a transcendent, for only such individuals are able to see it. Such persons have had their names inscribed in the Grand Bourne and will be presented in Upper Purity" 當傳骨相合仙之人有得見者太極書名奏之上清.[149] The same principle sometimes applied to a would-be disciple's ability to catch sight of a transcendent at all. Thus, the master Han Zhong 韓衆 could be depicted as saying to a man who had approached him hoping for instruction: "You must have the bones of a transcendent—that's why you were able to see me" 汝有仙骨, 故得見吾耳.[150]

This discourse of somatic signs as indicating the potential for cultivational attainment is not unique to Daoist texts. A meditation scripture translated by Kumārajīva in the early fifth century, for example, answers the question, "By what signs (*xiang* 相) can it be known that one who cultivates meditation has obtained 'oneness of mind' (*yi xin* 一心)?" (i.e., the first *dhyāna*) with a list of behavioral and experiential criteria. But the list also includes "having a sleek complexion" (*mianse yueze* 面色悅澤).[151] Some Confucian texts speak of sages' ability to read people's affective dispositions, or *qing* 情, as reflective of their self-cultivational potential.[152] Texts such as Liu Shao's 劉邵 (ca. 180–245) *Treatise on Human Character* (*Renwu zhi* 人物志) articulated methodologies for reading people's outward characteristics as signs of inward tendencies, to be used by those selecting men for official positions.[153] And Buddhists developed a range of methods by which practitioners might divine their karmic and, hence, soteriological status and prospects. For example, the *Scripture on Divining Requital for Good and Evil Deeds* (*Zhancha shan'e yebao jing* 占察善惡業報經), composed in China around 580–590, prescribes practices not only for ascertaining one's present karmic situation but also for discovering how it might play out in future life events. That is, the practices link karmic conditions with specific life outcomes in a way that seems unusual outside the context of *jataka* narratives, in which, similarly, contemporary events are causally (and quite precisely) linked to particular karmic roots in the past. But in *jataka* narratives this linkage is retrospective, whereas in *Scripture on Divining* it's prospective, predicting future events.[154]

Conclusion

Practitioners of all sorts naturally wanted to know where they stood on their long, gradual paths of self-cultivation. If there were obstacles hindering their progress, they wanted to be able to identify them. But ascertaining their status was no simple matter, and the obstacles were often opaque or outright unknowable, buried deep within themselves or scattered across their many-lifetimes-long karmic history. The self implied in texts and practices of the DIAGNOSTIC PARADIGM is fragmented, riddled with gaps in knowledge of itself, plagued by its own opacity—a karmic self stretched over many lifetimes but with no memory and no direct awareness of what it must confess to, or a federated self harboring congenital components actively trying to thwart its progress and violate the canons of practice. How, then, could practitioners discover their soteriological status? How could they discern the latent stumbling blocks? This was the fundamental concern addressed by the texts we have considered in this chapter. It was a concern pointedly captured by Shen Yue 沈約 (441–513) near the opening of a confession text he wrote: "From my birth in this lifetime back to the beginningless beginning [of my series of rebirths], if my transgressions were to be set side by side they could absolutely not be named or calculated, but the evidence is obscured amidst the causal conditions of bygone times—there is nothing by which to verify or bring them to light" 約自今生以前至于無始. 罪業参差固非詞象所算. 證昧往緣莫由證舉.[155]

One solution was for practitioners to view (some of) their dreams as holding the answers they sought. Since most dreams did not address dreamers' soteriological status clearly or explicitly, it was necessary to approach them through a logic of signs,[156] which is to say, to take certain of their elements as meaning things quite distinct from their surface content. For that, one needed a hermeneutic, a decoding system. That is what the texts glimpsed in this chapter provided. But it isn't the only thing those texts have in common.

In all of them, whatever mechanism makes it possible for dreams to be utilized in this way is left unspecified. The texts' concern lies with listing the signs and disclosing their meanings, not theorizing how they're produced. Yet although the production process remains a black box, its outputs are charted with utmost confidence. There's nothing tentative or conjectural about the dream-to-diagnosis correspondences the texts chart. They are precise. And the diagnoses are impersonal in that no matter who you are, if (for instance) you have taken bodhisattva vows or are about to perform a certain ritual sequence and you dream of X, the same diagnosis is indicated for you as for anyone else in the same situation. A large diagnostic dreambook such as *Explication of Dreams* has a clerical, bookkeeping feel.[157] No input whatsoever about the dreamer's emotional state or specific life situation is allowed for. This is yet another example of how the texts considered in this book don't usually view dreaming as a psychological phenomenon.

We can also see this feature as an argument about the nature of selves, of self-cultivational paths (of whatever sort), and of the relations between them, for texts of the DIAGNOSTIC PARADIGM work at two levels simultaneously. On one hand, there is the ability to consult the text for the diagnostic import of any particular dream. But on the other hand, there is also a macro-scale rhetorical effect, insofar as the text implies by its very nature that there is a total *system* of dreams and their meanings, a system that transcends any particular dreamer or individual circumstance, in terms of which one's progress can be mapped. *How* this is possible is nowhere explained, but *that* it's possible is assumed—and assumed under the aegis of the Buddha's or the gods' authority. In this way, these texts function not just as manuals but also as arguments.

But we can identify one factor that makes this approach to dreams possible, and it's this: the path of practice being walked by the texts' implied readers was a path well known to the texts' makers—it was a *common* path with shared signposts of progress, communally fixed criteria of success, and a collectively posited ultimate goal. Rather than being solipsistic accidents, then, dreams in these texts and practices are fashioned into a common ground on which the practitioner joins others on the same path. A dream of this sort isn't an idiolect; rather, any particular dream is a bit of *parole* participating in a shared *langue*. Each dream featuring the same signs speaks in the same manner to any and all who've learned from the text how to interpret the *parole* correctly. Dreaming is rendered into a standardized set of diagnostic signs stamped with the authority of tradition. In other words, in such texts dreaming is canonized. As for dream contents that fall outside their diagnostic lists, the texts say nothing. Unlisted dreams were the oneiric equivalent of the theological category of adiaphora.

Regarding meditative visions interpreted as symbolic signs of attainment, Eric Greene has observed that they were "at once personal experiences known only to the meditator *and* events whose meaning and consequences require[d] authoritative interpretation."[158] Similarly in the case of dreams as they're treated in texts built on the DIAGNOSTIC PARADIGM, quintessentially personal experiences known at first only to their dreamers had to be interpreted to become soteriologically relevant. Where did the authority of interpretation reside? Hypothetically it might have resided in a teacher, or in a text, but where it emphatically *didn't* reside was in dreamers themselves. It seems reasonable to imagine that in self-cultivational contexts, dreamers must sometimes have consulted their teachers for help in interpreting their apparently symbolic, coded dreams. But in the case of dreams, markedly unlike the case of meditative experiences analyzed by Greene, we have surprisingly few records of this sort of interaction. Greene emphasizes that meditators didn't themselves know—or have any way of discovering—what their meditative visions meant until informed by their teachers.[159] But in the case of the dream-related texts we've surveyed, there's no reason to think that a manual such as *Explication of Dreams* was any less available to dreamers themselves than to their masters.

In a thoroughgoing study of dreaming's roles in two major medieval compilations of monks' biographies, Christopher Jensen adduces many examples of masters and disciples discussing their dreams with each other or with peer practitioners, but in almost no cases are these dreams understood as symbolic and thus requiring sophisticated decoding.[160] That is, in my typology these dreams are almost entirely constructed on the VISITATION PARADIGM. When it comes to individuals' *coded* dreams it seems to have been primarily *texts* that were vested with the authority of reading them as signs of progress on a path.[161] A manual such as *Explication of Dreams* seems to obviate the need for a teacher where dream interpretation was concerned. It can be read as bidding to replace the teacher with a totalizing system for ascertaining one's progress based on one's dreams. In this respect it comports with other texts mentioned above that treat dreams and other experiential signs as substitute confirmatory mechanisms when a practitioner lacked teachers to initiate him or her. And it must have fit well into a society such as medieval China, where symbolic dream interpretation was very widely engaged in (under the PROSPECTIVE PARADIGM) as a way of divining the future, and where manuals were often consulted for this purpose.[162]

There is one other aspect of the rhetorical positioning shared by texts in the DIAGNOSTIC PARADIGM that we should ponder from the point of view of manuscript transmission and survival. Consider: The diagnosis arrives in coded form. The coded signal—that is, the dream image or event—must be deciphered to derive the correct diagnosis. And attaining a diagnosis is vital—it is a matter of success or failure on the path, even of life and death in the case of medical diagnoses. Yet, given the cryptic nature of the code and the otherwise recondite nature of what the encoded dream reveals when correctly interpreted, the interpreter would (the texts imply) have had no other way to arrive at the desired information. After all, with very few exceptions, it's not as if the signs' meanings were common knowledge, or something a practitioner could figure out independently. The language of dreams is too strange to allow for that. The seeming arbitrariness of the semiotic link between sign and meaning, and the lack of any explanation of how the signs and their correlations are generated, renders all such texts fundamentally *divinatory* in character, albeit with the technique trained not on the shape of future events but instead on opaque aspects of the practitioner's progress and current status.[163] But the seeming arbitrariness we've observed in many of the dream-to-diagnosis correlations has a further rhetorical function: it argues, in effect, that *these texts alone* are the necessary and sufficient hermeneutic technology. By this rhetorical gambit these texts and methods bade to ensure their survival in the manuscript era. And insofar as they still exist, they can be said to have succeeded in this, even when there remains little direct evidence for their actual use in medieval times.[164]

CHAPTER THREE

Spilling Over

Tucked among the pithy utterances the *Analects* (*Lunyu* 論語) attributes to the character Confucius is a curious lament:

> The Master has said: "Atrocious! I'm declining! It's been such a long time since the Duke of Zhou appeared in my dreams."[1]
>
> 子曰: 甚矣吾衰也! 久矣吾不復夢見周公.

What the master's actual experience might have been—and even the question whether he really existed—are not at issue for our purposes, nor is the much-debated question of when the text was formed.[2] Relevant here is that this remark was a notable instance of the many memorable things he was supposed to have said. The audience he's implied to have been addressing is one or more of his disciples. The topic, as is unfailingly the case in the *Analects*, is self-cultivation. The text in which the remark appears was preserved by the transgenerational lineage of practitioners of a certain path of self-cultivation, a lineage that looked back to Confucius as its main progenitor and counted his immediate disciples as its first generation.[3] Confucius was known primarily as a virtuoso self-cultivator, a man who could sum up his life as a sequence of stages in character development until at seventy he could finally "give free rein to my passions without once stepping over the line" 從心所欲不踰矩.[4] It was no small thing to portray such a figure as measuring his efforts on the yardstick of his dreams.

The remark appears in chapter 7, whose dominant theme is "the importance of a properly directed and sufficiently intense will or intention."[5] Its point, as Edward Slingerland observes, seems to be that "one's immersion in the culture of the Zhou should be so complete that it penetrates even into one's dream-life."[6] But is this all? If we bracket the psychological model of dreaming, we glimpse further implications—ones we might want to call ontological or even theological. Suppose dreaming isn't a mental event contained inside the dreamer's head but is instead a portal through which other agents may come to meet the dreamer. If that is so, then we can understand Confucius to be suggesting that the Duke has stayed away because he looks unfavorably on Confucius's recent efforts. That both readings are possible is typical of the ontological ambiguity of this and similar passages in the early Confucian corpus, such as the famous line, "'Sacrifice as if [they were] present' means that when sacrificing to spirits you should comport yourself as if the spirits were present" 祭如在, 祭神如神在 (in *Analects* 3.12),[7] or the elliptical wording with which the "Rightness in Offerings" ("Ji yi" 祭義) chapter of the *Records of Rites* describes ancestral spirits' arrival to the sacrificial banquet without so much as using any noun to refer to them.[8]

The compilers of *Annals of Master Lü* (*Lüshi chunqiu*) incorporated a similar passage about self-cultivation and dreaming. But for them the ontological door wasn't one to be left open:

> Confucius, Mozi, and Ning Yue, all of them men of service who wore commoners' clothes, reflected on the current state of the world and found nothing in it to match the methods of the ancient kings. So they studied these day and night. Anything that facilitated this study, they did. Anything that did not facilitate this study, they were unwilling to do. It is said that Kong Qiu and Mo Di would spend the entire day reciting, memorizing, and practicing, and at night would see King Wen and Duke Dan of Zhou personally, of whom they would ask questions. With wills as concentrated as this, what affairs could they not accomplish, what tasks could they not complete? Thus it is said: "When you focus and immerse yourself in study, the spirits will inform you." But it is not really a matter of spirits informing you, but of your own focus and immersion.[9]
>
> 孔, 墨, 甯越, 皆布衣之士也, 慮於天下, 以為無若先王之術者, 故日夜學之. 有便於學者, 無不為也; 有不便於學者, 無肯為也. 蓋聞孔丘, 墨翟, 晝日諷誦習業, 夜親見文王, 周公旦而問焉. 用志如此其精也, 何事而不達? 何為而不成? 故曰精而熟之, 鬼將告之. 非鬼告之也, 精而熟之也.

Whether it was presented as a matter of the practitioner's concentrated effort or of other beings' responses, or both (and we'll see this question broached again in other texts), we have to deal here with what I call the SPILLOVER PARADIGM of dreaming. It has four components. First, the dreamer is a self-cultivator whose waking practice is so assiduous that it *spills over* into his or her dream life. (Or his practice is so lacking that it fails to spill over or draws an admonitory or punitive dream response.) Second, even while dreaming the dreamer remains in the role being cultivated while awake; the dreamer stays in character. Dreaming here represents not a rupture with waking pursuits (as it does in the PURIFICATION PARADIGM) but a continuation of them. Third, the dream usually involves face-to-face interactions with other beings. Dreaming is a portal for encounters (in this respect resembling what I've termed the VISITATION PARADIGM), and the encounters stem directly from—and further—the practitioner's waking-life efforts (in this respect differing from the VISITATION PARADIGM). Fourth, unlike those in the DIAGNOSTIC PARADIGM, dreams of this sort are not symbolic. They constitute events in the world, not coded indications about something in the world, and their impact flows back into waking life.[10]

Stimulus and Response

Hundreds of medieval narratives arising from multiple communities of discourse and practice play out a key cultural scenario: that of "stimulus and response," or *ganying* 感應 (also *ganyu* 感遇, "stimulus and encounter,"[11] and *gantong* 感通, "stimulus and contact"). By key scenario, a term borrowed from anthropologist Sherry Ortner, I mean a typical pattern of action, experience, and narrative in terms of which many of a culture's transactions and events are framed.[12] This way of putting things assumes that "narratives are not just about experiences. Experiences are, in a sense, about narratives. . . . Narratives are not primarily after-the-fact imitations of the experiences they recount. Rather, the intimate connection between story and experience results from the structure of action itself. Many kinds of social actions . . . are organized and shaped by actors so that they take on narrative form."[13]

"Stimulus and response," then, was three things at once: a set of ideas, often implicit but occasionally theorized, about humans, the cosmos, and their interrelations; a type of narrative; and a perceived pattern of action and experience. *Ganying* can be summarized as the idea that elements of the normally unseen world respond—sensibly, strikingly, sometimes miraculously—to the stimulus of human devotional activity, religious merit, or moral character, or to the pointed lack thereof. The essential claim was that human beings and other denizens of the cosmos are woven together into a web of relations such that activity in one respect and locale will reverberate, triggering a response from an Elsewhere. The stimulus and response occur across some ontological or epistemological gap, so that beings or forces ordinarily undetectable become temporarily manifest in response to valorized human activity. The valorization may be positive or negative. That is, a response may be elicited by someone's especially assiduous performance of a devotional act or ritual, or by their violation of protocols or breach of proper bounds.[14]

The SPILLOVER PARADIGM of dreaming interfaces with this cultural scenario in two ways. First, the responses to waking actions arrive through dreams. Second, both the dreamer's actions and the oneiric response centrally involve the dreamer's self-cultivation. So, to return for a moment to the two examples introduced above, the *Lüshi chunqiu* passage is a case where certain individuals' waking-life efforts at self-cultivation were deemed so effective that they spilled over into their dreams—perhaps, or perhaps not (depending on one's ontology), eliciting responses through the portal of dreaming by the likes of King Wen and the Duke of Zhou. Conversely, *Analects* 7.5 is a case where a self-cultivator—no less a one than Confucius himself—is portrayed as weighing his own efforts and finding them wanting in light of their *not* spilling over into his dream life; and perhaps also, again depending on the ontology, finding his efforts wanting in view of the Duke's *failure* to appear in his dreams in response to his efforts.

The following story, included in Wang Yan's 王琰 *Records of Signs from the Unseen Realm* (*Mingxiang ji* 冥祥記 ca. 490),[15] can serve as a typical *ganying* narrative involving a dream response. I've inserted bracketed numbers to facilitate discussion of specific aspects of the tale.

[1] During the Song there lived Wang Qiu, styled Shuda, a native of Taiyuan. He served as governor of Fuling. Because in Yuanjia 9 [432–433] he was derelict in his duties in the commandery,[16] he was imprisoned and encumbered with a heavy chain that was fastened down tightly. [2] Qiu had earlier been vigorous in his [Buddhist] practice. Now that he was incarcerated [3a] he applied his mind diligently [in devotion]. There were over a hundred persons imprisoned with him, and many of them were hungry. [3b] Each time Qiu was given a meal, he distributed his food among them, meanwhile fasting and concentrating his mind to the utmost on [the bodhisattva] Guanshiyin.

[4] One night he dreamed he ascended a high seat, where he saw a monk who handed him a roll of scripture. The titles on it read "Chapter on Light" and "Chapter on Comfortable Conduct," and it also had the names of various bodhisattvas. Qiu took it, unrolled it, and read it. He forgot [on waking] the first bodhisattva's name but remembered that the second was Guanshiyin and the third was Dashizhi [Mahāsthāmaprāpta].[17] He also saw a wheel, and the monk said, "This is the wheel of the five paths."[18] [5] He then woke to find the chain severed. In his mind Qiu knew it had happened due to divine power, so he redoubled his concentration, and because of this[19] he refastened the chain. After three days of this he was pardoned.[20]

[1] 宋王球字叔達. 太原人也. 為涪陵太守. 以元嘉九年於郡失守繫在刑獄. 著一重鎖釘鍱堅固. [2] 球先精進. 既有囹圄 [3a] 用心尤至. 獄中百餘人並多飢餓. [3b] 球每食皆分施之. 日自持齋. 至心念觀世音. [4] 夜夢昇高座見一沙門. 以一卷經與之. 題云光明 [案 > 安] 樂行品. 并諸菩薩名. 球得而披讀. 忘第一菩薩名. 第二觀世音. 第三大勢至. 又見一車輪. 沙門曰: 此五道輪也. [5] 既覺鎖皆斷脫. 球心知神力彌增專志. 因自釘治其鎖. 經三日而被原宥.

[1] Anecdotes usually open by briefly introducing a protagonist and mentioning whatever specifics are needed to contextualize the events about to be narrated. Stories involving a response that delivers the protagonist from dire straits often state the problem to set the stage for the response.

[2] Sometimes background is given on the protagonist's past self-cultivational efforts. As here, these are usually habits of long standing: in effect, the field has long ago been seeded and watered. (There are exceptions, such as a case in which Guanshiyin appears in a dream to an innocent man who's been imprisoned, then releases him, but the man

has never seen or heard of the bodhisattva and has to be told by others who it was who'd appeared to him.[21] And the valorized practices involved can stretch over a lifetime or occur in a single night.[22]) Even more crucially, [3] the practices he undertakes in the immediate situation are specified. Rhetorically speaking, these urge that the unusual event the story is building toward be seen as a *response* to the protagonist's practices and not a coincidence. Wang [3a] "applies his mind diligently" (*yong xin you zhi* 用心尤至), presumably in contemplation or a firming of intention, while also [3b] donating his food to others (acts of giving being a key merit-earning practice in the Buddhist repertoire), observing a fast (*chi zhai* 持齋), and "concentrating his mind to the utmost" (*zhi xin nian* 至心念) on Guanshiyin. Each of these practices, as well as the practitioner's mental disposition and sincere intention, are things collectively valorized in the repertoire on which he draws and are repeatedly prescribed in scriptures.

These practices and mental dispositions trigger [4] the striking response in the form of a dream. (Sometimes, however, the response comes in waking life. A key aspect of the SPILLOVER PARADIGM is that the impact on the protagonist is the same whether the response arrives in waking hours or in a dream.) The dream has four key characteristics.

First, it's a face-to-face *encounter* with another being. Here, as in many other instances, that being is an unfamiliar, perhaps foreign, monk. Reading across many such narratives, one gains an impression of clouds of such figures hovering unseen around humans. They stand ready to respond with assistance, instruction, admonition, or reassurance when prompted by practitioners' actions. Usually they don't just appear and leave; they instruct, render aid, or confer an object that remains in the dreamer's possession upon waking. Dreaming is *contact*.

Second, the dream is a real event in the world, not a coded message about something in the world. It requires no interpretation, because it is not a sign of something else.

Third, the dream brings soteriologically efficacious instruction, sights and sounds, or objects. In Wang Yan's text we see several instances of this. In his dream Wang ascends an elevated seat of the sort mentioned in chapter 2—a ritual space where Dharma is taught, akin to the ordination platforms central to bodhisattva practice from the early fourth century on. The mysterious monk hands Wang a roll containing a sutra.

Sutra copies were the focus of much devotional activity and narrative. To copy, possess, recite, carry, or venerate one of them was to amass merit, perhaps prompting the response depicted here.[23] Wang "took, unrolled, and read it" (*de er pi du* 得而披讀), actions having intrinsic karmic benefit. The chapter titles he glimpses are unmistakably reminiscent of sections of actual sutras circulating in China at the time, sutras that prescribe the same practices Wang performs in the narrative—particularly "Chapter on Comfortable Conduct" ("Anle xing pin" 安樂行品), which is the title of the fourteenth chapter in Kumārajīva's translation of the *Lotus Sutra* (*Miaofa lianhua jing* 妙法蓮華經), completed less than three decades before the events narrated here. (Below we'll see a passage from this chapter that promises the same sort of dream Wang was having.) Two bodhisattvas are explicitly mentioned, and one of them—Sound Observer, or Guanshiyin 觀世音 (whose name itself reflects the *ganying* scenario)—was hugely important in both monastic and lay practice in China at the time.[24] Further, the sutra seen by Wang mentions "the names of various bodhisattvas" (*zhu pusa ming* 諸菩薩名). This is significant in light of the immense power claimed for the recitation of their names—power to actualize their presence and unlock their salvific potential.[25] In these ways Wang in the dream replicates precisely the devotional actions he habitually performed in waking life. This is what I mean by saying that his waking practice spills over into his dreams. And then there is the wheel, whose significance is glossed by the monk, lest we or the protagonist mistake it. This moment in the dream, odd though it is (in that the wheel usually functioned as a visual and conceptual *metaphor* for the workings of the rebirth process but is here glimpsed as a literal object), visually confirms a key Buddhist teaching not usually so directly verifiable in ordinary experience.

Fourth, the dream's effects flow back quite tangibly into waking life: the chain is severed. Wang doesn't hesitate to recognize this as a confirmatory response to his own practices and mental states, not an accident or the work of a fellow prisoner. He further intensifies his cultivational efforts. And so he gains release from his predicament.

We've considered this story as an illustration of the role dreams often played in the stimulus and response scenario. At this point we should pause to recall how these stories came to be and what kept them alive. Wang's dream was the experience of a single person, but this report of his experience and its aftermath was the product of many other people who shared a vital interest in such cases. It was these others, most of whom remain unknown to us by name, who told, retold, recorded, exchanged, compiled, and thus preserved this and many similar narratives for us to read. Each such anecdote constitutes a memorate, an artifact of collective memory. In the era of manuscripts, any given text might easily cease to be copied and transmitted and thus disappear. The sheer existence of large numbers of such records is testimony to the investment of narrative communities in their preservation. Further testimony may be found in the prefaces to tale collections, where compilers wrote explicitly of their efforts to gather such cases based on their desire to preserve and disseminate evidence of karmic retribution and of the efficacy of devotional action.[26] Scholars who continue to frame things as a question of "didactics," a matter of individual authors "using" such tales to "support ethical or religious teachings"—as though men such as Wang Yan (in this instance) *made up* stories out of thin air as colorful ways to illustrate doctrines and inculcate values otherwise unfamiliar to readers—misapprehend this genre of writing and thus fail to grasp its worth as a source for religious history.[27] When we read such a story, we should do so with its narrative community in mind—the network of interested parties who repeatedly told, recorded, copied out, and transmitted it because they saw it as vitally important.

The stimulus and response scenario was hardly original or unique to Buddhist settings in China. Hundreds of instances dating from at least the late Warring States forward[28] could be adduced from across the entire Chinese cultural repertoire. Elsewhere I've discussed a Confucian example in which the protagonist's sincere display of filial piety elicits a striking cosmic response.[29] To cite but one Daoist example, in Du Guangting's 杜光庭 (850–933) fifteen-roll compilation *Records of Numinous Verifications of Daoism* (*Daojiao lingyan ji* 道教靈驗記)[30] we find a story set during the Tang Kaiyuan period (713–742) in which a young girl named Yao Changshou 姚長壽, daughter of Yao Yuanchong 姚元崇, governor of Fengyi in modern Shaanxi, assiduously follows her parents' instructions to burn incense and light lamps before an icon of Laozi. One day while napping she dreams of seeing Laozi himself.[31] The deity is flanked by attendants, one of whom compliments her: "Your diligent cultivation of the practice of burning incense is truly exemplary. I will now orally bestow on you a stanza from the *Scripture of the Vitalizing Spirits of the Nine Heavens*" 爾之焚修, 精志可隨, 口授汝九天生神經一章.[32] He proceeds to do so, quoting ten verses that are matched verbatim by lines in that Numinous Treasure (Lingbao 靈寶) scripture:

The Grand Void is moved to offer a spiritual
  encounter 太虛感靈會
And commands me to produce a divine stanza. 命我生神章
One recitation penetrates the nine abysses, 一唱洞九玄
A second reverberates through heaven and earth. 二誦天地通
I am merged together with them, 混合自相和
And after the ninth round I become a
  transcendent lord. 九徧成仙公
The great sages praise the prime's
  auspiciousness 大聖 [贊 > 讚] 元吉
As I scatter flowers reverently beneath the
  Grand Void. 散華禮太空
The heavenly hosts look on delightedly, 諸天並懽悅
Nodding their heads as one to show their esteem.[33] 一切稽首恭

The opening and closing verses seem to have been chosen to fit the occasion: just as their speaker has moved the Void to respond (*gan* 感) with a numinous meeting and spurred the celestial assembly to express their approval, so has the young Changshou prompted their reactions by her pure devotion. Upon waking, she remembers the dream and the stanza and recounts both to her parents. Struck with wonder, they respond that her assiduous devotion with the incense and lamps must have elicited this bestowal of instruction (*chui jiao* 垂教) from the Most High and that she must have the bones of a transcendent (a notion discussed in chapter 2). A week later she again dreams of Laozi and his entourage and is told that her father will soon be summoned to serve in the palace of "a sage."[34] Yuanchong reacts with both delight and fear—delight because this is obviously an auspicious dream, but fear because he assumes Laozi is the intended "sage" and thus that this summons spells his imminent death. But it turns out that Emperor Taizong is the sage referred to by the girl's divine informant.

The stimulus can be negative as well as positive. The pattern remains the same: something the protagonist has or hasn't done in waking life triggers a dream response, whose results carry back into waking life. Here are two examples, drawn again from Du Guangting's *Records of Numinous Verifications of Daoism*. Zhang Rong 張融 was a Daoist who constantly practiced the copying of talismans and registers but habitually left them lying around where he ate and slept, so that they became disordered and sullied. He lacked a respectful mind and disregarded his fellow Daoists' warnings. He and his family developed terrible illnesses lasting many years. The Tiantai Daoist Lu Hanzhen 陸含真[35] heard someone talking about Zhang, so he went to see him. "The protocols and registers of the Three Caverns are celestial precious writs," he told him. "You are responsible for disrespecting them. Cleanse your heart and confess your sins, so that, even if you don't receive mercy while you live, you may avoid torture after you die." Zhang complied. Afterward he dreamed a golden-armored god with several hundred retainers gathered above him in the air, informing him that the crime he'd committed was serious enough that the eight-year reduction of his lifespan could not be undone but that, since he'd realized his mistake, at least the illness would be removed. Zhang "wrote down all these matters and posted the record on walls to warn others" 具以此事書牓於壁, 廣勸同人矣.[36]

The second example is more baleful still, yet again not unmitigatedly so. It concerns the Daoist cleric Zhang Renbiao 張仁表, who was a skilled debater but was deceitful and lacked sincerity. At length he fell ill, and doctors were unable to cure him. (The narrative links his deceitfulness and his incurable illness with the word *yin* 因, "and so," implying that the former was the cause of the latter. This, too, shows the stimulus and response scenario in action.) He dreamed he was arrested on the order of the Director of Allotted Lifespans (Siming 司命). He was bound by soldiers and horsemen and driven rapidly through brambles, the thorns ripping his clothes and flesh. At length they reached a black, iron-walled city covered with smoke and guarded by animal-headed, human-bodied figures with flashing teeth and sword-like fangs, "just like the paintings of the purgatories circulating in the world" 真世之所畫地獄狀也. (This aside argues the veracity both of the dream report and of waking-world depictions of the purgatories, by matching them up together. The dream wasn't just a haphazard mental creation involving nothing outside the dreamer's head, and the paintings reflect the realities of what returning travelers have reported.) Passing through a gate, they came to a vermilion palace. Zhang was told it was the palace of the Celestial Worthy of Grand Unity 太一天尊宮 and that they'd soon reach the director's bureau. Upon hearing the phrase "Grand Unity" he suddenly recalled having urged others during his debates to call on the Celestial Worthy of Grand Unity, Savior from Suffering (Taiyi Jiuku tianzun 太一救苦天尊). So he began invoking the Worthy in a loud voice. His captors laughed at him. Nevertheless, he persisted, tears soaking his robe.

Soon the Worthy appeared. Zhang prostrated himself, confessed his entire life's transgressions, and vowed repentance. The Worthy responded that sins of the mouth are the most heinous, for when one person speaks falsely, many others are led astray. Zhang couldn't be saved from perdition, the god said—his sins were too many—and his allotted lifespan had run out. (Here the story nearly obliterates the distinction between dream experience and waking life, including the experience of dying, so seamlessly are they dovetailed: Zhang is told that his allotted lifespan has expired, as if he has died and had his spirit summoned to the other world, yet earlier the text clearly says all this happened in a dream.) But the Worthy granted Zhang seven more years to live so that he could display the god's image to many in the world, exhorting them to goodness. He was sent back home and woke to find his illness improved. He used his wealth to commission a painting of the god at the Suming Abbey 肅明觀 in Chang'an, and "he wrote and circulated an account of his experience to awaken others" 傳寫其本，遍令開悟. Then, recalling his initial arrest, he revisited the site where it had occurred. He found traces of his blood and clothing on the brambles through which he'd been driven. As foretold, he died seven years later.[37]

That Zhang Renbiao found waking-world traces of his dream experience serves to confirm the reality of what had happened in the dream—a trope common as well in the VISITATION PARADIGM.[38] Conversely, Zhang Rong's dream confirms the effects of his waking behavior. Either way, both stories stress continuity across the waking/dreaming divide. Causes and effects flow full-strength in both directions. Dreams are events in the world, not just mental phenomena. Both men make and circulate written records of what had happened to them so as to alert others. Their dreams, initially private experiences, were thus converted into words and not so much "published" as laboriously transmitted along chains of interaction and networks of interpersonal connection. Extant anecdotes of these sorts are the work of many interested parties.

Scriptural Promises

Passages in a number of important scriptures promise readers that certain practices undertaken during the daytime will render even their dreams conducive to advancement on the path. Often this takes the form of an assurance that if practitioners fail to experience the promised visions or encounters while awake, they will have them in their dreams. Such passages in effect argue that the canons of waking practice can be extended into practitioners' dream lives.

For example, the *Sutra on Meditation on the Buddhas of the Present* (*Banzhou sanmei jing* 般舟三昧經/*Pratyutpanna samādhi sutra*), partially translated by Lokakṣema 支婁迦讖 in 179 and completed by 208,[39] offers "a *samādhi* in which one is brought face-to-face with the Buddhas of the present" 現在佛悉在前立三昧.[40] The bodhisattva Bhadrapāla asks the Buddha what kind of meditation bodhisattvas should practice so as to enjoy a long list of soteriological benefits, among them the promise that "they are never parted from the Buddhas, even in their dreams" 未曾離佛時，若於夢中亦不離佛. A passage in the first chapter, "Protection," expands on this promise. There the Buddha assures Bhadrapāla that, as a result of having practiced the meditation,

> as for the Buddhas, those gods among gods, the bodhisattvas will not only see them during the daytime, but at night in their dreams they will both see the Buddhas' bodies and [hear] each of the Buddhas tell them his name. Furthermore . . . as for sutras which these bodhisattvas have not yet recited and sutra rolls they have not previously heard, these bodhisattvas will, by means of the spiritual power of this meditation, obtain all the names of the sutra volumes in their dreams. There they will see them all and hear all the sounds of the sutras. If they do not obtain them in the daytime, then they will see and obtain them all at night in their dreams.[41]

諸佛天中天, 菩薩不但晝日見, 夜於夢中若見諸佛身, 若諸佛各各自說其名字. 復次. . . 是菩薩所未誦經, 前所不聞經卷, 是菩薩持是三昧威神, 夢中悉自得其經卷名, 各各悉見悉聞經聲. 若晝日不得者, 若夜於夢中悉見得.

The second chapter, "Practice," sketches out the contents of the meditation. After preparing themselves with a long list of behaviors, attitudes, and attainments, practitioners—monastic or lay, female or male—are to "keep the precepts in their entirety, settle down alone somewhere, and call to mind the presence of the Buddha Amitābha in the western quarter" 持戒完具, 獨一處止, 心念西方阿彌陀佛. They should "do this single-mindedly, either for one day and night or for seven days and nights. After seven days they will see the Buddha Amitābha. If they do not see him while awake, they will see him in a dream" 一心念若一晝夜, 若七日七夜, 過七日以後, 見阿彌陀佛, 於覺不見, 於夢中見之.[42]

Having issued this prescription, the text immediately deploys seven similes to clarify how the practice should—and shouldn't—be understood. Five involve dreaming.

(1) The practitioner should call to mind (*nian* 念) a Buddha the way a man while dreaming sees all his gold, silver, and jewels, and his loved ones and friends. On waking, he tells others about it, even shedding tears as he recollects it. (Dreaming affectively changes the dreamer. Although dream events aren't real, their affective impact lingers, and therein lies the benefit.)

(2) In his vision of the Buddha, the practitioner will see things without obscuration, all being laid open to him, just as in dreams one does not fail to see because of darkness or obstructions. (In dreams we gain clarities and powers not associated with waking. Although its objects aren't real, dreaming is in this way more efficacious than waking vision.)

(3) Because he has heard of Amitābha and his realm, the practitioner longs to see them and repeatedly calls them to mind, just as men who, having heard of beautiful courtesans they've not met in person, visit them in their dreams. (Dreams are a way of visiting distant places and people one has heard about. Dreams are stimulated by desire and can satisfy desire.)

And yet (4) the practitioner should realize that the Buddhas and realms he sees are empty of own-being, just as a man journeying in the wilderness dreams of eating and drinking but finds his belly empty upon waking. By reflecting on this emptiness he "attains happiness in dharmas which do not come into existence from anywhere" 得無所從生法樂. (Dream experiences are fictive in a way that waking experiences are not. Also: everything is empty, and the experience of waking from a dream to find it was "only" a dream and not "real" helps us realize this liberating truth.)

(5) The practitioner, having heard about distant Buddhas, constantly thinks on them (*nian* 念 again) the way a traveler experiences homesickness, returns home in dreams, and wakes to tell others. (Dreams afford us a bypass around the limitations of waking experience, allowing us to visit places and experience things unavailable in waking life.)

As we can already see, *Sutra on Meditation on the Buddhas of the Present* is at pains to clarify the ontological status of what one was supposed to experience in waking visions or dreams. The sutra counterposes the notion of emptiness against the richness of dreams and meditative experience as a strategy for avoiding attachment to what is seen and heard there. The visions and voices are valid perceptions, yet empty of own-being.[43] So insistent is the text on this point that it spends much more space reminding readers of the emptiness of the experiences than it does either on describing them or on prescribing what to do to achieve them. The vision or the dream, the text explains, is like a monk contemplating bones of the dead which he has mentally arrayed before himself. At times he contemplates them when they are green, or white, or black. "Nobody brings these bones to him, nor do these bones exist, nor do they come from anywhere. They exist only as thoughts produced by the mind" 其骨無有持來者, 亦無有是骨, 亦無所從來. 是意所作想有耳. Just so, in this meditation

> if one wishes to see the Buddha then one sees him. If one sees him then one asks questions. If one asks then one is answered; one hears the sutras and rejoices greatly. One reflects: "Where did the Buddha come from? Where did I go to?" And one thinks to oneself: "The Buddha came from nowhere, and I also went nowhere." One thinks to oneself: "The Three Realms—the Realm of Desire, the Realm of Form, and the Realm of the Formless—these Three Realms are simply made by thought. Whatever I think, that I see. The mind creates the Buddha. The mind itself sees him. The mind is the Buddha. . . . The mind belongs to me, the mind sees the

> Buddha. The mind does not itself know the mind, the mind does not itself see mind. . . . There is nothing in these dharmas that can be enjoyed; they are all made by thinking. If thinking is nothing but empty, then anything which is thought is also utterly nonexistent."[44]
>
> 作是念, 佛從何所來, 我為到何所, 自念佛無所從來, 我亦無所至, 自念三處, 欲處色處無想處是三處意所為耳. 我所念即見, 心作佛, 心自見, 心是佛. . . 心是我身, 心見佛, 心不自知心, 心不自見心 . . . 是法無可樂者, 皆念所為. 設使念為空耳, 設有念者亦了無所有.

It's a fine line that is being walked here. The mind's agency is stressed as an alternative to seeing things as "real," but mental agency is then relativized in its turn. You see Buddhas in this practice, and your doing so is clearly due to your own activity (and not a matter of other beings coming to visit you); but you don't create them as "real" things, either. Mental activity is compared to the fabrications of a conjurer (*huan shi* 幻師).[45] This ontological caution differs markedly from the stimulus and response scenario, which stresses the reality of dream contacts. But it's reminiscent of the *Annals of Master Lü* passage seen above. In both cases, daytime immersion and mental concentration are rewarded with oneiric face time with Buddhas or Zhou-era sages, during which one may pose questions and receive instruction directly from the source, yet the reader-practitioner is cautioned not to view the dream visitors as real.

In a variation on this sort of promise, several sutras state that if practitioners prove unable while awake to have the sorts of visions expected to follow from the scripture's prescribed actions, they will have equivalent encounters in their dreams. For instance, the *Mañjuśrī Parinirvāṇa Sutra* (*Wenshushili banniepan jing* 文殊師利般涅槃經), one of a group of contemplation sutras probably composed in China in the fifth century but traditionally attributed to Nie Daozhen 聶道真,[46] prescribes a "method of calling to mind the image of Mañjuśrī" (*nian Wenshu xiang fa* 念文殊像法) in which one is to visualize a beryl icon of the bodhisattva and recite his name over a period of one to seven days. Having done this, practitioners may expect to receive a visit from the bodhisattva while awake. If they do not, this is due to their residual karma. Even so, they should then be able to see Mañjuśrī in their dreams, where the bodhisattva will explain Dharma, enabling dreamers to reach the stage of non-regression.[47] Similar promises are made in at least two other fifth-century contemplation sutras, *Scripture on the Contemplation of the Bodhisattva Ākāśagarbha*[48] (*Guan Xukongzang pusa jing* 觀虛空菩薩經) and *Oceanic Scripture on the Samādhi of the Contemplation of the Buddha* (*Guanfo sanmei hai jing* 觀佛三昧海經).[49]

Other scriptures promise something similar: that self-cultivational efforts practitioners conducted while awake can and should extend into their dreams, and that what they do in dreams is equally effective. At one point in the Perfection of Wisdom sutras, for example, the question is raised whether a practitioner who increases in wisdom during the day continues to do so at night in his dreams 夜於夢中亦復益. The answer is yes, since the Buddha has taught that diurnal waking experience and nocturnal dream experience are non-distinct 晝日夜夢中, 佛說等無異.[50] Elsewhere these sutras assert that non-reversible bodhisattvas keep the ten precepts[51] and can even attain the three types of *samādhi* while dreaming.[52] A more ornately developed version of the same idea is found in the *Sutra of the Divinely Transforming Mantras of [the Bodhisattva] Sound Observer of the Unfailing Net* (*Bukong juansuo shenbian zhenyan jing* 不空羂索神變真言經), translated by Bodhiruci. There we find the promise that a practitioner who receives and puts into practice the secret mantra of the bodhisattva Sound Observer of the Unfailing Net will enjoy a long list of benefits.[53] Among these is the ability to "snare" or "procure" (*huo* 獲, a telling verb given the sobriquet of the bodhisattva to whom the sutra is dedicated) seven sorts of auspicious dreams (*shan meng* 善夢). Each involves entering the palace of a particular bodhisattva, receiving his seal or emblem (here termed *sanmei ye* 三昧耶), and in some cases receiving consecration (*dingshou* 灌頂).[54] Another passage promises that those who have received the consecration rite it prescribes will enjoy a succession of four auspicious dreams involving divine visits and cosmic visions, all briefly described.[55]

But I know of no scriptural passage that proffers more stupendous oneiric attainments than the final verses of the "Comfortable Conduct" chapter of the *Lotus Sutra*. On the heels of a long list of benefits we encounter these lines:

Or, in his dreams	若於夢中
He will see only[56] wondrous things.	但見妙事
He will see the Tathāgatas	見諸如來

Seated on their lion thrones,	坐師子座
Multitudes of monks	諸比丘眾
Surrounding them as they expound Dharma.	圍繞說法
He will also see *nāgas* and gods,	又見龍神
Asuras and the like,	阿修羅等
As numerous as Ganges' sands,	數如恒沙
Joining their palms in reverence	恭敬合掌
As he sees himself	自見其身
Expounding Dharma for them.[57]	而為說法
He will also see Buddhas,	又見諸佛
Their golden bodies replete with the marks,[58]	身相金色
Radiating infinite light	放無量光
Which illuminates all reality	照於一切
And speaking in Brahmic tones	以梵音聲
As they declare and expound all dharmas.	演說諸法
While a Buddha for the fourfold assembly	佛為四眾
Expounds the matchless Dharma	說無上法
[The dreamer] will see himself in their midst,	見身處中
Palms joined, praising the Buddha.	合掌讚佛
Hearing the Dharma, he will be delighted	聞法歡喜
And will perform offerings,	而為供養
Gain *dhāraṇis*,	得陀羅尼
And be confirmed in irreversible wisdom.[59]	證不退智
The Buddha, knowing that his mind	佛知其心
Is deeply entered upon the Buddha path,	深入佛道
Will confer on him the prediction	即為授記
That he will attain ultimate awakening:	成最正覺
"You, good son,	汝善男子
In a coming age	當於來世
Will attain limitless wisdom,	得無量智
A Buddha's great path.	佛之大道
Your realm shall be adorned and pure,	國土嚴淨
Broad and great, without peer.	廣大無比
You, too, shall have a fourfold assembly	亦有四眾
Listening to your teaching with palms joined!"	合掌聽法
He will also see himself	又見自身
Amidst mountains and forests	在山林中

Cultivating good dharmas 修習善法
And being confirmed in the unconditioned,[60] 證諸實相
Deeply entering meditative absorption, 深入禪定
Seeing the Buddhas of the ten directions, 見十方佛
Their golden-hued bodies[61] 諸佛身金色
Adorned with all the blessed marks. 百福相莊嚴
Having heard Dharma, he will expound it
for others. 聞法為人說
Ever will he have this sort of auspicious dream. 常有是好夢
He will also dream of being prince of a kingdom, 又夢作國王
Forsaking palace and loved ones 捨宮殿眷屬
And the wondrous delights of desire, 及上妙五欲
Journeying to reach a place of practice. 行詣於道場
Under a bodhi tree 在菩提樹下
Seated on a lion throne 而處師子座
His search for the way having surpassed
seven days, 求道過七日
He will attain the wisdom of all Buddhas. 得諸佛之智
Having completed the matchless path, 成無上道已
He will rise to turn the wheel of Dharma, 起而轉法輪
Teaching Dharma to the fourfold assembly. 為四眾說法
Through countless kalpas 經千萬億劫
He will expound the untainted Dharma 說無漏妙法
And convey to salvation limitless numbers
of beings. 度無量眾生
Afterward he will enter into *nirvāṇa* 後當入涅槃
As smoke dissipates once the lamp is put out. 如烟盡燈滅
If in the latter evil age 若後惡世中
He preaches this foremost teaching, 說是第一法
This man will obtain great blessings 是人得大利
Such as the merits spoken of above.[62] 如上諸功德

The passage begins by promising that practitioners' dream lives will be purified into a field of experience in which they "see only wondrous things" (*dan jian miaoshi* 但見妙事). The "wondrous things" are extraordinary indeed. And, like the Perfection of Wisdom passages discussed in chapter 2, they progress upward. In dreams, first of all, practitioners will see and hear Buddhas teach. Then they will see themselves instructing non-human beings in Dharma. Next, they will see themselves in the assembly as Buddhas teach. They gain the opportunity to perform offerings to the Buddhas, they acquire *dhāraṇis*, and they have their attainments confirmed (*zheng* 證) by Buddhas. But the list goes on. They will receive a prediction of their future Buddhahood from a living Buddha. In dreams they will see themselves going out to the forest, meditating, encountering Buddhas in their meditative visions, and afterward teaching others. Finally, in dreams they will replicate a Buddha's final rebirth: born a prince in a palace, they'll eventually depart, meditate under a bodhi tree, realize the truth, teach Dharma to others, and attain final *nirvāṇa*. The passage promises that the practitioner's dreams will become a fully efficacious platform for nothing less than the attainment of Buddhahood.

All this, and much else, is promised to "those who read this sutra aloud" (*du shijing zhe* 讀是經者). Throughout Kumārajīva's version the compound *dusong* 讀誦, "read (or recite) aloud," occurs more than sixty-five times, especially in the fourth through sixth rolls, mostly in passages urging readers or hearers to engage with the text thus.[63] Recitation is one of several practices focused on the sutra that the sutra repeatedly recommends, the others being "receiving and upholding" (*shouchi* 受持), involving storing the text in specially made cases, enshrining it in consecrated spaces, and handling it according to codes of purity), expounding (*jie shuo* 解說), copying (*shuxie* 書寫), and venerating the sutra with pure offerings (*gongyang* 供養).[64] These promised effects of reciting the sutra seem rhetorically designed to drive home, from yet another angle, that the sutra is an unrivaled repository of power and that interacting with it carries supreme soteriological benefit.[65] Still, *this* promise is stunning: if one but recites the sutra while awake, the otherwise inconceivably arduous work of attaining Buddhahood will be accomplished while one sleeps, in dreams.[66]

Zhou Ziliang's Dream Records

Introduction

We turn now to what is probably the most stunning example of the SPILLOVER PARADIGM among extant texts. *Records of Master Zhou's Communications with the Unseen World* (*Zhoushi mingtong ji* 周氏冥

通記) has come down to us in the Daoist canon and in several other editions.[67] It's a remarkable work, seemingly well preserved despite its antiquity, and is of a different genre than other texts we've reviewed to this point: in part it is a fragmentary journal of dreams and waking visions written in the first person.[68]

The Master Zhou of the title was Zhou Ziliang 周子良 (b. 497), a favored disciple of the master Tao Hongjing 陶弘景. During the years 515 and 516 Zhou recorded dozens of instances in which deities, most of whom had entered the repertoire through the Shangqing revelations to Yang Xi 楊羲 between 364 and 370, appeared to him in both waking visions and dreams. Shortly after Zhou died by self-administered elixir on December 6, 516, Tao Hongjing retrieved as many of these piecemeal records as he could find. He arranged them chronologically, added a running commentary and a sketch of Zhou's life and sudden death, and submitted these in four rolls to Xiao Yan 蕭衍, Liang Emperor Wu 梁武帝, in January 517.[69]

The work can be divided into four parts: Tao's narrative of the young master's life and death and of his relationship to Tao and other members of the Zhou clan (1.1a–7b); Tao's comments addressed to the ruler (with the latter's brief response, 1.7b–8b); Tao's compilation of all the scraps he could find of Zhou's records, with his own interlinear comments (1.8b–4.19a7); and a recipe for the Ninefold Perfected Jade-Liquor Elixir 九真玉瀝丹 (characterized by Strickmann as a "rudimentary vegetomineral compound") featuring locally obtainable powdered mushrooms and cinnabar,[70] which had been transmitted to the young man by the Perfected Zhou Ziyang 周紫陽[71] and which may or may not have been the elixir he used to end his life (4.19a8–20b).[72]

A timeline of events will prove helpful. According to his introduction, Tao first met Zhou Ziliang by chance in 508 (the seventh year of the Liang Tianjian 天監 reign period), when the latter was a lad of twelve. Thanks to a travel glitch, Tao wound up at the hall of a local Celestial Master parish in Yongjia 永嘉 commandery (in today's Zhejiang province), where Zhou was a recent initiate under the tutelage of his maternal aunt.[73] Zhou accompanied and served Tao during his subsequent travels until the eleventh year of Tianjian (512) found them back on Mount Mao. There, Tao bestowed scriptures on Zhou and formally initiated him as a disciple. In the fall of the twelfth year (513), members of Zhou's family, including his mother, aunt, and younger brother, joined him on the mountain, residing with him in an outbuilding of the temple.

It was apparently on the summer solstice of the fourteenth year (June 20, 515) that Zhou began to be visited by gods. That, at least, is the date of the first record he made that survived his death. Several months later he moved to the newly constructed, imperially sponsored hermitage named Scarlet Solarity 朱陽, where Tao resided. In the winter of that year, following the secret orders of his divine interlocutors but "on the pretext of convenience" (*tuo yi fangbian* 託以方便, 1.3a3), he built a separate structure (*bie yu* 別宇) and moved into it.

The latest vision recorded among the recovered papers occurred on the twenty-third day of the seventh month of Tianjian 15 (September 5, 516). Zhou consumed an elixir on the twenty-seventh day of the tenth month of that year (December 6, 516). So the records span a period of around fifteen months and leave off three months before his death. But Zhou had almost certainly made notes on additional dreams and visions—notes he was seen burning either ten days or one day before he died. As Tao explains while reporting his postmortem investigation, Zhou's assistant He Wenxing 何文幸 "said that on the sixteenth [or the twenty-sixth, i.e., either November 25 or December 5][74] Ziliang had burned two bundles of writings, perhaps a hundred sheets' worth, and would not allow anyone to see them" 云一 [or 二] 十六日燒兩束書, 可百餘紙, 不聽人見 (1.5a1–2). I'll return to this important detail below.

The Making of the Text

Before we delve into its contents, some remarks are in order on the processes—scribal, material, editorial, and commentarial—by which the text was created.

First, a clarification. We are talking about Zhou's dreams as he represented them and as Tao Hongjing redacted and commented on them. As with any account in any era, we have no access to another person's dreams except through what the dreamer says or writes about them. That we might somehow tease out which of Zhou's reported dreams actually occurred is an impossible research agenda, though the text's seemingly intimate first-person voice might beguile us into trying.[75] What we have to work with is a text, not some sort of oneiric raw material. Wang Jiakui 王家葵, who knows the text much better than I do, has argued—without being able to prove definitively, as he grants—that it was "fabricated" (*wei zao* 偽造) by Tao Hongjing in response to the complex Buddho-Daoist tensions during the reign of Liang Emperor Wu.[76] This could mean a number of things, from emphasizing Tao's role in transforming fragmentary records scrawled on slips of paper into the chronicle of revelations it now appears to be, right down to claiming that Tao invented the entire thing as a sort of "novel"[77] (*xiaoshuo* 小說 in its modern, not its early medieval, sense)—including the fact of Zhou Ziliang's very existence (though this would've been risky since the emperor could easily have sent someone to investigate).[78]

I fear that the modern construct of authorship here risks obscuring aspects of the textual process we seek to understand. Even if the strongest version of this claim were true and "Zhou Ziliang" was just an invented voice into which Tao dubbed his own claims, the text would be no less significant for my purposes as a vividly detailed record of the sorts of things that could be credibly claimed about dreams in relation to self-cultivation in the early sixth century. To imagine that we might sort out which bits "really happened" is, I think, to mistake the nature of narratives of past events.[79] And Tao certainly made no effort to hide his role in fashioning the text. His handiwork is evident in every line. In fact, *any* transmitted dream record from the manuscript era can only have been the work of many hands. Unless we're talking about an autograph document inserted into a tomb and only recently recovered, no sixth-century record of dreams that reaches our eyes can have been the unmediated production of the dreamer. It's just that in this case we know the initial mediator's name and we know a lot about how he (claims to have) carried out his work of textual assemblage.

Tao tells us that his disciple wrote piecemeal records of dreams and visions, most of which began by noting the date. We do not know what, if anything, Zhou had planned to do with these records, why he made them, or why he left (some of) them behind,[80] but his inclusion of dates gives the sense of a progressive series of revelations through time, some of which built upon or presupposed earlier ones in the sequence. Zhou himself left no arrangement or introduction. It's Tao who placed the entries in temporal sequence and framed them within a narrative, written in his own voice, of the young man's short life and early demise.

We do know three things about Zhou's scribal practice (or Tao's representation of it). First, he wrote in varying colors of ink on different colors, sizes, and types of paper. The reason is unclear. It might simply have been a matter of the availability of materials. In any case, in his comments Tao meticulously enters the type of paper and color of ink used, and sometimes the style of characters as well. The copies of *Declarations of the Perfected* that Tao had prepared and Zhou recopied[81] were similarly color-coded.[82] Second, Zhou sometimes returned to his notes and emended them. Tao writes: "Also, in his records there are many blacked out and emended graphs, indicating that he first wrote something down hastily and later thought better of it and changed it. Earlier in Lord Yang's writings there had been many similar instances" 又諸記中往往有黯易字, 當是受旨時匆匆, 後更思憶改之, 昔楊君迺中多如此 (1.17b–18a). Third, with few exceptions both writers carefully noted which records were of waking visions and which were of dreams; for example, he wrote: "Here it says [Fan Jian] 'came,' so it wasn't a dream" 此云來則非夢 (4.4b). At one point Tao even takes pains to specify:

> According to these documents, all the incidents labeled "dreams" were seen in sleep, while all those where it's noted explicitly "I saw such-and-such on day X" were direct waking visions, but it's unclear whether he was seated inside or was somewhere outside when he had them. From the eighth month of the *yiwei* year [August 515] onward he was traveling [in dreams] to various locations, so in those cases it was a matter of his spirit leaving but his body not moving [1.17b].
>
> 按尋記, 凡標前云夢者, 是眠中所見, 其有直云某日見某事者, 皆是正耳覺時其見, 但未知為坐為外耳. 從乙未年八月以後, 遊行諸處, 此皆是神去而身實不動也.

Tao also entered a running count following each month's entries. For example: "The three entries to the right record events of the sixth month. One is termed a vision, and two are termed dreams" 右三條, 六月中事. 一條云見, 二條云夢 (4.18a6). Finally, he sums up the statistics near the end of the work: "a combined total of one hundred and nine entries, [of which] sixty-three entries read 'I saw,' forty-six entries read 'I dreamed'" 一白九條; 六十三條云見, 四十六條云夢 (4.19a5). However, his count appears to be off by a few entries, and in several cases it's unclear whether a given entry describes a vision or a dream.[83]

Awake or asleep, Zhou was frequently visited by deities, and what he learned in those two sets of encounters fit together seamlessly. In other words, he seems to have received exactly the same kinds of instruction in dreams as in waking visions—a striking instance of the SPILLOVER PARADIGM at work. I detect no difference in the contents or tone of the two types of entries. The interesting question, then, is: Why were both Zhou and Tao so scrupulous about noting whether each experience occurred while Zhou was asleep or awake?

The answer is unclear. But some passages in Shangqing texts imply a visionary hierarchy based on the practitioner's degree of advancement. Topmost were those who could interact with Perfected ones in waking experience; next were those who could do so only in dreams; at the bottom were those not advanced enough to see the gods at all.[84] It was not, then, that one saw different beings or received different sorts of information in the two states. Rather, the ability to have waking visions or dream encounters was correlated to one's degree of progress in self-cultivation. And the reason for the difference, as we saw in chapter 1, was the Perfected ones' purity: for them to appear directly to an uncultivated person would be an affront to their dignity and risk polluting them. (Recall that dreaming was seen as *contact*.) But it's unclear how this hierarchy relates to Zhou Ziliang's case since his records indicate he was able to have both kinds of experience regularly, though not immediately: in one early instance he records having heard a voice without seeing the speaker, and upon waking he is told by a lesser god that the reason is because "that was a Perfected personage. It is not yet appropriate for you to see him, so he instructed you from a distance" 是真人爾, 未宜見之, 故遙相告爾 (2.5b). Each divine visitation, in any case, confirmed his progress on his path toward deification.

An important aspect of the textuality of *Records of Master Zhou's Communications with the Unseen World* is Tao Hongjing's specification about how the work should be ritually treated:

> These *Records* contain many secret names of Perfected [ones] and transcendents as well as their teachings and precepts. Just as one does with other scriptures and [divine] declarations, one must purify the table on which [the *Records*] are placed and the cloth with which they are touched.

> One must bathe and burn incense before viewing them. If one wants to copy them for transmission [to others], one must also first make announcement to all the Perfected as well as to the Mystic One himself.[85] It is not permissible to write them out haphazardly or [mix them with] other documents [1.6a7–8].[86]
>
> 此記中多有真仙諱字, 并諸教戒, 便同依經誥之例, 皆須淨案淨巾沐浴燒香, 乃看之. 若欲傳寫, 亦應先關告眾真及玄人, 不得皆悠悠外書記也.

The comment reminds us that, whatever experiences Zhou Ziliang may have had, they were accessible to others only through the material objects he had left behind as mediated and refashioned through Tao Hongjing's salvage, rearrangement, introduction, and commentarial interventions.[87] With these lines Tao sought to ensure that the work would be viewed and treated as a body of divine revelations, on a par with *Declarations of the Perfected* and the many other sacred texts of the Upper Purity corpus. In this he can be said to have succeeded, insofar as the text was incorporated into subsequent Daoist canons.

One other notable aspect of the textuality of the *Records* is the very frequent use of the ellipsis (*yun yun* 云云). I discuss this in "The Esotericizing Dynamic" below.

Dreams as Direct Encounters

All but two of the dream accounts Zhou Ziliang left behind share two key features: they involve direct encounters with other beings, and they have something to do with the young man's self-cultivation. I begin with a single illustration. For modern readers, even a brief passage such as this one requires considerable explanation of the personae and places mentioned. Throughout, both when translating and when transposing the corresponding Chinese text, I place Tao Hongjing's commentarial insertions within parentheses. (As is common with old texts, bits of what was once Tao's commentary occasionally appear to have crept up into the main text—or, more often, the other way around.) Square brackets enclose my own clarifications.

> On the twelfth of the eighth month I dreamed I traveled by chariot inside [the] Huayang [cavern heaven] together with the Lord Certifier of

> Registers. We were attended by thirty jade maidens who strummed celestial music. We called on the Southern Perfected in the Cinnabar Citadel, where I was instructed by her and so on. I was further instructed by [the Perfected of the] Grand Prime. He showed me the register of transcendents and so on. (The administrative seats of these two Perfected Ones are both at Greater [Mount] Huo.)[88]
>
> 八月十二日, 夢與定錄君於華陽內共乘車, 侍玉女三十人, 奏天樂, 造南真於丹城, 南真見告 云云. 因又告太元, 太元示以仙籍 云云. (二真府並在大霍也.)

Zhou Ziliang here makes a dream journey into one of the ten major cavern heavens (*dongtian* 洞天) ubiquitous in Daoist (especially Shangqing) lore—the one called Huayang heaven 華陽天, whose mouth was situated at the central peak of Mount Mao.[89] He accompanies Mao Gu 茅固, the middle of the Mao brothers, often referred to by his title in the otherworld administration, Lord Certifier of Registers 定錄君. Entertained as they ride by an ensemble of divine female musicians, they reach the Cinnabar Citadel 丹城, a southern locale mentioned in the revealed hagiography of the Perfected Zhou Ziyang 周紫陽.[90] There they call on Lady Wei, Perfected of the Southern Marchmount 南嶽魏夫人, also known as Wei Huacun 魏華存, who had been the subject of a revealed Shangqing hagiography.[91] She had received Celestial Master revelations from Zhang Daoling 張道陵 and had been Yang Xi's principal tutor, and was therefore a key bridge between the Celestial Master and Upper Purity traditions.[92] Zhou Ziliang is "instructed by" (*jian gao* 見告) her. Though we're told that it took place, we're not privy to the subject matter of this instruction. Whatever it was, it's replaced by the ellipsis 云云, which appears twice even in this brief an entry.

In the same dream Zhou is instructed by yet another key Shangqing deity, Mao Ying 茅盈, the eldest Mao brother, among whose titles were Perfected of the Grand Prime 太元真人 and Lord Supervisor of Lifespans 司命君. During this tutorial, whose contents are again elided, the god shows Zhou the "register of transcendents" (*xian ji* 仙籍), a list of those who'd already joined their ranks or were destined to do so. Zhou might well have glimpsed his own name there.

Finally, Tao Hongjing comments that Lady Wei and Mao Ying both had their administrative seats at Mount Huo 霍山 (in today's southern

Anhui province), which since the Han era had been deemed the Southern Marchmount rather than Mount Heng 衡山 much farther south in Hunan.[93]

Consider what does and doesn't transpire in this brief passage. What does transpire is nothing less than sublime: Zhou comes face-to-face with three key Shangqing deities; traverses a cavern heaven to reach another mountain; enjoys celestial music; and inspects a register of transcendents. And he receives instruction from two of his divine interlocutors. Easily lost sight of is what doesn't transpire: neither Zhou nor Tao questions what meaning the dream might have or whether it can be taken at face value. It's not treated as a sign of anything, including Zhou's own psychology. Zhou narrates an event, and Tao supplements Zhou's account not with speculation about Zhou's state of mind but with a factual detail to help the reader understand its logic: that it made sense for Zhou to meet Lady Wei and Mao Ying at Mount Huo because that's where their bureaux are located. This is the SPILLOVER PARADIGM at work: Zhou's dream is represented as an event that directly continued and furthered his waking-life efforts to cultivate himself. He just happens to have been asleep when it occurred. Throughout, Tao treats Zhou's records as a source of factual information about the workings and layout of the unseen world, using them to fill in gaps in what was already known (through *Declarations of the Perfected* and other texts) or trying, and sometimes failing, to square them with previous revelations.

By my rough count, Zhou interacts with at least thirty named deities in his dreams, most of them over multiple evenings—not to mention the many others he encountered in waking visions.[94] These include most of the other major Perfected beings featured in *Declarations* (including Mao Zhong 茅衷, often referred to as Lord Protector of Lifespans 保命君; the now deified Yang Xi; Xu Mi 許謐; the Perfected Consort of Ninefold Florescence 九華真妃; Lady Wang of Purple Tenuity 紫微夫人; Zhou Yishan 周義山, also known as the Perfected of Purple Yang 紫陽真人; and the Lord Azure Lad of Fangzhu 方諸青童君). They also comprise pre-Shangqing transcendents, such as Wang Yuan 王遠, Han Zhong 韓衆, and Tang Gongfang 唐公房, who'd been co-opted into the Shangqing pantheon.[95] More strikingly, through Zhou's dream records, Tao Hongjing and subsequent readers were introduced to previously unknown deities and at least one uncharted cosmic destination: Yin Citadel Palace 陰城宮,

which Zhou found to harbor "transcendents of the Dayou [cavern heaven], none of whom I recognized" 大有仙人, 而自不識 (Tao comments, "I've not yet seen Yin Citadel Palace mentioned anywhere" 未見陰城宮所出處 [4.9a9–10]). The newly encountered deities include a certain Xu Xuanzhen 徐玄真 (who, Tao surmises, must be an officer in the realm of the dead), two officials based at Mount Daheng with the title Grandee 大夫, and one Master Hong, Transcendent of the Central Marchmount 中嶽仙人洪先生. None of these deities, Tao comments, had been previously known from the Shangqing revelations or otherwise.

Not only did deities visit Zhou Ziliang on Maoshan through the portal of dreams. As we've seen, Zhou also traveled to other locales, usually accompanied by one or more gods.[96] Such journeys—and the ability to accomplish them rapidly—were an affordance unique to dreaming, since in his waking visions Zhou remained on Mount Mao. His farthest destinations include the divine palaces on such blessed eastern isles as Fangzhu 方諸 (dream-visited twice in the same week, 4.5a–b) and Penglai 蓬萊 (4.5b, 4.6b–7a). Fangzhu was associated with Lord Azure Lad 青童君, frequenter of the pages of Shangqing writings and associated with (among other things) a "method of lying down in the Dipper" (*wo dou zhi fa* 臥斗之法) so as to absorb its energies.[97] The following four excerpts are typical examples of Zhou's dream travels to divine locales:

> On the twenty-first of the eighth month I dreamed I traveled with the Lord Protector of Lifespans [Mao Zhong] to Penglai, where we met Zhou dafu [Zhou Dabin 周大賓].[98] We also reached a vermilion terrace with purple chambers, outfitted with a gigantic gatetower with [gates on] blue hinges. They said this was the Bureau Overseeing Yin and that someone named Tao [i.e., Tao Hongjing] would soon be made director of its southeastern palace sector.[99] We then set off again. . . . (Zhou dafu is [Zhou] Dabin. *Declarations of the Perfected* says that the Lord Overseer of Yin is in charge of all matters in the world pertaining to water. The topic appears in the "Traditions of Lord Ma." It was not previously known that that bureau is located on Penglai.[100] On Lesser Fangzhu there are many who serve the path [of Buddhism]. This, too, is mentioned in *Declarations of the Perfected*) [4.5b–6a].[101]

> 八月二十一日, 夢與保命至蓬萊, 見周大夫. 又至一朱臺巨闕青軒紫房, 云是司陰府, 陶某近正應肩治此東南一玄宮中. 因復行. . . . (周大夫, 即大

賓. 真誥亦云: 在蓬萊, 司陰君主天下水事, 事出馬君傳. 前不知那治在蓬萊. 小方諸多事道, 事亦出真誥.)

On the fifth of the ninth month, I dreamed I went again to Penglai. I first stopped in to see the Supervisor of Lifespans [Mao Ying]. I was instructed by him as follows: "Before taking a divine elixir it is first necessary that one's name be inscribed in the register of transcendents. Only then can one take the elixir" and so on. I continued on to Penglai and saw Zhou dafu. He was eating a certain herb shaped like sophora incense but purple colored. I was instructed: "You are not yet able to eat this. When you are able to eat it you will have become one such as I." He was referring to the matter of "fire jujubes and exchanged pears." And so on. ("Fire jujubes and exchanged pears" appear in *Declarations of the Perfected*, but I do not know what sort of divine marvel these fruits are) [4.6b–7a].[102]

九月五日, 夢又至蓬萊, 先過司命. 司命見告: 服神丹應, 先須名上仙籍, 乃得服之. 云云. 乃至蓬萊見周大夫, 食一草, 狀如槐香而紫色, 見告云: 子未得食此, 得食此, 便如吾耳. 及火棗交梨事. 云云. (火棗交梨出真誥中. 亦竟不知此果是何神奇.)

On the sixteenth of the eighth month [September 9, 515] I dreamed I traveled to Fangzhu, where I saw the Azure Lord's headquarters. I did not see the Azure Lord himself. I did see Han Taihua and Lady Song of the Cinnabar-and-Blue Residence. I was instructed in essentials of divine transcendence and techniques for abandoning one's bodily form and so on [4.5a9–b1].[103]

八月十六日, 夢至方諸, 見青君府, 不見青君. 乃見韓太華, 丹青館宋夫人, 見告神仙之要, 委形之術云.

On the nineteenth of the eighth month I again dreamed of visiting Fangzhu. I arrived just as the Azure Lord was starting out on an excursion, with Lord Yang [Yang Xi], Lady Nine Blossoms, and Transcendent Marquis Xu [Xu Mi] accompanying him. So we called on Marquis Han and I was instructed regarding the matter of the registers and so on. (This "Han" is the keeper of the registers in the eastern palace, mentioned in the previous roll. His given name is Huiqi) [4.5b2–4].

八月十九日, 又夢造方諸, 正見青君出遊, 楊君九華及許仙侯皆從. 因造韓侯見告簿籍事. 云云. (韓即前卷所云東宮典錄籍者, 名惠期也.)

A partial list of other destinations Zhou visits in his dreams would include two palaces, Yixian 易遷 and Tongchu 童初, where female and male transcendents dwell;[104] a mountain called Cinnabar Dragon 丹龍, which harbored caverns and "many transcendents and Perfected ones" (*duo xian zhen* 多仙真) and whose shape was flat and circular, "not like the mountains of the human realm" 異於人間;[105] the Hidden Dragon Palace 玄龍宮 of the Lady of Purple Tenuity, located in the north (4.5a); a thatched lodge for traveling transcendents on Mount Daheng 大衡山 (4.6a); and the gilded and gem-studded palaces of Mount Tongqiao 桐橋山, to which he traveled alone (4.7b). In making these journeys to far-off, inaccessible places and recording them once he'd returned and awakened—but also in *not* detailing the esoterica he'd learned there—Zhou Ziliang joined the ranks of performers of a long-established cultural role I've elsewhere termed the *long-distance specialist*: one who, having traveled vast distances, returns home bearing exotic knowledge otherwise inaccessible to most people.[106]

Above I said that almost all of Zhou's dreams involve encounters in the direct mode—that is, he and Tao both treated them straightforwardly as events that happen to have occurred during sleep, not as opaque symbolic messages. The few exceptions to this rule are instructive. One of these comes in a statement Zhou makes about his recent dreams. In the first roll Tao Hongjing relates new behaviors that caused Zhou's family to worry:

> On the day of the summer solstice of the fourteenth year [June 20, 515] Zhou suddenly retired to recline in his chamber before noon. He conferred with spirits for a long time before emerging. His aunt didn't know what he'd been up to and questioned him closely about his strange behavior. . . .[107]
>
> Now the Zhou family had originally served profane gods, so the family elders all feared that Zhou might have been bewitched by some of these deities taking on the guise of Daoist spirits. Some family members even declared that they themselves were in danger of contamination by perverse *qi*. They therefore interrogated Zhou closely. He would only answer: "They might after all be *louluo* dreams. There's no way of knowing for sure. If you're all so worried about it, you can break relations with me." At this, none of the family members could decide what to do. They

decided to let the matter go for the time being and wait to see how things would develop [1.2a–b].[108]

以十四年乙未歲五月二十三夏至日於廨忽未中寢臥, 彌淪良久乃起出. 姨母不解所以, 深加辯切. . . . 周家本事俗神, 姨舅及道義咸恐是俗神所假, 或謂欲染邪氣, 亟相蹙問, 唯答云: 許終是婁羅夢, 無所知究, 自懷愁慮, 為復斷隔耳.於是眾人莫測可否, 相與縱置, 聽看趣向.

Noticing Zhou's sudden withdrawal from normal ways of interacting and eating (on which more below) and knowing that he'd begun having visionary and oneiric contact with Others, his family fears he's being beset by precisely the sorts of polluting dreams seen in chapter 1. That "profane gods" (*su shen* 俗神) or "perverse *qi*" (*xie qi* 邪氣) might masquerade as proper Daoist spirits was to be expected. Could his dreams be demonic incursions? His response to these challenges is telling. He offers his family an out by inviting them to look upon his experiences not as the direct encounters with Daoist deities that he claimed they were but as some sort of indirect, confusing dream signal, a message or event that couldn't be taken at face value. One meaning of the binome *louluo* 婁羅 is *weiqu* 委曲, "turned and twisted," labyrinthine—*indirect*.[109] He himself sees his dreams as straightforward interactions whose meanings are self-evident, but he's giving his family the option of dismissing them as muddled signals of no great import.

Then there is an account in which Zhou dreamed he was standing at the foot of a mountain peering up at two figures, one of whom appeared to be Mao Zhong, Lord Protector of Lifespans, and the other one Laozi, seated on a throne. The two were conversing but, Zhou writes, "I couldn't understand what they were saying. In a little while I woke up. I do not understand why I encountered these two personages" 某亦不解其語, 須臾便覺, 竟不知此二人後何所適.[110] Zhou was apparently so accustomed to receiving instruction or evaluation during his dream encounters that this dream of seeing two gods only from afar, speaking to each other but not to him, puzzled him.

The only other exception to the rule comes when Zhou records having dreamed he cut up meat and ate some goose fat, then adds: "I don't understand what this means" (*wei ke jie ye* 未可解也 [4.18a]). Tao Hongjing explains the dream by recalling that there had been an official event that day at which goose fat was served. But Zhou seems surprised by his failure to "understand" it precisely, I think, because he was accustomed to direct dreams needing no decipherment and having to do with his self-cultivation, whereas cutting meat and eating goose fat held no clear relevance.[111]

As we've seen, Tao Hongjing, too, treats Zhou's dreams and visions straightforwardly as events yielding important information about the other world—that is, as revelation. He rarely assesses Zhou's dreams as reflections of the young man's state of mind—with one notable exception. Zhou had written:

> On the twenty-fifth of the eighth month [September 18, 515] I dreamed I entered [the] Huayang [cavern heaven] and called on the Certifier of Registers. I inquired of him whether next year's tenth-month date could be extended. He answered that it could be. And so on.
>
> 八月二十五日, 夢入華陽, 造定錄, 諮來年十月可保得申延不. 答云可爾. 云云.

"Next year's tenth-month date" refers to the day the gods expected the young man to act on their summons and ascend to the heavens to take up the post awaiting him. Zhou is here asking whether his assigned date of death-and-ascent can be postponed. A note of anguish is detectable in Tao's comment on this passage:

> This means Ziliang had the intention of remaining in the world longer. Although when he [here] made this request he was at first told it would be permissible, it seems that later he must have gone back and asked again whether it could be extended and was denied. He therefore departed after all in the tenth month. [4.6a7–9]
>
> 此其猶欲留世意. 所以發此請, 雖初云可爾, 恐後復相請, 卻審得申者, 則不應, 十月果去也.

This instance, too, exemplifies the SPILLOVER PARADIGM, for it shows that a vital concern Zhou had while awake—his being summoned to die much earlier than his preallotted lifespan would have called for, a summons to which he'd initially reacted with surprised dread ("my face showed my fear" 子良便有懼色)—carried over directly into his dreams.[112]

Dreams as Training Ground

Almost all of Zhou's dream records feature what we might call scenes of evaluation and instruction. We see him being taught, sized up, chided, or tested by residents of the unseen realm as he performs his nascent divine identity before them,[113] much as elite young men were sized up in this world, as glimpsed in a letter written in the 470s by Wang Sengqian 王僧虔 to his sons:

> You've unrolled your *Laozi* as far as about five feet from the beginning of the scroll and don't yet know what Wang Bi has said or what He Yan's argument is, where Ma Rong and Zheng Xuan differ. . . . Yet you are already grandly swishing your yak-tail whisks and referring to yourselves as "masters of conversation." What if Magistrate Yuan were to command you to speak of the *Changes*, or Secretary Xie to incite you to speak of the *Zhuangzi*, or Mr. Zhang from Wuxing to sound you out in a discussion of the *Laozi*? Do you really suppose that at that point you would be able to backtrack and say, "I never read them"? Conversation is thus like archery: when the earlier shooter has hit the target, the later ones must be able to hit it as well.[114]
>
> 汝開老子卷頭五尺許, 未知輔嗣何所道, 平叔何所說, 馬, 鄭何所異 . . . . 而便盛於麈尾, 自呼談士, 此最險事. 設令袁令命汝言易, 謝中書挑汝言莊, 張吳興叩汝(言)老, 端可復言未嘗看邪? 談故如射, 前人得破, 後人應解, 不解即輸賭矣.

But for Zhou Ziliang the stakes were inordinately higher. And every one of his divine interlocutors had most definitely already "hit the target."

We glimpse this sort of evaluative moment when the divine Zhou Ziyang suddenly in mid-conversation (during a waking encounter one day) asked Zhou Ziliang his name. "Flustered and pressed" 倉卒 by the unexpected question, the young man could only manage to produce the name he'd been born with, not the Daoist one he'd been assigned (which was Zhou Taixuan 周太玄, byname Xuling 虛靈).[115] At this the god exploded in rage and cried: "How could you be so negligent?"[116] We also find entries such as these:

> On the twenty-fifth day of the ninth month I suddenly[117] saw Zhang Lijin in a dream. He ordered me to recite the *[Scripture of] the Dao and Its Power* and so on.[118]
>
> 九月二十五日,忽夢見張理禁,令誦道德云云.
>
> On the second of the tenth month I dreamed I saw Master Hong. I was ordered by him to recite the Incantation of the Grand Immaculate and so on.[119]
>
> 十月二日,夢見洪先生,見令誦太素祝云云.

These directives might simply be exhortations to incorporate recitation of these texts into his habitual practice, but the locution "ordered me to recite" (*ling song* 令誦) suggests rather that they were tests of Zhou's ability to produce these texts from memory on command.

Elsewhere Zhou's progress on the Upper Purity path is appraised by his divine interlocutors. Sometimes he's chided, other times complimented or encouraged, but in every case he is urged to continue applying himself:

> On the twenty-fourth day of the sixth month I was in the southern grove during the daytime when I dreamed of a man of around sixty . . . who had not come previously. . . . He approached, sat, and said: "The excellence of your virtue has moved those of us in the spirit realm" [2.17a–b].[120]
>
> 六月二十四日,晝外南林,夢一人,年可六十許. . . 未嘗來也. . . . 進坐,乃言曰:德秀之美,感乎幽冥.
>
> On the eighteenth [of the intercalary month] I dreamed that the Lord Supervisor of Lifespans [Mao Ying] asked me: "Do you want to become a transcendent?" I replied: "Yes, I really do wish to become a transcendent." "Then why do you not practice [arts of] transcendence?" and so on [4.12a10–12b1].
>
> 十八日,夢大司命君,問曰:子欲仙不?答:實願仙.云:願仙,何不學仙?云云.

On the fifth of the tenth month I saw in a dream the Lord Certifier of Registers, who said: "You are progressing in your self-control and have excelled at observing the prohibitions and regulations. Do not slacken your resolve" [4.8b8–9].

十月五日, 夢見定錄君, 云: 比來多諸進御, 善自禁節, 勿縱志也.

On the eleventh [of the twelfth month] I dreamed I saw Lady Han [Han Taihua 韓太華夫人], who told me: "Recently your diligence has been exemplary. You are more and more acquiring the characteristics of a Perfected one" [4.11a9–10].

十一日, 夢見韓夫人云: 比者情志落落, 彌入真相.

On the third of the intercalary month I dreamed I saw Lady Han [again]. She said, "It would be good for you to stop leaving traces in this world" [4.12a3–4].

閏月三日, 夢見韓夫人云: 世上方無復蹤如可.

On the second day of the first month of the *bingshen* year [February 19, 516] I dreamed of visiting Xiaoyou [cavern] heaven.[121] There I saw Lord Wang, who said: "Why are you still dallying among humans? Your name is already established. Do not linger on the worldly path" [4.13b5–7].[122]

丙申年正月二日, 夢造小有天, 見王君云: 爾何遑遑於人間, 名已定, 勿虧頓於世路.

The text is similarly rich with scenes of instruction—dreams or waking visions in which the young adept has some esoteric information transmitted to him, is given a rare substance, or simply gains the opportunity to observe something hitherto unknown about the mysteries of the divine world. In all such scenes the term *gao* 告 (or, when Zhou is the grammatical subject, the passive form *jian gao* 見告), which I perhaps undertranslate as "instruct," seems to be used as a verbal marker of a new bit of revelation. In these passages it's not just a matter of a deity saying something (in which contexts we find the verbs *yun* 云 and *yue* 曰) but is instead a moment when divine truth is being revealed or a new string of divine speech is being formally uttered, to be recorded by the human scribe.

Zhou Ziliang has new and strange substances bestowed on him in his dreams. Among them are "nocturnal light excrescence" (*yeguang zhi* 夜光芝, 4.4b) and "dragon transcendence excrescence" (*longxian zhi* 龍

仙芝, 4.4b);[123] a certain "seed" (*zi* 子) the size of a goose egg, which he's told to ingest as a stopgap until he becomes qualified to ingest a nine-cycle elixir (4.13a); and a mysterious herb called "*qing* 青 something or other" (Tao notes that Zhou had erased the second character of the name—a detail to which I return below), something to tide him over until he's ready for the unnamed fruit he sees Zhou Dabin eating but is told he's not yet ready for (4.16a). These gifts signify both the gods' esteem for his progress and their judgment that he isn't yet ready for more advanced comestibles. This sort of dietary index of self-cultivational advancement would have seemed unremarkable to most readers. It extended into dreamland a mode of practice familiar to all Daoist adepts in the waking world, whereby one increasingly substituted rare, exotic, celestial, or divinely synthesized materials—or simply pure *qi*—for a mortal's ordinary diet.[124]

Zhou Ziliang also records having conversed with various divine tutors on methods of practice. Virtually every personage he encounters in his dreams has something to teach him or some feedback to offer. Over the fifteen-month period covered in the records, he is instructed piecemeal by a whole cloud of senior deities who've taken an interest in him—again a reflection of the social world he'd glimpsed and participated in thanks to his association with his elite master. He receives instruction on a method (attested elsewhere in the Shangqing corpus) of reclining in the Dipper and actualizing its two invisible stars (4.9a, 4.9b, 4.10b, 4.15a). He is warned by a certain Commander Fan 范帥 not to take lightly the "wicked demons that are on the move hither and yon" (*e mei hengxing* 惡魅横行) spreading disease.[125] He is cautioned about two particular false practitioners traveling in the area deceiving people, including descriptions of their appearance (right down to their teeth and visible birthmarks), behavior, and even their road songs.[126] Such itinerant practitioners, tricksters, and raconteurs were a familiar phenomenon, and in these two dreams Zhou is admitted into the circle of those able to discern the fraudsters from the genuine.[127]

Mostly, though, his descriptions of what he was taught in his dreams are quite vague. He "had bestowed on [him] secret methods of transformation" (*jianshou yinbian fang* 見授隱變方) by two deities previously unknown to Tao Hongjing (4.6a3). He benefited from discussions with divine interlocutors of certain "Daoist methods" (*daofa zhi shi* 道法之事,

4.5b9) and unspecified "matters of divine transcendence" (*shenxian shi* 神仙事, 4.6a5). At the Bureau of the Overseer of Lifespans he was "instructed at great length" (*gao dayou suo yan* 告大有所言, 4.8a), and on another occasion at the same site he "was told many pure and mysterious matters concerning the Jade Purity [heavens]" (*gao yuqing qingxuan shi* 告玉清清玄事, 4.11a). These elliptical references are not haphazardly written. They form part of a complex rhetorical strategy discussed in the next section.

But Zhou's sessions with his many divine tutors weren't just in lecture format, as it were; there were opportunities for questions and discussion. In waking visions he asks about his aunt's persistent ill health and about relocating his father's tomb.[128] In dreams he is promised divine assistance in dealing with a spate of banditry in the area (3.14b, 4.17a9). When he requests permission to move his residence on the mountain, he is at first warned against his choice of site because of what seemed to be an old tomb and what Tao terms an abandoned "place of mediumistic practice" (*wu changchu suo* 巫場處所) nearby. But another of the gods accompanies Zhou to the site to inspect it. They confirm the god's prior warning that "stale vapors" (*gu qi* 故氣) linger there in the form of a hideous creature called the *dadu* 大都, but Zhou is advised that although it frightens most people away, he himself will suffer no harm by living there.[129] Zhou inquires about his master's prospects, and although the gods are clearly impressed with Tao Hongjing and make a point of mentioning a divine office that awaits him, their evaluation is at times mixed.[130] In several dreams Zhou brings up the severe drought plaguing his region (a drought Tao confirms in his commentary), and the gods are seen to respond, eventually bringing the badly needed rain (2.15b–16a, 2.18a, 4.8a–b, and 4.11a). Zhou's most pressing concern was, of course, his own unexpectedly early summons to divine office, his petition to extend that deadline (mentioned above), and the efforts to, as one interlocutor explained, "begin the removal of your name from the ledgers of death and re-register your name among the living" 始得除君死錄, 更紀生名 (2.18a). All this and more unfolds in the young adept's dreams.

The Esotericizing Dynamic

Several lineages of Daoist teachings and techniques were built around the controlled transmission of knowledge that was to be kept secret from all save the initiated. These lineages constituted a geographically dispersed, organizationally loose esoteric tradition.[131] Initially at least, Upper Purity texts were transmitted in this fashion. As a form of cultural discourse, however, secrecy is often more complex than it might seem. One example of this complexity is a strategy Hugh Urban has characterized as "advertising the secret," in which "the claim to possess very precious, rare, and valuable knowledge [is made], while simultaneously partially revealing and largely concealing it. For a secret is only worth anything if someone knows you have a secret."[132] When we survey not only the initially esoteric Daoist scriptures themselves but also the narrative traditions that accumulated around their practitioners, what we find is an important textual record of discursive strategies, social behaviors, and ritual practices that created tension between secrecy regarding texts and methods on the one hand and an often extravagant display of their results on the other. A kernel of esoteric knowledge is kept hidden from the uninitiated while at the same time the existence of that knowledge as well as insiders' access to it are disclosed, often flamboyantly. It's by this outward-facing display of results, abilities, and other behaviors culturally marked as unusual—behaviors associated with whatever role the practitioner is performing (transcendent-to-be, wonder-working monk, master of esoterica)—that those not privy to the secrets can recognize the adept as an adept. This gestalt of concealment-and-display is something I previously termed the esoteric dynamic. Since my earlier publications on this topic, I've come to prefer *esotericizing* to stress that what's at issue is not a particular body of subject matter but a repertoire of cultural ways of acting that have the effect of framing, and limiting access to, some technique or body of knowledge. I intend a parallel with Catherine Bell's use of *ritualization* to refer to a "way of acting that is designed and orchestrated to distinguish and privilege what is being done in comparison to other, usually more quotidian, activities"[133] or "a way of acting that distinguishes itself from other ways of acting in the very way it does what it does."[134]

Under the SPILLOVER PARADIGM, dream records often transport readers and hearers into scenes not commonly accessible in ordinary waking life—scenes triggered by the dreamer's work of self-cultivation. (At the simplest level, of course, any oral or written dream report does this much, if only in that it relates private experience otherwise unknowable by others.) But an esotericizing dream record does this in an unusual way. In showing an audience what the dreamer experienced, it leaves much out. (Again, any dream report does this much, since there must always remain a gap between the dream as experienced and the narrative and language in which it's related to others and to oneself.) But not only does it leave much out: it does so deliberately and signals clearly and repeatedly that it is doing so. The excluded content is likely to be the crucial details not otherwise knowable by audiences.

Here I will show that *Records of Master Zhou's Communications with the Unseen World* is an especially interesting and complex example of the esotericizing dynamic at work. One reason for its complexity is the number of voices and perspectives refracted through it.

Let's start with Emperor Wu. By its own account, the entire text begins its life as Tao Hongjing's report to the ruler of the recent happenings on Mount Mao. These comprise not only Zhou Ziliang's experiences, his life and sudden demise, but also several "anomalous events" (*yi shi* 異事, 1.7b5) at sites where Zhou had practiced. These include a white turtle found with strange graphic markings on its shell, a new shoot growing impossibly fast from a bamboo plant, and a mysterious white powder—deemed by onlookers to be the "sweet dew" (*gan lu* 甘露) traditionally signaling divine approval of an emperor's reign—suddenly covering several large cypress trees near the ritual altar used by Zhou. Tao Hongjing mentions by name several witnesses to these phenomena.[135] His commentary shows that he intended these passages to be read as favorable omens signaling divine approval of Emperor Wu's reign. At one point he even quotes a text known as the *Chart of Auspicious Responses* (*Ruiying tu* 瑞應圖).[136] He thus provides the emperor with not only a report of omens but also ready-made favorable interpretations of them. In effect, the text subsumes Zhou Ziliang's entire story as yet another auspicious omen. The emperor's brief response acknowledging his receipt is entered into the text (1.8a3–5), as is a mention of his having unrolled its four scrolls and examined them within the inner palace (1.8a9–10). Emperor Wu is thus inscribed within the frame of the text as both its primary intended audience and its first reader. He is decidedly an outsider to the events at Mount Mao, but one who is afforded a glimpse of them through the text. Incidentally, this was by no means the first literary exchange between Emperor Wu and Tao Hongjing; in 504, for example, the two men had had the same dream regarding Tao's fashioning of an elixir on Mount Mao under imperial sponsorship,[137] and in 505 the emperor had commissioned fine swords to be produced under Tao's supervision.[138]

Another perspective is that of Zhou Ziliang's family members. Some passages show how his behaviors appeared to them and how they reacted. We don't hear their voices except in depictions of their interactions with Ziliang—most poignantly his mother's cry, "What have you done? What have you done?" (*he yi, he yi* 何意, 何意) as she rushes into his chamber to find him dying on the floor. This scene memorably exploits the dramatic possibilities of the esotericizing dynamic. We see a young man who is performing his esoteric role to the fullest right up until the moment of death. *He* knows that he's answering the divine summons he'd received more than a year earlier. His relatives, not privy to that summons, have no way to understand Ziliang's actions. The insider and outsider perspectives converge there on the floor of his chamber. Confused and horrified outsiders to the real program he's enacting, his mother, aunt, and brother can only look on uncomprehendingly as before expiring he adjusts his cap to prepare for his imminent appearance in the celestial court.[139]

In effect, every passage involving Zhou Ziliang enacts this same dynamic. In some scenes we get privileged glimpses of the divine encounters in light of which his outward actions would make sense. In others, we see those same actions as they appeared to mystified onlookers:

> On the day of the summer solstice of the fourteenth year [June 20, 515] Zhou suddenly retired to recline in his chamber before noon. He conferred with the spirits for a long time before finally emerging. His aunt did not understand why he had done this and questioned him closely. Zhou told her a bit of what he had seen, as recorded below in his transcripts. [1.2a8-b1]
>
> 以十四年乙未歲五月二十三夏至日於癬忽未中寢臥, 彌淪良久乃起出. 姨母不解所以, 深加辯切, 乃頗說所見, 具如別記.

He "told her *a bit* of what he'd seen" 頗說所見—but hardly all. Ziliang revealed just enough to staunch the questions from his aunt, who was a practicing Celestial Master Daoist not privy to Upper Purity secrets.

Thanks to the text, we know, as his aunt did not, some of what happened in that chamber. The text then reports:

> For the next forty or fifty days, Zhou was seen to act very strangely indeed. He would habitually close the curtains and bar the door to his chamber, not letting anyone enter. Alone in his room, he burned incense. Each day he ate only a single cup-measure of honey-sweetened rice. [1.2b1–3]
>
> 自爾於四五旬中大覺為異. 恆垂簾掩扉, 斷人入室, 燒香獨住. 日中止進一升蜜餐.

To his family his behavior is "strange" or "altered" (*yi* 異). He closes himself up in his room, granting family members access only to the outward traces of his practice—the smell of incense, the sight of the closed curtains and door. His diet shifts, and this, too, is visible to his family though its rationale is not. Such reduction of food intake had been a staple of the way of transcendence for several centuries.

Finally, consider Tao Hongjing. It's his narrative that frames the text. He positions himself as the curator of new revelations about the workings of the unseen world, information he carefully fit, piece by piece, beside what he already knew about Upper Purity from the fourth-century records he'd previously sifted through and assembled. Tao wasn't the direct recipient of the revelations (although some of them concerned him), yet without his activity it's likely no one else would ever have seen them. Compared to every other reader of the text, Tao is an insider with respect to his knowledge of Shangqing materials, his relationship with the young visionary, and his familiarity with the *bodhimanda* at Mount Mao. He is a necessary mediator. And yet even he finds himself very much on the outside looking in at mysteries he was not privileged to learn straight from the gods. There was much in Zhou Ziliang's experience that neither he nor we are privy to, and Zhou made sure to make his master—and any future readers—aware of this fact.

Why did Zhou record his visions and dreams at all? If he'd wanted to ensure that they would remain entirely secret he could simply have refrained from writing them down, or he could have destroyed all the records he'd made. Yet he did write them down, and although he burned some of them shortly before his death, he made a point of being seen doing so:

> Wenxing [an assistant] said that on the sixteenth [or the twenty-sixth, i.e., either November 25 or December 5[140]] Ziliang had burned two bundles of writings, perhaps a hundred sheets' worth, and would not allow anyone to see them [1.5a1–2].
>
> 文幸云一十六日燒兩束書, 可百餘紙, 不聽人見.

Tao speculates that Zhou "may have burned those [records] that contained matters he was not permitted to reveal" 亦可是焚不可顯出者也 (1.5b6). Shortly after Zhou's death, Tao sent people to inspect Zhou's residence hoping to find records, but "not a scrap was ever found" (*yong wu yi zha* 永無一札, 1.5a1). But then we have this:

> On the morning of the first day of the eleventh month [December 10], I personally went to the cavern of Yankou peak to see what I could find. I found a large letter-case that had been sealed and thrown inside. Climbing to an overhanging precipice I was able to snag and retrieve it. I then did obeisance, respectfully requesting permission, and returned with it. When I opened it I saw that it was indeed a record of instructions he had received. For the fifth month there were only four entries dating from the summer solstice forward. The records for the sixth and seventh month were complete. From the eighth month to the end of the seventh month of this year there were only scattered entries, briefly outlining what had occurred and saying only "and so on." I cannot fathom how he could have experienced further events such as those of the sixth and seventh months and still not preserved a record of them or else not written them down in detail but only abbreviated them in this way. As I think on these things now I fear that we will never know more. How could we?[141] [1.5a3–10]
>
> 十一月旦甲子試自往燕口山洞尋看, 果見封投一大函. 登崎嶽鉤取, 拜請將還, 開視, 即是從來受旨. 五月唯有夏至日後四事, 六月七月並具足, 從八月後至今年七月末, 止疏目錄, 略舉事端, 稱云[云] 而已. 未測亦並有事, 如六七月, 而不存錄, 為當不復備記, 止徑略如此邪? 今以意求, 恐是不復疏之. 何知爾?

This is a revealing passage. Zhou burned some records but sealed others in a case and threw it into the mouth of a nearby cave, where he perhaps anticipated his master might go looking for traces. Many a Daoist story relates how some rare substance or secret writing might, with great difficulty, be retrieved from a cavern.[142] Then there is Tao's reaction upon opening the case, arranging the dated slips of paper chronologically (something he doesn't here describe doing but must have had to do given his seriatim comments on the many small slips of paper Zhou had used), and poring over their contents. At first the entries are detailed and explicit, but then they grow increasingly sparse and laconic. What's more, Tao bemoans Zhou's progressively frequent use of the ellipsis (*yunyun* 云云) to stand in for details he'd decided to omit *yet wished to signal he'd omitted*. The ellipsis thus performs the esotericizing dynamic at the level of the sentence. Most occurrences of these ellipses are typeset in today's printings as though they were part of Tao's commentary, but I think in fact all of them were written by Zhou himself. They point to a "more" that he'd experienced but was deliberately withholding from the records he left behind.

Other passages, increasingly frequent as we move down the calendar, signal even more explicitly that there was much else Zhou could have written down but either chose or was instructed not to. All of the following passages concern dream experiences (Tao's comments are again enclosed in parentheses):

> I was told much, but I am unable to write it all down. (This must have been something quite marvelous [4.8a2–3].[143])
>
> 告大有所言, 非可具記. (此應有奇事也.)
>
> I dreamed I went to the place of the Overseer of Lifespans and was informed by him of many pure and mystic affairs concerning Jade Purity and so on. (What was discussed must have been extraordinarily elevated. What a pity he did not at least summarize it [4.11a7–8].)
>
> 夢往司命處, 告玉清清玄事. 云云. (此所論殊高, 恨不略說也.)
>
> I was ordered by the Lord to take some *qing*— (This character has been rubbed out and can never be known [4.16a3–4].)
>
> 君見令取青□. (此一字章漫, 永不可識也.)

> I again dreamed of meeting Marquis Han, the Lady of Purple Tenuity, Lord Yang, the Certifier of Registers, and others. They thoroughly explained for my benefit matters of human nature and lifespan, moral cause-and-effect, and the sources of sin and fortune. If I wrote it all out in detail it would require three or four sheets of paper. (Not to hear of this is again especially regrettable [4.18a10–b2].)[144]
>
> 復夢見韓侯, 紫微, 楊君, 定錄等, 多為論性命之致, 因緣罪福之源. 若疏此可三四紙許. (不聞此, 亦為殊恨也.)

The teacher's frustration is palpable.

These aspects of Zhou's writing practice mirror a pattern we can detect in his face-to-face interactions with his teacher over the months when he was encountering gods. Consider this description by Tao of his disciple's behaviors:

> Even when questioned he would answer briefly or evasively so as not to reveal the directives of the Perfected. Because of this I simply stopped asking after a while. After we moved to Scarlet Solarity I would ask him to direct appropriate questions to the Perfected. Later I would repeatedly inquire as to whether he had received an answer and he would always say "not yet," thus keeping the words of the Perfected secret. Looking at his records now, I see that he did indeed receive answers. It must have been that he was afraid to relay responses to such questions because people would have given him thank-you gifts and then everyone would have come to rely on him for information. Then, if he failed to ask the Perfected, he would be blamed by people; but if he did ask, he would violate the Perfected ones' instructions. This is why he was so secretive about the whole thing.[145]
>
> 或有訪問, 皆依違末略, 初不顯詔. 又師經一過, 因辭訪移朱陽. 及有所當事後, 屢問蒙答, 以不每云, 未報, 遂不顯言. 今料視, 定已有答. 尋此當是恐問便有酬者, 則人人因託不少. 若不為問, 則被人責, 若悉為問, 便忤冥旨, 是以皆匿隱之.

We see the same pattern in his final actions before dying: although he obviously ingested some elixir or other, he took great care to conceal which one:

> The kettle was checked. It seemed to smell only of ordinary wine. His earthenware basin had been washed out and was odorless. No traces of medicinal substances were found anywhere. In the end there was no fathoming what he had used. (According to the records, he had obtained a drug method. Perhaps this is what he used.)[146]
>
> 檢溫鐺中猶如常酒氣, 瓦盆中已被水盪, 無氣, 都不見藥蹤迹, 竟不測何所因託. (檢記中得藥方, 或疑脫是此.)

Whatever caused his death, Zhou took pains to conceal it. Tao Hongjing writes that no one saw Zhou burying any elixir ingredients or heard him grinding materials with a mortar and pestle, and he speculates that perhaps Zhou did the preparations somewhere else and that the wine he let his younger brother glimpse him heating (mentioned at 1.3b8) was a ruse to cover his tracks (雖見溫酒, 亦或假以亂之耳言, 4.20b).

To the very end, Zhou Ziliang was positioning himself as the insider with respect to his family and even his teacher. Tao Hongjing positioned himself as the insider with respect to the emperor and others at court, yet he was outside the innermost circle of knowledge Zhou had received directly from the gods. And the text positions itself as the selective discloser but ultimate guardian of divine secrets with respect to any and all readers, including us.

Conclusion

The texts we've seen in this chapter all recommend, promise, or portray the extension of diurnal self-cultivational practice into sleep by means of dreaming. Let's conclude by considering why this extension must have seemed so attractive.

First, whether or not one was a full-time religious practitioner, the anxiety about how one was progressing on the path—an anxiety seen in full measure in chapter 2—must have been acute. The stakes were high, yet one could never be quite sure where one stood. Being able to continue cultivating oneself while asleep, taking advantage of oneiric overtime, must have seemed attractive on these grounds alone.

Second, as we saw in chapter 1, some dreams put practitioners in a state of pollution, placing them at odds with the canons of practice to which they'd committed themselves. Extending one's waking-life vigilance and assiduity into sleep, rendering one's dreams into a purified space of practice, had the soteriological side effect of converting a danger zone into an opportunity. A whole category of possible self-cultivational pitfalls was thereby closed up.

Third, dreaming opened the door to certain encounters and experiences not obtainable while awake, even for the most diligent. One could receive face-to-face, personalized instruction in real time. One might enjoy direct, unmediated access to long-deceased masters and denizens of other worlds. Geographic and cosmic distance, historical and cosmic time—in dreams such gaps could be easily, if only temporarily, bridged.[147]

Fourth, if waking-life self-cultivation involved, among other things, learning to perform a role, then dreaming offered other stages, other audiences, and almost unlimited scope for such performance. Awake, you might be a layman or laywoman practicing veneration of a sutra such as the *Lotus* that had long ago and far away been preached by Gautama Buddha. But in dreams you could become a Buddha yourself. Awake, you might be a young girl diligently lighting incense and lamps before a votive image of Laozi. In dreams you could be paid a visit by Laozi and receive a direct bestowal of sacred verses. Awake, you might be a young practitioner observing numerous regulations and cultivating yourself in a mountain community, even being taught in visions by divine beings or receiving revelations not available to others. In dreams you could continue experiencing even more intense versions of such encounters while visiting cosmically distant sites inaccessible to mortals.

We should not forget that all these affordances of dreams became possible because dreaming wasn't seen as a solely psychological occurrence. Dreams were interactive events. They carried consequences as tangible and momentous as any waking-life event might, sometimes more. In the SPILLOVER PARADIGM dreams were fashioned into a self-cultivational platform charged with great potential.

The self presupposed under texts of the SPILLOVER PARADIGM is a performed self. Dreaming afforded practitioners an added, more glorious, and even cosmic stage on which to perform. In their dreams practitioners could *act now* as a Buddha, a sage, a Perfected one. In a religious landscape characterized by slow, gradual paths of self-cultivation toward eventual, distant goals, SPILLOVER dreams afforded a sudden alternative in which practitioners might close the otherwise persistent gap between their current status and their projected goal[148]—but only until the dream ended and the curtain rose once again.

CHAPTER FOUR

Not Dreaming, Waking Up, and Not Minding the Difference

For all their differences, the three paradigms of dreaming we have considered share four basic features. Most obviously, each starts from the putative occurrence[1] of a dream seen as significant for the self-cultivator, whether directly, as an event impacting the dreamer's life and practice, or symbolically, as a coded index of progress or of a problem. Second, each sets dreamers into relationship with something other than themselves. In direct mode (under the PURIFICATION and SPILLOVER PARADIGMS) dreams involve consequential interactions with other beings. In indirect mode (under the DIAGNOSTIC PARADIGM) dreams are a message in a cryptic but interpersonally shared language, indicating where the practitioner currently stands as measured on some evaluative yardstick.

Third, each paradigm treats dreams by setting them into some relation to waking life. That is, dreams are taken account of in terms of how they relate to wakeful self-cultivation; they are responded to insofar as they impinge on the dreamer *qua* practitioner. When Confucius laments his failure to dream of the Duke of Zhou, he does so not just because dreaming of the Duke brings intrinsic pleasure but because *not* dreaming of him means something about his self-cultivational progress. When people have foul dreams, not only are the dreams unpleasant, but they also put the dreamers in a state of ritual pollution, rendering them unable to play their collectively defined roles. Decoding diagnostic dreams matters because the messages derived from the decoding process reveal how dreamers are faring in their self-cultivational efforts. Meeting gods in dreams matters because these meetings further practitioners' waking-life efforts. These are examples of what I mean by saying that dreams are approached in relation to waking life. Fourth, then, each paradigm assumes, and plays back and forth across, the difference between being awake and dreaming. It's this difference that lent dreaming its power to impinge on projects of self-cultivation. It's the otherness of dreaming that afforded it leverage for self-cultivators who spent most of their time awake.

But these three paradigms do not exhaust the types of relationship attested in the archive between dreaming and self-cultivation. Beyond them lie at least three other positions I'd like to note briefly in this chapter as this book moves toward its close. First, we find *not dreaming* tagged as a mark of self-cultivational attainment, a limit-attribute of sages. In such passages, what is it, we wonder, that is deemed sagely about not dreaming? Second, we find *the contrast between dreaming and waking* used in certain arguments. What are those arguments, and how is the dreaming/waking dyad used to make them? Third, we find the idea that *wise persons attach no importance to the difference* between waking and dreaming—that the distinction between these states is relative, trivial, or meaningless. What's the point of relativizing or erasing the distinction?

None of these passages takes up dreaming as a topic of inquiry in its own right. None offers approaches to particular types of dreams, or methods for harnessing some dreams' power or curbing their danger. In fact, none addresses particular dreams at all except as fictive examples. Rather, the handful of passages we'll look at exploit the *general phenomenon* of dreaming as a rich vein of concrete analogies and rhetorical gambits while mounting arguments about other matters. Nevertheless, these passages, too, are examples of how dreaming and self-cultivation were placed into relation with each other, in that they use the phenomenon of dreaming to instruct on matters wise persons should understand.

Not Dreaming

From at least the compilation of *Zhuangzi* forward, texts of various persuasions over many centuries asserted that sages or fully realized persons don't dream. Jean-Pierre Diény has thoroughly documented this theme from its earliest traces in the archive all the way into the Ming period and beyond.[2] Focusing on just a handful of telling passages, my goal here is to tease out what they portray as sagely about not dreaming.

To my knowledge, the earliest examples date from the late Warring States and early Han. One of the best known comes in *Zhuangzi* chapter 6:

> As for the genuine humans of old: *their sleep was without dreaming*, their waking without cares. They found one food as sweet as another and breathed from their depths. . . . The genuine humans of old did not know to prefer life, did not know to despise death. They emerged without delight and went back in without a fuss. They were content to leave as briskly as they came. They did not forget whence they had come, did not try to find out where they would end. They were pleased with the gift they had received but forgot it as they gave it back. This is what's called not letting the mind repel[3] the Way, not using what is human to "help out" heaven. This is what's called the genuine human.[4]
>
> 古之真人, 其寢不夢, 其覺無憂, 其食不甘, 其息深深. . . . 古之真人, 不知説生, 不知惡死; 其出不訢, 其入不距; 翛然而往, 翛然而來而已矣. 不忘其所始, 不求其所終; 受而喜之, 忘而復之. 是之謂不以心捐道, 不以人助天. 是之謂真人.

"Sleep without dreaming, be awake without worries" seems to have been a Zhuangzian adage, recurring in chapter 15:

> With the sage, his life is the working of heaven, his death the transformation of things. Stilled, he and Yin share a single power; moving, he and Yang share a single flow. He will not, to gain advantage, make the first move; will not, to avoid trouble, take the first step. Only once stirred does he respond; only once pressed does he move; only when he has no choice does he rise up. He discards knowledge and purpose[5] and follows the patterns of heaven. So he incurs no disasters from heaven, no entanglement with things, no opposition from people, no blame from ghosts. His life is like a floating, his death like a resting. He does not ponder or scheme, does not plot for the future. He is a person of radiance yet does not dazzle, is trusted without promising. *His sleep is without dreaming*, his waking without cares. His spirit is pure and unmixed, his cloudsouls unwearied. In emptiness and nothingness, calm and indifference, he joins with the power of heaven.[6]
>
> 聖人之生也天行, 其死也物化; 靜而與陰同德, 動而與陽同波; 不為福先, 不為禍始; 感而後應, 迫而後動, 不得已而後起. 去知與故, 循天之理, 故無天災, 無物累, 無人非, 無鬼責. 其生若浮, 其死若休; 不思慮, 不豫謀;

光矣而不耀，信矣而不期；其寢不夢，其覺無憂；其神純粹，其魂不罷．虛無恬惔，乃合天德．

These passages obviously aren't empirical observations based on sleep studies of somnolent sages. They enlist dreaming as an example in order to make a larger set of points. In them, non-dreaming doesn't stand alone as a goal to aim for, nor is any intrinsic rationale provided for it. Instead, it forms part of an ensemble of traits. We must consider those other traits and how non-dreaming relates to them.

When we do, it turns out that non-dreaming is associated with having no preferences or attachments, even to life over death, and with accepting changes that are beyond our control. Above all, not dreaming while asleep is paired with not worrying while awake.[7] Dreaming, then, is at bottom a sign of anxiety about outcomes.[8] It occurs in those who prefer life and fear death, seek to spy out the future (perhaps by consulting diviners), and kick against the constant stream of change. Dreaming is something done by people who resemble the hot metal in *Zhuangzi*'s metalsmith analogy, interrupting its transformation to leap up and demand a single preferred outcome.[9] Stop being such a person and you'll be free of worries and of anxious dreaming.

Incidentally, scholars inclined to read works like this as what conventionally counts as "philosophy" might startle at the phrase "no blame from ghosts" (*wu gui ze* 無鬼責) in the *Zhuangzi* 15 passage. But vengeful ghosts, including family members suffering in the afterlife who might harm their living relatives in the course of seeking relief, were of real concern to many. The passage anticipates the sort of "underworld lawsuit" (*zhong song* 塚訟) perhaps best documented in the fourth-century case of Tao Kedou 陶科斗 and the Xu 許 family.[10] Just as the sage avoids such entanglements, so he avoids dreaming.

In a *Huainanzi* passage that incorporates some of these *Zhuangzi* lines, non-dreaming is again linked with non-attachment, with being imperturbable because one flows with life's constant changes. But non-dreaming is there characterized in terms of the soul-journey model.[11] Genuine humans, the text says,

> take birth and death to be a single transformation, the myriad things to be a single place. They merge their essence with the root of Grand Purity and

> roam in the land of No Place. They have essence but do not use it, have spirit but do not set it in motion. They match tallies with the unhewn block of the Great Chaos, stand in the midst of Utmost Purity. For this reason *their sleep is without dreaming*, their knowledge does not put forth sprouts, their whitesouls [need] not be restrained, their cloudsouls do not soar aloft.[12]
>
> 以死生為一化, 以萬物為一方, 同精於太清之本, 而游于忽區之旁. 有精而不使, 有神而不行, 契大渾之樸, 而立至清之中. 是故其寢不夢, 其智不萌, 其魄不抑, 其魂不騰.

Dreaming is to sleeping as being disturbed by stimuli is to waking. One wants to avoid such stirrings while awake and while asleep. While awake, they generate emotions; while asleep, they trigger dreams. This is similar to *Zhuangzi*'s use of non-dreaming but isn't quite the same. It also anticipates later prescriptions of active measures to prevent the souls from escaping during sleep, as seen in chapter 1.

A *Xunzi* passage (in the chapter "Dispelling Blindness" ["Jie bi" 解蔽]) again links dreaming to other kinds of mental disturbance, for which emptying, concentrating, and quieting the mind is the cure:

> How does a person know the Way? I say: through the mind. How does the mind know? I say it is through vacuity, concentration,[13] and stillness.
>
> The mind never stops storing up things; nonetheless there is what's called being empty. The mind is forever two-fold; nonetheless there is what's called being single-minded. The mind never stops moving; nonetheless it has what's called being still.
>
> People from birth have awareness. With awareness, they have focus. To focus is to be storing something. Yet there is what's called being empty. Not letting what one is already storing interfere with what one is about to receive is called being empty.
>
> The mind from birth has awareness, and with awareness comes perception of differences. These differences are known at the same time, and when they are known at the same time, this is to be two-fold. Yet there is what's called being single-minded. Not letting one thing interfere with another is called being single-minded.
>
> When the mind sleeps, it dreams. When it relaxes, it moves about of its own accord. When put to use, it forms plans. Therefore, the mind is always moving. Yet there is what's called being still. Not letting dreams and worries disorder one's understanding is called being still.[14]

> 人何以知道? 曰: 心. 心何以知.曰: 虛壹而靜. 心未嘗不臧也, 然而有所謂虛; 心未嘗不兩也, 然而有所謂壹; 心未嘗不動也, 然而有所謂靜. 人生而有知, 知而有志; 志也者, 臧也; 然而有所謂虛; 不以所已臧害所將受謂之虛. 心生而有知, 知而有異; 異也者, 同時兼知之; 同時兼知之, 兩也; 然而有所謂一; 不以夫一害此一謂之壹. 心臥則夢, 偷則自行, 使之則謀; 故心未嘗不動也; 然而有所謂靜; 不以夢劇亂知謂之靜.

Here there is no claim that wise people don't dream, just that they don't let dreaming upset them or cloud their capacity to know. Not being disturbed by dreams is here linked *not* to accepting changes with equanimity but to emptying, concentrating, and quieting the mind. But emptying the mind might be a way to come to accept changes with equanimity.

Despite their differences, all these passages construe dreaming as a perturbation akin to excessive sensory stimulation. It's a contact with something, a contact that might stir one up, when stillness is to be preferred. In the face of culturally dominant views of dreams as visitations from other beings or signs predicting the future, these passages argue that wise practitioners are unconcerned about predictions and shut the door to oneiric visitors.

"Sages don't dream." Yet, as we saw in chapter 3, no less a figure than Confucius was said to have lamented how long it had been since he'd dreamed of the Duke of Zhou. Unless one were willing to dismiss either the claim about sages or the *Analects* report about Confucius, this idea presented a problem for those invested in Confucius' sagehood. Early medieval commentators therefore glossed *Analects* 7.5 creatively. In compiling *Exposition of the Meaning of the Analects* (*Lunyu yishu* 論語義疏), Huang Kan 皇侃 (488–549) incorporated several earlier commentaries to form a work that is "now almost our only window into *Analects* interpretation from the third to the sixth centuries."[15] Folded into a single passage we find two interpreters' hermeneutical handiwork:

> The sage perceives with unmediated clarity and never relies on dreams or mental images. That he nonetheless says he dreamed is a matter of his sharing in the manner of the things of the world to indicate [its] decline.

So it is that Li Chong [d. ca. 362[16]] says, "The sage is without mental images—how could he have dreams? This must be a matter of his being pained at the daily decline of the virtue of the Zhou and being grieved that the way and its teaching is not practiced. Therefore he lodges his sadness in [lamenting his] 'not dreaming' and gives issue to his sighs in [referring to] the *fenghuang*."[17]

然聖人懸照, 本無俟夢想, 而云夢者, 同物而示衰故也. 故李充曰: 聖人無想, 何夢之有. 蓋傷周德之日衰哀, 道教之不行. 故寄慨於不夢, 發歎於鳳[鳥 >] 凰也.

For Huang Kan and Li Chong, Confucius' lament had not been straightforward. He had merely "adapt[ed] his mode of expression to the circumstances, expectations, and capacities of those he addresse[d]."[18] In other words, in bemoaning his failure to dream of the Duke of Zhou Confucius had resorted to what Buddhists called an expedient device, a lie that helps less advanced others arrive at the truth. The sage had "lodged" (*ji* 寄) or "entrusted" (*tuo* 託) his meaning into indirect speech that clued-in readers would know not to take literally,[19] just as the cosmos does with the simulacra (*xiang* 象) that figure in people's dreams.[20]

Waking Up

By medieval times, awakening (*jue* 覺 or *wu* 悟) had become a pan-Asian metaphor for a seminal sort of self-cultivational attainment. The metaphor entails that most people are by default "asleep" under the sway of dream-like delusions they can only recognize as such once they've woken up. In this way, too, dreaming proved good to think about and good to persuade with. Again I confine myself to mentioning just a few examples.

I begin with a *Huainanzi* passage useful for its pairing of the awakening metaphor with an anecdotal example. Each helps bring the other into focus:

You once happen on the form of human being and are especially pleased. But the human condition has a thousand alterations and ten thousand transformations, never reaching its limit, wearing out and then renewing again. Can its joys ever be counted? Compare this to dreaming we're a bird and flying in the sky, dreaming we're a fish and disappearing into the depths. *While we're dreaming we don't realize it's a dream. Only after waking do we recognize it was a dream.* Only after the great awakening will we realize that this present moment was one big dream. In the beginning before I was born, how would I have known the joy of being alive? Now in this moment when I've not yet died, how would I know that being dead isn't also joyful?

Formerly Gongniu Ai suffered from a cyclical illness. Every seven days he would metamorphose into a tiger.[21] Once his older brother opened his door and entered to spy on him, and when he did, the tiger snatched and killed him. Thus his patterns and markings became those of a beast, his fingernails and teeth shifted and changed, his intent and mind altered, his spirit and form metamorphosed. *When he was a tiger, he didn't realize he'd ever been a human being, and when he was a human being he didn't realize he'd ever been a tiger.* These two alternated in opposition, yet each found joy in the form it took. [Similarly,] cleverness and stupidity, "rights" and "wrongs" displace each other endlessly, and who knows from whence they sprout?[22]

一範人之形而猶喜. 若人者千變萬化而未始有極也, 弊而復新, 其為樂也, 可勝計邪. 譬若夢為鳥而飛於天, 夢為魚而沒於淵, 方其夢也, 不知其夢也, 覺而後知其夢也. 今將有大覺, 然後知今此之為大夢也. 始吾未生之時, 焉知生之樂也? 今吾未死, 又焉知死之不樂也?

昔公牛哀轉病也, 七日化為虎. 其兄掩戶而入覘之, 則虎搏而殺之. 是故文章成獸, 爪牙移易, 志與心變, 神與形化. 方其為虎也, 不知其嘗為人也; 方其為人, 不知其且為虎也. 二者代謝舛馳, 各樂其成形. 狡猾鈍惛, 是非無端, 孰知其所萌.

The passage, like so many others in *Zhuangzi*, *Huainanzi*, and *Liezi*, concerns the ceaseless transformation (*hua* 化) of things and our attitude toward it. At any given point in the endless series of transformations that make up our existence, we cling to our current state and dread the next. We can't yet know what the next state will be like. Things change, and we change, and then, having landed in the new state, we realize there was no reason to dread it. This constant gaining of new perspectives is analogized to realizing, once we've awakened, that what seemed real was in fact a dream. Only in the wake of transformation do we come to see the former state with new eyes. Only from a different vantage point can we look back and see clearly where we were. And we can never know for sure whether any present state is like a dream—that is, whether it's something we'll realize only later, from some future viewpoint, was limited in some way we will only then have come to see.

Death is the elephant-in-the-living-room transformation. Seen from this side, it may seem the greatest of disasters. But we can widen this perspective. There was a time before we were born. Perhaps then we dreaded the transformation into human form, but now we know its joys. Now that we know life's joys we dread dying, but how do we know that greater joy doesn't await us on the other side of this next great change? We won't know until we're there. From there we may look back and wonder why we'd ever clung to life.

This analogical use of the transition from dreaming to waking only works in one direction, hitching itself to time's never-ceasing sequence of transformations. But the ensuing parable of the were-tiger Gongniu Ai transposes the same message into a back-and-forth alternation. In each state the transforming subject doesn't realize it was ever anything but itself, and there are joys to be had in both states. These joys are made possible by the subject's "not realizing" (*bu zhi* 不知), because this forgetting of one's former state makes comparison of the two states impossible. There's no third viewpoint from which the subject might undertake such a comparison. And someone else trying to point it out might come in at the wrong time and be eaten.

The line about the "great awakening" (*da jue* 大覺) and "big dream" (*da meng* 大夢) transposes this transformation of perspective into a spatial or scalar mode. There is now some "greater" (*da* 大)—no longer a succession of transformations in a linear series but a leap up to some new plane. But, like other passages built on this trope, there's always the hanging possibility that what from here we expect to be an absolute and final awakening will turn out from some yet wider, later perspective to have been another big dream. The succession of such realizations continues indefinitely, and each becomes possible only when we've reached the point where it can happen.[23] Here's another example, this one from *Zhuangzi*:

> How do I know that loving life is not a delusion? How do I know that in hating death I'm not like a man who, having left home in his youth, has forgotten the way back? . . . . How do I know that the dead don't wonder

> why they ever longed for life? He who dreams of drinking wine may find himself weeping the next morning; he who dreams of weeping may in the morning find himself going out to hunt. While he's dreaming he doesn't realize it's a dream, and in his dream he may even try to interpret a dream. Only after waking does he realize it was a dream. And only at the great awakening shall we know that this was all a big dream. Yet fools think they're awake, so confident that they know who they are—"lords," "herdsmen," how dense! You and Confucius are both dreams, and I who call you a dream am also a dream. This saying of his,[24] the name for it is "a flight into the extraordinary." If once in ten thousand ages a great sage comes along who knows its explanation, it will have happened as though between morning and evening.[25]
>
> 予惡乎知說生之非惑邪. 予惡乎知惡死之非弱喪而不知歸者邪. . . . 予惡乎知夫死者不悔其始之蘄生乎. 夢飲酒者, 旦而哭泣; 夢哭泣者, 旦而田獵. 方其夢也, 不知其夢也. 夢之中又占其夢焉, 覺而後知其夢也. 且有大覺而後知此其大夢也, 而愚者自以為覺, 竊竊然知之, 君乎, 牧乎, 固哉! 丘也與女, 皆夢也; 予謂女夢, 亦夢也. 是其言也, 其名為弔詭. 萬世之後而一遇大聖, 知其解者, 是旦暮遇之也.

Such passages invite us to consider that there's perhaps no end to the succession of imaginable scalar leaps and transformations after which we may realize that what we'd felt so certain of wasn't so at all. We'd just been dreaming, and from this viewpoint it's dreaming and waking all the way out, indefinitely.

Other passages assure us that there really is such a thing as a great, ultimate awakening, opening out into a *nirvāṇa* where all transformations finally and definitively cease. As reported by Ji Zang 吉藏 (549–623), Yu Fakai 于法開 (ca. 310–370) maintained that

> the three realms are a lodging in the long night, wherein mental consciousness is the protagonist of the great dream [of existence]. All impressions of existence which we now perceive are things seen in that dream. Upon awakening, delusory consciousness is extinguished, and the three realms are realized to be empty.[26]
>
> 三界為長夜之宅, 心識為大夢之主. 今之所見群有皆於夢中所見. 獲曉即倒惑識滅, 三界都空.

After *that* awakening, there was nowhere to go but out.

Not Minding the Difference

Finally, there are passages that relativize the very distinction between dreaming and waking. They do so, once more, in the course of making arguments meant to be instructive. Here's an example from the *Liezi* 列子 (formed 300–330[27]):

> In the south corner of the far west there is a land . . . called Gumang. The *qi* of Yin and Yang do not meet there, so there's no distinction between cold and heat. The light of the sun and moon do not shine there, so there's no distinction between day and night. Its people don't eat or wear clothes and they sleep most of the time, waking once in fifty days. They think that what they do in dreams is real, and what they see while awake is unreal.
>
> The realm equidistant from the four seas is called the Central Kingdom. It goes north and south across the [Yellow] River, east and west over Mount Tai, for more than ten thousand miles. Yin and Yang are balanced there, so there is alternation of cold and heat. Darkness and light are divided there, so there is alternation of day and night. Of its people some are wise and some foolish. The myriad things there thrive and multiply, there are many kinds of skill and talent, there are rulers and ministers to oversee them, ceremonies and laws to support them. What they do is past telling and counting. They wake and sleep in alternation. They think that what they do while awake is real, and what they see in dreams is unreal.
>
> In the north corner of the far east there is land called Fuluo. Its climate is always hot, for the excess of the light of the sun and moon shines there. Its soil will not grow fine crops; its people eat herbs and roots and fruits from the trees, and do not know how to cook with fire. By nature they are hard and fierce, the strong oppress the weak, they honor the victor and do not respect [what is] right. They travel at a gallop most of the time and seldom rest. They are always awake and never asleep.[28]

西極之南隅有國焉 . . . 名古莽之國. 陰陽之氣所不交, 故寒暑亡辨; 日月之光所不照, 故晝夜亡辨. 其民不食不衣而多眠. 五旬一覺, 以夢中所為者實, 覺之所見者妄.

四海之齊謂中央之國, 跨河南北, 越岱東西, 萬有餘里. 其陰陽之審度, 故一寒一暑; 昏明之分察, 故一晝一夜. 其民有智有愚. 萬物滋殖, 才藝多方. 有君臣相臨, 禮法相持. 其所云為不可稱計. 一覺一寐, 以為覺之所為者實, 夢之所見者妄.

東極之北隅有國曰阜落之國. 其土氣常燠, 日月餘光之照. 其土不生嘉苗. 其民食草根木實, 不知火食, 性剛悍, 彊弱相藉, 貴勝而不尚義. 多馳步, 少休息, 常覺而不眠.

The relative priority, even the "reality," of waking and sleeping states is simply an accident of geography. In some lands it is the dream that's "real" (*shi* 實) and the waking state that's "unreal" (*wang* 妄). There are even folk who, never sleeping and constantly alert, lack any doorway out of this hot, strife-torn world—a terrifying image. A wise person, then, relinquishes the notion that there's any weight to the difference between waking and dreaming and perhaps spares a moment of gratitude for being able to experience both.

The difference between dreaming and waking is, in other words, just another of the culturally prioritized distinctions readers are urged to set aside. A well-known passage from the sixth chapter of *Zhuangzi* drives the point home with a parabolic narrative:

> Yan Hui said, "I'm improving!"
>
> Confucius said, "What do you mean?"
>
> "I've forgotten about humaneness and dutifulness."
>
> "That's good, but you're not there yet."
>
> Another day he saw Confucius again.
>
> "I'm improving!" he said.
>
> "What do you mean?"
>
> "I've forgotten about the rites and music."
>
> "That's good, but you're not there yet."
>
> Another day he saw Confucius again.
>
> "I'm improving!"
>
> Confucius said, "What do you mean?"
>
> "I just sit and forget."
>
> Confucius looked very startled. "What do you mean, just sit and forget?"
>
> "I let organs and members drop away, dismiss perception and intellect, cast off bodily form, expel 'knowledge,' and just go along with the Great Thoroughfare. This is what I mean by 'just sit and forget.'"
>
> Confucius said, "If you go along with it, you must have no more preferences. If you let yourself be transformed, you must have no more constants. You really are a 'worthy man' after all![29] Oblige me by accepting me as your disciple."[30]

顏回曰：回益矣. 仲尼曰：何謂也？曰：回忘仁義矣. 曰：可矣，猶未也. 他日復見，曰：回益矣. 曰：何謂也？曰：回忘禮樂矣. 曰：可矣，猶未也. 他日復見，曰：回益矣. 曰：何謂也？曰：回座忘矣. 仲尼蹵然曰：何謂坐忘？顏回曰：墮肢體，黜聰明，離形去知，同於大通，此謂坐忘. 仲尼曰：同則无好也，化則无常也. 而果其賢乎！丘也請從而後也.

As would have been obvious to most readers, humaneness (*ren* 仁), dutifulness (*yi* 義), the rites (*li* 禮), and music (*yue* 樂) were nothing less than the four pillars of the Confucian program for personal and societal improvement. Each of these domains was based on the making of distinctions and the marking of boundaries. In forgetting these, Yan Hui arrives at the ability to let go of his attachment to his bodily form and to what passes for "knowledge," instead "just going along with the Great Thoroughfare" (*tong yu datong* 同於大通), submitting fully to the unceasing process of change that is life-and-death-and-life in this world. Confucius obligingly fills in for us some of what this means: no more preferences (*wu hao* 无好) for one state of being over another, letting oneself be transformed (*hua* 化) without attachment or resentment, relinquishing all constants (*wu chang* 无常) one might have insisted on and clung to.

It's in light of such passages that I understand the lesson obliquely conveyed in what is perhaps the most famous passage in the Chinese archive concerning a dream:

> Once Zhuang Zhou dreamt he was a butterfly, flitting and fluttering around, happy with himself and doing as he pleased, not knowing he was Zhou. Suddenly he woke and there he was, unmistakably Zhou. But he didn't know if he was Zhou who had dreamt he was a butterfly, or a butterfly dreaming he was Zhou. Between Zhou and the butterfly there is necessarily a distinction! This is what's known as the transformation of things.[31]
>
> 昔者莊周夢為胡蝶，栩栩然胡蝶也. 自喻適志與. 不知周也. 俄然覺，則蘧蘧然周也. 不知周之夢為胡蝶與，胡蝶之夢為周與. 周與胡蝶則必有分矣. 此之謂物化.

It's not that Zhuangzi literally does not know whether he's a butterfly or a human being but that he is relaxed about feeling as though he's one or the other at different times. While dreaming he's a butterfly he soars aloft happily, "not knowing he's Zhou" (*bu zhi Zhou ye* 不知周也). This loosening of his sense of identity spills pleasantly back into waking life, where he can entertain the instructive thought that maybe it's the other way around. (It's still as Zhuang Zhou, though, that he entertains this thought.) "There must be a distinction" (*bi you fen* 必有分) between Zhuang Zhou and the butterfly, waking and dreaming, but which side of the distinction you're on at any given moment is of no consequence. It changes from moment to moment, and each state has its joys. (Recall: "When he was a tiger, he didn't realize he'd ever been a human being, and when he was a human being he didn't realize he'd ever been a tiger. These two alternated in opposition, yet each found joy in the form it took.") "This is what's known as the transformation of things" 此之謂物化. And the recommended attitude toward this never-ceasing transformation from one state to another is acceptance, here exemplified in Zhuangzi's reaction to his dream.

EPILOGUE

Fish Traps and Rabbit Snares

In many respects this is a book about how communities of self-cultivational practice tried to come to grips with a type of human experience that is as ubiquitous as it is capricious, unpredictable, and (normally) uncontrollable. For communities organized around forming selves and subjectivities of specific sorts, each dedicated to inducting individuals into a particular habitus through collective norms, rules, and disciplines, dreaming—a quintessentially private, personal mode of experience—had to be addressed in some way. However insistently these communities strove to impose specific form on practitioners' waking moments, their dreams remained a pocket of stubborn resistance, a domain of experience studded with the constant potential for formlessness and lawlessness, for personal experiences outside the canon. And so, although these communities' responses to dreaming took many shapes, one shape they didn't take was disinterested theoretical speculation. Practitioners' dreams were of urgent concern.

They might intrude on practice in counterproductive ways. Foul dreams breached practitioners' carefully cultivated selfhood and exposed them to pollution, thereby blocking their progress on the path. Communities prescribed ritual responses to close the breach, restore practitioners to a state of purity, and bring them back into alignment with the canons of practice. This set of understandings and approaches makes up what I've termed the PURIFICATION PARADIGM of dreaming as it relates to self-cultivation. But dreams might also further practice. Under the SPILLOVER PARADIGM, dreaming was so well assimilated to waking self-cultivation projects that it served to continue and further them by other means. In theory, at least, practitioners could glide smoothly between waking and sleeping life, with even their dreams fully integrated into their ongoing self-transformation thanks to the assiduity of their waking practice. But this was a pinnacle only seldom reached, it seems, an ideal more often approached asymptotically than fully realized and sustained. Even Confucius could be represented as failing to achieve the spillover effect consistently. And even Zhou Ziliang recorded dreams whose relation to his self-cultivational quest he was unable to discern. In some respects these two paradigms, PURIFICATION and SPILLOVER, resemble two sides of a single coin: dreams either interrupt or further waking-life practice—directly (that is, non-symbolically) so in either case.

By contrast, in the DIAGNOSTIC PARADIGM some dreams, at least, could be made to further self-cultivational practice, but interpretive work was required to make the dream speak to practitioners' concerns. On their surface, dreams' relevance to one's waking efforts was by no means clear. Their strange language required interpretation. And, even then, not just any dream could be read as pertinent to the practitioner's status or progress, for no hermeneutic system, not even one as extensive as *Explication of Dreams for Bodhisattvas* with its more than six hundred oneiric signs, could possibly encompass every possible dream image. There was always a residue of adiaphora.

The approaches to dreams taken under the PURIFICATION and DIAGNOSTIC PARADIGMS turn out, perhaps surprisingly, to have two commonalities. In both, first of all, dreams created work for someone to do; dreams had to be processed, whether by acts of purification or of interpretation. And in both, secondly, a text (or teacher) was needed to supply the collectively sanctioned method for processing the dream. It was essential to both these paradigms that the response to the dream be guided by tradition, by methods and texts already grounded in the repertoire and bearing the mantle of communal authority. Under both paradigms, dreams were subsumed under a canon, an always sizable body of stipulations not of the dreamer's own individual making. That was what these two types of responses to dreams were fundamentally about.

Seen from this vantage point, the SPILLOVER PARADIGM is the outlier. There, dreams are not necessarily so easily assimilable to tradition: they might end up modifying tradition. They might bid to inject newly revealed information about the unseen world, new methods of self-cultivation, or newly revealed works into the scriptural canon.[1] Among the documents investigated here, *Records of Master Zhou's Communications with the Unseen World* is the most robust example of this scenario. But even in such cases, dream accounts' success in introducing novelty depended on their reception by larger communities of practitioners. Under this paradigm, then, any given dream had the potential to change a canon of practice or perhaps even, in rare cases, to launch a new one. But the dream's effect was inescapably a function of its reception—first by the dreamer and then, even more crucially, by many other parties. Until that time, it remained just one individual's dream.

As is so often the case, the *Zhuangzi* and *Liezi* texts stand in oblique relationship to the projects and concerns on which this book has mainly focused. With their privileging of wandering (*you* 遊) and staying on the move, their valuation of only temporarily lodging in any one vantage point, and their preference for roaming "outside the realm" (*fang wai* 方外) rather than remaining within its demarcated borders, they are fundamentally not friendly to canons of any kind. In these texts, dreaming isn't a danger to be responded to, a coded message, or even a spilling over of waking pursuits into the nocturnal domain, but a way of getting "outside the realm"—and it is dreaming's alterity with respect to waking life that makes it so. What dreamers bring back with them isn't any specific new information but a refreshing loosening of their grip on the little certainties structuring quotidian life, a reminder that at any point we are liable to awaken from our dogmatic slumber and realize that the fixities of canon and culture that we'd taken for granted were, after all, no more substantial than dreams. Dreams do not need to be assimilated. They are less a series of lumps demanding to be smoothed out than exit ramps or ladders out of the matrices of culture, tradition, and convention. In opening doors to these wider possibilities, these texts work like wedges to pry readers loose from the mesh of tradition, or the web of culture, with which they have become too accustomed. Like what they argue concerning dreaming, these texts themselves are fundamentally therapeutic in character.

But this too, in its own way, amounts to an assimilation of dreaming—a way of making dreaming serve a human agenda, even if the agenda is reminding us that no canon is ever really closed, that no scheme of order, nor any single way of mapping what we too naïvely take to be reality, can be considered final. And this book's mapping of some of the self-cultivational uses of dreams in China must similarly be regarded as provisional. I am reminded of another inimitable *Zhuangzi* passage:

> The fish trap exists because of the fish; once you've gotten the fish, you can forget the trap. The rabbit snare exists because of the rabbit; once you've gotten the rabbit, you can forget the snare. Words exist because of meaning; once you've gotten the meaning you can forget the words. Where can I find someone who has forgotten words, that I might have a word with them?[2]
>
> 荃者所以在魚, 得魚而忘荃. 蹄者所以在兔, 得兔而忘蹄. 言者所以在意, 得意而忘言. 吾安得忘言之人而與之言哉?

Happily, dreams are ever so much more elusive than fish and rabbits. The best we might hope for is to momentarily catch them only to release them back into the wild—or watch amusedly as they escape through our fingers and splash back into the stream of time (which physicists say is not what it seems, either). In any case, what this book has pondered isn't dreams themselves but the latticework of ideas and practices—the equivalents of so many fish traps and rabbit snares—within which dreams were deemed meaningful. But by studying closely the handiwork that went into their construction we have, I hope, come to better understand some of the fascinating and poignant interfaces between dreaming and self-cultivation, and between experience and culture, in a distant era.

APPENDIX A

The Initial List of Dream Signs in Explication of Dreams for Bodhisattvas (Pusa shuomeng jing 菩薩說夢經)

In my translation below, I give the signs (or items) in the sequence in which they appear in part 2 of the sutra, adding numerals and omitting the iterations of "Next, Vajra Obliterator . . . " 復次金剛摧 prefacing almost every item.[1] With some exceptions, I present this list as if the sutra contained no further passages to help the reader better understand what each involves. But in a non-trivial number of cases, what is found in part 3 of the sutra (or the main body, the detailed unpacking of each dream sign) does not correspond to this list. This is true in four respects: (1) items appear in part 3 that aren't listed in part 2 at all; (2) conversely, a few items in part 2 lack a counterpart in part 3; (3) the sequence sometimes varies; and (4) in some instances the sense of the line in this initial listing of signs changes or is clarified upon reading its corresponding passage in part 3, as indicated in my notes. Following each item is a reference indicating the page, register, and line number in the Taishō edition where the corresponding passage (if any) in part 3 begins, at least in my judgment. (This isn't always completely clear since both the wording and the sequence often differ.) At the end is listed one passage in part 3 that has no corresponding items in part 2.

Translation

1. In a dream you see the[2] Tathāgata come and speak personally with you; you see his marvelous body. 夢見如來身共語見妙身.

2. In a dream you see the Tathāgata. He is silent.[3] 夢見如來默然.
3. In a dream you see the Tathāgata with his head covered, seated. 夢見如來覆頭坐.
4. In a dream you see the Tathāgata sitting with his back to you. 夢見如來背坐.
5. In a dream you see the Tathāgata, colored red.[4] 夢見如來身紅色. [82a6]
6. In a dream you see the Tathāgata with his body drawn upon in many colors. 夢見如來彩色畫身. [82a9]
7. In a dream you see the Tathāgata walk away. 夢見如來去.[5] [82a11]
8. a dream you see the Tathāgata explaining the Dharma to others. 夢見如來為他說法.[6] [82a22]
9. In a dream you see the Tathāgata exercising his divine powers by walking in midair. 夢見如來神通虛空中行. [82b3]
10. In a dream you see the Tathāgata attain parinirvāṇa. 夢見如來般涅槃.
11. In a dream you see the Tathāgata's body cremated. 夢見闍維如來身. [82b14]
12. In a dream you obtain a relic of the Tathāgata's body. 夢得如來舍利. [82b19]
13. In a dream you obtain a hair of the Tathāgata. 夢得如來髮.
14. In a dream you see a stupa of the Tathāgata that you haven't seen before. 夢見如來未曾見塔. [82c4]
15. In a dream you see a stupa of the Tathāgata richly bejeweled and ornamented.[7] 夢見如來寶莊嚴塔.
16. In a dream you see a stupa to the Tathāgata's divine powers. 夢見如來神通塔.[8] [82c14]
17. In a dream you see the Tathāgata radiating light. 夢見如來光.[9]
18. In a dream you hear the Tathāgata's voice but don't see his body. 夢聞如來聲不見身. [82c21]
19. In a dream you present offerings to the Tathāgata. 夢中供養如來.[10] [82c24]
20. In a dream you see [a stupa to[11]] the Tathāgata being adorned with flowers and incense paste. 自夢見花鬘香塗覆如來 [上 > 塔].[12] [83a6]
21. In a dream you see the Tathāgata wearing a soiled robe. 自夢見如來著垢膩衣.

22. In a dream you hear Dharma that you've never heard before. 自夢聞未曾聞法. [83a17]
23. You dream that you are explaining for someone Dharma that you haven't heard before. But when you wake up, you can find no way to express it, and you no longer remember it. 自夢為人說未曾聞法.寤已無所顯示.乃至不念. [83a25]
24. You see an unfamiliar Dharma master. 又見未曾見法師.
25. You dream that you are seated on the Dharma seat explaining the Dharma to others. 自夢坐法座為他說法.
26. You dream that you have attained [the state of] fearlessness. 自夢得無畏.
27. In a dream you see a place of [Buddhist] practice. 自夢見道場. [83b25]
28. In a dream you see the Tathāgata walking straight along. 夢見如來經行.
29. In a dream you see the Tathāgata turning the wheel of Dharma. 夢見如來轉法輪.
30. In a dream you see the stupa [at the site of the] Tathāgata's *parinirvāṇa*. 夢見如來般涅槃塔.[13]
31. You dream of obtaining the Tathāgata's robe. 夢得如來衣.
32. You dream of obtaining the Tathāgata's alms bowl. 夢得如來鉢. [84a12]
33. You dream simply of the Tathāgata. 夢獨見一如來.
34. In a dream you see the Tathāgata encircled by a great many people. 夢見如來多人圍繞.
35. In a dream you see the Tathāgata's canopy.[14] 夢見如來蓋.
36. In a dream you see the Tathāgata's leather slippers. 夢見如來革屣.
37. In a dream you see the Tathāgata sitting. 夢見如來坐.
38. You dream of presenting the Tathāgata with food. 自夢與如來食.
39. You dream of presenting the Tathāgata with robes. 自夢與如來衣.
40. You dream of presenting the Tathāgata with flowers. 自夢與如來花. [84c24]
41. You dream of entering mountains. 自夢入山.
42. You dream of yourself naked. 自夢裸形.
43. You dream of walking in one of the four intermediate directions.[15] 自夢四維行. [85a14]

44. In a dream you see a place you've never seen before. 自夢見未曾方.
45. You see yourself in a dream walking through muddy water. 自夢濁水中行. [85a29]
46. In a dream you see clouds and rain. 自夢見雲雨.
47. In a dream you see the ground shake. 夢見地猺.[16] [85b14]
48. In a dream you walk among a pack of wild dogs and wolves in the wild. 自夢在豺狼野干中行.[17]
49. You dream that you are ill. 自夢病. [85c1]
50. You dream you are falling off a mountain with nothing to hold onto. 自夢墮山無所依仗. [85c6]
51. You dream you are tied up and taken to be executed. 自夢被縛將殺. [85c23]
52. You dream of walking among daggers and swords. 自夢刀劍中行.
53. You dream of walking in midair. 自夢虛空中行.
54. You dream of holding a lit torch in your hand. 自夢手捉炬火.
55. You dream of the Bodhisattva escaping the palace and leaving the city. 夢見菩薩踰宮出城.
56. You dream of obtaining sutras. 自夢得經. [86a29]
57. You dream of hearing the sound of *dhāraṇīs*. 自夢聞陀羅尼聲.
58. You dream of hearing the sound of *samādhi*. 自夢聞三昧 [夢>聲].[18]
59. You dream of hearing the sound of Mahāyāna[19] sutra(s) [being recited]. 自夢聞方廣經聲.
60. You dream of hearing the sound of a certain Dharma master's voice. 夢某甲法師聲. [86b26]
61. You dream of obtaining a *gāthā* in a dream.[20] 自夢夢中得偈. [86c5]
62. You dream of having a sutra expounded for you in a dream. 自夢夢中得經說.
63. You dream of hearing the sounds of Dharma treasure.[21] 自夢聞法藏聲. [no counterpart in part 3]
64. In a dream you hear the name of a Tathāgata in another world. 自夢聞他方世界如來名. [86c24]
65. In a dream you hear the name of some bodhisattva in another world. 自夢聞他方世界某甲菩薩名.
66. You dream of setting off to sea. 自夢入海去.

67. You dream of a bunch of gems. 自夢集寶.
68. You dream of being atop Mount Sumeru. 自夢在須彌山頂. [87a21]
69. You dream of ascending a mountain. 自夢上山.
70. You dream of summiting a mountain. 自夢上到山頂.
71. You dream of climbing a tree. 自夢上樹.
72. You dream of seeing a dragon or elephant.[22] 自夢見龍象.
73. You dream of riding a dragon or elephant. 自夢乘龍象.
74. You dream of riding a horse. 自夢乘馬.
75. You dream of performing an act of truth. 自夢發真實誓願.
76. In a dream you see trees bearing fruits. 自夢見果樹.
77. In a dream you see flowering trees. 自夢見花樹.
78. In a dream you see an unfamiliar city. 自夢見未曾見城. [88a2]
79. In a dream you see Anavatapata Lake.[23] 自夢見阿耨大池. [88a9]
80. In a dream you see a celestial being. 自夢見天子.
81. In a dream you see a dragon.[24] 自夢見龍. [88a24]
82. In a dream you see yourself leaving Jambudvīpa.[25] 自夢見餘閻浮提去.
83. In a dream you see yourself wearing a white robe.[26] 自夢見著白衣.
84. In a dream you are wearing gems in your hair. 自夢寶鬘在頭.
85. In a dream you see flowers in your hair. 自夢見花鬘在頭. [88b27]
86. In a dream you pick up scattered flowers. 自夢取散花.
87. In a dream you play a drum while others amuse themselves. 自夢打鼓餘人作樂. [88c12]
88. In a dream you see a solar or lunar eclipse. 自夢見日蝕月蝕.
89. In a dream you smear yourself with filth. 自夢以不淨自塗. [88c26]
90. You dream of being a king. 自夢作王.
91. In a dream you are a minister to a ruler and walk among his entourage. 自夢作王輔相在大眾中行.
92. You dream of riding through a grove. 自夢乘乘往園林中去. [89a18]
93. In a dream you see a town in an unfamiliar land where the monks live in town among the lay people. 自夢見未曾見方土聚落僧坊房舍人眾.
94. You dream of obtaining a canopy.[27] 自夢得蓋. [89b2]
95. You dream of expounding the Dharma for many people. 自夢為多人說法. [89b9]

96. In a dream you enter a town. 自夢入聚落.[28] [89b25]
97. You dream of donating a bridge.[29] 自夢施繫橋梁. [no equivalent in part 3]
98. You dream of riding[30] on a boat. 自夢乘船.
99. You dream of clouds, thunder, and lightning. 自夢見雲雷電.
100. You dream of obtaining weapons and donning armor.[31] 自夢得刀著鎧杖. [89c21]
101. You dream of obtaining a vessel. 自夢得器物. [89c27]
102. You dream of showing sentient beings the path. 自夢示眾生道.
103. You dream of entering a grove. 自夢入園林中.
104. In a dream you see a mass of grains. 自夢見眾穀聚.
105. You dream of healing living beings of their illnesses. 自夢治眾生病. [90a26]
106. In a dream you hear a voice conferring prediction of [your] eventual Buddhahood. 自夢受記聲.
107. You dream of attaining enlightenment. 自夢覺道.
108. You dream of obtaining a full pitcher. 自夢得滿瓶. [90b17]

The following sign appears in the main body of the text but not in the initial list of signs:

In a dream you see yourself in the midst of a quarrel. 夢中自見在鬪訟中 [85b23]

On the Number of Primary Signs

Why are there 108 primary signs? This number surely wasn't haphazardly chosen. The number 108 is a Harshad number (an integer divisible by the sum of its digits), and in many Buddhist contexts it signals completion or totality. It figures in the numbers assigned to cycles of cosmic time.[32] In Indo-Iranian astronomy and astrology, parts of which were appropriated in China in early medieval times, 108 was the number of stations along the ecliptic.[33] By some reckonings it was the total number of types of passions or afflictions 煩惱;[34] by others, the total number of internal feelings 內受,[35] or the number of types of *samādhi*.[36] It is the number of beads most often found in Buddhist rosaries.[37] In two *dhāraṇī* sutra compilations, one made in the sixth century and the other in the seventh, 108 is the number of times one is to chant an incantation. In the *Compendium of Dhāraṇīs* (*Tuoluoni jijing* 陀羅尼集經, completed in 654)—a text that features an initiation ritual in which the blindfolded initiate throws a flower into a *maṇḍala*, resulting in a special affiliation with the corresponding deity—this mandate is given no fewer than 141 times,[38] while in the Liang-era *Assortment of Dhāraṇīs* (*Tuoluoni zaji* 陀羅尼雜集) it's given twelve times.[39]

When it comes to *Explication of Dreams*, perhaps the closest analog—for there, too, it is a matter of *signs*—is that 108 was by some accounts the number of auspicious symbols on the soles of Buddhas' feet. This seems to have been primarily a Theravāda tradition, evidenced in Sri Lanka, Thailand, and Cambodia, but lists of auspicious signs on the Buddha's feet or body propagated throughout Asia.[40] Lists of the thirty-two marks (*lakṣaṇa*) and eighty attributes (*anuvyañjana*) appear in several Chinese sutra translations. However, I know of no sutra in Chinese that lists 108 marks on the Buddha's feet or body.[41] Comparing the list of bodily marks given by Skilling to the dream signs in *Explication of Dreams*, I find nothing to suggest that the signs in *Explication* were drawn from lists of Buddhas' somatic marks.[42]

APPENDIX B

A Close Comparison of Chinese Versions of the Chapter on the Diagnostic Use of Dreams in Perfection of Wisdom Texts

The following comparison across multiple translations of the same scriptural chapter is presented because it spotlights the different specific ways in which practitioners' dream lives were portrayed as diagnostic indices of bodhisattvas' self-cultivational practice.

The first sign. The gist is that, even when dreaming, the practitioner remains steadfast in the role of bodhisattva.[1] This has three components: he does not succumb to the temptation to prematurely exit the path by becoming an *arhat* or *pratyekabuddha*; he remains fixed on the goal of Buddhahood (心悉常在佛 as Lokakṣema has it, 心志常在佛 per Zhi Qian); and he regards all dharmas as being "like things seen in a dream," meaning insubstantial, lacking own-being. Lokakṣema's expression of this third component (夢中視) is so terse that its meaning becomes clear only when compared to Zhi Qian's rewrite (諸法夢中視). Other versions add standard analogies for the non-substantiality of dharmas: Mokṣala, for example, has "he regards all dharmas as like dreams, like echoes, like illusions, like heat from a flame" 視諸法如夢, 如響, 如幻, 如熱時焰.[2]

The second sign. The main idea is that the bodhisattva in a dream sees himself as being not only in the audience as the Buddha discourses, but also the foremost disciple there. This was an opportunity so prized that it spurred the notion that, although Gautama departed long ago, there are other worlds where one might now encounter an active Buddha.[3] Kumārajīva (larger sutra) expands the audience to include non-humans: "*devas*, *nagas*, 'ghosts and spirits,' *kinnaras*, and so forth" 天, 龍, 鬼神, 緊那羅等. Mokṣala adds assurance that the Dharma heard in the dream is correct: 所說不失法則. The outlier is *Mohe banruo chao jing* 摩訶般若鈔經, where *the dreamer* is the one expounding Dharma "like a Tathāgata, arhat, or fully enlightened Buddha" 如怛薩阿竭阿羅訶三耶三佛.

The third sign. There is a divide between translations that place the dreamer in the role of a Buddha preaching from midair and those (such as Mokṣala's) that put him in the audience looking upward as a Buddha preaches. The passages in the former group vividly convey the oneiric experience of inhabiting the role of Buddha: the dreamer "looks around to see his own halo a span wide" (還自見七尺光 in Lokakṣema, Zhi Qian, and *Mohe banruo chao jing*). Kumārajīva's translations are split across these alternate understandings. His rendition of the smaller sutra accords with the first three, adding an embellishment about what the dreamer thinks during the dream as he sees himself preaching as a Buddha; but his larger sutra and *Da zhidu lun*, like Mokṣala's version, have the dreamer "see[ing] the Buddha with his thirty-two marks and eighty characteristics . . . radiating light and leaping into midair " 見佛三十二相,八十隨形好 . . . 放大光明踊在虛空 to address the audience.

The fourth sign. The earliest two versions (those of Lokakṣema and Zhi Qian), as well as *Mohe banruo chao jing*, give a shorter list of the disturbing phenomena seen in a dream without provoking a fearful response. To this list Mokṣala adds, "or if he sees the death of his parents, siblings, close friends, or acquaintances" 若見喪失父母兄弟親友知識, and Kumārajīva's larger sutra is similar. Kumārajīva's smaller sutra lacks this passage entirely.

The fifth sign. All versions except Zhi Qian and Kumārajīva's larger sutra have the dreamer not only "forming the thought" 作是念 but also "issuing a vow" 發願 that, once he has attained Buddhahood, the realm he creates will contain nothing polluted, vile, or evil 惡. And in all versions, the practitioner forms this resolve and utters the vow within the frame of the dream. The main difference comes in the enumeration of the ills seen in the dream that spur the bodhisattva's response. Lokakṣema, Zhi Qian, and *Mohe banruo chao jing* list only animals devouring each other and people falling ill,[4] whereas the other versions mention the standard three unfortunate paths: rebirth in the purgatories, rebirth as a *preta* or ghost, and rebirth as an animal.

The sixth sign. It's here that the texts diverge most. One difficulty hinges on whether the dream from which the practitioner has awakened was, as Conze puts it in a bracketed insertion, "a prophetic dream."[5] That is, did the bodhisattva dream that his town was on fire and then wake to find it really was so? Lokakṣema's version, which is extremely hard to parse, initially gives the impression that the dream wasn't necessarily about a burning city. The point isn't that the practitioner dreamed of an event that now is coming true in the waking world, but rather that the bodhisattva has received in a dream a sign of his irreversibility and now intends to test its veracity by doing something while awake. "When this *bodhisattva-mahāsattva* has awakened from his dream[s], if he sees that his city is on fire, he forms this thought: 'If I compare this to what I saw in my dream[s], using it as a sign [?], I was unafraid upon seeing it, and this was a sign sufficient to show that a *bodhisattva-mahāsattva* is *avivartika* [non-retrogressing]'" 是菩薩摩訶薩於夢中覺已, 若見城郭火起時, 便作是念: 我於夢中所見, 用是比, 用是相, 見不怖, 用是比, 用是相, 行具足 菩薩摩訶薩如是, 是為阿惟越致相.[6]

Then we come to the point: "I will now thoroughly investigate whether this is any different from the fire that has now broken out in the city" 今我審應審至審, 是所向者, 當無異今是城郭火起. Much hinges on the "this" 是 here. Rather than seeing it as referring to the city fire in the dream as compared to the city fire in waking life, I think it refers to the speaker's having been indicated in the dream to be an irreversible bodhisattva. He will now test that indication by performing a *truth act* in the waking world (more on truth acts in a moment): "By virtue of [this truth about] me, let this fire be completely extinguished and not reignite" 用我故, 悉當滅, 悉當消, 悉當去, 不復現. If the fire dies out, this confirms his irreversibility and previous receipt of a prediction of Buddhahood. If the fire persists, this indicates that he hasn't yet received such a prediction. And "if the fire gods burn down one dwelling here and there, or one hamlet here and there" 設火神燒一舍置一舍, 復越燒一里置一里, this means that "[the retribution for] members of those households having abandoned the Dharma in previous lifetimes has now arrived" 其家人前世時斷經故所致. They will now see this plainly for themselves, and because of this the evil karma will be dissolved (是輩之人所作宿命悉自見, 宿命所作惡於是悉除賜, 從是以來斷經餘殃悉盡, 是宿命惡悉消). *And*, unfortunately for the bodhisattva, this is *also* a sign that he hasn't yet attained irreversibility or realized unsurpassed enlightenment (知是菩薩摩訶薩未得阿惟越致, 阿耨多羅三耶三菩).

Similarly to what Conze's translation implies, Zhi Qian seems to view the dream from which the dreamer has awoken as involving an urban wildfire. "Upon waking from [such a?] dream and seeing his city on fire, the bodhisattva forms this thought 於夢中寤已, 若見城郭火起時便作是念: 'Just like this was the sign I saw in my dream. Seeing it, I was unafraid, and this was a sign that I am an irreversible bodhisattva'" 可於夢中可見是相. 見之不怖, 用是相行具足, 是為不退轉闓士. "Let me now examine whether what I saw then is any different now. The fire that's broken out should be completely extinguished and not appear again" 今我審應是所向者, 當無是異變. 火起當滅, 悉消去不復見.

But Mokṣala makes the fires seen in the dream those *of the purgatories* (菩薩夢中見泥犁中火燒湯煮). It's those fires that the dreamer tries to extinguish with his act of truth (如我所見, 泥犁中火即當滅去)—after he has woken up (覺已念言). If they go out, this confirms that he's been predicted to attain Buddhahood ([以 > 已] 受記莂). But if the fire spreads from house to house or hamlet to hamlet, this indicates that those householders' previous sin of rejecting Dharma has now met its retribution. So Mokṣala skips from the fires of the purgatories, seen while asleep, to the dreamer's urban surroundings in the waking world, which are now similarly on fire.

Kumārajīva's larger sutra[7] similarly takes the fires to be those of purgatory (夢中見地獄火燒眾生)—but the dreamer performs the act of truth while still asleep. If the purgatorial fires die out, this is a sign of irreversibility. But during the day he performs a similar act when he sees a wildfire burning in his town. If the fire goes out, this is a sign that he has previously received a prediction of Buddhahood; if not, it's an indication that the people whose houses are burning are receiving retribution for having previously rejected Dharma.

Kumārajīva's smaller sutra differs yet again. Having seen in a dream a sign of his irreversibility on the path, he finds upon waking that his city is on fire. He performs the truth act to test the validity of the oneiric sign he'd received. If the fires go out, the bodhisattva knows that he's previously received a prediction of his own perfect enlightenment and will not retrogress. But if they don't, he knows that he has *not* yet received such a prediction (若火不滅, 當知是菩薩未得受記). *And* if the fire skips some houses and burns others, this indicates that the incinerated homes are those of people who in previous lives rejected Dharma, and the fire constitutes their karmic retribution for that. But somehow this, too, constitutes a sign that the dreamer *is* an irreversible bodhisattva. On all these points *Mohe banruo chao jing* agrees, but its wording differs.

The seventh sign. In all versions this event occurs while the bodhisattva is awake. Essentially, he performs an exorcism as a truth act. If the demon departs, this is a sign of his irreversibility and future attainment of Buddhahood. If not, then he's not yet irreversible. The only significant differences—interesting in light of our discussion of agents of pollution in chapter 1—concern the vocabulary describing the spirit's assault on its human host: "descended upon" 所下 and "seized" 所持 in Lokakṣema, "taken" 所取 in Zhi Qian, "seized" 所持 in Mokṣala and in Kumārajīva (larger), and "infused upon" 所著 in Kumārajīva (shorter). The passive voice is telling.

APPENDIX C

A Collection of Incubatory Spells in Three Dongshen Registers of Red Writs of the Most High (Taishang chiwen dongshen sanlu 太上赤文洞神三籙)

My attention was drawn to this text by an intriguing summary and paraphrase of one of its prescribed methods published by Michel Strickmann in 1988.[1] The scripture's preface claims it was compiled by no less an authority than Tao Hongjing, but in fact it's been plausibly argued to postdate the 930s, and the preface is probably a forgery.[2] Hence it falls outside this book's temporal scope. But given the relative paucity of textual information in the archive on ancient and medieval incubation methods, as well as the incompleteness of Strickmann's characterization, I include it in this brief appendix.

Here is what Strickmann had to say about the text. He noted that the text's instructions are "exceedingly laconic" and stressed that his "unravelling" of the method was "tentative." In fact, he gave a fair idea of what the first method, or spell, entailed (found at 6a10–6b9) without commenting on the ones following it. Strickmann's paraphrase reads as follows:

> The . . . priest uses a young child as a medium. He puts the child to sleep [by unspecified means]. Just before doing so, he twice recites the name of a deity called "The Immovable One," then takes a piece of black paper, folds it in two, and has the child hold it between his teeth. Then he wraps the child's head in a piece of cotton cloth and puts it to sleep. Next he inhales twice and recites: "I send the four great spirit-generals to apprehend the jade maidens who have beguiled the souls." He then blows his breath into the mouth of the sleeping child.

> Next a second person goes to sleep or is put to sleep. Presumably this is the person who is the object of the priest's concern. . . . Once [the man for whom the ritual is being performed] has been tucked in, the priest draws breaths from the five directions and blows them over the patient's body, lightly, as if blowing on a cup of tea. Then he sits down once more and recites again, "O Lord Immovable,"[2] his invocation to the presiding deity. He next goes to look at the patient and then recites: "I send the four great spirit-generals to apprehend the souls which have been beguiled by the jade maidens. I call them swiftly to return!" Then he calls out the sleeper's personal name and awakens him.[3]

The passage is labeled "Method of the patriarchs for treating nocturnal dreams in which, having roamed to various regions, one's cloudsouls have been beguiled by jade maidens" 祖師入夜夢遊諸境玉女迷魂法. It reads:

> 第一試: 法門令小兒睡, 先念呪二曰不動尊聖攝. 以黑紙上疊了, 令小孩兒口咬之. 二帛蒙頭, 先取睡臥. 二口氣念呪曰: 追四大神將勾迷魂玉女. 念畢, 吹睡小兒口內以兩手大拇指去睡人三思臺上分捻. 又其人自睡. 又取五方氣吹在身上, 如二椀茶間. 自端坐, 念不動尊聖攝, 去尋之, 見了, 再念追四大神將勾玉女迷魂, 吾喚速來歸. 喚小名起來.[4]

The passage is indeed "exceedingly laconic," and Strickmann's paraphrase is unobjectionable. "Lord Immovable" 不動尊聖 is clearly a Daoist appropriation and slight re-titling of Acala 不動明王, the Immovable Wisdom King, a demon king incorporated into esoteric Buddhism as the emissary of Vairocana and a central figure in the esoteric rites Amoghavajra (704–774) deployed in service to the Tang imperial house. Amoghavajra's *Trisamaya Scripture* is "the locus classicus for Acala rites."[5] The term *she* 攝 is here used in a way unfamiliar to me, either as a noun meaning "spell," a counter word for spells, or a marker for where a spell ends.

What Strickmann omitted was that the text goes on to list eleven more spells (*zhou* 呪), all of which function to induce a dream on a particular theme or topic. Here is the list of themes:

2. To dream of leaving home 第二去家夢
3. To dream of dispatching someone 第三去遣人夢
4. To dream of crossing a river by raft 第四過河筏夢
5. To dream of overlooking mountain areas 第五觀山境夢
6. To dream of entering a female person 第六入陰人夢
7. To dream of entering a male person 第七入陽人夢
8. To cause someone to dream of journeying among clouds 第八令人遊雲夢
9. To cause someone to dream of journeying home 第九令人遊家夢
10. To cause someone to [be able to] wash their eyes and see ghosts and spirits in dreams 第十令人洗眼見鬼神夢
11. To cause someone to dream of journeying into the nine empyrean realms 第十一令人遊九霄夢
12. To become able to dream of whatever you like[6] 第十二一切去者隨意夢

One thing seems clear: this appears to be a list of spells for dream control—either the practitioner's own dreams or his clients' dreams, or perhaps both. As for the divine beings apparently named in some of the spell texts themselves, as far as I can tell they are all *hapax legomena*.

Further research is needed on this text—and on other discussions of incubation perhaps buried in the Chinese archive and waiting to be brought to light.

Notes

Introduction

1. The exception is lucid dreams, which aren't dealt with here since I have found no clear record of them in the archive (though there are a few spells to induce dreams of specific sorts, as discussed in appendix C).
2. For pithy evocations of the oddness of the dreams vis-à-vis waking life, see the passages quoted from David Linden and Eva Brann in Campany, *Dreamscape*, 16.
3. This is a core passage from the famous *Great Learning* (*Daxue* 大學, perhaps better translated as *The Greater Practice*) chapter of *Records of Rites* (*Li ji* 禮記). See *Da xue* 981; translation in Goldin, "Han Law," 4–5, from whose discussion I have benefited.
4. *Master Redpine's Petition Almanac* (*Chisongzi zhangli* 2.3b–4b; translation in Kleeman, *Celestial Masters*, 356–57).
5. *Analects* 10.4. See *Lunyu jijie yishu* 5.22a–b; translation modifying Slingerland, *Analects*, 99–100.
6. From *Records of Signs from the Unseen Realm* (*Mingxiang ji* 冥祥記) as anthologized in *Fayuan zhulin* 53:875a; translation modifying Campany, *Signs from the Unseen Realm*, 197.
7. From *Recent Accounts from the Talk of the Ages* (*Shishuo xinyu* 世說新語); translation and Chinese text in Chen, *Anecdote*, 132.
8. From *Traditions of Divine Transcendents* (*Shenxian zhuan* 神仙傳) as quoted in TPGJ 7.3; translation in Campany, *To Live as Long*, 263. Another anecdote occurs in *Liezi* 列子 in which an individual is evaluated for his self-cultivational attainment or potential by being scanned by a specialist while standing in the light; the one being scanned is one Long Shu 龍叔, and the scanner is the physician Wen Zhi 文摯. See *Liezi jishi* 129–30 and Graham, *Book of Lieh-tzu*, 82–83.
9. As I was nearing completion of the manuscript for this book, I stumbled back upon a passage in which, as was so often the case, Michel Strickmann had anticipated this idea: "La vie éveillé des moines était rigoureusement réglementée. La moindre action était ritualisée, et les activités humaines ordinaires leur étaient en grande partie interdites. Leur vie oneirique constituait donc un défi au système. À tout le moins, il fallait des critères pour évaluer l'importance morale des choses vues ou des actes accomplies en rêve" (*Mantras et mandarins*, 294).
10. In fact, there exists a study that proceeds roughly in this fashion except insofar as it focuses on a single anthology of texts: Lin Fu-shih, "Religious Taoism and Dreams." For a brief critique of Lin's approach see Campany, *Dreamscape*, 165n6.
11. See Campany, "On the Very Idea of Religions," "Chinese History and Writing about 'Religion(s),'" "Religious Repertoires and Contestation," "'Religious' as a Category," and "Two Religious Thinkers." All these studies offer both critiques and constructive alternatives.
12. Smith, *Drudgery Divine*, 117–18, emphasis added.
13. Elsewhere I've shown how the model of "religions" as repertoires and imagined communities can be used to characterize and better understand interreligious competition. See Campany, "Religious Repertoires and Contestation."

14. For more on what I mean by this—and for a discussion of alternatives to seeing religions as organic wholes or as containers of ideas and practices—see Campany, "On the Very Idea of Religions."
15. Smith, *Relating Religion*, 368–72. Compare Campany, "'Religious' as a Category," 336–37.
16. This book thus operates for the most part at a middle level between close and distant reading. In this respect my approach resembles that of Hunter, *Poetics of Early Chinese Thought*.
17. For extensive discussion and copious examples in the cases of texts, images, and artifacts see Gentz, "Defining Boundaries," and Meyer, *Documentation and Argument* and "Device for Conveying Meaning." See also Kern, "Formation of the *Classic of Poetry*" and "'Xi shuai'"; Hunter, "To Leave or Not to Leave," 11–12, and *Confucius Beyond the Analects*; Krijgsman, "Traveling Sayings" and "Rise of a Manuscript Culture," 176, adopting the term "gobbets" (based on Griffiths, *Religious Reading*, 49–54) to denote short strings of memorizable text; Boltz, "Composite Nature of Early Chinese Texts" (he prefers "units" and "building blocks" for the bits of text that circulated independently and are now found emplaced across multiple documents in the archive); Schwermann, "Collage-Technik"; Capitanio, "Sanskrit and Pseudo-Sanskrit Incantations"; Lewis, *Writing and Authority*, 58; Ledderose, *Ten Thousand Things*; S. Huang, "Media Transfer and Modular Construction"; and Pettit and Chang, *Library of Clouds*, 140–68. To my knowledge, this fruitful line of inquiry has not yet been applied to show the modularity of Chinese ritual and self-cultivational practice. This book takes a few small steps in that direction.
18. Palumbo, *Early Chinese Commentary*, 6.
19. Compare this phrasing: "When medieval Chinese Buddhists are understood to be, first and foremost, simply medieval Chinese people (and not avatars of ideology, foreign or domestic), then it is clear that the common store of Chinese culture was as rightfully theirs as it was the Daoists'" (Copp, *Body Incantatory*, 57).
20. Whether initially composed there or (in the case of many Buddhist texts) translated from works originating elsewhere is beside the point here. By "China" I mean not the geographic area now so designated but the Sinographic cosmopolis (to adapt a term of Sheldon Pollock's) or Panhuaxia (to use Alexander Beecroft's term) of persons who participated to some extent in the writing system now termed "Chinese," the common if loose and variegated set of old touchstone texts, and the many key terms, values, genres, macro-narratives, writing and other practices, personages, and names that were baked into that writing system and those texts. See Pollock, *Language of the Gods*, 10–19; Beecroft, *Authorship and Cultural Identity*, 9; Sen, "Yijing and the Buddhist Cosmopolis"; and Campany, *Dreamscape*, 3 and 166n8.
21. Among the many studies that could be cited on text-making, writing, and reading in China ca. 300 BC–800 CE, see for example S. Nichols, "Introduction: Philology in a Manuscript Culture"; Krijgsman, "Inquiry into the Formation of Readership," "Rise of a Manuscript Culture," "Traveling Sayings," and "A Self-Reflexive Practice" (see 76n1 for a useful list of further works); Nugent, *Manifest in Words*; Tian, *Tao Yuanming and Manuscript Culture* (note in particular the startling example related at pp. 7–8); Zhang Hanmo, *Authorship and Text-Making*; Waring, "What the Single Bamboo Slip"; Matthias Richter, *Embodied Text* and "Textual Identity"; Meyer, *Documentation and Argument* and *Philosophy on Bamboo*; Gentz, "Defining Boundaries"; Hilgert, "Text-Anthropologie"; Nylan, "Toward an Archaeology of Writing"; Kern, "Ritual, Text, and the Formation of the Canon," "Creating a Book," and "Xi

shuai"; Harper, "Textual Form of Knowledge"; Yates, "Soldiers, Scribes, and Women"; C. Cook, "Education and the Way"; Barbieri-Low, "Craftsman's Literacy"; Li Feng and Branner, eds., *Writing and Literacy*; Antje Richter, *Letters and Epistolary Culture*; Sanft, *Literate Community* and *Communication and Cooperation*; Hunter, "To Leave or Not To Leave" and *Confucius beyond the Analects*; Shaughnessy, Tsinghua Manuscript *Zheng Wen Gong wen Tai Bo*"; Kornicki, *Languages, Scripts, and Chinese Texts*; Drège, *Les bibliothèques en Chine au temps des manuscrits* (especially 143–73) and *Le papier dans la Chine impériale*; Tsien, *Written on Bamboo and Silk*; Teiser, *Scripture on the Ten Kings* and "Literary Style"; Chen Ruifeng, "Three Short Indigenous Chinese Buddhist Scriptures"; Rong Xinjiang, *Eighteen Lectures on Dunhuang*; Hao Chunwen, *Dunhuang Manuscripts*; Galambos, *Orthography of Early Chinese Writing* and "Punctuation Marks"; and Campany, *Signs from the Unseen Realm*, 17–30, and "Miracle Tales as Scripture Reception."

22. See for example Barbieri-Low, "Craftsman's Literacy"; Yates, "Soldiers, Scribes, and Women"; Sanft, *Literate Community*; and Cutter, "Shen Who Couldn't Write."
23. One of the most satisfactory musings on the complex relationships between extant texts and lineages of masters and disciples, at least in the early period, may be found in Lewis, *Writing and Authority*, 53–97 (though I fear his terminology of "school" is anachronistic).
24. I've learned much from the deft consideration of textual religious cultures in Suit, *Qur'anic Matters*; Lowe, "Discipline of Writing" and *Ritualized Writing*; Jan Yün-hua, "Power of Recitation"; Kuo Li-ying, "La récitation des noms de Buddha"; and Hsu, "Practices of Scriptural Economy," among other works.
25. Blackburn, "Text and the World," 153.
26. Saussy, "Reading From, Reading Into," 206.
27. Here drawing on Fish, "Literature in the Reader," among many other discussions.
28. I first absorbed this strategy for thinking about almost any religious text, practice, or teaching from Davis, *Dojo*.
29. To mention just one spectacular, though idiosyncratic, example of unexpected reception, see Ginzburg, *Cheese and the Worms*.
30. For a salient case of reception-as-destruction see Hubbard, *Absolute Delusion*.
31. Addressing the complexities of this idea and the many ways in which it's been approached is impossible here, but among the studies that have informed my thinking are Tompkins, "Introduction"; Fish, "Literature in the Reader" and "Yet Once More"; Culler, "Literary Competence"; Darnton, "First Steps Toward a History of Reading"; Poulet, "Criticism and the Experience of Interiority"; Bennett, "Texts in History"; Mailloux, "Interpretation and Rhetorical Hermeneutics"; Behr and Fuehrer, "Einführende Notizen zum Lesen in China"; Bennett, "Texts in History"; Carter, "Narrative Readings"; and Iser, *Implied Reader* and "Reading Process."
32. See for example the passages discussed in Campany, *Dreamscape*, 49–52, 61–63.
33. There's a non-negligible number of cases in the archive in which two or many people experience the "same dream" 同夢 on the same night. See Campany, *Dreamscape*, 146 and 213n65.
34. See for example James, *Varieties of Religious Experience*; Proudfoot, *Religious Experience*; Jay, *Songs of Experience*; and Taves, *Fits, Trances, and Visions*. On the persistent, fundamentally Protestant nature of "religious studies," see especially J. Z. Smith, *To Take Place*, 96–117, and "Tillich['s] Remains." Slingerland (*Mind and Body*, 277) misses the point: the claim isn't that Protestantism is taken as "representative of the Western tradition as a whole" but that its emphasis on experience and doctrine and its denigration of ritual as "empty" have profoundly shaped the model of religion

operative (often unconsciously) in much academic work not only in Western societies but also worldwide.

35. Regarding certain esoteric Buddhist rituals of ordination Sharf comments, "A meditative state or liberative experience is identified not on the basis of privileged personal access to its distinctive phenomenology, but rather on the basis of eminently public criteria" ("Experience," 107). See also Sharf, "Buddhist Modernism," and Greene, *Chan Before Chan*.
36. On "specialness" as marking religious experiences see Taves, *Religious Experience Reconsidered*, and Campany, "'Religious' as a Category."
37. Sharf criticizes the common practice of "treating the reports [of religious experiences] as if they provided unmediated access to some originary phenomenal event." This stance, he writes, "fails to grasp the rhetorical logic of appeals to experience. The word 'experience,' insofar as it refers to that which is given to us in the immediacy of perception, signifies that which by definition is nonobjective, that which resists all signification. In other words, the term experience cannot make ostensible a something that exists in the world. The salient characteristic of private experience that distinguishes it from 'objective reality' is thus its unremitting indeterminacy. At the same time, the rhetoric of experience tacitly posits a place where signification comes to an end. . . . The category experience is, in essence, a mere placeholder that entails a substantive if indeterminate terminus for the relentless deferral of meaning" ("Experience," 113). I would have to agree. See also Fitzgerald, "Experience."
38. Orsi, *History and Presence*, 251.
39. Orsi, *History and Presence*, 60, emphasis in original.
40. On individuals' "beliefs" as a non-promising subject for historical research (and a subject of fairly recent origin) see in particular Eidinow, "The (Ancient Greek) Subject"; Needham, *Belief*; and W. C. Smith, *Believing*.
41. The foregoing lines have been shaped by J. Z. Smith, *Imagining Religion*, 36–52, and Satlow, "Tradition."
42. Carruthers, *Craft of Thought*, 2.
43. See Orzech, "Tantric Subjects," 28, on the liturgical creation of a new subject with an alternate subjectivity. Compare Brindley, *Individualism*, 29ff. on "bodily conformism," although it wasn't just bodies that were brought into alignment—it was the whole person, comprising mind, intention, speech, action, and habit.
44. See Hamar and Inoue, eds., *Faith in Buddhism*, and note especially the chapter by Kósa, "Trusting Words," a study of the semantics of *xin* 信 in pre-Buddhist Chinese texts. Kósa concludes that it means "to consider something or someone trustworthy," and not, for example, to assent to doctrinal propositions.
45. Humphrey and Laidlaw, *Archetypal Actions*, 8. See also Eidinow, "The (Ancient Greek) Subject," 64. Peter Burke (*Historical Anthropology*, 223–38) offers useful general observations of the denigration of ritual in many areas of life in the early modern period. "Many people . . . have associated ritual with the shadow rather than the substance, the letter rather than the spirit, the outer husk rather than the inner kernel" (224). This "repudiation of ritual" is hardly unique to early modern Europe (Burke lists examples at 225–26), but it remains the case that the Reformation saw "a great debate, unparalleled in scale and intensity, about the meaning of ritual, its functions, and its proper forms" (227). The impact of this debate wasn't limited to religious contexts; Burke adduces many instances of critiques of ceremony in universities, courts, and even everyday life (232–37).
46. Coakley, "Introduction," 8–9. The Asad quotation is from his "Remarks on the Anthropology of the Body," 48.

47. Krais, "Gender and Symbolic Violence," 169–70, citing Bourdieu, *Logic of Practice*, 56. See Mauss, *Techniques, technologie et civilisation*, 365–94; Asad, "Remarks on the Anthropology of the Body"; Postone, LiPuma, and Calhoun, "Introduction," 4; and Taylor, "To Follow a Rule." Importantly, note Asad's correction to the idea (asserted for example in Jackson, "Knowledge of the Body") "that bodily awareness is at once primordial and universal" (ibid., 48n11); cf. Sahlins, *Western Illusion*, 107, 110.
48. See Brindley, "Capturing the World"; Makeham, *Name and Actuality*, xii, 131, and passim; and for a lovely collection of the relevant texts, see Johnston and Wang Ping, *Mingjia*.
49. See Hadot, *Philosophy as a Way of Life* and *What Is Ancient Philosophy*; Foucault, *Hermeneutics of the Subject* and *Technologies of the Self*; Denecke, *Dynamics of Masters Literature*; and Hunter, *Poetics of Early Chinese Thought*, 172.
50. On the notion of affordances and its usefulness in thinking about cultural constructions of dreaming see Campany, *Dreamscape*, 25–26, 145–55, 159–60.
51. In arriving at this concept and these ways of characterizing it I've drawn on various works. Lakoff and Johnson speak of "systematicity" (*Metaphors We Live By*, 7–9) and "experiential gestalts" (ibid., 81) as well as, importantly, relations of "entailment" between multiple metaphors (ibid., 9). They also speak of "coherence" (ibid., 87–96) but point out that it's not the same thing as consistency in a narrow sense (ibid., 43–45). Johnson observes, "There is a logic of image-schematic structure" (*Meaning of the Body*, 139), and speaks of image schemas as "having internal structures that give rise to constrained inferences" (ibid., 144). Bourdieu speaks of "practical coherence" that is something generative (*Logic of Practice*, 86, 92), and he observes that "practice has a logic which is not that of logic" (*Outline of a Theory of Practice*, 109; cf. Bourdieu, *Logic of Practice*, 86), and this seems somewhat close to what I mean by practical logic. But elsewhere he uses the phrase "practical logic" to mean "a feel for the game" that "works outside conscious control and discourse" (*In Other Words*, 61), and this is *not* what I intend by the phrase. Some readers might insist that my attention to cultural models and practical logic smacks of "structuralism" and ignores the extent to which different groups competed for power and prestige. To them I would respond as does Marshall Sahlins: "We are not soon likely to hear an end to poststructuralist litanies about the contested and unstable character of cultural logics: about categories and perceptions that are different for women and men, chiefs and commoners, rich and poor, this village and that, yesterday and today. All the same, not everything in the contest is contested. . . . In order for categories to be contested at all, there must be a common system of intelligibility, extending to the grounds, means, modes, and issues of disagreement. It would be difficult to understand how a society could function, let alone how any knowledge of it could be constituted, if there were not some meaningful order *in* the differences" ("Goodbye to *Tristes Tropes*," 15). In this book I am operating at the level of the "common system of intelligibility."
52. Schmid, "Revisioning the Buddhist Cosmos," 300–301.
53. Schmid, "Revisioning the Buddhist Cosmos," 301.
54. The quoted phrases are drawn from Crippen and Schulkin, *Mind Ecologies*, 7.
55. See Slingerland, *Mind and Body*, 283–84.
56. The quoted phrases are from Lakoff and Johnson, *Metaphors We Live By*, 5.
57. Some examples of attention to the metaphors that structure Chinese thought and practice include Zhou Boqun, "Subtle and Dangerous"; Allan, *Way of Water*; Buckelew, "Pregnant Metaphor"; Despeux, "Symbolic Pregnancy"; Pankenier, "Weaving Metaphors"; Slingerland: "Conceptions of the Self," "Metaphor and Meaning," and

Effortless Action; Csikszentmihalyi, *Material Virtue*, 141–60; Behuniak, "Hitting the Mark"; Geaney, *Epistemology of the Senses*; Anderl, "Metaphors of 'Sickness and Remedy'"; Raphals, "Body, Mind, and Spirit," 549–50; Bokenkamp, "What Daoist Body?"; Raz, "Birthing the Self"; and Campany, *To Live as Long*, 18–60, "On the Very Idea of Religions," "Buddhism Enters China," and "'Survival' as an Interpretive Strategy."

58. See the collection of early glosses in *Wang Li gu Hanyu zidian*, 30; this array of English analogs mostly draws from Kroll, *Student's Dictionary*, 419.
59. See for example Slingerland, *Effortless Action*, 46, 50, 52–55, 265–66, and the many passages adduced in Weingarten, "Self-Cultivation."
60. See Lakoff and Johnson, *Philosophy in the Flesh*, 267–89.
61. Lakoff and Johnson, *Philosophy in the Flesh*, 268.
62. For a discussion of this passage and its implications see Slingerland, "Conceptions of the Self," 335. On various ways in which the subject-self metaphor system plays out in some seminal early self-cultivation texts in China, see Graziani, "Subject and the Sovereign," and Ahrens, "Conceptual Metaphors of the 'Self.'"
63. See Campany, "On the Very Idea of Religions," 291–305. *Dao* is by far the most common metaphor for ensembles of practices and their goals, but we also find others, some of them involving crossing a body of water (e.g., "wading across the ford" 涉津流 as something one does as a practitioner, or "ferrying across" 渡 as something a salvific being does for others).
64. See Buswell and Gimello, "Introduction," 1–9. But elsewhere Gimello veers off course, as it were, by positing individual practitioners' *experiences* as the test of whether the practices "actually work[ed]" ("Mārga and Culture," 372), as if personal experiences were the sole criterion of success in monastic practice.
65. There is one additional idiom of practice we will see in chapter 1 that seems quite literal and hardly metaphorical at all, and that is the *demonological*, where it's a matter of exogenous beings (seemingly) literally attacking or invading the practitioner. But the matter is complex and would bear further reflection elsewhere. The practical logic involved might be the same regardless of whether the individual practitioner interpreted a text's instructions, or the demons involved, as metaphorical or as literal.
66. Useful overviews of notions of the body include Lewis, *Construction of Space*, 13–76; Elvin, "Between the Earth and Heaven"; and Bokenkamp, "What Daoist Body?"
67. See Buckelew, "Pregnant Metaphor"; Despeux, "Symbolic Pregnancy"; and Raz, "Birthing the Self."
68. Verellen, *Imperiled Destinies*, 7. But the idea of the rather precisely quantifiable deduction of *time* from one's allotted lifespan due to transgressions is evidenced much earlier—see Campany, "Living Off the Books" and *To Live as Long*, 47–60.
69. See Schipper, *Corps taoïste* and "Taoist Body"; Sivin, "State, Cosmos, and Body"; and Bokenkamp, "What Daoist Body?"
70. See for example the cases from the domain of eating and cooking discussed in Sterckx, "Sages, Cooks, and Flavours."
71. See for example M. Brown, *Politics of Mourning*; J. Chen, *Anecdote*, chapters 3–6, and "On Mourning and Sincerity"; Knapp, *Selfless Offspring* and "Accounts of Filial Sons"; and Radice, "Method Mourning."
72. See respectively Campany, *Making Transcendents*; Greene, *Chan Before Chan*, 21–56; and Chen Jinhua, "Meditation Traditions."
73. "Several ordination platforms seem to have been designed to emphasize the intimate presence of the Buddha. These should be considered along with the fact that the *vinaya*, Chan, and esoteric traditions from which the participants in this movement

derived all emphasized *direct lineal succession from the Buddha*" (McRae, "Daoxuan's Vision," 93, emphasis added).

74. See Kleeman, *Celestial Masters*, 240–324, on "the Daoist citizen," a role which began with the receipt of a register 籙 upon first initiation as a child, then ascended through higher ranks to that of libationer 祭酒 and beyond. See also Schipper, "Taoist Body," 374–81.
75. See for example Knapp, *Selfless Offspring* and "*Ru* Reinterpretation of *xiao*."
76. For further thoughts on these audiences and communities of estimation see Campany, *Making Transcendents*, 28–30.
77. *Analects* 2.4; translation roughly following the French of Lévi, *Entretiens de Confucius*, 8.
78. See for example C. Cook, *Ancestors*, 204–41.
79. This is something I tried to demonstrate in some detail in *Making Transcendents*.

Chapter 1

1. *E meng* 惡夢 should not be confused with *e meng* 噩夢 as used in the *Rites of Zhou* (*Zhou li* 周禮) to name one of six categories of dreams pertaining to oneiromancy. (On the passage, see Campany, *Dreamscape*, 53, and the works cited at 180n79.) *E* 噩 is usually defined as frightful or alarming and, so far as I am aware, is never used as an alternate way of writing 惡 (or vice versa). In his commentary on the *Zhou li* passage, Zheng Xuan 鄭玄 (127–200) opines that 噩 here means 驚愕, or "startling." Even this seems distinct from the modern usage of "nightmare." And while 惡夢 appears hundreds of times in the archive, 噩夢 appears only rarely, usually in quotations of or allusions to this *Zhou li* passage.
2. In fact this notion is not newly or uniquely modern (see, e.g., the discussions of Wang Chong's and other theories in Campany, *Dreamscape*, 49–52, 61–63), but it is predominantly so.
3. *Oxford English Dictionary*, s.vv. "nightmare" and "mare." See also Hall, "Evidence for *Maran*." For a study of contemporary dreams involving "encounters with nocturnal pressing spirits" at the intersection of cultures and human physiology, see Adler, *Sleep Paralysis*. My thanks to Chris Jensen for this reference.
4. *Oxford English Dictionary*, s.v. "evil"; and compare Onions, *Oxford Dictionary of English Etymology*, and Skeat, *Etymological Dictionary*, s.v. "evil."
5. *Wang Li gu Hanyu zidian*, 320. On Xu Shen, see CL, 1714–15 (I adopt Knechtges's and Chang's translation of the title of Xu's work).
6. HYD 7:552.
7. See Zürcher, *Conquest*, 23, 36. Dating and attribution based on Nattier, *Guide*, 102–9.
8. *Da zhidu lun*, 25:80a; Pu Chengzhong, "Notes," 36–37. On the importance of this text in China, see McBride, "Dhāraṇī and Spells," 93–94. On its place both in East Asian Buddhism and in modern Buddhology, see Zacchetti, *Da zhidu lun* (a book that only became available as I was completing work on this manuscript). On Nāgārjuna's place in the *imaginaire* of Chinese Buddhism, see Young, *Conceiving*, and BEB 2:727–34.
9. *Chengju guangming sanmeijing*; see Pu Chengzhong, "Notes," 36–37, and on the text's date and linguistic style see Nattier, *Guide*, 94–102.
10. Harbsmeier, "Authenticity," 177, citing Yang Bojun, *Lunyu yizhu*. Michael Nylan observes that in early classicist texts 惡 usually means "ugly" rather than "evil" or "substantially flawed" ("Living Without Sin," 62).
11. See Harper, "Wang Yen-shou's Nightmare Poem," 255n62, 269, 273, and "Note on Nightmare Magic," 72–73.

12. *Zhen'gao* 8.12a5–6. Lady Right Blossom, thirteenth daughter of the Queen Mother of the West 西王母, would soon be betrothed to the official Xu Mi. On the dating of these particular lines, see Bokenkamp, *Fourth-Century Daoist Family*, 108–14, and for a slightly different translation see idem., 120. This line was incorporated verbatim by Du Guangting 杜光庭 (850–933) into his much later hagiography of the goddess (*Yongcheng jixian lu* 5.3b6–7). Regarding other Daoist methods involving headrests and objects placed inside, see Campany, *To Live as Long*, 337–38, 517–18.
13. According to Stephen Bokenkamp, "there is no direct evidence in the form of queries from Sima Yu that he ever received any of the materials Yang's Perfected marked for him," but indirect evidence (involving the manner in which certain pages had been copied) suggests they may have been displayed at court during his brief reign (personal communication, 4 September 2020).
14. See Campany, "Secrecy and Display"; "Long-Distance Specialists"; and *Making Transcendents*, 88–129. More on the esotericizing dynamic in chapter 3.
15. See Wilms, *Divine Farmer's Classic*, 301. Many later pharmacopoeias, including Sun Simo's 孫思邈 *Essential Prescriptions for Urgent Ills* (*Beiji qianjin yaofang* 備急千金要方, written between 650 and 659), incorporate versions of this passage. I explain more on 魘 below in the section "Expunging Dream Pollution." "Wood fragrance" 木香, the root of *Aucklandia lappa*, was similarly recommended for apotropaic purposes; see Wilms, ibid., 54.
16. *Shexiang* is mentioned several times in chapter 17 of *Baopuzi neipian*, including a passage in which Ge Hong, after listing several effective apotropaia, writes: "If you are [headed into mountains and] end up unable to obtain any of these [other] medicinals, to simply wear a pouch of good fresh deer musk at the belt is also quite effective" 若卒不能得此諸藥者，但可帶好生麝香亦佳, *Baopuzi neipian* 307). This type of musk also figures in many medicinal recipes and in other pharmacopoeia; for a listing of its mentions in medical manuscripts found at Dunhuang and in Turfan, see Despeux, ed., *Médicine*, 1201.
17. On the medicinal use of spices and fragrances generally, see Di Lu and Vivienne Lo, "Scent and Synaesthesia."
18. See Li Jianmin, "Contagion," 203, and Strickmann, *Chinese Magical Medicine*, 111.
19. See Li Jianmin, "Suibing."
20. See Li Jianmin, "They Shall Expel," 1113–23. These entities are discussed below in the section "Dream Agents and Idioms of Practice."
21. See Li Jianmin, "Contagion," 203, and "They Shall Expel," 1123.
22. 感生死之氣 may refer obliquely to *saṃsāra* while still evoking contact with death pollution. My thanks to Stephen Bokenkamp for this suggestion.
23. *Zhubing yuanhou lun jiaozhu*, 690–91, modifying Li Jianmin, "Contagion," 203. 而方不皆顯其名也 could also mean "but [medical] methods do not reveal all of their names."
24. *Zhubing yuanhou lun jiaozhu*, 695, translation modifying Li Jianmin, "Contagion," 203.
25. This is depicted in an anecdote attributed to *Youming lu* 幽冥錄 (ca. 440) and preserved in TPGJ 320/17.
26. Or "painting on tiles and writing talismans," as understood in Tian Xiaofei, *Family Instructions*, 83. On talismans (*fu* 符), an important technological component of self-cultivational practice and of material culture throughout the period considered here, see Raz, *Emergence of Daoism*, 127–76; Bumbacher, *Empowered Writing*; Steavu, *Writ of the Three Sovereigns*, 49–62; Robson, "Signs of Power"; Copp, "Manuscript Culture"; Mollier, "Talismans"; Campany, *To Live as Long*, 61–69, 78–79, 192–93.

27. *Yanshi jiaxun*, 98; see Li Jianmin, "Contagion," 201.
28. *Huangdi jiuding shendan jingjue* 1.1a4–5; see also Pregadio, *Great Clarity*, 85, and Campany, *To Live as Long*, 39. On this scripture see TTC, 378–79. Cf. the similar passage in *Taiji zhenren jiuzhuan huandan jing yaojue* 4b9–10, translated in Pregadio, *Great Clarity*, 85. On this latter text see TTC, 102–3. On Daoist bathing practices see Ding Huang, "Daojiao de muyu tanjiu."
29. "If any of the personal entourage or the six relatives come to see the sick practitioner, they must not include in their midst any individual who takes meat, wine, or the five pungent herbs. Should such a person be present, he or she must never be allowed to approach the patient's side. Otherwise the dying person will lose right mindfulness, demons and spirits will disturb him, and the patient, dying in delirium, will plummet into the three unfortunate rebirth paths" 行者等眷屬六親若來看病, 勿令有食酒肉五辛人. 若有, 必不得向病人邊. 即失正念, 鬼神交亂, 病人狂死墮三惡道. *Guannian Amituofo xiang haisanmei gongde famen* 47:24b29–c2; translation modifying Stevenson, "Pure Land Buddhist Worship," 378–79. On Shandao see Atone, "Shan-tao"; Cheung, "Comparative Study"; Pas, "Shan-tao's Interpretation" and *Visions*; Chappell, "Chinese Buddhist Interpretations" and "Formation of the Pure Land Movement."
30. *Taiping jing hejiao*, 90; translation modifying Hendrischke, *Scripture on Great Peace*, 209.
31. The same advice appears at *Zhen'gao* 10.7a10–b1, where Tao Hongjing adds a note explaining that "high" in this case means three *chi* 尺 (about thirty inches) or higher. Another discussion of regulations for sleeping (specifically the wearing of clothing and the placement of shoes) appears in *Zhoushi mingtong ji* 1.14a; cf. the other sources cited in ZSMT, 84.
32. Compare the passage at *Zhen'gao* 10.7b2–5: "The rooms where people sleep should be *sheng*. If they're *sheng* then they're receptive to numinous *qi*; if not, then they will receive stale *qi*. And when stale *qi* disorders people's homes, then whatever they engage in will not succeed and whatever they attempt will not come to pass. They should also bathe themselves frequently. If they don't, there is no hope for them" 人臥室宇當令潔盛, 盛則受靈氣, 不盛則受故氣. 故氣之亂人室宇者所為不成, 所作不立. 一身亦爾當數洗沐澡潔, 不爾無冀, on which Tao comments interestingly: "The word *sheng* means 'pure.' The Central Kingdom originally had no word for 'pure,' so *sheng* was used. This is true throughout all the scriptures" 盛字是淨義. 中國本無淨字, 故作盛也. 諸經中通如此. *Sheng* 盛 usually means "hale, thriving, flourishing, exuberant" (Kroll, *Student's Dictionary*, 410).
33. *Nai* 乃 carries considerable force here: only because of his illness-induced delirium was he able to see the demon's normally invisible machinations. In line with the god's explanation of the physics of the process, I understand 下 as indicating that the demon bored through the wall near the floor.
34. *Zhen'gao* 15.9b2–5. My translation differs slightly from the partial one in Nickerson, "Great Petition," 253n14.
35. Copp, *Body Incantatory*, 145–47. Closely related was the Buddhist discourse that characterized right knowledge and divine power as "perfuming" their surroundings—a discourse that gave form to ritual practice in (for example) the use of perfume boxes as reliquaries (see Brown, "Bodily Relics," 200–201; also relevant is the technical Buddhist discourse on the relationship between karma and consciousness as one of "perfuming": see DDB, s.v. *xunxi* 熏習). Writing about his travels (in the years 629–645) to Buddhist sites in Central and South Asia, Xuanzang often described stupas and other shrines as emitting light, music, pleasant fragrance, fire, and

smoke, and as healing sickness and triggering other miraculous events (see Beal, *Si-Yu-Ki*, 1:60, 66, 67, 94, 101, 103, 121, 138; also Drewes, "Revisiting," 108–9). On *dhāraṇīs*, in addition to the Copp book see Overby, "Why Don't We Translate Spells"; McBride, "Dhāraṇī and Spells" and "Practical Buddhist Thaumaturgy"; Copp, "*Dhāraṇī* Scriptures" and "Notes on the Term *Dhāraṇī*"; Sørensen, "Spells and Magical Practices"; Bokenkamp, "Sources," 464–65; and Strickmann, *Chinese Magical Medicine*, 89–122.

36. See S. Cook, *Bamboo Texts*, 697–702; Puett, "Innovation as Ritualization," 28, and "Theodicies of Discontinuity," 57–58; Brindley, "Music, Cosmos," 21.

37. *Mengzi* 6A15, translation modifying Geaney, "Guarding," 121. See also Geaney, *Epistemology of the Senses*.

38. *Xunzi jijie*, 17.309. My translation of the first phrase modifies Geaney, "Guarding," 121; cf. Hutton, *Xunzi*, 176.

39. See Greene, "Pratītyasamutpāda," 253–57. On the Buddhist emphasis on vigilance regarding the "doors" of the senses see for example Holt, *Discipline*, 73–81; Kalupahana, *History*, 32. Har Dayal writes: "It is almost impossible to give an adequate idea of the vehemence and pertinacity with which Buddhist writers have preached the duty of curbing, controlling, suppressing, crushing and conquering the senses" (*Bodhisattva Doctrine*, 122).

40. An intriguing exception is the Mohist corpus, where the senses are sometimes metaphorically construed as "five roads" 五路. See Johnston, *Mozi*, 526–27.

41. "Moral decay, strategic failure, political ineptitude, and social perversion were equated with foul and putrid influences, the stench of which would disgust both the spirit world and human society" (Sterckx, *Food, Sacrifice, and Sagehood*, 169). Conversely, "Scent as a conduit for contact with the spirit world is a recurring theme in sacrificial liturgy, ritual song, and temple hymns" (ibid., 170).

42. On birth itself, and newborns, as polluting to the mother and others who came in contact, see Kinney, *Representations*, 167–68. Wang Chong's chapter on the "Four Avoidances" 四諱 discusses pollution dangers of pregnancy, birth, and nursing; see *Lunheng jiaoshi*, 975–78.

43. *Sun zhenren beiji qianjin yaofang*, 3.16a10–b2; translation modifying Yates, "Medicine," 165–66. On Sun Simo (Simo is also read Simiao) see Sivin, *Alchemy*, 81–144.

44. *Sun zhenren beiji qianjin yaofang*, 3.17a6; translation following Yates, "Medicine," 166. Compare the cautions against looking at (*shi* 視) what is ritually incorrect (*fei li* 非禮) in the Warring States-period text "Gentleman's Performance of Ritual" (*Junzi wei li* 君子為禮) attested in bamboo slips purchased by the Shanghai Museum; see Csikszentmihalyi, "Ethics and Self-Cultivation," 541.

45. Harper, *Early Chinese Medical Literature*, 379. See also Yates, "Medicine," 161; Milburn, "Marked," 12–13; Choo, "Lump," 187; Kinney, "Dyed Silk," 27–28; Furth, "From Birth to Birth," 170; Bokenkamp, "Simple Twists."

46. On the complex problems surrounding what counted as "Confucian" in this period and what this label means—problems that will crop up again at the outset of chapter 3 (where more discussions of this issue are cited)—see Nylan, *Five "Confucian" Classics*, 2–3.

47. Geaney, "Guarding," 123. Yates further explains that "music for Xunzi was something that could flow like a noxious vaporous essence or *qi* 氣 through a person's bodily orifices, penetrating the boundaries of the sense organs, and reaching ultimately the heart-mind" ("Purity and Pollution," 502). On the cosmological and political significances of boundaries and surfaces in late imperial times, see Zito, "Silk and Skin."

48. *Xunzi jijie* 20.379, following Geaney's translation ("Guarding," 123); cf. Hutton, *Xunzi*, 218.
49. *Xunzi jijie* 16.303, again following Geaney's agreeably literal translation (123); cf. Hutton, *Xunzi*, 171.
50. See Rom, "Polyphonic Thinking"; Brindley, "Cosmic Power of Sound"; and Ashmore, "Art of Discourse."
51. This idea is expressed, for example, in this passage from *Discussions at the White Tiger Hall* (*Baihu tong*, 1st–3rd centuries?): "Music is used to simulate heaven, the rites are used to model earth. There is no human being who does not contain the *qi* of heaven and earth and the nature of the five constants. Therefore, music is that by which [people] are purified and their pollution reversed; the rites are that by which their corruption is dammed up and their excesses given limits" 樂以象天, 禮以法地. 人無不含天地之氣, 有五常之性者. 故樂所以蕩滌, 反其邪惡也; 禮所以防淫泆, 節其侈靡 (*Baihutong shuzheng*, 93–94; cf. Yates, "Purity and Pollution," 502–3). On the difficulty of dating the *Baihutong* see ECT, 347–50. Even non-Ruist writers focusing on the relationship between language and reality stressed this essential social and self-cultivational function of rites and music; see for example Johnston and Wang, *Mingjia*, 72–73.
52. Cf. Yates, "Purity and Pollution," 502n35, and compare the rendition (with Chinese text) in Knoblock and Riegel, *Annals of Lü Buwei*, 423.
53. *Xunzi jijie*, 170; translation modified from Yates, "Purity and Pollution," 508.
54. See the remarks in Csikszentmihalyi, "Ethics and Self-Cultivation," 523–25. Note, however, that in translating the characteristic phrase 禮坊民所淫 from this chapter Csikszentmihalyi psychologizes it—"ritual serves as an embankment dam to prevent the rise of the people's depraved *thoughts*" (525, emphasis mine)—weakening, or certainly altering, the argument embedded in the line.
55. The single sustained treatment I'm aware of at this writing is Yates, "Purity and Pollution"; see also several essays by Li Jianmin treating this topic as it relates to medical texts, and Schipper, "Purity and Strangers." Verellen, *Imperiled Destinies*, 60–67, treats ritual pollution in Daoist liturgical practice, and C. Cook, "Moonshine and Millet," treats purification in the context of feasting in ancient times. Lowe, *Ritualized Writing* and "Discipline of Writing," are seminal studies of pollution ideas and purification practices surrounding the copying of Buddhist sutras in eighth-century Japan. Kim, "Filth," instructively treats many aspects of pollution discourse and practice in medieval Japan.
56. See Douglas, *Purity and Danger*, 132.
57. This oversight is recognized in Yates, "Purity and Pollution," 499–500. Where I render 淫學流說 in *Annals of Master Lü* as "learning that pollutes and theories that corrupt," Knoblock and Riegel give "wayward learning and heterodox theories" (*Annals of Lü Buwei*, 423). Their translation not only occludes the pollution discourse at work in the passage (and projects an "orthodoxy" model where it doesn't belong) but also misses the register in which the impact of such learning on people is denounced. Where (following Yates) I render 防淫除邪 in *Xunzi* as "dike against pollution and exorcise the noxious," Watson gives "prevent licentiousness and wipe out evil," while Hutton has "prevent licentiousness and eliminate perversity" (Watson, *Hsün Tzu*, 49; Hutton, *Xunzi*, 78). Patricia Ebrey (*Confucianism and Family Rituals*, 27) notes that some *Li ji* passages similarly compare rituals to "dikes that keep people from impulses toward lawlessness and licentiousness." As Yates observes, such translations of words like *yin* 淫 and *xie* 邪 not only sanitize the pollution discourse out of them but also reroute their reference, construing them as "pertaining to the inner feelings or

character of the individual, rather than to any heteropathic agent external to him" ("Purity," 500). In the *Records of the Hidden and Visible Realms* (*Youming lu* 幽冥錄) story of men who used old coffin wood to fashion carriages, where I render 注連凶禍 as "infusion-caused disasters"—*zhulian* being an unmistakable reference to pollution that clings to those who've been contacted (see Li Jianmin, "Contagion," 201–5)—Zhang Zhenjun gives "the series of disasters never stopped" (*Hidden*, 90), missing the plain sense of the text.

58. See Kinney, *Representations*, 167–73.
59. On slaves and convicts as socially dead and hence polluting, see Yates, "Slavery," 299, 316–18. On views of physically deformed or mutilated persons, see Milburn, "Marked," and Chapman, "Unwholesome." On ethnic others as impurifying, see Abramson, "Deep Eyes," 205, 314–15, 397.
60. Douglas, *Purity and Danger*, 35.
61. Douglas, *Purity and Danger*, 160. See also Douglas, *Implicit Meanings*, 47–59.
62. J. Smith, "Towards Interpreting Demonic Powers," 429–30.
63. The passage occurs in the inner chapters 內篇, conventionally dated to around 320 BCE, but for a trenchant critique of this dating see Klein, "Were There 'Inner Chapters'?"
64. *Zhuangzi jijie*, 11; translation modifying Graham, *Chuang-tzu*, 50, emphasis added. See also Campany, *Dreamscape*, 41.
65. My thanks to Alice Cheang for pointing out the range of meanings of *jiao* 交.
66. The three Lords Mao are as follows: the eldest, Mao Ying 茅盈, often referred to by his title in the Shangqing-imagined celestial imperium as the Lord Director of Lifespans 司命君; the middle, Mao Gu 茅固, byname Jiwei 季偉, often referred to as the Lord Certifier of Registers 定錄君; and the youngest, Mao Zhong 茅衷, byname Sihe 思和 (Tao Hongjing provides his given name at *Zhen'gao* 7.4b9), often referred to as Lord Protector of Lifespans 保命君. They'll appear again in chapter 3.
67. *Zhen'gao* 7.6b10–7a7; Yoshikawa and Mugitani, *Zhen'gao jiaozhu*, 231; translation is that of Bokenkamp, *Ancestors and Anxiety*, 142.
68. Compare the moment in some Buddhist narratives of the Buddha's descent from the heaven of the thirty-three (where he'd been preaching to his departed mother) when the gods, accompanying him in his descent to earth, are unable to bear the stench of humanity. The Buddha emits a sandalwood fragrance that dispels the miasma and allows the gods to continue their descent (Schopen, "Fragrance," 13).
69. For a list of terms see Yates, "Purity and Pollution," 493–94.
70. See T. Wilson, "Sacrifice," 271–77, one of the few adequate discussions of this important aspect of religious practice in China.
71. Exactly how the adoption of a different bodily form protects the god from impurity is unclear. On reading this passage, Chris Jensen (personal communication) suggested that perhaps the god "slips on Xu Hui's form like a disposable glove." On simulacra as they relate to dreams, see Campany, *Dreamscape*, 75–79.
72. For a summary of this jumbled text (which skips over the passage translated here), see Shinohara, "Removal of Sins," 253–72. See also Swanson, "Dandala, Dhāraṇī, and Denarii." On the terms *vaipulya*, *vaidalya*, or *vaitulya* (often rendered into Chinese as 方等 or 大方等) as designations for certain sutras, see Karashima, "Who Composed," and Skilling, "Vaidalya," 84–97. Whatever its shades of meaning in Indic texts, in China the term came to be used early on as a classifier for Mahāyāna sutras: see Zacchetti, "Notions and Visions," 93–96.
73. This god appears among the characters listening to the Buddha's preaching of other Mahāyāna sutras, such as the *Lotus* (see, e.g., *Zheng fahua jing* 9:130b7).

74. Malignant or incompetent officials are a threat from which many of our texts promise to protect their upholders, as we'll see below. In Indic contexts the expression being translated here probably just referred to government personnel of all kinds and levels, and 縣官 may have been understood similarly by Chinese readers (see Loewe, "Organs of Han Imperial Government"). It could have also been read as specifically indicating local-level officers—the sort that ordinary people were most likely to encounter.
75. *Da fangdeng tuoluoni jing* 21:654b1–21.
76. P2682 (available electronically at https://gallica.bnf.fr/ark:/12148/btv1b83033424/f1.image.r=Pelliot 202682) contains a medieval version of the demonological text *Baize jingguai tu* 白澤精怪圖, including illustrations of demons. A thorough description of its contents may be found in Kalinowski, ed., *Divination et société*, 455–58; see also Harper, "Demonography."
77. *Baopuzi neipian*, 308, mentions a *Baizetu jiudingji* 白澤圖九鼎記. See also Campany, *Strange Writing*, 42, 123; Jiang Shaoyuan, *Zhongguo gudai lüxing*, 40–41, 56; Poo Mu-chou, "Ritual," 307.
78. See Harper, "Demonography" and "Spellbinding." As Harper writes, "We are dealing . . . not with the textual history of a single document. . ., but with the identification of a sub-class of demonographic literature ascribed to White Marsh" ("Note on Nightmare Magic," 71).
79. My translation is partially indebted to Harper's in "Note on Nightmare Magic," 72, and "Textual Form of Knowledge," 54.
80. For an account of the excavation and overview of the relevant texts, see Harper, "Demonography," 462–70.
81. The graph *gao/*kaw* 皋 can mean "announcement" and functions here to open the frame of the incantation, compelling its recipients to pay attention.
82. For the template's "so-and-so" (*mou* 某) the dreamer is to substitute his or her own name.
83. There is a pun here between the text's "broadcloth" (*fu* 幅) and "blessings" (*fu* 福) and "wealth" (*fu* 富). Textiles were themselves, of course, a form of wealth.
84. Translation modified from Harper, "Textual Form of Knowledge," 52; cf. Harper, "Note on Nightmare Magic," 72–73. Photographs, transcriptions, and annotations of the Shuihudi daybook passages may be consulted in *Shuihudi Qin mu zhujian*, plates 134–35 and pages 210 and 247. See also the listings in Harper and Kalinowski, eds., *Books of Fate*, 449, 452. On this passage and others involving Qinqi and similar early dispellers of nightmares see also Liu Zhao, *Chutu jianbo wenzi*, 203–6, 213–16. On early exorcistic practices more generally see Harper, "Spellbinding" and "Demonography," and Poo Mu-chou, "Ritual," 305–9. On post-dream exorcisms in early modern times see Vance, "Exorcising Dreams and Nightmares."
85. Both characters are non-standard. The first is 豸 + 今, and the second is 立 + 奇.
86. The main difference is that the Dunhuang text advises readers to go over dream polluters' heads, in effect, and speak directly with their superior, as will be seen below.
87. Incidentally, one might wonder why such texts would have been entombed with deceased persons. Were the dead thought to continue to dream within their tombs, causing their souls to wander outside its confines? Alain Thote surmises that common reasons for burying texts in tombs might have included these: "First, the placement of manuscripts with texts of a technical nature was intended to personally benefit the tomb occupant by permitting the deceased to engage in activities in the otherworld in the same manner as during life. . . . Second, manuscripts placed in

tombs may have benefited the tomb occupant indirectly as objects imbued with apotropaic properties that protected the deceased from negative influences and harm that arose post-mortem" ("Daybooks," 16–17).

88. The Shuihudi B passage simply ends with the incantation, leaving implicit the hoped-for result.
89. See, for example, Yates, "Medicine for Women," 150–51; Schafer, "Bathing," 59–60; Lin Fushi, "Medical Knowledge and Uses of Hair." On hairstyles and hats see Dien, *Six Dynasties Civilization*, 312–14.
90. Abramson, "Deep Eyes," 334.
91. Harper, "Note on Nightmare Magic," 73n7.
92. In the sense developed in Austin, *How to Do Things*, and Searle, "What Is a Speech Act?" For a direct application of their theory of performative speech to religious liturgy see Udemmadu and Umezi, "Language of the Sacraments."
93. Harper, *Early Chinese Medical Literature*, 165. For discussions and examples of breath magic see Harper, ibid., 163–67, and Harper, "Wang Yen-shou's Nightmare Poem," 279–80. See also the passage at *Baopuzi neipian jiaoshi* 114, translated in Campany, *To Live as Long*, 285.
94. For a bit more on Qinqi see Yan Changgui, "Daybooks," 227–28.
95. Sahlins, *Western Illusion*, 92.
96. P2682 recto, https://gallica.bnf.fr/ark:/12148/btv1b83033424/f8.item.r=Pelliot 202682.
97. *Hou Han shu*, 3127–28. See further Bodde, *Festivals*, 75–138; Nishioka, "Akumu no zō"; Knechtges, *Wen xuan*, 290–97; Harper, "Textual Form of Knowledge," 55. Note the further mentions of dreams in Bodde, *Festivals*, 79, 82, 85, 97–98.
98. Respectively, Harper, "Textual Form of Knowledge," 54 (where the graph 常 is omitted), and Harper, "Nightmare," 72.
99. Harper, "Note on Nightmare Magic," 73n7.
100. See Campany, "Meanings of Cuisines" and *Making Transcendents*, 62–87.
101. On transcendents neither needing food offerings nor accepting payment for services, see Campany, *Making Transcendents*, 171–75, 181–83. On what the "reciprocity" structuring many divine-human relations in the ancient world was—and wasn't—see the astute remarks in Eyl, *Signs*, 170–212, who argues that reciprocity (both between gods and humans and among humans of unequal status), unlike market exchange, did not seek precise equivalence for goods or services, was asymmetrical, and demanded things like respect and honor from humans. Reciprocity amounted to the assumption that people and gods share mutual interests and care for one another, not that offerings and prayers constituted a mere business transaction. Eyl argues that the apostle Paul "engage[d] in reciprocity with God, especially linking faithfulness to powers of divination and wonderworking" (198), but that this relationship was not a matter of the well-known formula *do ut des* ("I give so that you will give") to which ancient religiosity is often reduced by conservative scholars seeking to distance early Christianity from it so as to make their imagined version of Christianity appear "unique" and detached from its milieux. Whether Eyl's insight applies in the Chinese case merits further investigation.
102. Thus Strickmann (*Mantras et mandarins*, 295) and the Taishō editors. Sørensen ("Central Divinities," 104) attributes the translation to Amoghavajra.
103. Other troubles (jealous enemies and social disharmony) are also mentioned; from the wording it's unclear to me whether these are in addition to the foul dream or are its subject.
104. *Xukongzang pusa wen qi fo tuoluoni zhou jing* 21:562c.
105. Here termed "seals" 印, short for "hand seals" 手印 or *mudrās*.

106. *Tuoluoni jijing* 18:885a. See Orzech and Sørensen, "*Mudrā*, Mantra, Mandala," 80.
107. See the extensive discussion and translation in Harper, "Wang Yen-shou's Nightmare Poem," and Campany, *Dreamscape*, 35–36.
108. "In your mouth" is implicit in *Sun zhenren beiji qianjin yaofang* and *Taiqing Daolin shesheng lun*; the *Yunji qiqian* version (35.13b) makes it explicit with 以含水向東方噀之.
109. Here quoting the version in *Taiqing Daolin shesheng lun* 11b5–7. As noted in TTC, 362, this is a Tang work with similarities to chapters 81–83 of *Sun zhenren beiji qianjin yaofang* (in which the corresponding passage is found at 81.16a5–7). Closely similar lines appear in *Yunji qiqian* 35.13b.
110. Compare the method recommended in a Dunhuang text written in Tibetan and translated into Chinese in Zheng Binlin and Yang Ping, *Dunhuang ben mengshu*, 209–14, where upon waking one first washes one's face, then transfers the pollution of the dream into a piece of wood and, pronouncing an incantation, burns it. Peachwood in particular had long been viewed as especially effective in repelling unclean spirits, something frequently mentioned in texts and also attested to by archeological discoveries of apotropaic peachwood figurines in tombs. (See, for example, Yan Changgui, "Daybooks," 230.) It's natural, then, to find that some methods prescribe writing talismans on peachwood planks to expel dream-causing demons; see, for example, the passage in *Yunji qiqian* 81.17a–18b discussed and partially translated below.
111. *Yangxing yanming lu* 1.19a (and cf. *Yunji qiqian* 32.16b). On this text see TTC, 345–36, and Stanley-Baker, "Cultivating Body." The same injunction is found elsewhere, such as *Dongxuan lingbao daoxue keyi* 2.13a6–7.
112. *Liji jijie* 114; cf. Legge, *Sacred Books, Part 3*, 103, and Yates, "Purity and Pollution," 525–26.
113. *Xunzi jijie* 381. Again I depart from less literal, more moralizing renditions, such as those found in Watson, *Hsün tzu*, 116, and Hutton, *Xunzi*, 220 (whose "foul doctrines" for 惡言 particularly obscures the meaning).
114. Poirier, "This Is Good Country," 117.
115. See Mageo, "Theorizing Dreaming," 20. For more on the impacts and implications of the telling of dreams, see Campany, *Dreamscape*, 74, 127–29.
116. On this text see Campany, *Dreamscape*, 80–87, and works cited there.
117. My transcription is based on the digitized image of the manuscript at http://gallica.bnf.fr/ark:/12148/btv1b8300230n/f16.item.r=P 203908 [8 March 2022] and the one given in Zheng Binglin, *Dunhuang xieben*, 177. In translating this passage I consulted Drège and Drettas, "Oniromancie," 387. The last couple of lines seem out of place, perhaps added as an afterthought (see Zheng Binglin, *Dunhuang xieben*, 202n263).
118. The manuscript has two characters, 赤 and 陽, each followed by a mark (resembling a semicolon) that indicates a previous character or phrase is to be repeated. Hence, several scholars have transcribed this phrase as 赤赤陽陽. However, Zheng Binglin argues that we should instead read it as 赤陽赤陽 (*Dunhuang xieben*, 202n261). Drège and Drettas say, on the other hand, that Zheng's transcription is mistaken ("Oniromancie," 389n43). Based on the discussion of repetition marks in Galambos ("Punctuation Marks," 345–46), as well as on a text in *Yunji qiqian* 81.17a–18b prescribing a similar incantation—which has the wording 日出東方,赫赫堂堂 (this method too involves the use of three talismans, although they're different ones)—I fear Zheng Binglin is wrong on this point.
119. See Knoblock and Riegel, *Annals of Lü Buwei*, 98.
120. On the line in the "Quli" 曲禮 chapter of *Li ji* that reads 齊者不樂不弔, "One who is purifying himself [before a sacrifice] must neither listen to music nor offer condolences

[to the recently bereaved]" (*Liji jijie* 75), James Legge felt it necessary to comment, "What would distract the mind from this [preparation for the sacrifice] must be eschewed" (*Sacred Books, Part 3*, 87n3). I submit that while mental focus was certainly a component of both the preparation for the rite and its performance (as Zheng Xuan 鄭玄 notes in his commentary), the main point of the line was to underscore the need for the ritualist to maintain ritual purity. Exposure to music or the bereaved would put him in a polluted state and thus disqualify him from performing his proper role.

121. The "Awakening at Cheng" chapter of *Yi Zhou shu* 逸周書 similarly has the Zhou king and his son "bowing to the auspicious dream" (*bai jimeng* 拜吉夢) after interpreting it in the royal temple. See Shaughnessy, "Of Trees," 606.
122. Sahlins, *Western Illusion*, 92.
123. See Kohn, "Kōshin," parts 1–3, and Pregadio, ed., *Encyclopedia of Taoism*, 446–47.
124. *Yunji qiqian* 81.17a–18b.
125. The removal of impurity and illness by means of washing of the intestines (or, more broadly, the intestines as the specific locus of impurity in the body) was something of a trope in early medieval texts. See for example *Baopuzi neipian jiaoshi*, 224; Campany, "Meanings of Cuisines," 41–42, 48; Lewis, *Construction of Space*, 48; Salguero, "Flock of Ghosts," 96–97, 101, 104–5; Gjertson, *Miraculous Retribution*, 18–19; Campany, *Making Transcendents*, 80, 82, and *Signs from the Unseen Realm*, 132–33; Wright, *Studies*, 65.
126. Such uses of specific dream images are the subject of chapter 2. Here the focus is on the purificatory response to foul dreams, but these passages are examples of the co-presence of multiple paradigms in the same passages.
127. *Taishang lingbao wufu xu* 2.23b6–24b8, seemingly the source for the unattributed passage (with the modification noted) in *Yunji qiqian* 82.5a–b. Both passages go on to mention the three worms 三蟲 as well. On this text see Raz, "Creation" and *Emergence of Daoism*; and TTC, 232–33.
128. *Taishang lingbao wufu xu* 2.23b7–24a2.
129. Both the DZ and ZHDZ editions give *lan chu* 爛出, which would have its own practical logic, but I suspect this might be an error for *lian chu* 煉出, "to refine away"—which would be an example of this metallurgical metaphor's application to the exorcistic and purification process.
130. Elsewhere we'll see seals deployed for other purposes. On the use of seals in Daoist, Buddhist, imperial, and other rituals, see Strickmann, *Chinese Magical Medicine* and "Seal of the Law"; S. Huang, "Daoist Seals"; Copp, *Body Incantatory*, 44–54, and "Manuscript Culture"; Orzech, "Tantric Subjects," 29–36; and Barrett, "Images of Printing."
131. *Zhengyi fawen xiuzhen zhiyao*, 19b–20a, modifying the translation in Strickmann, "Seal of the Law," 19. On this text see TTC, 488.
132. The text is lost except in quotations, including the extensive ones in *Secret Instructions for Ascent to Perfection* (*Dengzhen yinjue* 登真隱訣), Tao Hongjing's annotated anthology of instructions for a wide range of practices compiled between 492 and 514 (see TTC, 201–5). See Cedzich, "Organon"; Kleeman, *Celestial Masters*, 354; and Verellen, *Imperiled Destinies*, 20, 85, 94, 110. Compare the passage at *Yunji qiqian* 45:10b–11a in a section of protocols for presenting oneself at the courts of the Perfected on specified days. Also compare *Yunji qiqian* 45.16a–18a, an incantation for use when lying down to sleep 寢臥時祝 (but it does not mention dreams); the main deities to whom the incantation is addressed in this case are those of Fengdu 酆都 and the Six Heavens.
133. *Wu* 忤 has the further sense of "refractory," implying an agent has willfully transgressed bounds.

134. *Dengzhen yinjue* 3.13a. I emend 冢 to 家 per Tao Hongjing's suggestion. My translation partly borrows from that in Bokenkamp, "Image Work."

135. *Baopuzi neipian jiaoshi*, 324. The Auxiliary star (*fuxing* 輔星, Alcor [80 Ursae majoris]) was the minute companion or assistant to the sixth in the series of seven stars of the Northern Dipper (see, e.g., *Jin shu* 11.291); in Daoist frameworks it was often seen as an assistant specifically to the Dipper-god known simply as the Perfected Person 真人. Several contemplative practices involving the star are prescribed in *Shangqing wozhong jue*, a text attributed to Tao Hongjing but probably a later, condensed version of Tao's *Dengzhen yinjue* done by someone else (see TTC, 628). For example, see *Shangqing wozhong jue* 1.1b–2a (where the adept receives texts from the god inhabiting the star and has his name inscribed in the rolls of the blessed that are kept there), 2.3a–b, and 3.4a–b (where the adept visualizes the gods known as the Three Ones descending from the Auxiliary star to take up residence in the Three Palaces within his person). On related practices and ideas, see Stanley-Baker, "Palpable Access," 120–22; Robinet, *Méditation*, 192–95, 301–13; Andersen, "Talking," 2n3.

136. A critique of the practice in the early Celestial Masters' *Daode jing* 道德經 commentary, *Xiang'er zhu* 想爾注, suggests that the practice wasn't new in Ge Hong's day. See Bokenkamp, *Early Daoist Scriptures*, 89, 144n26.

137. See for example Roth, *Original Tao*, 1–9. *Taiping jing* has much to say on *shouyi* and already recognizes a diversity of recommended methods for it (see *Taiping jing hejiao*, 409–10, and Kaltenmark, "Ideology," 41–43). See also Xiao Dengfu, "Daojiao shouyi xiuchifa."

138. See Kleeman, *Celestial Masters*, 99–100, and Campany, *To Live as Long*, 246–47.

139. *Baopuzi neipian jiaoshi*, 324.

140. Versions of the passage appear (with or without attribution) in *Shangqing wozhong jue* 2.6b6–7a10, *Shangqing xiuxing jingjue* 4b6–5b10, *Shangqing xiuxing yaoshi jing* 5a6–6b4, *Zhengyi fawen xiuzhen zhiyao* 2b5–3b5, *Ziting neibi jue xiuxing fa* 6a1–7b1, *Daodian lun* 4.4b3–5b1, *Yunji qiqian* 45.20a–b, and elsewhere.

141. I follow a Sinological convention in translating *xuan* 玄 thus, but as Paul Kroll has explained, "The specific quality of *xuan* is to be translucent, in the strict sense of 'allowing the passage of light, yet diffusing it so as not to render bodies lying beyond clearly visible'" ("Between Something and Nothing," 409, quoting the *OED*).

142. One of the nine palaces in the head, a crucial site in Daoist practices of many sorts. See Yamada Toshiaki, "Deigan kyūkyū setsu kō"; Kakiuchi Tomoyuki, "Tōbu kukū no zaishi to Tai'itsu"; and Pregadio, ed., *Encyclopedia of Taoism*, 775–77.

143. Reading 守 for 受, per the wording in *Zhengyi fawen xiuzhen zhiyao*.

144. The Xinwenfeng reprint of the Shanghai woodblock reprinting of the canon has 閣 here, but Yoshikawa and Mugitani give 闕 (*Zhen'gao jiaozhu*, 293), and I follow them. The yellow gatetowers were sometimes glossed as the point midway between the eyebrows, as for example (and not coincidentally) in the Shangqing rewrite of the *Scripture of the Yellow Court* (*Huangting jing* 黃庭經), which has 安在黃闕兩眉間 (*Taishang huangting neijing yujing* 10a). Cf. *Huangting neijing yujing zhu* 34b5–6. (On the *Huangting jing* see more below.)

145. See the next passage, which I understand to be instructing the practitioner on how to recognize the auspicious dream response as such.

146. The 夜 in this line seems to imply that the subsequent dream might be expected on the same night—as confirmation that the practitioner's removal of the dream pollution was successful.

147. This pattern—that one has a certain sort of dream, then notes one's mental or attitudinal response to it upon waking, and from that response ascertains whether the dream was auspicious or not—recurs in several texts discussed in chapter 2.
148. The three primes (*sanyuan* 三元) are the three regions of the body, centered on the head, the heart, and the region between the navel and the pubis. See Bokenkamp, *Early Daoist Scriptures*, 326n.
149. *Zhen'gao* 9.16a7–18a1; Yoshikawa and Mugitani, *Zhen'gao jiaozhu*, 293–95. My translation is partially indebted to the one given in Bokenkamp, "Image Work."
150. As suggested in Bokenkamp, "Image Work."
151. *Zhen'gao* 18.8a5–6; cf. Bokenkamp, "Image Work," 4. For an excellent discussion of the case of Tao Kedou and what it reveals about the dangers inherent in relations between the living and the dead, see Bokenkamp, *Ancestors*, 130–57. On the Dark Warrior and his representation on tomb walls and on other material objects, see Major, "New Light"; Ding Changyun, "Daojiao de siling chongbai"; and Pregadio, ed., *Encyclopedia of Taoism*, 908–11. On some of his later vicissitudes see Giuffrida, "Representing," and Seaman, *Journey*.
152. See further Campany, *Dreamscape*, 13–18, 32–33.
153. Shangqing methods often urge the severance of family ties because of the trouble they could bring. See Bokenkamp, *Ancestors*, 130–57, and Campany, "Sword Scripture." By the mid-fifth century Lingbao masters were similarly urged to leave their families; see Bokenkamp, "Early Lingbao Scriptures." And writings concerning practitioners of transcendence arts similarly depict familial relations as a source of trouble; see Campany, *Making Transcendents*, 186–98.
154. Compare the etiological overkill built into the Celestial Master petitioning ritual, in which the performer was to tick off a long list of the possible causes of a family's troubles, since neither the family nor the petitioner knew for sure what they were. For examples see Nickerson, "Great Petition," 239–40, 261–62, and Verellen, *Imperiled Destinies*, 52, 84, 101–2. For an excellent discussion of the practice of petitioning see Kleeman, *Celestial Masters*, 353–73.
155. See Pregadio, ed., *Encyclopedia of Taoism*, 835–36; Komjathy, "Mapping," 70–71; Baldrian-Hussein, "Yellow Court," 208.
156. The characterization is that of Isabelle Robinet, in Pregadio, ed., *Encyclopedia of Taoism*, 511. On the *Huangting jing* see also Maspero, *Taoism*, 489–95; Robinet, *Méditation*, 85–149; Schipper, *Le corps taoïste*, 178–91; Schipper, *Concordance*; Kroll, "Body Gods"; Carré, *Livre de la cour jaune*; Baldrian-Hussein, "Yellow Court." The outer scripture predates the Shangqing revelations of the 360s (see TTC, 96–97). A scripture by its title is mentioned in the *Lives of Notable Transcendents* (*Liexian zhuan* 列仙傳) as having been recited by the transcendent Zhu Huang 朱璜 (see *Liexian zhuan*, 153–54, and Kaltenmark, *Lie-sien tchouan*, 177–79). It appears in Ge Hong's catalog of scriptures (*Baopuzi neipian jiaoshi*, 334), as well as in his characterization of a man he considered to be a bogus practitioner (if also a talented raconteur), Cai Dan 蔡誕 (see *Baopuzi neipian jiaoshi*, 348–50, and Campany, *Making Transcendents*, 140). The "outer" scripture does contain the lines 明堂四達法海源, 真人子丹當吾前, 三關之中精氣深, 子欲不死修崑崙 (*Taishang huangting waijing jing* 1.1b6–7), but only the inner scripture explains the term *san guan* 三關.
157. See TTC, 184–85.
158. *Taishang huangting neijing yujing*, 4b.
159. *Taishang huangting neijing yujing*, 6b. Compare Maspero, *Taoism*, 494n109, and Baldrian-Hussein, "Yellow Court," 208. An unannotated translation of these passages may be found in Carré, *Livre*, 55, 58; unfortunately, however, without any com-

mentary explaining their significance the text reads like something out of an Ezra Pound poem, a sequence of striking but empty images. For the Daoist master and ritual reformer Lu Xiujing 陸修靜 (406–477), the three barriers were body, mouth, and mind (see Verellen, *Imperiled Destinies*, 165).

160. See for example the illustration based on an Eastern Han tomb brick in Nanyang, Henan province, given in Zhao Chengpu, ed., *Nanyang*, illustration no. 150.
161. As noted above, the spot midway between the two eyebrows was designated as the yellow gatetowers.
162. For a translation of Guṇabhadra's *Gaoseng zhuan* biography, see Shih, *Biographies*, 148–56 (my translation was done independently); for a summary, see DB, 189–90. Regarding his recitations and translations of sutras, see Glass, "Guṇabhadra"; Radich, "Triad of Texts"; Lettere, "*Guoqu xianzai yinguo jing*"; Boucher, "Hīnāyāna Zealot," 87, 95n10.
163. *Gaoseng zhuan* 50:344c22–29. The story was also incorporated into *Fayuan zhulin* 53:1030 and *Chu sanzang jiji* 55:106. An alternate translation and discussion may be found in Jensen, "Dreaming Betwixt and Between," 301–3.
164. Precisely this phrase appears in Dharmarakṣa's translation of the *Lotus Sutra* (*Zheng fahua jing*, 10:129c) in the chapter devoted to the bodhisattva Guangshiyin 光世音 (as he is there named). For translations of Kumārajīva's version of the passage see Hurvitz, *Lotus Blossom*, 314–15, and Robert, *Lotus*, 366–67.
165. *Fayuan zhulin* 53:988b; compare ibid., 409b, and *Gaoseng zhuan* 50:350c. The story in which this excerpt appears is translated and discussed in Campany, *Signs from the Unseen Realm*, 132–33.
166. *Dili sanmeiye budong zunshengzhe niansong bimi fa* 21:16a12–29. On Amoghavajra and his context see Goble, *Chinese Esoteric Buddhism*.
167. On this standard feature of Mahāyāna sutras sée Schopen, *Figments*, 209–10, and Drewes, "Revisiting," 113–22, 134–35.
168. *Fangguang banruo jing*, 8:50c–51a; *Mohe banruo poluomi jing*, 8:289c; *Daoxing banruo jing*, 8:435b; *Da mingdu jing*, 8:485a; *Mohe banruo chao jing*, 8:517a; *Xiaopin banruo poluomi jing*, 8:545a; and *Da zhidu lun* 25:474a.
169. *Zengyi ahan jing* 2:806a (on this work see Palumbo, *Early Chinese Commentary*); *Shiyi xiangsinian rulai jing*, 2:861a–b; *Da fangbian fo baoen jing*, 3:129; *Faju jing*, 4:561c; and *Faju biyu jing*, 4:581c. Compare the promise that if one attains the mind of compassion, polluting dreams will cease, in *Chengshi lun* 32:336c and *Jietuo daolun* 32:435a.
170. *Da fangdeng daji jing*, 13:143a, 166c, 249b, 327b; *Pusa nianfo sanmei jing*, 14:823a; and *Beidou qixing huma fa*, 21:458c.
171. *Azhapoju guishen dajiangshang fo tuoluoni shenzhou jing*, 21:184a. See Strickmann, "Seal of the Law," 39, and Despeux, "Buddhist Healing Practices," 139–40.
172. *Zunsheng pusa so wen yiqie zhufa ru wuliangmen tuoluoni jing*, 21:847c.
173. *Hailongwang jing*, 15:146c. The same idea in reverse shows up in *Da zhidu lun* 25:155c, where a consequence of killing living beings is having polluting dreams.
174. *Chaoriming sanmei jing*, 15:547c.
175. *Jinguangming jing*, 16:335b, 349b, 349c, 350b; *Hebu jinguangming jing*, 16:360a, 386c, 392b, 392c, 393c; *Jinguangming zuishengwang jingshu*, 39:320b, 320c; *Shiyi mian shenzhou xinjing yishu*, 39:1101b; and *Guanding jing* 21:501a.
176. *Si tianwang jing*, 15:118b. On this sutra see Sørensen, "Divine Scrutiny," and Mochizuki, *Bukkyō kyōten*, 393–400.
177. *Guanding jing* 21:503a: those who wear a set of twenty-five spirits' names (灌頂章句善神名) will be protected from weapons, demons, black magic, etc., and from polluting dreams, disasters, local officials, and anomalies. *Guanding jing* 21:505b (and cf.

21:510a): wearing these seven divine kings' names at the waist, one won't be troubled by ominous bird calls, polluting dreams, wild beasts, sprites, and aberrations. *Guanding jing* 21:519c: in a long list of types of demons, one is termed "demons who cause polluting dreams" 為惡夢鬼. *Guanding jing* 21:534a: when beset by ominous bird calls, demons, anomalous beings, corpse-pathogens 尸邪, etc., in the night, venerate Bhaiṣajyaguru and you will be protected. For an overview of this sutra see Strickmann, "Consecration Sūtra."

178. On this text see Strickmann, *Le taoïsme*, 60–61; Robinet, *La révélation*, 2:101–110 (where one may find a detailed analysis and comparison with other texts); and Bokenkamp, *Early Daoist Scriptures*, 275–372, the best available treatment. My translations quote or closely follow his.

179. This way of describing their motion, *liudang* 流蕩, itself suggests pollution—a flowing out beyond proper bounds.

180. Not only was blood a polluting substance in many circumstances, but early Daoists also rejected blood sacrifice to non-ancestral spirits as polluting and pernicious. See Raz, *Emergence of Daoism*, 91–126; Verellen, *Imperiled Destinies*, 25, 27; and Kleeman, *Celestial Masters*, 96–97, 257–58.

181. As Bokenkamp notes, the River Sire (He Bo 河伯) was god of the Yellow River and as such oversaw the Yellow Springs, one of several ancient destinations of souls of the dead. His domain and the Three Offices 三官 were dreaded sites where days, months, or years were deducted from one's lifespan as punishment for sins. On the system implied here see Campany, "Living Off the Books."

182. Translating *xie* 邪, "bent" or "twisted" *qi*-based pathogens. See Strickmann, "Seal of the Law," 20n31.

183. *Huangtian shangqing jinque dijun lingshu ziwen shangjing*, 8b–11a; translation modified from Bokenkamp, *Early Daoist Scriptures*, 324. This passage also appears in *Shangqing xiuxing jingjue* 3b, *Shangqing xiuxing yaoshi jing* 4a, *Shangqing taiji zhenren shenxian jing* 16a–b, and *Yunji qiqian* 54.7a. The same model, but with a different suggested response, underlies this brief passage: "When you dream of something polluting, you should the next morning notify the Most High. This is first to rectify your cloudsouls and whitesouls and, second, to eradicate the unpropitious" 夢惡者, 明旦當啓太上, 一以正魂魄, 二以 [所 > 折] 除不祥 (*Zhen'gao* 7.15b10–16a1).

184. *Huangtian Shangqing jinque dijun lingshu ziwen shangjing*, 11a–b, closely following Bokenkamp, *Early Daoist Scriptures*, 326.

185. Terminology also seen elsewhere, such as *Dongshen badi miaojing jing* 14b.

186. As Bokenkamp notes, these are the traditional directional animals. "They have a long history as demon-quellers and are to be found . . . represented on the walls of tombs. The dragon and tiger have even been found, represented in shell, in a Neolithic burial site" (*Early Daoist Scriptures*, 325n).

187. *Huangtian Shangqing jinque dijun lingshu ziwen shangjing*, 10b1–11a7, slightly modifying Bokenkamp, *Early Daoist Scriptures*, 322–26.

188. A trope going back—but in reverse direction—to the parable of Hundun 渾沌 in the seventh chapter of *Zhuangzi* (*Zhuangzi jijie* 75; Watson, *Complete Works of Chuang Tzu*, 97), where this sealed-up figure has seven holes bored into him by his well-meaning but benighted guests. See Girardot, *Myth and Meaning*, 21–46.

189. This is seen, for example, in the "method for driving off the three corpses by sending down the most high from the Palace of Purple Tenuity" 紫微宮降太上去三尸法 prescribed in *Yunji qiqian* 83.10b–11b. See Kohn, "Taoism in Japan," 391–96, and "Kōshin," parts 1–3. This method is not to be confused with the notion that sages don't dream, which is discussed in chapter 4.

190. One attempt at a comprehensive treatment may be found in volume 5 of de Groot's *Religious System*. See also Poo Mu-chou, ed., *Guimei shenmo*, and Wu Kang, *Zhongguo guishen jingguai*.
191. See Allan, *Way of Water*, 87–92.
192. This idea is also discussed in Campany, *Dreamscape*, 44–45, 47–49.
193. *Taiping jing hejiao*, 51–52; translation modifying Hendrischke, *Scripture on Great Peace*, 129–30.
194. *Taiping jing hejiao*, 57–60; translation modifying Hendrischke, *Scripture on Great Peace*, 143–45. A lovely passage in *Huainanzi* instructively sets *xie* in parallel with *guo* 過: "Sorrow and joy are perversions of potency, pleasure and anger are excesses with respect to the Way, fondness and loathing are fetters of the mind" 夫悲樂者德之邪也, 而喜怒者道之過也, 好憎者心之 [暴 > 累] 也 (*Huainanzi jishi* 519, following the editor's emendation; translation modifying Major et al., *Huainanzi*, 246).
195. I reproduce the line as given in Stein manuscript 6825 and as photographically reproduced in *Laozi Xiang'er zhu jiaozheng*—except that it reads 靈 where most editions have 虛. Both Rao Zongyi and Bokenkamp implicitly treat this as a copyist's error. On this text's place in Celestial Masters organization and ideology, see Kleeman, *Celestial Masters*, 79–96. For a superb study and translation see Bokenkamp, *Early Daoist Scriptures*, 29–148.
196. Here is a case where translating *e* as "evil"—especially when in apposition to *shan* 善, or "good"—is justified. But the sense of pollution lurking beneath the word should be borne in mind. Incidentally, here and elsewhere in Stein 6825, *xie* 邪 is written with the loan graph 耶.
197. "Conduct" is an interpretation of what this line refers to. In this context, what the heart "produces" or "makes" (*wei* 為) could just as well be understood as thoughts or intentions.
198. *Laozi Xiang'er zhu*, 6; translation modifying Bokenkamp, *Early Daoist Scriptures*, 78. For a discussion and alternate translation, see Kleeman, *Celestial Masters*, 94–95.
199. Verellen, *Imperiled Destinies*, 64. Similar beings are treated in Chang Chaoran, "Killing Spirits" and "Laizi sizhe de yangsha."
200. See Li Jianmin, "Contagion," 205–8.
201. These are the five classicist texts established as canonical during the Han and (in legend) associated with the figure of Confucius: *Book of Changes*, *Documents*, *Odes*, *Records of Rites*, and *Spring and Autumn Annals*. On them see Nylan, *Five "Confucian" Classics*.
202. *Laozi Xiang'er zhu*, 22; translation modifying Bokenkamp, *Early Daoist Scriptures*, 104–5.
203. See Li Jianmin, "Contagion" and "They Shall Expel Demons"; Verellen, *Imperiled Destinies*, 64–65; and Stanley-Baker, "Drugs, Destiny, and Disease," 126–28.
204. On the perils of family connections see Verellen, *Imperiled Destinies*, 78, 101, 120–21; Bokenkamp, *Ancestors*; and Campany, "Sword Scripture." On *gui* and their depredations generally see Chang Chaoran, "Killing Spirits" and "Laizi sizhe de yangsha"; Cedzich, "Ghosts and Demons"; Poo Mu-chou, "Zhongguo gudai gui lunshu de xingcheng," "Taming of Ghosts," and "Culture of Ghosts"; de Groot, *Religious System*, 465–1185 (on the beings) and 929–1185 (on apotropaic methods); Strickmann, *Chinese Magical Medicine*; Hu Baozhu, *Believing in Ghosts and Spirits*; and Campany, "Ghosts Matter" and *Garden of Marvels*, index s.v. "ghost."
205. For collections of passages mentioning this term, see Lin Fu-shih: "Shi mei" and "Renjian zhi mei."

206. See Campany: *Strange Writing*, 253–55, *To Live as Long*, 153, 161–68, 252–55, 319–21, *Making Transcendents*, 165–68, *Garden of Marvels*, index s.vv. "demon" and "fox spirits"; Gundersen, "Attacked by Māra," 6–8, 46–60; Benn, "Another Look," 77–80.
207. I've learned much about hybridity in premodern times from Bynum, *Metamorphosis and Identity*. For a general treatment of the corpses and worms see Miyakawa Hisayuki, "Dōkyōteki shintairon ni okeru shichu to konpaku." For examples of visual illustrations see *Taishang chu sanshi jiuchong baosheng jing* 7a–14a and S. Huang, "Daoist Imagery," 35.
208. For Butler, "The abject designates . . . precisely those 'unlivable' and 'uninhabitable' zones of social life which are nevertheless densely populated by those who do not enjoy the status of the subject, but whose living under the sign of the 'unlivable' is required to circumscribe the domain of the subject. This zone of uninhabitability will constitute the defining limit of the subject's domain; it will constitute that site of dreaded identification against which—and by virtue of which—the domain of the subject will circumscribe its own claim to autonomy and to life" (*Bodies That Matter*, 3). See also Mrozik, "Materializations of Virtue," 16–17; Langenberg, *Birth in Buddhism*, 75–93; L. Wilson, *Charming Cadavers*, 53; Kristeva, *Powers of Horror*; and McNicholl, "Generative Power of Disgust." All these worms and corpses infesting the practitioner are in these senses the practitioner-subject's abject, at once "constitutive outside" and also "inside" much more literally than Butler intends.
209. See *Yunji qiqian* 13.12b–14b and 81.15b–17a. On the related systems of sin reportage and penal lifespan deduction, which figured across the religious landscape, see, among others, Kohn, "Counting Good Deeds" and "Kōshin" parts 1–3; Kleeman, *Celestial Masters*, 83–89; Verellen, *Imperiled Destinies*; Rotman, *Thus Have I Seen*, 9–12; Zürcher, *Buddhism in China*, 625–26; Brokaw, *Ledgers*; and Campany, "Living Off the Books" and *To Live as Long*, 47–60.
210. See for example *Yunji qiqian* 83.7a–b.
211. This is seen in a method anthologized in *Yunji qiqian* 82.2b–3a, where nothing is said about their causing polluting dreams but where the practitioner, after performing a ritual expulsion, is to "return to bed and lie down. You should have a responsive dream in which personages come to apologize, bid farewell, and depart, after which [the disturbance] stops. If not, then they have not yet left" 還牀臥, 當應夢見人辭謝去者, 止. 不爾未去.
212. Precisely as predicted in other texts, as we'll see shortly. The best example comes just two pages down, in the lines "After three days he may have spells of wailing loudly during the day or feeling troubled or dazed" 或自於日中大哭, 煩惱恍惚.
213. *Yunji qiqian* 82.14b–17a. The narrative seems, then, to have been intended as a cautionary tale to warn readers of the wiles of the corpses, who may go to such lengths to convince their hosts to let them stay.
214. In some Buddhist texts, too, worms inhabit the human body, whether literally or in meditative imagery; but rather than teaching methods for expelling them, the texts recommend worms among many other contemplative reminders of impurity and impermanence. See L. Wilson, *Charming Cadavers*, and for examples in an indigenously written scripture see Greene, *Secrets*, 116–17, 130–33, 186–87, 264–66.
215. Anthologized in *Yunji qiqian* 82.8b–10a.
216. Identifications follow Wilms, *Divine Farmer's Classic*, 312, 252, and 268 respectively. On wolfsbane used both as a therapeutic drug and as a poison, see the superb discussions in Obringer, *L'aconit et l'orpiment*, 91–143, and Y. Liu, *Healing with Poisons*, 46–52.
217. The term is *li* 痢, usually meaning dysentery.

218. Compare the "Method Used by Transcendents for Expelling the Three Worms and Subduing the corpses" 仙人下三蟲伏尸方 in *Taishang lingbao wufu xu* 2.23b–24b and *Yunji qiqian* 82.5a–b. There, too, dreams are used diagnostically, and the cure involves a mixture of substances, although the whole process requires two hundred days. For further examples of methods for expelling the corpses, see Campany, *To Live as Long*, 49–52.
219. Zhiyi 智顗 (538–597) was a notable exception. He distinguished between ordinary demons and their effects on humans, on the one hand, and Māra and his effects, on the other. Ordinary demons cause diseases of the body, while Māra afflicts practitioners' minds, disrupting their progress. See *Mohe zhiguan* 46:107c and Swanson, *Clear Serenity*, 1335.
220. See Gundersen, "Attacked by Māra"; Kamitsuka, "Ma no kannen," and its partial translation in Kamitsuka, "Concept of Māra"; Bollée, "A Note on Evil"; Liu Shufen, "Zhonggu sengren de famo wenshu"; Liu Yi, "Early Medieval Concepts of Demon Troops"; DeCaroli, *Haunting*; Boyd, *Satan and Māra*; Giddings, "Structuralist Examination"; Mollier, *Une apocalypse taoïste* and "Visions of Evil"; Karetzky, "Māra"; Bareau, "L'allégorie de la mort"; Zhiru, *Savior Bodhisattva*, 89–97; McBride, "Esoteric Buddhism and its Relation to Healing," 210–14; Lopez, *Hyecho's Journey*, 124–25; Lettere, "*Guoqu xianzai yinguo jing*," 135–38; M. Nichols, *Malleable Māra*; and Campany, "Taoist Bioethics."
221. I adopt the distinction drawn in Kim, "Filth."
222. *Chufan* 觸犯 has the literal sense of being "touched and violated."
223. *Taiwei lingshu ziwen xianji zhenji shangjing* 1a–3b, mostly quoting Bokenkamp, *Early Daoist Scriptures*, 362–66. I've also consulted the ZH edition (1:304–5) and Pelliot 2751 (https://gallica.bnf.fr/ark:/12148/btv1b83021869/f3.item.r=Pelliot 2751).
224. For examples, see the stories listed in the index to Campany, *Garden of Marvels*, s.vv. "animal spirit" and "demon, sexual congress with."
225. Many examples are translated in Campany, *To Live as Long*; see also Campany, *Making Transcendents*, 54–55.
226. Some exceptions are discussed in Campany, *Dreamscape*, 49–52, 54–55.
227. Kim, "History of Filth." I quote from the unpaginated abstract.
228. See Campany, *To Live as Long*, 18–75.
229. On the separation of pure from soiled articles see Yifa, "Chinese Vinaya Tradition," 128–29. On the boundary-fixing ritual and its constituting of a monastic community as a single body, see the important discussion in Jung, "Natural Land."
230. See Carruthers, *Craft of Thought*, 34–38.
231. P. Brown, *Body and Society*, 231–32.

Chapter 2

1. On this work and the eras from which its source texts derived, see TTC, 943–45.
2. *Hu* 忽 means "suddenly," to be sure, but also often connotes "unexpectedly" or "for no apparent reason." Here, the unexpectedness underlines that these dreams warrant attention as signs or simulacra (*xiang* 象). On the meanings of *xiang* in contexts of dream interpretation, see Campany, *Dreamscape*, 75–79, 120–21.
3. As seen in chapter 1, medicinal compounds were often prescribed to expel the corpses.
4. The five types were tattooing, amputation of the nose, amputation of one or both feet, castration (of men) or sequestration (of women), and execution.
5. *Yunji qiqian* 83.8a–b, partially incorporating the paraphrase in Strickmann, "Dreamwork," 35.

6. For more on such rituals, see Raz, *Emergence of Daoism*, 105–16, and Campany, *To Live as Long*, 39–41.
7. See for example Chapman, "Rhetoric and Ritual"; Bodde, "Cosmic Magic"; Huang and Chang, "Evolution and Decline"; Loewe, *Divination*, 191–213; Raphals, *Divination and Prediction*, 140; and Campany, "Two Religious Thinkers," 189–202.
8. For examples, see Campany, *Dreamscape*, 81–84.
9. This rhetorical feature dates back to dream divinations recorded in Shang oracle bone inscriptions. See Campany, *Dreamscape*, 34, 173n10.
10. See the discussion in Campany, *Dreamscape*, 47–49, and the example presented below.
11. Peirce, *Collected Papers*, 228.
12. See Peirce, *Essential Peirce*, 13–17, and Liszka, *Semeiotic*, 18–52.
13. On the PROSPECTIVE PARADIGM, see Campany, *Dreamscape*, 93–131.
14. For more, see Campany, *Dreamscape*, 80–87, 89–91, 163.
15. I am reminded of a memorable line in Claude Lévi-Strauss: "Comprendre consiste à réduire un type de réalité à un autre; . . . la réalité vraie n'est jamais la plus manifeste; . . . la nature du vrai transparaît déjà dans le soin qu'il met à se dérober" (*Tristes tropiques*, 62).
16. Pelliot 3017 is a list of corrections to the *Ratnakūṭa* collection (on which see more in the ensuing discussion and the following note), titled 金字大寶 [積] 經內略出交錯及傷損字數. On the first sheet of this manuscript, a few minor emendations (regarding the images seen under sign numbers 100 and 101) are listed under *juan* 15 and 16, corresponding to brief passages in the *Pusa shuomeng jing*. Beside the heading as given in *juan* 15, interestingly, the attribution to Dharmarakṣa is repeated. See https://gallica.bnf.fr/ark:/12148/btv1b83007111/f1.item.r=大寶積經.zoom.
17. In the Taishō canon the text is to be found at 11:80c–91b; in the ZHDZ edition, which I've also consulted, it appears at 8:524–42. Several parts of the *Ratnakūṭa* are attested in Dunhuang manuscripts, including a beautiful, complete copy on a paper scroll (still attached to its wooden roller, S351) of *juan* 117, comprising the first half of *Baofa pusa hui* 寶髻菩薩會 / *Ratnacūḍaparipṛcchā*, corresponding to 11:657a–665a; see Pagel, *Bodhisattvapiṭaka*, 435. But, to my knowledge, this dream text is unattested among Dunhuang manuscripts—except in P3017, discussed in the previous note.
18. On the *Ratnakūṭa* see Pedersen, "Notes"; Pagel, *Bodhisattvapiṭaka*; Chang, *Treasury* (which translates selected portions); Silk, "*Mahāratnakūṭa* Tradition"; and Nattier, *Good Men*, 31–37.
19. There is at least one extant Tibetan version: see Harrison, "Mediums," 137–38, and Esler, "Note d'oniromancie." At this writing I am uncertain how closely the Chinese and Tibetan version(s) resemble each other, but judging from Harrison's rather sketchy characterizations it seems there are significant differences. For example, Harrison writes that the recommended practice "usually turns out to be text-recitation" (ibid.), whereas the Chinese version seldom mentions this remedy; he says that the Tibetan text comprises 106 signs, whereas the Chinese has 108, a much likelier total (for reasons discussed in appendix A). Esler writes of another Tibetan text whose list of 108 dream signs was drawn from a Tibetan version of the *Ratnakūṭa*. It's unclear to me whether Harrison and Esler are discussing the same text or different ones. Some portions of a Tibetan *Ratnakūṭa* appear to have been translated from the Chinese rather than from an Indic text, but I don't know whether this work on dreams should be counted among them (Nattier, *Good Men*, 34–35). Eric Greene has commented briefly on the Chinese text (see *Chan Before Chan*, 143–44).
20. See Forte, "Bodhiruci," 97–98; Pagel, *Bodhisattvapiṭaka*, 64–66; and Nattier, *Good Men*, 32.

21. See Forte, "Bodhiruci," and Weinstein, *Buddhism*, 44.
22. Forte, "Bodhiruci," 103.
23. *Kaiyuan shijiao lu*, 55:570b2–4. On *hui* 會 and *pariṣad* as denoting textual units, see Nattier, *Good Men*, 35.
24. *Kaiyuan shijiao lu*, 55:584b2–6. See also the listings in Tokiwa, *Gokan yori Sōsei ni itaru yakkyō sōroku*, 604, 637.
25. "A close examination of its textual phrasings shows that it is of a rather different sort from Dharmarakṣa's sutras" 細詳文句與竺法護經稍不相類, Zhisheng observes (*Kaiyuan shijiao lu*, 55:584b2–7). On Dharmarakṣa's textual productions see Boucher, "Dharmarakṣa" and "Buddhist Translation Procedures."
26. On the nature of Zhisheng's catalog, see Tokuno, "Evaluation," 52–58; on its impact, see Wu Jiang, "Chinese Buddhist Canon," 37. On Fei Changfang and his catalog, see Radich, "Fei Changfang's Treatment"; Tokuno, "Evaluation," 43–47; and Storch, "Fei Changfang's Records."
27. In kindly commenting on my manuscript at this point, Chris Jensen noted that diagnoses of the dreamer's karmic condition and diagnoses of the condition of his indwelling spirits "draw on different underlying logics of how dreams would come to contain such information." Quite so, but my emphasis here is on the common diagnostic structure and function of all such texts. And I would here mention a point made again below, that the logics of *exactly* "*how* dreams come to contain such information" are usually left completely unaddressed in such texts—a feature I see as fundamental to their rhetorical positioning vis-à-vis readers.
28. See *Chu sanzang jiji* 55:62a–c and Zürcher, *Buddhist Conquest*, 196–97.
29. On it see Zürcher, *Buddhist Conquest*, 54, 186, 366n283; Lu, "Analogy of Pots"; and Deleanu, "An Shigao's Translation."
30. On it see Nattier, "Proto-History."
31. On it see Nattier, *Guide*, 137–39, and Wolf, "Ritual Refashioned," 184–86. On Zhi Qian's life and work see Nattier, *Guide*, 116–48, and BEB 2:818–25.
32. On some of these texts see Nattier, "Proto-History." On the bodhisattva path generally see Dayal, *Bodhisattva Doctrine*; Pagel, *Bodhisattvapiṭaka*; Williams, *Mahāyāna Buddhism*, 200–208; and Hirakawa, "Rise of Mahāyāna," 64–69. On some of its Daoist appropriations see Bokenkamp, "Stages of Transcendence," and Funayama, "Buddhist Theories."
33. In that the text clearly assumes a reader already well versed in the stages of the bodhisattva path and familiar with the basic practices, the statement that *Explication of Dreams* was included in the *Ratnakūṭa* in order to "furnish the collection with a text that systematically classifies, and sets in a well-designed scheme, practices that are elsewhere haphazardly cited" (Pagel, *Bodhisattvapiṭaka*, 101–2) is not an accurate characterization of its contents, as noted by Harrison, "Mediums," 136n37.
34. Hoping to clarify some of the rough passages, I compared the two versions closely, but they are nearly identical. On the importance of consulting editions across both canons when doing close work on texts, see Deleanu, "Transmission," 25–26. Deleanu's article also contains an excellent guide to the maze of Chinese Buddhist canons (pp. 7–13). The *Zhonghua dazang* edition of *Explication of Dreams* is based on the Jin 金 canon version found in the Guangsheng monastery 廣勝寺 in Shanxi province in 1933, and therefore dates to between 1139 and 1172, when its woodblocks were carved; it is collated with at least seven other editions. See Zacchetti, *In Praise*, 99–100. The Taishō edition is based on the second edition of the Korean canon (1236–1251), and it, too, is collated with at least seven other editions.
35. For example, in the part 3 passage corresponding to the sixth sign (seeing in a dream a painted icon of the Buddha), we first read that any of the first five bodhisattva

stages might be indicated, but shortly afterward we're told that any of the first *six* signs might be indicated. Several other entries are internally inconsistent in similar ways.

36. For a listing of works on physiognomy in China, see Campany, *Dreamscape*, 184n8, to which should be added Kohn, "Textbook of Physiognomy" and "Mirror of Auras."
37. I obtained this number by counting the sub-signs in part 3 and adding that total to the 108 main signs.
38. On the *Oneirocritica* see the superb edition, translation, and study in Harris-McCoy, *Artemidorus' Oneirocritica*. It is, however, not so much a straight dreambook (as I use the term) as it is a commentary on dreambooks. It goes far beyond listing dream signs and their meanings.
39. On these works see Lackner, *Der chinesische Traumwald*; Drettas, "Le rêve mis en ordre"; Strassberg, *Wandering Spirits*; Vance, "Textualizing Dreams"; and Struve, *The Dreaming Mind*.
40. J. Z. Smith, *Imagining Religion*, 44.
41. Smith, *Imagining Religion*, 47.
42. For more on dreambooks across many cultures and in China, see Campany, *Dreamscape*, 80–87.
43. Gethin, "Mātikās," 165. Compare Radich, *The Mahāparinirvāṇa-mahāsūtra*, 152n414; McDaniel, "Philosophical Embryology," 94–95; and Ronkin, *Metaphysics*, 27–30, 65, 145, focusing on relationships between *mātikā*s and the development of *abhidharma* texts and teachings. On Chinese receptions of such lists see Dessein, "Abhidharma in China."
44. Gethin, "Mātikās," 153 and 161.
45. Artemidorus similarly claimed completeness for his massive compilation of dream signs and their meanings. See Harris-McCoy, *Artemidorus' Oneirocritica*, 19–21.
46. The cult of relics and stupas appears in signs 12–16, 30–32, and 36. The dreamer sees or hears the (or a) Buddha in 1–4, 7–11, 17–21, 28–29, 33–34, 37–40, and 55. The dream involves offerings 供養 or ornamentation 莊嚴 in 19, 20, and 38–40. Icons figure in items 5 and 6. Hearing or expounding Dharma factor in 8, 22–23, 25, 60, and 62. Hearing sutras or spells figures in 57–59, 61, 63. Other continents or worlds feature in 64, 65, and 82.
47. See for example Hureau, "Buddhist Rituals," 1227–32; Zürcher, *Buddhism in China*, 150, 297–98; Janousch, "Emperor as Bodhisattva"; and Rothschild, *Emperor Wu Zhao*.
48. On this aspect of the *Ratnakūṭa* see Nattier, *Good Men*, 121–27. Sign 83, in which one dreams of oneself dressed as a layperson, implies that the reader is expected to be a monk or nun.
49. Throughout my discussion of this text I will have recourse to the masculine first-person pronoun, since it's an individual dreamer who is being addressed and described in each entry and since repeatedly writing "he or she" would be cumbersome. But there is little that would prevent us from picturing a female practitioner as the one being addressed in any given passage.
50. *Bu jing* 不淨 strongly suggests feces, but later the entry speaks of "blue-green (or gray) mud/paste" 青淤泥, perhaps euphemistically.
51. *Qianshen* 前身, literally "previous body" (or bodies), a standard term for a being's past rebirths.

52. This *pusa* 菩薩 seems extraneous, unless it means that *as a bodhisattva* the practitioner has cultivated transgressive actions, or unless grammatically the entire group of phrases modifies "bodhisattva" (copula form).
53. Throughout this discussion I provide the location of particular passages in (first) the *Taishō* and (second) the *Zhonghua dazang* editions.
54. One item in part 3, which corresponds to item 45 in the initial sign list and reads 自夢見在濁水中去 (85a29–b3/ 531a13–18), lacks this opening formula.
55. In the initial list, dreaming of hearing the sound of a *dhāraṇī* 自夢聞陀羅尼聲 appears in position 57, but the corresponding entry in part 3 appears between entries corresponding to numbers 62 and 64. (Item 63 in the initial list, 自夢聞法藏聲, has no counterpart in part 3.)
56. For an exception to this rule, in the case of the 91st sign (自夢作王輔相在大衆中行 in the initial list, 夢王前若輔相前若大衆中 in the corresponding passage in part 3) different specific actions are prescribed according to which of the eight possible stages one might have reached, but the text provides no way of ascertaining which of the eight stages it might be.
57. Eighteen entries are quite brief, containing little or no elaboration on the main sign.
58. This translation of *bu san* 不散 is tentative. Since to *san* 散 one's hair was to untie it and let it hang down loosely, perhaps *bu san* here refers to a hair still curled up rather than long and straight.
59. This final line is interesting for perhaps implying that bodhisattvas might enter *samādhi* while dreaming—a notion by no means unique to this text (as seen below) and exemplifying the SPILLOVER PARADIGM investigated in chapter 3. Or else it involves *dreaming of* being in *samādhi* without actually being so. It's possible to understand the places where the hair is obtained as correlated with moments in Siddhartha's final rebirth.
60. See *Guanfo sanmei hai jing* 15:660a28–c28 and Yamabe, "Visionary Repentance," 34–35 (and on this sutra generally see Yamabe, "Sūtra on the Ocean-Like Samādhi"). Other examples of the seemingly (and unusually) non-arbitrary nature of signs indicative of attainment are discussed in Greene, *Chan Before Chan*, 93–95. As Greene aptly puts it, such signs and images "often seem designed to tempt one's inner hermeneute into action" (94).
61. That is, without dwelling further on it.
62. These are the standard six perfections of the bodhisattva. See Dayal, *Bodhisattva Doctrine*, 165–269.
63. Gregory Schopen has argued that recollection of former lives often involved remembering rebirth in one of the unfortunate destinies, because this then effected a change in one's behavior as a human while also letting one enjoy the rare opportunity to amass merit (*Figments*, 190–220).
64. This sign does not appear in the initial list of 108, so I leave it unnumbered.
65. 經行處 is a standard translation of the Sanskrit *caṅkramana*, a walkway used by monks on monastery grounds. My thanks to an anonymous reader for this suggestion.
66. This phrase corresponds to the second item in the initial list of signs. See appendix A.
67. Compare the seventh sign in the initial list.
68. There are textual variants at this point.
69. Confession is also recommended in items 11 and 50. Repentance of one's transgressions 悔過 is prescribed in item 56.
70. *Vīrya* is prescribed in items 7, 10, 28, 36, 38, 53, 56, 66, 86, 87, 100, 102, and 107. *Vīrya* and the other perfections are also sometimes mentioned diagnostically, where (for example) it's a failure in respect of vigor or giving (as in item 72) that is blocking the practitioner's progress.

71. Items 4, 10, 28, 43, 47, 73, 76, 88 (without hope of recompense), 90, and 91.
72. Items 5, 6, 8, 10, 23, 44, 49, 50, 62, 73, 81, 90, 91, 92, 97, and 102. Robert Buswell has observed that "the quality most fundamental to [advancing on] the mārga [i.e., on the path] is *dāna*" ("Path to Perdition," 126). Jan Nattier has similarly noted that "from the very beginning of Buddhist history, the act of giving (*dāna*) to members of the Buddhist monastic community was seen as the merit-making activity par excellence" ("Realm of Akṣobhya," 88).
73. Forbearance is prescribed in items 9, 34, 46, 59, 81, and 100; behavioral discipline in items 62, 74, 90, and 95; skill in means in items 60, 81, and the entry that opens with the phrase 在鬪訟中 (which lacks a corresponding item in the list of primary signs in part 2); and contemplation in item 54.
74. 信 is recommended in items 50, 59, 70, 72, 87; 大悲 (or 慈) in 105, 106, 107; 無礙心 in 49, 60; 無畏 in 47. Holding a lamp is recommended in 11, keeping silence in 57, eliminating arrogance in 65 (on the special importance for bodhisattvas of maintaining humility, see Boucher, *Bodhisattvas*, 56–58, and Nattier, *Good Men*, 135–36, 173–74), and 念佛 in 93.
75. The translation reflects my sense that the term *sheli* 舍利 can refer both to parts of the body remaining among the ashes after cremation and, in a stricter sense, the hard, crystalline grains often stored in reliquaries. "Buddhist relics may be seen not as the leftover but as the essence that is extracted from the dead, cremated body" (Strong, *Relics of the Buddha*, xvi). "Death and cremation reduce the person to its 'essential ingredient,' *dhātu*. They extract . . . the ore (*dhātu*) from the dross" (Schopen, "Relic," 257). See also E. Wang, "Of the True Body."
76. Literally "a hand" 手; I suspect that 指 has dropped out and so translate accordingly.
77. "Without support" 無依 here might refer to the metaphor describing forest-dwelling (vis-à-vis monastery-dwelling) monks as not relying on anything (see Nattier, *Good Men*, 300, and Drewes, "Forest Hypothesis," 79). If so, this passage can be read as advising a monastery-dweller (or householder) to leave for the forest. Alternatively, Deleanu has noted the emphasis in Perfection of Wisdom sutras on "practicing without a support," a notion he does not further clarify ("Preliminary Study on Meditation," 69); he also writes of the Perfection of Wisdom emphasis on achieving "a high degree of awareness with no emotional support, i.e., attachment" (ibid., 77). Compare Conze, *Eight Thousand Lines*, 215–17: acts of will and deeds can arise only with "objective support," and the bodhisattva regards all dharmas as without support, that is, as lacking own-being. Yet another possibility is that 無依 here qualifies the six perfections—that they are outside the causal bonds of karma (my thanks to an anonymous reader for this suggestion). Other concepts regarding "support" for bodhisattvas are discussed in Pagel, *Bodhisattvapiṭaka*, 378n174, but I don't think they are the ones intended here.
78. This is not an ordinary chair (on which see Kieschnick, *Impact*, 241–49), nor a corded chair (*shengzuo* 繩坐) used for seated meditation (on which see Greene, *Chan Before Chan*, 43), but an ornamented, ceremonial seat resting on an elevated dais (hence its complete name, *gaozuo* 高座), occupied by the monk who is preaching Dharma or expounding a sutra to an audience. This usage is attested in China from at least the late second century (see Zürcher, *Buddhist Conquest*, 343n212) and was applied to ritual furnishings in both monastic and household spaces (see McRae, "Daoxuan's Vision," 93, and Campany, "Abstinence Halls," 4 and 13n22). On indigenous "seats" 坐 or "spirit seats" 神坐 in religious contexts see Harper, "Seat of Taiyi."
79. In accordance with several editions, I read 今 here instead of 令.

80. Donner and Stevenson explain: "The obstacle of retribution refers to limitations of physical or mental endowment as well as environment that arise from karmic influences of the past" (*Great Calming*, 282n282).
81. Sorting out such lists can be challenging. For example, there is also a standard list of "three obstructions" 三障: those of defilements 煩惱 (*fannao/kleśa*, on which more in a moment), karma 業, and retribution 報. See *Da zhidu lun*, 25:100a10–11; Greene, *Secrets*, 172–73; and Swanson, *Clear Serenity*, 338–39. And even these are variously defined: the "obstruction of deeds" 業障 often refers to the five sins of instant retribution (patricide, matricide, killing an arhat, splitting the sangha, or spilling the blood of a Buddha, on which see Silk, "Good and Evil"). Given the frequency of their mention in *Explication of Dreams*, I think it is very unlikely that the text understands 業障 as referring to these sins of instant retribution, and I maintain that, instead, it simply means karma. On some historical reasons for the multiplicity and complexity of such lists, see Cox, "Attainment," 63–65.
82. Lamotte, "Passions," 91. In many texts there are, further, "impregnations or latent odors of the passions [or "habituated tendencies of affliction," DDB], *kleśa-vāsanā* in Sanskrit, *fannao xi* 煩惱習 in Chinese (also *xiqi* 習氣, *yuqi* 餘氣, *canqi* 殘氣) . . . secondary residues of the passions which remain in the mind after the destruction of the passions and determine an irrational, seemingly impassioned behavior. It is thus that a sesame seed perfumed by a flower retains the flower's scent when the latter is no more" (ibid.). None of these further terms appears in *Explication of Dreams*. See also Dessein, "Of Seeds and Sprouts," 19, 26, and "Contaminants," 76; Bronkhorst, "The Buddha and the Jainas" and "Did the Buddha Believe"; and Greene, *Chan Before Chan*, 176–77, who notes the early Buddhist claim that "liberation does not result from destroying bad karma directly, through . . . painful austerities . . . , but by using the Buddhist path of precepts, meditation, and wisdom to become free of the mental impurities (*kleśa*) in whose absence past karma lacks the power to cause rebirth." According to Cox, "abandoning and preventing the future arising of defilements" is the ultimate goal of Buddhist practice, at least as understood in later Sarvāstivādin Abhidharma texts (Cox, "Attainment," 66).
83. The other entries in which *fannao* are mentioned are 57, 64, 69, 79, 88, 91, 102, 103, and the entry appearing in sequence after the fifty-sixth and starting at 86b7, beginning with 菩薩夢中聞得法功德聲.
84. All but one of the nine instances of this phrase in the entire Taishō canon occur in *Explication of Dreams*.
85. For example, Donner, "Chih-i's Meditation on Evil."
86. See Zacchetti, "Prajñāpāramitā Sūtras," 181. In the *Perfection of Wisdom in 8,000 Lines* Māra appears often, especially in chapters 11, 17, 21, 24, and 27. His obstructive activity sometimes seems desperate, as when he places dirt on the high seat that has been prepared for the Buddha to preach from, thus impurifying it and delaying the proceedings while water is fetched to clean up. See Conze, *Eight Thousand Lines*, 295–96, and Shinohara, "Removal of Sins," 255–57. Other discussions of Māra were cited in chapter 1, in the section "Dream Agents and Idioms of Practice."
87. By "testing" mountain-dwelling seekers of transcendence, for example, in Ge Hong's writings. See Kamitsuka, "Concept of Māra," 36, and Gundersen, "Attacked by Māra," 54.
88. *Shichan boluomi cidi famen* 46:506c5; see Gundersen, "Attacked by Māra," 64. On this work see Swanson, *Clear Serenity*, 2135; Zhiyi's shorter manual on meditation (*Xiuxi zhiguan zuochan fayao*) is "an abbreviated and updated version of this work."
89. See Swanson, *Clear Serenity*, 1393–1409, translating *Mohe zhiguan*, 46:115b–117a.

90. In the initial list of signs (in both editions of the canon) the dream involves presenting these offerings *to a Tathāgata*. Also, there the incense is in paste 塗, not powder 末, form.
91. Here *dāna* is translated as 施, whereas a few characters earlier it's transliterated as 檀.
92. I've mostly relied on Zacchetti, "Prajñāpāramitā Sūtras." See also Zacchetti, *In Praise*, 1–140. Treatments of Chinese translations of *prajñāpāramitā* literature may be found in Zürcher, *Buddhist Conquest*, 339–40n182; Tsukamoto, *History*, 369–85; and Ch'en, *Buddhism*, 58–60. To better understand the contexts of these passages I have consulted Conze's *Eight Thousand Lines*, 227–29, and *Large Sutra*, 431–34, although of course his translations are based on Sanskrit and Tibetan texts that don't necessarily match up closely with these Chinese renditions.
93. See Falk and Karashima, "First-Century *Prajñāpāramitā* Manuscript: *parivarta* 1" and "First-Century *Prajñāpāramitā* Manuscript: *parivarta* 5"; and Strauch, "Early Mahāyāna."
94. See Zacchetti, "Prajñāpāramitā Sūtras," 184–87.
95. On it see Karashima, "Was the *Aṣṭasāhasrikā*"; Zacchetti, "Prajñāpāramitā Sūtras," 182; Nattier, *Guide*, 80. I have also consulted Karashima's exacting *Critical Edition* and *Glossary*.
96. See Nattier, *Guide*, 136–37, and "Who Produced"; Zacchetti, "Prajñāpāramitā Sūtras," 182–83; and Zürcher, *Buddhist Conquest*, 48–51.
97. See Nattier, *Guide*, 62, 97; Zacchetti, "Prajñāpāramitā Sūtras," 184, 189; and Zürcher, *Buddhist Conquest*, 62, 64.
98. See Zacchetti, "Prajñāpāramitā Sūtras," 183, and *In Praise*, 38–39; and Karashima, *Glossary*, ix. On Zhu Fonian see also Nattier, "Re-Evaluating."
99. See Nattier, *Guide*, 97, and Zacchetti, "Prajñāpāramitā Sūtras," 189.
100. For a partial translation that doesn't include the section of interest here, see Shi Huifeng, "Kumārajīva's *Xiaopin*."
101. On this text see, most recently, Zacchetti, *Da zhidu lun*. Were it not lacking the relevant section, *Guangzan jing* 光讃經, the translation by Dharmarakṣa's team of the *Larger Perfection of Wisdom*, would also warrant discussion here. See Zacchetti, *In Praise*, 51–62.
102. The chapter is, however, assigned different titles across the versions.
103. Prajñāpāramitā sutras appropriate the earlier tools for praxis in the Buddhist repertoire but remain focused on Buddhahood—not *arhat*-ship—as the goal. One was mostly to engage in the same practices while redirecting the expected effects. This was probably the original "skill in means." See Deleanu, "Preliminary Study on Meditation," 69, and Zacchetti, "Prajñāpāramitā Sūtras," 174. On bodhisattvas' irreversibility see Gilks, "No Turning Back."
104. The texts considered here uniformly use 相 to designate these signs.
105. Conze gives, "It is another mark if, even in his dreams, he *sees himself as a Tathagata*" (*Perfection of Wisdom in Eight Thousand Lines*, 227, emphasis added). This presumably fits the wording of the later Sanskrit version he was working from, but, as we can see in the detailed comparison offered in appendix B, only one of the much earlier Chinese versions agrees.
106. The versions differ as to whether the dreamer, as a member of the audience, sees the Buddha preaching from midair, or whether the dreamer sees himself as a Buddha preaching. For a comparative analysis, see appendix B.
107. This aspiration is an example of what has been termed "remodelling the world"—the notion that, because of their achievements, Buddhas can design their future

realm to specifications of their choosing. The absence of the three unfortunate paths of rebirth is a fixture of such discussions. See Sasaki, "Remodelling"; Nattier, "Indian Roots," 185–87, and "Realm of Akṣobhya," 81–84.

108. As Karashima notes (*Critical Edition*, 357n156), in the Sanskrit and Tibetan versions the fire's spread from house to house results from *the bodhisattva's* past karma, as reflected in Conze's translation (*Eight Thousand Lines*, 228–29). He opines that this is the result of a later redaction.

109. Good starts on this sort of analysis have been made in Teiser, "Ornamenting" and "Literary Style," and Wolf, "Ritual Refashioned."

110. Burlingame, "Act of Truth," 429.

111. Khoroche, *Once the Buddha*, 258n6. See also Kimbrough, "Reading the Miraculous Powers," 19 and passim; W. N. Brown, "Duty as Truth" and "Rg Veda 10.34"; Nattier, "Realm of Akṣobhya," 87; Thompson, "Truth-Acts in Vedic"; Wayman, "Hindu-Buddhist Rite of Truth"; and Kong, *Saccakiriyā*.

112. Austin, "Performative-Constative," 13.

113. Note that Austin and Searle do allow for the possibility that a given performative utterance may be "infelicitous" or may "misfire" because of being incorrectly formed, uttered by the wrong person or at the wrong time or in the wrong setting, etc. In fact, they spend much ink trying to sketch the general conditions under which speech acts may be infelicitous: see Austin, *How To Do Things*, 14–52, and "Performative-Constative," 14–15; and Searle, "What Is a Speech Act?"

114. See Campany, *Dreamscape*, 47–49.

115. *Mohe zhiguan* 46:107b20–25; translation modifying Swanson, *Clear Serenity*, 1334.

116. This notion is not without precedent: for an example, see Campany, *Dreamscape*, 44–45.

117. See Orzech and Sørensen, "*Mudrā*, Mantra, Mandala," 80.

118. *Tuoluoni jijing* 18:809b.

119. *Tuoluoni jijing* 18:825c.

120. These are the three aspects of dream incubation outlined in Patton, "Great and Strange Correction." For a superb study of incubation in the ancient Mediterranean world, see Renberg, *Where Dreams May Come*.

121. As this manuscript was going to press, I learned of a recent study of what seems to have been an obscure Qing-period compilation titled *Secret Book for Requesting Dreams* (*Qimeng mishu* 祈夢秘書): see Zhang, "Incubating Prognostic Dreams."

122. No method for interpreting the resultant dream is prescribed in the text, perhaps because it was expected to be a direct divine visitation needing no decoding.

123. *Dongshen badi miaojing jing* 11b–12a. On this text see TTC, 266–69, and Steavu, *Writ of the Three Sovereigns*, 219–24, who gives a detailed outline of its contents. On other Sanhuang divination prescriptions see Andersen, "Talking."

124. *Shangqing taishang huangsu sishisi fang jing* 12a–b; *Yunji qiqian* 46.18b–19a. On this scripture, which accounts for most of roll 46 of *Yunji qiqian*, see TTC, 179.

125. *Tuoluoni jijing* 18:854c.

126. *Tuoluoni jijing* 18:814c. Yet another interesting incubation method is prescribed in *Xukongzang pusa wen qi fo tuoluoni zhou jing* (early sixth century) 21:563b (not 593b as indicated in Strickmann, *Mantras et mandarins*, 474n10), but since it's designed to secure direct visions of Buddhas rather than to elicit diagnostic signs, I bypass it here.

127. On these sutras, the differences among them, and their histories, see Sørensen, "Spell of the Great, Golden Peacock Queen," and the brilliant study by Des Jardins, *Le sūtra de la Mahāmāyūrī*. Yijing worked from a different version of this sutra than

the ones reflected in earlier Chinese translations. The Japanese monk Myōe recorded a dream in which he saw two great peacock kings (or queens?) adorned with jewels which spoke Dharma verses; each of the peacocks bestowed a sutra on him, and when he woke he found his pillow soaked with the tears of joy he'd shed in his dream. See Girard, *Un moine de la secte Kegon*, 118–19, and Tanabe, *Myōe the Dreamkeeper*, 161–62.

128. *Da kongque zhou wang jing* 19:476c.

129. This sutra is discussed at length in Shinohara, "Removal of Sins," and Kuo Li-ying, "*Da fangdeng tuoluoni jing.*" On the sutra and related confession and repentance practices see Bodiford, "Matara"; Greene, *Chan Before Chan*, 181–82; Hubbard, *Absolute Delusion*, 21–24; Jensen, "Dreaming Betwixt and Between," 134–37; Kuo Liying, *Confession*; Yamabe, "Visionary Repentance"; Adamek, "Addressing the Mind"; Stevenson, "Four Kinds of Samādhi," 61–67; and Donner, "Great Calming," 337. On Daoist rites with similar functions see Bokenkamp, "Sackcloth"; Verellen, *Imperiled Destinies*; and Pregadio, ed., *Encyclopedia of Taoism*, 1001.

130. *Da fangdeng tuoluoni jing* 21:652a, translation modifying Swanson, *Clear Serenity*, 1651.

131. Most of the relevant chapter of the text is translated or summarized in Swanson, *Clear Serenity*, 1651–57. Several examples of discussions of dream incubation in Tibetan Buddhist texts are discussed in Young, *Dreaming in the Lotus*, 137–46.

132. On this text see Willemen, Dessein, and Cox, *Sarvāstivāda Buddhist Scholasticism*, 229–39, and BEB, 1:99.

133. I translate *xiang* differently in these opening lines for consistency with usage throughout chapter 2 and because of what these translations are likely to mean to Anglophone readers. But "marks" and "signs" in this context amount to the same thing.

134. Literally "if one is *unable* (*bu neng* 不能) [to respond] in these ways."

135. *Apidamo da piposha lun* 27:886a5–19, modifying the translation in Buswell, "Path to Perdition," 111–12. On this text's place among Abhidharma treatises translated or written in Chinese, see BEB, 1:88–102.

136. And the stakes are high, for the interlocutor has just claimed that there are some who, even if they perform a large quantity of wholesome actions, will *still* be unable to plant the seeds of liberation. How to know whether one is among them?

137. See Teiser, *Scripture on the Ten Kings*, 103n5, and Salguero, "Fields of Merit," 342.

138. See for example *Guannian Amituofo xiang haisanmei gongde famen* 47:24b, translated in Stevenson, "Pure Land Buddhist Worship," 378. For further studies of this phenomenon and its textual traces in early medieval China and Japan, see Mai, "Visualization Apocrypha"; Stone, "With the Help of 'Good Friends'" and *Right Thoughts*; Horton, "Mukaekō." Voluminous records of cases of individuals' rebirth in pure lands were also circulated and collected in texts of the "traditions of rebirth" (*wangsheng zhuan* 往生傳) genre. See Lai, "Legends of Births"; Sharf, "On Pure Land Buddhism," 290–91; and Mai, "Visualization Apocrypha," 30–39.

139. Greene, *Chan Before Chan*, 111. On these see Funayama, "Rikuchō jidai ni okeru bosatsukai," 14–21, and Groner, "Ordination Ritual."

140. *Fanwang jing* 24:1008c; translation modifying Yamabe, "Visionary Repentance," 19. See also Yamabe, "Bonmōkyō"; Kuo Li-ying, *Confession*, 56–58; Stevenson, "Four Kinds of Samādhi," 61–67, 71; Zürcher, *Buddhism in China*, 625; Robson, "Sin," 83; Groner, "Ordination Ritual"; Adamek, "Addressing the Mind"; Kuramoto Shōtoku, "Hokuchō jidai ni okeru hōdōzan to kōsōgyō"; and Ōtsuka Nobuo, *Indo shoki mikkyō seiritsu katei no kenkyū*, 225–78. Other texts issue similar prescriptions.

141. See Greene, *Chan before Chan* and *Secrets*.

142. See *Pusa shanjie jing* 30:1014a, and the translation in Yamabe, "Visionary Repentance," 31. The text was originally the fifth roll of *Pusa shanjie jing* and was included in the Taishō canon under that title). On Guṇavarman see *Gaoseng zhuan* 340a–342b; DB 190–91; Heirman, "Chinese Nuns"; Funayama, "Guṇavarman"; and Greene, *Chan Before Chan*, 50. The history of the translation of this and similar texts is complex; see for example Adamek, *Mystique*, 419n53.

143. See *Xiuxi zhiguan zuochan fayao* 46:463a6–15; translation in Swanson, *Clear Serenity*, 1668).

144. See *Gaoseng zhuan* 50:336c19; Greene, *Chan Before Chan*, 111; Yamabe, "Visionary Repentance," 19–20; and Shih, *Biographies*, 104. On Dharmakṣema see Chen Jinhua, "Indian Buddhist Missionary"; DB 123–24; and Zürcher, *Buddhism in China*, 558.

145. See, for instance, the passage from the "Hundred Diseases Precepts" 百病律 section of *Regulations from the Dark Metropolis* (*Xuandu lüwen* 8a–b) discussed in Verellen, *Imperiled Destinies*, 100. On the date of this text and what it reveals about abbeys or monasteries at the time it was compiled, see Jiang Boqin, "Xuandu lü niandai."

146. See for example the passage translated from the *Scripture and Instructions of the Nine Elixirs of the Yellow Thearch* (*Huangdi jiuding shendan jingjue* 1.1b2–10) in Pregadio, *Great Clarity*, 161. See also Campany, *To Live as Long*, 40, 207.

147. See for example Campany, *Making Transcendents*, 102–4, 132–33; Campany, *To Live as Long*, 140–41 and 389–90 (on the case of a woman identified only as "Cheng Wei's wife"), 259–70 and 456–63 (on Wang Yuan and Cai Jing—Wang also rejects a Mr. Chen for transmission after having him stand facing the sun and scrutinizing him for unspecified signs). A similar line occurs in the hagiography of Yan Qing (see ibid., 346–47 and 528–29). The relevant line from Cheng Wei's Wife story is picked up in *Xiulian dadan yaozhi* 2.12b1.

148. *Shangqing jiudan shanghua taijing Zhongji jing* 27a; *Wushang biyao* 31.14b. On this scripture see TTC, 164–65, and Robinet, *La révélation*, 2:171–74.

149. *Taishang yupei jindang taiji jinshu shangjing* 2b; compare the similar passage at 26a: 有金名列於上清精丹感於九天得見此經. On this text see TTC, 176–77, and Robinet, *La révélation*, 2:213–18. Cf. *Wushang biyao* 31.14b–15a. Compare the passage in *Shangqing housheng daojun lieji* 6a–b, translated in Bokenkamp, *Early Daoist Scriptures*, 350–51.

150. *Shenxian zhuan* hagiography of Liu Gen 劉根 as anthologized in *Taiping guangji* 10.2; cf. Campany, *To Live as Long*, 243, and *Making Transcendents*, 132–34.

151. *Zuochan sanmei jing* 15:277c13–14; see also Yamabe and Sueki, *Sutra on the Concentration*, 44, and Greene, *Chan Before Chan*, 66–67. Compare the discourse on sages having facial "glossiness" 睟, "brilliant whiteness" 皜皜, etc., discussed in Csikszentmihalyi, *Material Virtue*, 154–57.

152. See Csikszentmihalyi, *Material Virtue*, 236–39.

153. On this text and its author see CL 554–57 and Shryock, *Study of Human Abilities*.

154. On this work see Moro Shigeki, "*Senzatsukyō* no seiritsu to juyō"; Kuo Li-ying, "Divination, jeux de hazard et purification"; Guggenmos, "*Qian* Divination," 51–54; Zhiru, *Savior Bodhisattva*, 84–89; Strickmann, *Chinese Poetry*, 80–81; Lai, "The *Chan-ch'a ching*"; and Makita, *Gikyō kenkyū*, 108–14. The second *juan* has been translated in Rulu, *Teachings of the Buddha*, 108–18. Although it falls beyond my historical scope, a marvelous example of how this text and its prescribed practices figured in the life of an individual practitioner during the Ming-Qing transition has been closely studied in McGuire, "Seeing Suchness." We have further evidence of its use in the form of a manuscript copy dating to ca. 1000–1200 and recovered in 2005

from Xixia grotto temples in the Shanzuigou valley; see http://www.kaogu.cn/en/Publication/New_books/2013/1025/30004.html. On divination in Buddhist contexts see Guggenmos, "List of Magic and Mantic Practices"; Strickmann, *Chinese Poetry*, 76–86; and Yang Gang and Anderl, "Prognostication." In monastic biographies, however, prognosticatory dreams are almost always direct rather than symbolic and thus don't require interpretation. See Yang Gang and Anderl, "Prognostication," 13n31, and Jensen, "Dreaming Betwixt and Between," 119–20, who notes that some dream stories in these texts even have an "anti-oneiromantic character."

155. *Guang hongming ji* 52:331b17–19. On this text see Wu Pei-Yi, "Self-Examination," 11–13 (but this line isn't translated there). On the special ability to recollect previous lives (*jātismara*) see Demiéville, "Sur la mémoire des existences antérieures"; de la Vallée Poussin, "Le Bouddha et les abhijñās"; and Schopen, *Figments*, 190–220.
156. Borrowing the phrase from Schaberg, "Logic of Signs."
157. Compare this characterization of the language used in Seneca's *De ira* (book 3): "Seneca uses terms related not to juridical but to administrative practices, as when a comptroller looks at the books or when a building inspector examines a building" (Foucault, *Technologies of the Self*, 33).
158. Greene, *Chan Before Chan*, 106–7.
159. Greene, *Chan Before Chan*, 108–9.
160. Jensen, "Dreaming Betwixt and Between." Jensen adduces the few exceptions that prove this rule at pp. 107–10.
161. My wording here is partly indebted to these lines in Greene, *Chan Before Chan*: "If, as Sven Bretfeld cogently suggests, the classical Buddhist *mārga* treatise is a literary genre that gives narrative meaning to Buddhist doctrine by setting each aspect of it within a timeless story of meditative progress from ordinary being to liberated saint, texts such as the *Five Gates* and *Chan Essentials* can be said to do just the opposite: they provide the tools that enable the particular, concrete experiences of individual meditators to be deemed instances of something normatively valuable. Rather than explaining where within an ideal meditator's experience each normative doctrinal truth will be realized, these texts explain what normative attainment a given concrete experience is the sign of. Seen in this light, these texts are neither descriptions of the experiences of past meditators nor prescriptions designed to produce or inculcate normatively sanctioned experiences, but something akin to handbooks for the interpretation of meditative experience" (97–98).
162. On the interpretation of coded dreams see Campany, *Dreamscape*, 92–131. On *manuals* of dream interpretation (including references to their use in practice) see ibid., 73, 80–82, 83–85, 90.
163. Compare Greene, *Chan Before Chan*, 81, 89.
164. This lack of evidence of use is true of *Explication of Dreams* though certainly not of most dream interpretation manuals that have survived. In his comprehensive study of dreaming's roles in medieval monks' lives as reflected in the two major pre-Song biographical collections, Jensen ("Dreaming Betwixt and Between") finds not a single instance in which a monk is depicted as consulting a manual to interpret his own or someone else's dream. But the archive certainly doesn't lack examples of other dreamers consulting manuals (see Campany, *Dreamscape*, 73, 80–82, 83–85, 90).

Chapter 3

1. *Analects* 7.5; *Lunyu jijie yishu* 4.11b; translation following Lévi, *Entretiens de Confucius*, 43.
2. For two recent positions see Hunter, *Confucius beyond the Analects*, and Goldin, "Confucius and His Disciples." Other important recent studies of the figure and

ever-shifting textual representations of Confucius include Nylan and Wilson, *Lives of Confucius*; van Norden, ed., *Confucius and the Analects*; Goldin, ed., *Concise Companion to Confucius*; and Hunter and Kern, eds., *Confucius and the Analects Revisited*.

3. The unity of the "Confucian" tradition and the centrality of the figure of Confucius to it have both been thoughtfully reexamined in recent years: see for example Csikszentmihalyi and Nylan, "Constructing Lineages"; Csikszentmihalyi, *Material Virtue*, 22–32; Loewe, *Dong Zhongshu*; and Cheng, "What Did It Mean to be a *Ru*?" But, as Sarah Allan has remarked, "the term *ru* [儒] is common in pre-Han as well as Han texts and the *ru* are clearly associated with Confucius. . . . The *ru* were 'Confucians' in the sense that they were defined by their adherence to the figure of Confucius, whom they took as the 'master' (*zi* 子). There was not yet an idea of philosophical lineage or a requirement of philosophical consistency, but there were teachers and students. All of Confucius' students—and his students' students—would have been *ru* by definition" (*Buried Ideas*, 144–45; see also Allan, "Not the *Lun yu*," 125–26, 142–43). I'm inclined to follow Allan on this, though the point makes little difference for my purposes since, whatever else he was, "Confucius" was clearly a figure emblematic of a concern for self-cultivation, even in texts (such as many *Zhuangzi* passages) that mock him and his followers for the ways they went about it.
4. *Analects* 2.4; translation roughly following the French of Lévi, *Entretiens de Confucius*, 8; cf. Slingerland, *Confucius: Analects*, 9.
5. Slingerland, *Confucius: Analects*, 65. For further comments on the passage see Fukatsu Tanefusa, "Kodai chūgokujin no shisō," 954–55, and Ong, *Interpretation of Dreams*, 60–62.
6. Slingerland, *Confucius: Analects*, 65.
7. *Analects* 3.12; translation is that of Slingerland, *Confucius: Analects*, 21. Recent discussions of the delicate place of divine or spirit-related matters in early Confucian discourse include Allan, "Not the *Lunyu*," 117, 125, 140 (on the tension between the way *Analects* is often read and an ostensibly "Confucian" text like the Chu bamboo-slip manuscript *Zigao*); Gentz, "Past as a Messianic Vision," 6–10; Csikszentmihalyi, *Material Virtue*, 41–42, 238–40; and T. Wilson, "Spirits and the Soul."
8. Not even a term meaning "ancestor," much less "spirit" or "ghost," is used. What sparing references there are to the recipients of sacrifice are elliptical—yet they are also unmistakable: the sacrificer will see "those for whom the vigil is employed" 其所為齊者, "he will certainly see something indistinctly in the place where [the spirit-tablet] is" 僾然必有見乎其位, and he will hear "his" (or her, 其) movements and sighing (*Liji jijie* 1208–9). This verbal indirection is heightened in the two major English translations available, James Legge's of over a century ago (Legge, *Sacred Books, Part 4*, 211) and Irene Bloom's, which closely follows Legge's (Bloom, "The Meaning of Sacrifices," 339–40); both sprinkle forms of "to seem" as a kind of ontological softener throughout the passage, and both inexplicably convert every "must see" 必有見 / 聞 to "will *seem to* see/hear," perhaps because the passage violated their expectations of what a Confucian text should be saying. It should also be noted that what looks like ontological reticence might instead have simply been deferential reference, much as the ruler was often referred to obliquely as "the one above" 上. For a corrective reading and discussion of the passage see T. Wilson, "Spirits and the Soul," 193–94.
9. Chinese text based on Knoblock and Riegel, *Annals of Lü Buwei*, 618. In translating I've consulted ibid. and Slingerland, *Confucius: Analects*, 65. On the date and authorship of *Annals* see ECT, 324, and S. Cook, "The *Lüshi Chunqiu*." Ning Yue is

mentioned in only a few early sources (including two other passages in *Lüshi chunqiu*—see Knoblock and Riegel, *Annals of Lü Buwei*, 361–62, 618–19), in which he is portrayed as a commoner who applied himself diligently and offered wise counsel. A work in one roll is attributed to him under the Scholars (*ru* 儒) subsection of the Masters (*zi* 子) section of the *History of the Han* bibliographic treatise (*Han shu* 30:1725).

10. I discuss three further instances of the SPILLOVER PARADIGM in Campany, *Dreamscape*, 37–40—one of them Confucian, the other two Buddhist in orientation. Importantly, that dreams under this paradigm constitute "real events in the world" needs qualification in the case of some (but not all) Buddhist texts considered below, in that, for such texts, nothing can be said to be "real" that lacks own-being (*zi xing* 自性), as do dreams. But then again, in such texts no other events in the contingent world enjoy own-being either, so dream events are no less real than others.
11. A good sense of what this term entailed can be gained from Verellen, "Encounter as Revelation," a study of Du Guangting's 杜光庭 (850–933) *Traditions of Encounters with Divine Transcendents* (*Shenxian ganyu zhuan* 神仙感遇傳).
12. See Ortner, "Patterns of History," 60–63.
13. Mattingly, *Healing Dramas*, 19. For further discussion see Campany, *Making Transcendents*, 11–13; *Signs from the Unseen Realm*, 47–48; and *Strange Writing*, 116, 212, 258, 308, 322, 367–68.
14. For further discussion of *ganying* see Sharf, *Coming to Terms*, 77–136; Verellen, "Encounter as Revelation," 369–72; and Campany, "Real Presence," 264–65, and *Signs from the Unseen Realm*, 31–32, 49, 54–55.
15. On Wang Yan and his *Mingxiang ji* see Campany, *Signs from the Unseen Realm*.
16. There is apparent mention of this incident in *Song shu* 5.81.
17. On this bodhisattva see Mochizuki, *Bukkyō daijiten*, 3294b–3297a; Hou, "Buddhist Pantheon," 1123; Hureau, "Translations," 770; and Wong, *Chinese Steles*, 145–147, 172, 177.
18. These are the five paths of rebirth. On this textual and visual motif see Teiser, *Reinventing the Wheel*. For an excellent reflection on the significance of its relative rarity in the Chinese archive (and on the significance of five versus six paths in that archive), see Schmid, "Revisioning the Buddhist Cosmos."
19. That is, because he knew that he had divine protection and would eventually be freed.
20. Translation based on *Fayuan zhulin* 23.459b–c, except that in the line starting with 球心知神力, I follow TPGJ 110.26 in reading the final graph as 志 instead of 到. For more on the passage (including other versions) see Campany, *Signs from the Unseen Realm*, 205–7. The story is translated and discussed in Teiser, *Reinventing the Wheel*, 121–26; my translation differs significantly, as explained in Campany, *Signs from the Unseen Realm*, 206n717.
21. See *Xi Guanshiyin* item 21 (in Makita, *Rikuchō kōitsu Kanzeon ōkenki no kenkyū*, 34–35), discussed in Campany, "Real Presence," 240.
22. For an example of a practice stretching over a practitioner's lifetime and stimulating a response, see Campany, "Miracle Tales as Scripture Reception," 37–38; for instances of practices engaged in intensely during a single night, see Campany, *Signs from the Unseen Realm*, 171, 189–90.
23. See Lowe, *Ritualized Writing*; Teiser, *Scripture on the Ten Kings*; Campany, "Notes on the Devotional Uses" and "Miracle Tales as Scripture Reception."
24. See Chün-fang Yü, *Kuan-yin*, 1–262; E. Wang, *Shaping the Lotus Sutra*, 221–28; and Campany: "Real Presence," "Earliest Tales," and *Signs from the Unseen Realm*, 49–51.

25. See for example Jan Yün-hua, "Power of Recitation"; Kuo Li-ying, "La récitation des noms de Buddha"; and Campany, "Real Presence," 248–50.
26. See Campany, "Real Presence," 266–67, and *Signs from the Unseen Realm*, 63–68.
27. The locutions in quotation marks happen to appear in Lin Fu-shih, "Religious Taoism and Dreams," 107, but the misapprehension is widespread. For further discussion see Allen, *Shifting Stories*, 18–30; Dudbridge: *Religious Experience and Lay Society*, 16–17, *Portrait of Five Dynasties China*, 200–253 (specifically the notations regarding informants), and *Books, Tales and Vernacular Culture*, 105–12; Gjertson, *Miraculous Retribution*, 93–98; and Campany: *Making Transcendents*, 21, 32–33, 216–58, *Signs from the Unseen Realm*, 17–30, "Miracle Tales as Scripture Reception," 27–28, and *Garden of Marvels*, xxiv–xxxiv.
28. And arguably much earlier than that, though the question of just how far back is beyond the scope of this discussion. One has only to think of the conception of heaven and of "percipient ghosts" in the *Mozi* 墨子 materials (on the latter of which see recently Gibas, "Mozi and the Ghosts") and the steady drumbeat of events being read as signs of cosmic responses to human action (see, e.g., Schaberg, "Logic of Signs," not to mention the vast literature on omens and portents).
29. See Campany, *Dreamscape*, 37–38, on the *Jin shu* biography of Liu Yin 劉殷.
30. On this text and its compiler see Verellen, *Du Guangting* and "Evidential Miracles"; TTC, 419–20; and Miyazawa, "Dōkyō reigen ki ni tsuite."
31. This narrative is one of more than two dozen in the text featuring "verificatory responses" by Lord Lao 老君. See the list in Miyazawa, "Dōkyō reigen ki ni tsuite," 14–16.
32. Its title in the canon is *Dongxuan lingbao ziran jiutian shengshen zhang jing*. On it see TTC, 220; Bokenkamp, "Sources," 480 (my translation of its title follows Bokenkamp's); and Kobayashi, *Rikuchō dōkyōshi kenkyū*, 217–40. Three commentaries on it, dating from the thirteenth–fourteenth centuries, have come down to us (see TTC, 725–26).
33. In the scripture these lines appear at 10b5–8.
34. *Daojiao lingyan ji* 10.3a–6b; a much-truncated version appears in *Yunji qiqian* 119.15a. Most of the story is taken up with a lengthy and detailed dialogue between the emperor and Yao Yuanchong, who says of himself that he "doesn't know books" but is good at hunting.
35. He is mentioned elsewhere in Du Guangting's writings.
36. *Daojiao lingyan ji* 12.10a–11a (story 131 in Miyazawa's numbering).
37. *Daojiao lingyan ji* 5.1a–3a; *Yunji qiqian* 118.5b–7b. I've consulted the partial translation in Verellen, "Evidential Miracles," 240–43. On Jiuku tianzun see Yusa Noboru, "Tōdai ni mirareru Kyūku tenson shinko ni tsuite," and Mollier, *Buddhism and Taoism*, 174–208.
38. For more examples of such waking-life confirmations of the reality of dream events, see Campany, *Dreamscape*, 135–41.
39. On the history of this version of the sutra and its relation to others, see Harrison, *Pratyutpanna Samādhi Sūtra*, 4–5, and "Earliest Chinese Translations," 145–50; and Nattier, *Guide*, 73–89. For studies of this and similar texts see Harrison, "*Buddhānusmṛti*" and "Commemoration and Identification." On Lokakṣema's work and significance see Zürcher, *Buddhist Conquest*, 35–36, and *Buddhism in China*, 428, 433–34, 443–44; and Tsukamoto, *History*, 98–103.
40. *Banzhou sanmei jing* 904b.
41. *Banzhou sanmei jing* 13:913a16–21, modifying Harrison, *Pratyutpanna Samādhi Sūtra*, 61. In what follows I silently modify Harrison's translation.
42. *Banzhou sanmei jing* 13:905a; Harrison, *Pratyutpanna Samādhi Sūtra*, 17–18.

43. See Harrison, *Pratyutpanna Samādhi Sūtra*, 3. On this aspect of the sutra's teaching see also Harrison, "*Buddhānusmṛti*," 46–51; Deleanu, "Preliminary Study on Meditation"; Ducor, "Les sources de la Sukhāvatī," 392–93; and BEB 1:223–24.
44. *Banzhou sanmei jing* 13:905c–906a.
45. 13:903c12–15. In view of this and similar passages Harrison comments: "The bodhisattva path was to some extent an exercise in creative visualization," that it may have "constitute[d] a kind of dream, a dream deliberately engaged in, of unlimited power, bliss and freedom from the shackles of our ordinary reality, of purity and perfection." Not that it was an idle or user-friendly exercise; on the contrary, it was "a heroic activity, pursued with relentless discipline and determination, day and night. . . the most strenuous mental asceticism, . . . a regime of stringent ritual exercises from which there is little or no rest at any time, even in one's sleep" ("Mediums and Messages," 144–46).
46. Quinter ("Visualizing") argues that the standard attribution of the translation to Nie Daozhen (a collaborator of Dharmarakṣa) is baseless and that the text was in fact part of a wave of indigenously composed fifth-century sutras prescribing methods of visualization and contemplation.
47. *Wenshushili banniepan jing* 14:481a; see also the translation in Quinter, "Visualizing," 111–12.
48. *Guan Xukongzang pusa jing* 13:677c8–9.
49. *Guanfo sanmei hai jing* 15:663a10, 665c29–666a4, 666b12–16, 666c9–11, and 666c26–29. On this and the previously mentioned sutra see also Greene, "Visions and Visualizations," 322–23.
50. *Da mingdu jing* 8:496c7–11; for a critical recension of the passage in Lokakṣema's version see Karashima, *Critical Edition*, 332–33. See also Conze, *Eight Thousand Lines*, 215. The text goes on to raise the question whether deeds done in dreams have karmic effects and answers thus: Insofar as the Buddha has taught that ultimately all dharmas are like a dream, then (from the standpoint of ultimate reality) the dreamer's deed will not be added to his heap of karma. But (from the standpoint of empirical reality) it *will* be added if, after waking, the practitioner consciously forms the desire to carry out the deed committed in his dream.
51. *Da mingdu jing* 8:494c14–15; cf. Conze, *Eight Thousand Lines*, 201. One of the vows of the future Buddha Akṣobhya is not to have emissions of semen even while dreaming (see BEB 1:214).
52. These three *samādhi*s are those of emptiness, signlessness, and non-contrivance (DDB s.v. 三三昧). *Da mingdu jing* 8:587b22; see also Swanson, *Clear Serenity*, 385.
53. On the translator see Forte, "South Indian Monk Bodhiruci," and Orzech, Sørensen, and Payne, eds., *Esoteric Buddhism*, 267–68, 271–72. On Amoghapāśa Avalokiteśvara 不空羂索, an esoteric form of the bodhisattva Sound Observer, and texts and iconography associated with him, see the excellent studies by Wong: "Bukong Juansuo Guanyin xintan" and "The Case of Amoghapāśa."
54. *Bukong juansuo shenbian zhenyan jing* 20:382c.
55. *Bukong juansuo shenbian zhenyan jing* 20:386b–c.
56. Agreeing with Robert's "dans ses rêves même / il ne verra que des choses sublimes" (*Le Sûtra du Lotus*, 263) and not Hurvitz's "Or, in a dream, he may simply see wondrous sights" (*Lotus Blossom*, 203).
57. Agreeing with Robert's "et il se verra lui-même / en train de leur prêcher la Loi" (*Le Sûtra du Lotus*, 264) and not Hurvitz's "To whom, showing his body, / He preaches the dharma" (*Lotus Blossom*, 204).
58. That is, the set of distinctive characteristics possessed by all Buddhas' bodies.

59. Not, I think, "and bears direct witness to unreceding knowledge" (Hurvitz, *Lotus Blossom*, 204). As seen in chapter 2, irreversibility is a key stage on the bodhisattva path, after which the practitioner's eventual realization of Buddhahood is assured.
60. That is, confirmed 證 in (his understanding of) the ultimate, unconditioned reality (not, I think, "bearing direct witness to the marks of reality" [Hurvitz, *Lotus Blossom*, 204] and not "attestant les aspects réels [Robert, *Le Sûtra du Lotus*, 264]). See DDB, s.v. 實相.
61. The text shifts here from four- to five-character lines.
62. *Miaofa lianhua jing* 9:39b20–c17, Kumārajīva's translation of the *Lotus*, consulting Hurvitz, *Lotus Blossom*, 203–5, and Robert, *Le Sûtra du Lotus*, 263–65.
63. Reading *aloud* is almost certainly implied; see Nugent, *Manifest in Words*, 133, and Campany, "Miracle Tales as Scripture Reception," 35–38. Less certain is whether these passages imply or assume that the recitation was to be done *from memory* (see Nugent, *Manifest in Words*, 74–75), although we have good evidence (some of which will be glimpsed below) that some scriptures were recited from memory. See also Kieschnick, *Eminent Monk*, 114–15, 141; Jensen, "Dreaming Betwixt and Between," 83; Greene, *Chan Before Chan*, 29, 50; McMahan, *Empty Vision*, 87–90, 194; Seymour, "Buddha's Voice"; and Dachille, "Inscribing the Corpus." But the recitation of sutras "from memory" often had marked elements of improvisation, as argued in McGovern, "Protestant Presuppositions." Beyond narrowly Buddhist contexts, recitation of texts from memory was ubiquitous and highly prized in Chinese culture: see for example Nugent, *Manifest in Words* and "Structured Gaps"; Tian Xiaofei, "Yu Xin's 'Memory Palace'"; and Krijgsman, "Inquiry into the Formation of Readership."
64. These are the focus of chapter 19, "Merits of the Dharma Preacher," but are repeatedly enjoined throughout the text. See Stevenson, "Buddhist Practice and the *Lotus Sutra*," 138–43, and Teiser and Stone, "Interpreting the *Lotus Sūtra*," 45–48.
65. Many have noted the *Lotus Sutra*'s unusually high degree of self-referentiality: it insists repeatedly on its own authority and spends a great deal of textual space instructing readers on how they should respond to it and what benefits they'll enjoy when they do (see Bielefeldt, "Expedient Devices," 65; Teiser and Stone, "Interpreting the *Lotus Sūtra*," 18; and Campany, "Miracle Tales as Scripture Reception," 26). For a rhetorical reading of the sutra see Cole, *Text as Father*.
66. It's also noteworthy that in Lokakṣema's version of the *Perfection of Wisdom in 8,000 Lines*, all of the auditory experiences that set the bodhisattva Sadāprarudita on his path toward Buddhahood occur in his dreams. See *Daoxing banruo jing* 470c20 ff.; Karashima, *Critical Edition*, 464–67; and (for comparison) Conze, *Eight Thousand Lines*, 277 ff.
67. All recensions, including the earlier critical edition and modern Japanese translation in Mugitani Kunio and Yoshikawa Tadao, *Shūshi meitsūki kenkyū* (hereafter SSMT), are incorporated in the recent annotated, critical edition of Wang Jiakui, *Zhoushi mingtong ji jiaoshi*, on which I have greatly relied. I cite passages from this latter work by its abbreviation (ZSMT) followed by page number. References to specific passages in the scripture itself appear in brackets and are keyed to the recension in the Xinwenfeng reprint of the Ming canon (DZ 9:45–81). Segments of the text are translated and introduced in Bokenkamp, "Answering a Summons." Russell, "Revelation and Narrative," approaches it from a literary perspective, focusing on how Zhou's encounters with deities "functioned as a vehicle for personal, subjective expression" (36).
68. In genre it somewhat resembles works by the Japanese monks Myōe 明恵 (1173–1232) and Keizan 瑩山 (1264–1325). On Myōe and his dream journal see Tanabe, *Myōe the Dreamkeeper*; Girard, "Le journal des rêves de Myōe"; and Girard, *Un moine de la*

secte Kegon, a superb, complete translation and study. On Keizan see Bodiford, "Keizan's Dream History," and Faure, *Visions of Power*, 124–27.

69. On Emperor Wu and his religious, literary, and political involvements, see Tian Xiaofei, *Beacon Fire*; Jansen, *Höfische Öffentlichkeit*; Bo Juncai, *Liang Wudi*; Strickmann, "On the Alchemy of T'ao Hung-ching" (esp. 155–59) and "Taoist Confirmation"; Janousch, "Emperor as Bodhisattva"; Chen Jinhua, "*Pañcavārṣika* Assemblies"; and Chittick, *Patronage and Community* and *Jiankang Empire* (esp. 295–323).
70. Strickmann, "On the Alchemy of T'ao Hung-ching," 159–61, gives a close paraphrase of the recipe.
71. On his self-dictated hagiography, *Ziyang zhenren neizhuan*, see TTC, 197–98; Robinet, *La révélation*, 2:385–88; Porkert, *Biographie*; J. Miller, *Way of Highest Clarity*, 103–60; and Pettit and Wells, "Revelation," 3.
72. Extant evidence doesn't permit us to identify what actually killed Zhou Ziliang, if in fact he did die of elixir poisoning and if the details of his death were actually as reported in the text (both of which are far from certain). Medically speaking, if this was the elixir Zhou ingested then the mushrooms would likely have compromised his liver and the mercury in the cinnabar would have affected the brain, but neither is likely to have dispatched him anywhere near as rapidly as whatever he swallowed on the day of his death, which did its work, according to Tao, "in only half the time it takes to eat a meal" 當半食頃耳 (translation in Bokenkamp, "Answering a Summons," 193)—unless the variety of mushrooms he used was really that acutely toxic. On the knowledge of mushrooms in early medieval times, see Lu Di, "Ancient Chinese People's Knowledge of Macrofungi" and "Ping daojiao dianji 'Zhong zhicao fa' de ziranshi jiazhi." Lu Di mentions one variety of toxic mushroom said to work as quickly as snake venom on those who ingested it ("Ancient Chinese People's Knowledge of Macrofungi," 45). On the use of mushrooms in self-cultivational contexts see Strickmann, "Notes on Mushroom Cults," and Steavu, "Marvelous Fungus." The recipe does clearly warn, "If you wish to ascend to the heavens rapidly, ingest all of it; you will die at once. If you wish to remain in the world for the time being, you should take it in small doses. When there's none left, you, too, will become a transcendent" 若欲速登天, 可併服之, 即死矣. 若欲且留世, 當稍服之, 盡亦仙矣 (4.20a5–6). A final consideration is that there was always a large and carefully orchestrated dose of mystery, theater, and deception in *shijie* and alchemical techniques; see Campany, "Sword Scripture" and *Making Transcendents*, 153–58.
73. On the history and geospatial coordinates of this administrative unit see http://maps.cga.harvard.edu/tgaz/placename/hvd_32276.
74. Versions vary on this point: DZ 1.5a1–2 and ZHDZ 246b have 一十六日 (corresponding to November 25), while SSMT 16 and ZSMT 32 have 二十六日 (corresponding to December 5); neither of these modern editions comments on the discrepancy. The *Mice huihan* 秘冊匯函 woodblock print edition done in the Ming Wanli period (1573–1620), p. 5a, has 二十六日. (On the discrepancies between this and the DZ edition see ZSMT 18.) Translating the passage, Bokenkamp gives November 25 ("Answering a Summons," 194).
75. On this general historiographic point see Campany, *Dreamscape*, 27–28.
76. Wang's excellent annotated edition is *Zhoushi mingtong ji jiaoshi*; see ZSMT 279–344. Wang admits the lack of definitive proof at p. 280.
77. A locution Wang uses at ZSMT 344.
78. As Wang notes at ZSMT 281.
79. See Campany, *Making Transcendents*, 263–65.
80. More on this in "The Esotericizing Dynamic" below.

81. At one point Zhou mentions explicitly to one of his divine interlocutors that he had copied out some or all of *Zhen'gao*: see 1.15a9 and ZSMT 13, 94.
82. On this aspect of Tao's scribal and editorial practice see Bokenkamp, *Fourth-Century Daoist Family*, 46–53.
83. For the three entries starting on 1.12a and running to 1.17a, Tao adds a note saying that these are all "rather confused dreams only, not direct and clear" 凡此三條, 皆髣彿夢耳, 不正分明. But it's unclear to me which entries he's referring to, since none of them contain the word 夢. Perhaps something dropped out of the text here. I found at least one instance where, unless I'm mistaken, Tao's count was off: in the span of text Tao is discussing, concerning events of the second month, he says there are six entries in all, five of them concerning waking visions and one recording a dream. But in that span there are three dream records, not one (4.16b6). Also, at one point Tao notes regarding the previous series of nine entries that some are visions 見 and some are dreams 夢 (4.4b1), but 夢 isn't used in any of them, at least as they now appear, so how does he know this?
84. See Bokenkamp, "Image Work" and *Ancestors and Anxiety*, 138, 154.
85. *Xuanren* 玄人 here refers to Zhou Ziliang in his now apotheosized state as one among the ranks of Perfected persons. See ZSMT 1–2n1, commenting on the text's opening words, 玄人周子良.
86. Modifying the translation in Bokenkamp, "Answering a Summons," 195–96.
87. "Materiality is a precondition for the social circulation and temporal persistence of experiences and ideas" (Keane, "On the Materiality of Religion," 230).
88. *Zhoushi mingtong ji* 4.5a; ZSMT 236; SSMT, 201.
89. On the cavern heavens see Soymié, "Lo-feou chan"; Verellen, "Beyond Within"; and Schafer, *Mao Shan*, 6–7. This was not Zhou's only dream journey into the Huayang heaven.
90. See *Ziyang zhenren neizhuan* 8a8; ZSMT 239n7.
91. This was *Traditions of Lady Wei of the Southern Marchmount* (*Nanyue Wei furen zhuan* 南嶽魏夫人傳), no longer extant except in quotations. See Robinet, *La révélation*, 2:399–405; Pregadio, ed., *Encyclopedia of Taoism*, 1031–32; and Robson, *Power of Place*, 187–212, 373–75.
92. As noted in Robinet, *La révélation*, 2:405, and Kleeman, *Celestial Masters*, 247, 250.
93. See Robson, *Power of Place*, 59–70.
94. We would do well, however, to heed the cautions issued in Bokenkamp, "Daoist Pantheons," when trying to list Daoist deities definitively.
95. On Han Zhong see Campany, *To Live as Long*, 243, 356; on Wang Yuan, ibid., 259–70, 456–63; on Tang Gongfang, ibid., 215–18, 432–33, and Campany, *Making Transcendents*, 104–5, 232–43.
96. His one unaccompanied dream journey is to Mount Tongqiao 桐橋, whose bejeweled palaces he describes (4.7b1–6).
97. On Fangzhang and the Azure Lad, see Schafer, *Mirages*, 109–17; Kroll, "Azure Lad," 79; and T. Smith, "Ritual and the Shaping of Narrative," 553. The Azure Lad is visited again in an "eastern palace" (probably another trip to Fangzhu) in a later dream (see 4.17a–b). Fangzhu was alternately named Fangzhang 方丈; see Pregadio, ed., *Encyclopedia of Taoism*, 788–90. On Penglai see Schafer, *Mirages*, 51–60; T. Smith, "Ritual and the Shaping of Narrative," 554; and Campany, *Making Transcendents*, 121–25, 172, 182, and *To Live as Long*, 226, 261. On "lying down in the Dipper" see TTC, 191; Mollier, *Buddhism and Taoism*, 163–65; and Robinet, *Méditation taoïste*, 281–328.
98. Zhou Dabin shows up at four points in the DZ: twice in *Dongxuan lingbao zhenling weiye tu* (25a and 27b; this text is also incorporated into the *Daozang jiyao*), once

in *Shangqing zhongjing zhu zhensheng bi* (642b), and once in *Wushang biyao* (42:541a).

99. This is one of several small inconsistencies in the text, as explained in ZSMT 240n14.
100. This line is probably misplaced; see ZSMT 241n17.
101. Wang Jiakui explains that since the *Declarations* passage Tao refers to mentions that many inhabitants of Lesser Fangzhu "uphold the way of Buddha" 奉佛道, our text's "many who serve the path" 多事道 should be understood similarly (ZSMT 241n18). Regarding the Shangqing notion that the inhabitants of Fangzhu practiced the Buddhist path, see Bokenkamp, "Buddhism in the Writings of Tao Hongjing."
102. The phrase 火棗交梨 does appear in the second roll of *Zhen'gao*, but, as Wang Jiakui points out, there it's probably used metaphorically. Either Tao Hongjing failed to grasp that, or he hoped to prevent Emperor Wu from understanding the reference (ZSMT 245n2).
103. I omit Tao's note, which explains that this Han Taihua had been mentioned in *Declarations of the Perfected* and provides information on his otherworld appointments (on him see also ZSMT 240n11). He gives no information on Lady Song, and I find no mention of her elsewhere.
104. 4.7a. It's Tao who explains what these palaces are. He adds that he doesn't know which direction they lie in.
105. 4.7a. Tao explains that it lies to the south and is a palace established by the Southern Perfected 南真, a shortened reference to Lady Wei of the Southern Marchmount 南嶽魏夫人, who appears frequently in Zhou's dreams.
106. See Campany, "Long-Distance Specialists."
107. I discuss the elided passage below.
108. Translation mostly following Bokenkamp, "Answering a Summons," 192.
109. Interestingly, HYD 4:371a cites this *Zhoushi mingtong ji* passage as exemplifying one of the several meanings of the term 婁羅 but punctuates it differently: 許終是婁羅, 夢無所知究, which would make this a general statement about the nature of dreams. They define it by binome as *weiqu* 委曲, "turned and twisted." Bokenkamp quite reasonably translates 婁羅夢 as "false dream," but I intend to bring out other relevant nuances of the expression. On Zhou's family's worry that his communications might be with profane gods see Stein, "Religious Taoism and Popular Religion," 54–55.
110. 1.17a–b; ZSMT 105.
111. In light of Liang Emperor Wu's attempted vegetarian reforms, Wang Jiakui (ZSMT 299) cites this passage as evidence supporting his theory that Tao Hongjing concocted the entire story.
112. 1.11a4–5; the passage is translated in Bokenkamp, "Answering a Summons," 198.
113. On the performative nature of Shangqing scriptures and practices see Campany, "Shangqing jing de biaoyan xingzhi."
114. *Nan Qi shu* 33.598, slightly modifying Ashmore, "Art of Discourse," 202. The analogy with archery is interesting since "the ideological importance of archery in the Western Zhou period is hard to overstate. Later texts and Western Zhou inscriptional materials accord with one another in identifying archery as a key skill of an accomplished aristocrat" (Childs-Johnson, ed., *Oxford Handbook of Early China*, 417). Nylan summarizes what the *Yili* 儀禮 section on archery has to say (*Five Confucian Classics*, 179–80). Behuniak, "Hitting the Mark," discusses archery as a source of metaphor in early Confucian texts. The article opens with this fine passage from Yang Xiong 揚雄's (53 BCE–18 CE) *Model Sayings* (*Fayan* 法言): "Cultivating yourself: take it as your bow. Rectifying your thoughts: take it as your arrows. Establish-

ing correctness: take it as your target. If you settle yourself before releasing, the shot will hit the target" 修身以為弓, 矯思以為矢, 立義以為的, 奠而後發, 發必中矣 (*Fayan yishu*, 84; compare Bullock, *Yang Xiong*, 57, and Behuniak, "Hitting the Mark," 588).

115. As related at 2.4b10.
116. 3.9a4; translated in Bokenkamp, "Answering a Summons," 202.
117. As pointed out in a note near the outset of chapter 2, *hu* 忽 often connotes "unexpectedly" in contexts such as this.
118. 4.8a4–5; ZSMT 244. As Tao explains in a subsequent note (4.8b3–4), this deity was also known as Zhang Xuanbao 張玄寶 and served in the region's celestial bureau in charge of rainfall.
119. 4.8b6–7; ZSMT 248. Tao comments: "It's unclear which scripture this [incantation] comes from" 未詳此出何經. Master Hong is introduced at 2.7a10 and 2.8a5–6 as "the transcendent of the Central Marchmount, Master Hong" 中嶽仙人洪先生. Tao notes that he doesn't appear in *Declarations of the Perfected*.
120. This gentleman proceeds to introduce himself as Xu Xuanzhen 徐玄真, a transcendent currently occupying a certain administrative position. He goes on to lament that his body lies coffinless and exposed in a cave on the south face of Mount Songgao but, having mentioned this, at once urges Zhou not to concern himself with it—a pointed contrast to the many anecdotes in which a ghost appears to a living person to lament the state of his remains and to ask for help (see Campany, "Ghosts Matter," 26–27, and *Garden of Marvels*, index s.v. "reburial").
121. 小有天 was the name of yet another cavern heaven. See ZSMT 262n1 and the brief passage cited from a work titled *Taisu zhenren Wang jun neizhuan* 太素真人王君內傳 in TPYL 40.1b. This seems to be that text's sole extant passage, although the Perfected of the Grand Immaculate 太素真人 himself is mentioned several dozen times in other works.
122. To this set of passages we can add an earlier dream in which he first hears a stentorian voice speaking a brief bit of instruction 告 but sees no one. He then wakes to find the officer usually referred to as Deputy Zhao 趙丞, that is, Zhao Weibo 趙威伯, one of four deputies assisting Mao Zhong, explaining to him that "that was a Perfected. *It is not yet appropriate for you to see him*, so he instructed you from afar" 是真人爾, 未宜見之, 故遙相告爾 (2.5b, emphasis added). I suspect (but at this writing haven't yet confirmed) that this Zhao Weibo is none other than the Zhao Sheng 趙昇 of *Traditions of Divine Transcendents (Shenxian zhuan* 神仙傳), who, like his fellow deputy Tang Gongfang (who also figures notably in *Traditions*), had by now been promoted to important posts in the Upper Purity administration. In *Traditions* Zhao is one of two top disciples of Zhang Ling 張陵 and passes seven arduous tests of his faith. See Campany, *To Live as Long*, 352–54.
123. On the term *zhi* 芝 (automatically rendered as "mushrooms" by some scholars, erroneously in my view) and my rationale for translating it as "excrescence," see Campany, *To Live as Long*, 26–30.
124. See Campany, "Meanings of Cuisines" and *Making Transcendents*, 62–87.
125. 4.17b–18a. This Commander Fan, who describes himself as "overseer of ghosts and spirits in the bureau of the Certifier of Registers" 定錄府鬼神之司 (1.12b2–3), is first introduced and described in a waking appearance at 1.12a–15b, one of the text's longest passages. Tao supplies his given name, Jiangwu 疆五, at 1.15b3.
126. 4.15a–b, 4.16a–b. In the former case Tao Hongjing frets that once the impostor learns of the detailed description circulating about him, he will change his appearance.
127. See further Campany, *Making Transcendents*, 136–42, 147–48, 155–58, 178–80, 259–63.

128. See the long passage translated from the first roll in Bokenkamp, "Answering a Summons," 197–99.
129. 4.9b–10b, and see ZSMT 253n10.
130. At one point Tao is characterized as "sometimes faithful but sometimes not, and enjoys testing people" 陶某或信不信, 多好試人. This naturally causes Tao some consternation and soul-searching in his comment (4.10a). Like his pupil and like the initial circle of Shangqing revelation recipients, Tao, too, received a divine summons to join the Perfected earlier than his preallotted lifespan would have dictated. See Strickmann, "On the Alchemy of T'ao Hung-ching," 161, and Bokenkamp, "Answering a Summons," 195, where Zhou learns that the summons had been canceled.
131. For an overview of what this secrecy entailed and examples of how it was constituted in discourse and practice see Campany, "Secrecy and Display" and *Making Transcendents*, 88–108. See also Tsai, "Opening Up the Ritual Casket." On these dispersed lineages of transmission see Raz, *Emergence of Daoism*.
132. Urban, "Torment of Secrecy," 235.
133. Bell, *Ritual Theory*, 74.
134. Bell, *Ritual: Perspectives and Dimensions*, 81.
135. This series of reports runs from 1.6a8 to 1.7b5.
136. There were a number of texts in circulation with this or similar titles, and the emperor was surely familiar with at least some of them. See Lipiello, *Auspicious Omens*.
137. See *Huayang Tao yinju neizhuan* 2.5a5–6a2 and Strickmann, "On the Alchemy of T'ao Hung-ching," 143–44.
138. See Strickmann, "On the Alchemy of T'ao Hung-ching," 156–59, and Campany, "Sword Scripture," 48–49.
139. 1.4a1; the dramatic passage is skillfully translated in Bokenkamp, "Answering a Summons," 193.
140. See note 74 above on the textual variants at this crucial juncture.
141. I follow the suggestions and emendation in ZSMT 32–35 and modify Bokenkamp, "Answering a Summons," 194–95.
142. To mention one example, Ge Hong writes of a scarcely accessible mountain outcropping where "excrescences" (*zhi* 芝) grow and where someone had carved an inscription touting their benefits. "Many practitioners of the Dao have given long thought to this place but feel that it is unapproachable. Perhaps only by affixing a bowl to the end of a bamboo or wooden pole, and stretching it across, might one catch and collect some. No one has yet been able to do even this, but, judging by the inscription, someone in an earlier age must have been able to get some" (Campany, *To Live as Long*, 27, translating *Baopuzi neipian jiaoshi* 198). For several examples of scriptures in caves, see Campany, "Secrecy and Display."
143. The wording used by both Zhou and Tao might be read as implying that Zhou didn't write it down not because it was lengthy but because it was something secret.
144. Compare two entries involving waking visions (4.18b) in which we similarly glimpse Tao's frustration. The first instance concerns "cyclic disasters of heaven and earth—once more so much material that I was unable to record it" 多論天地災橫之事, 亦甚多不可記. Tao: "This matter is very difficult to understand. He should have explained it!" 此事理難, 當說. (For a sense of just how difficult this matter is to understand, see Bokenkamp, "Time After Time"; Zürcher, *Buddhism in China*, 165–254; and Li Fengmao, "Liuchao daojiao de zhongmo lun.") In the second record Zhou writes of "seeing a group of thirty Perfected ones. We discussed much concerning the basis of human self-regulation and many methods for confessing grave sins. Furthermore, we discussed matters pertaining to the fashioning of nine-cycle elixirs

and so on" 見眾真凡三十人, 多論人治身之本, 謝殃之法甚多. 亦復論作九轉事云云. Tao: "That this item was not disclosed is cause for the most profound regret" 此條不顯為恨最深.

145. 1.6a; translation in Bokenkamp, "Answering a Summons," 195.
146. 1.4b7–9, adapting Bokenkamp, "Answering a Summons," 194.
147. See the discussion of "revelatory" modes of Buddhist scriptural genesis in Campany, "Buddhist Revelation," 20–21.
148. The tension between "sudden" and gradual approaches to self-cultivation has long been recognized as an important feature of Chinese culture. For a collection of studies centered on this theme, see Gregory, ed., *Sudden and Gradual*.

Chapter 4

1. Or *feared* occurrence, in the case of polluting-dream prophylaxis.
2. Diény, "Le saint ne rêve pas."
3. *Juan* 捐 also can mean "contribute to," which would parallel *zhu* 助 in the next phrase. Either way, the point is the same.
4. *Zhuangzi jijie*, 55–56; translation adapted from Watson, *Complete Works of Chuang Tzu*, 77–78, and Graham, *Chuang-tzu*, 84–85; emphasis added.
5. Or human precedent (*gu* 故).
6. *Zhuangzi jijie*, 133; translation adapted from Watson, *Complete Works of Chuang Tzu*, 168–69, and Graham, *Chuang-tzu*, 265–66, with emphasis added. Passages at least superficially similar can be found in the *Upaniṣads*; see Olivelle, *Saṃnyāsa Upaniṣads*, 240, 262.
7. As Diény puts it, "Zhuangzi établit un parallèle entre l'absence de rêve dans le sommeil et l'absence de souci dans sa vie éveillée" ("Le saint ne rêve pas," 130).
8. As noted in Graziani, *Fictions philosophiques*, 292–95.
9. *Zhuangzi jijie* 64; Watson, *Complete Works of Chuang Tzu*, 81; cf. Campany, *Dreamscape*, 162–63.
10. On this case see Bokenkamp, *Ancestors and Anxiety*, 130–57. On Daoist methods addressing this concern see also Campany, "Sword Scripture."
11. As it sometimes is in *Zhuangzi*, too; see Campany, *Dreamscape*, 41–44.
12. *Huainanzi jishi* 524–25, emphasis added. For a different translation see Major et al., *Huainanzi*, 249.
13. Or "oneness" or "single-mindedness."
14. *Xunzi jijie* 395–96; translation modified from Rickett, *Guanzi*, 23–24, and Hutton, *Xunzi*, 228.
15. Ashmore, *Transport of Reading*, 114. On this text see also Jian Boxian, *Jincun nanbeichao jingxue yiji kao*, 239–46, and Makeham, *Transmitters and Creators*, 77–167.
16. Li Chong served as Imperial Editor, in which capacity he introduced the four-part bibliographic classification that, with some modifications, is still used today. See *Jin shu* 2388–91 and CL 477–80.
17. *Lunyu jijie yishu* 4.3a; translation modified from Ashmore, *Transport of Reading*, 124. The mention of the *fenghuang* 鳳凰, whose name is often rendered as "phoenix," alludes to *Analects* 9.9, where "Confucius" laments the non-appearance of this sign of a sage-king's rise. See Diény, "Le Fenghuang," and Lipiello, *Auspicious Omens*, 133–34.
18. Ashmore, *Transport of Reading*, 124.
19. On the use of these terms in early medieval *Analects* commentaries see Ashmore, *Transport of Reading*, 123.
20. John Makeham discusses Huang Kan's commentarial appropriation of the Buddhist notion of expedient devices (though Huang doesn't use *fangbian* 方便 to name

them); see *Transmitters and Creators*, 155–56. On dreams as consisting of cosmically fashioned "simulacra" see Campany, *Dreamscape*, 69–131. The Buddha, too, was a sage who was often asserted not to have dreamed once he had attained enlightenment, but space doesn't allow me to develop the point further. An excellent survey of theories of dreaming in the Sino-Japanese Buddhist canon may be found in Girard, *Un moine de la secte Kegon*, xix–xxxv, and a fine overview of theories and roles of dreaming in the Buddhist tradition (especially in Tibetan texts) may be found in Young, *Dreaming in the Lotus*.

21. He and his affliction are mentioned in no fewer than five chapters in Wang Chong's *Lunheng* 論衡 or *Arguments Weighed in the Balance*, those titled "Wu xing" 無形, "Qi guai" 奇怪, "Zao hu" 遭虎, "Lun si" 論死, and "Si wei" 死偽.
22. *Huainanzi jishi* 96–100; translation modifying Major et al., *Huainanzi*, 86–87, with emphasis added. The passage incorporates phrases found in what are now chapters 6 and 2 of *Zhuangzi*.
23. As Jean-Pierre Diény puts it, "Sa figure mystérieuse [that is, the "great sage" 大聖 mentioned in the passage about to be quoted] personnifierait donc l'aboutissement indéfiniment reculé du grand éveil" ("Le saint ne rêve pas," 145).
24. This refers back to the statement heard by the other interlocutor in this imagined dialogue from "the Master," Confucius.
25. *Zhuangzi jijie* 24–25; translation adapted from Graham, *Chuang-tzu*, 59–60, and Watson, *Complete Works of Chuang Tzu*, 47–48.
26. *Zhongguan lun shu* 42:29b3–7; translation modified from Zürcher, *Buddhist Conquest of China*, 142, 368n11, and Radich, "A 'Prehistory' to Chinese Debates," 108. Radich notes that the opening line seems to have been a slogan circulating in Yu's day.
27. Dating based on Graham, "Date and Composition," and Barrett, "Reading the *Liezi*."
28. *Liezi jishi*, 64–65; translation adapted from Graham, *Book of Lieh-tzu*, 67.
29. I concur with Watson that this is probably a humorous reference to *Analects* 6.11: "The Master has said: 'What a worthy man was Hui!'" 子曰：賢哉，回也.
30. *Zhuangzi jijie* 68–69; translation adapted from Watson, *Complete Works of Chuang Tzu*, 90–91, and Graham, *Chuang-tzu*, 92. This passage, too, was collected into the *Huainanzi*; see Major et al., *Huainanzi*, 468–69, where it's supplemented with a tag from *Daode jing* 10.
31. *Zhuangzi jijie* 26–27; translation based on Graham, *Chuang-tzu*, 61, and Watson, *Complete Works of Chuang Tzu*, 49. For a partial list of interpretations of this passage that I've found persuasive, see Campany, *Dreamscape*, 215n4.

Epilogue

1. Several examples of relevant passages are translated and discussed in Campany, "Buddhist Revelation."
2. *Zhuangji jijie* 244; modifying the translation in Watson, *Complete Works*, 302. I can't read these lines without thinking of Wittgenstein's "Er muß sozusagen die Leiter wegwerfen, nachdem er auf ihr hinaufgestiegen ist" (*Tractatus Logico-Philosophicus*, 150).

Appendix A

1. In the Taishō edition this list runs from 11:81b3 to 11:81c27; in the ZHDZ edition, from 8:525a9 to 8:526a5.
2. Although throughout this list I use the definite article, the being designated in this way need not be Gautama but might be any Buddha, since all have the same set of identifying marks (other than their names) and teach the same Dharma.

3. These first two items lack corresponding interpretive comments in part 3. But two phrases occurring in the comments on item 7 in part 3 more or less match up with these two initial signs. (Partially matching item 1 in the initial list is 見如來行去迴顧共語說空 in item 7 in part 3, indicating the dreamer has reached the tenth stage. Partially matching item 2 is 見如來默然, indicating the fourth stage.) Item 7 is formatted differently from the surrounding items, suggesting that some textual problem or redaction occurred at this point.
4. In the main body, this and the next item are explicitly about seeing *an icon* of a Buddha with the specified characteristics. (In the passage corresponding to item 5, we have 夢見如來泥像; in the one corresponding to item 6, we have 夢中見如來畫像.) Also, the key phrase in item 5 is 如來身紅色 in the initial list, whereas the main body has 如來泥像—an icon *made of mud*. This blurring of descriptions of the Buddha's body with descriptions of his icons can perhaps be read as suggesting something important about the manner in which icons were conceived and treated: that they are not distinct from the Buddha himself. Or else it simply owes to either (1) someone's misunderstanding during the process of translating the sutra or (2) scribal errors in the text's subsequent reproduction and transmission (or both).
5. In part 3 this becomes simply 見如來行, but in the final sub-sign it is 見如來行去.
6. In the opening line of the corresponding portion of part 3, it's *the dreamer himself* who is doing the preaching (82a23). But the rest of the passage speaks of the Buddha as the expounder, as in the initial list.
7. Donating or applying "ornamentation" 莊嚴 to stupas, icons, temples, and ritual spaces—or, in an only slightly less concrete sense, even to individual persons, for example in a healing liturgy designed to bestow merit earned by performers of the rite upon a sick person—was part of the basic repertoire of devotional acts. See Teiser, "Literary Style" and "Ornamenting."
8. Translation tentative. The term 神通塔 here and in the corresponding passage in part 3 is a *hapax legomenon*, at least as far as the Taishō canon is concerned.
9. At the corresponding position in the main body there is no counterpart to this item. Instead we find that the previous entry (82c13–21) is worded anomalously and that the text then skips on to an entry corresponding to item 18. Two references to seeing the Buddha radiating light do occur in the main body passage corresponding to item 9.
10. In both editions the initial list has "In a dream you see the Tathāgata's body" 夢見如來身 (Taishō 81b12–13 / ZHDZ 525a20–21). I emend the line to conform to the corresponding passage in the main body (Taishō 82c27–28 / ZHDZ 527b15).
11. In the main body (starting at Taishō 83a6 / ZHDZ 527c4) it's a *stupa* 塔 that's being so adorned. I emend accordingly. This segment of part 3 is again anomalous with respect to most of the rest of the text.
12. On the importance of incense, and more generally of fragrances, in Buddhist liturgy and lore, see Schopen, "Fragrance."
13. The phrase 般涅槃塔 is rare in the canon, occurring in only four other passages. In *Ayuwang zhuan* 50:104c22 it clearly denotes a stupa built by Aśoka at *the site of* the Buddha's *parinirvāṇa*. I translate accordingly.
14. Compare item 94. Canopies or parasols over altars, seats, platforms, carriages and other conveyances were important elements of ritual spaces. They are mentioned numerous times in *Explication of Dreams* both as images seen in dreams and as objects for donation. In iconography, the Buddha is often depicted sitting on an elevated seat surmounted by a canopy. Donating canopies and parasols was a form of "ornamenting" ritual spaces and a common way of earning merit (see Teiser, "Ornamenting"). For examples of canopies see Dien, *Six Dynasties Civilization*, 203–5, 301–3, 372–73.

15. Southeast, southwest, northeast, and northwest.
16. Emending the Taishō version's 旋 to 猺 per ZHDZ 531b7.
17. This item lacks a counterpart in the main body. Wild dogs (or dholes) and wolves 豺狼 are mentioned nowhere else in the text. Huilin's 慧琳 compendium of pronunciations and glosses, *Yiqiejing yinyi* 一切經音義 (807), contains a rather lengthy comment on this passage (see 54:377b). This Huilin is not to be confused with the fifth-century former monk turned Confucian apologist and fixture at court who went by the same name; see Zürcher, *Buddhist Conquest*, 15, 372n385, and Ch'en, *Buddhism*, 139, 207.
18. The Taishō edition reads 三昧夢; both ZHDZ (525b21, and cf. 534a10) and CBETA give 三昧聲. I emend accordingly. The phrase "sound of *samādhi*" 三昧聲, while uncommon, is attested in a couple of interesting passages. In *Da fangdeng daji jing* (in a portion attributed to Narendrayaśas, active in the second half of the sixth century) it appears in a long list of sounds that the Buddha causes to rain down on the palace of the *asuras* 阿修羅, converting them to faith in the Dharma (13:308c–309a). (On a rainmaking ritual prescribed elsewhere in this sutra see Capitanio, "Dragon Kings," 76.) In the *Sutra of the Questions of the King of the Great Tree Kiṃnaras* (*Dashu jinnaluowang suowen jing* 15:374), attributed to Kumārajīva, in the course of extolling the musical skill of the king of the *kiṃnaras* 緊那羅 (celestial musicians with hybrid bodies, possibly etymologically related to the English "chimera"), the Buddha lists the many sounds their music contains. Among them are no fewer than forty-six distinct varieties of "*samādhi* sounds." At this writing I remain unsure whether the phrase means sounds that produce or facilitate *samādhi*, sounds emitted by (someone in) *samādhi* (unlikely), or neither.
19. 方廣, like 方等, usually translates the Sanskrit *vaipulya*, which in turn usually refers to Greater Vehicle sutras as contrasted with others. See Zacchetti, "Notions and Visions," 93–96.
20. Items 61 and 62 seem to be instances of dreaming within a dream, unless (much less likely) the extra phrase is a copyist's error. The phrasing is identical across the Taishō and ZHDZ editions; neither lists variant readings.
21. This uncommon expression perhaps means the sound of sutras being recited.
22. This dream content partially overlaps with that of sign 81 below.
23. In part 3 this becomes 夢中見阿耨龍王池. In Buddhist cosmology, the Cool Lake (Anavatapta) is situated in the center of Jambudvīpa 閻浮提, from which four great rivers flow. See Gao, "Idea of the Anavatapta," and Kloetzli, *Buddhist Cosmology*, 28. This lake was the setting for a text collecting recitations in which each member of a group of disciples of the Buddha, and then the Buddha himself, "describe one or more karmically important act[s] that he had performed in a previous life and explains how the karma from that action led him to his current exalted state as an arhat and disciple of the Buddha" (Salomon, *Buddhist Literature*, 199). On the very early Gāndhāran manuscripts containing versions of this text, see the magnificent critical edition in Salomon, *Two Gāndhārī Manuscripts*, as well as Salomon, *Buddhist Literature*, 199–228.
24. This item partially overlaps with sign 72.
25. In Buddhist cosmology, Jambudvīpa is the southernmost of the four continents surrounding the central cosmic mountain Sumeru and the one on which we live.
26. That is, dressed as a layperson rather than as a monk or nun.
27. See the note to item 35.
28. In part 3 this becomes 若自夢見初立城郭.
29. Donating bridges was an important act of karmic merit for both monks and layper-

sons, prescribed in sutras from the third century forward. See Kieschnick, *Impact*, 199–214.

30. Some editions write 集船, others 乘船; I follow the latter. See ZHDZ 8:542b2–3.
31. Following variants listed in both the Taishō and ZHDZ editions, I emend 力 to 刀 and 仗 to 杖. In part 3 this becomes 若夢莊嚴得刀.
32. See Baumann, *Divine Knowledge*, 85.
33. See Kotyk, "Early Tantric Hemerology," 15–16, and "Sinicization," 10n15.
34. DDB s.v. 百八煩惱.
35. See, for example, *Da zhidu lun*, 25:202.
36. See Lamotte, "Sūtra composite," 114; *Da zhidu lun*, 25:97.
37. See Kieschnick, *Impact*, 116–38, and Tanabe, "Telling Beads."
38. See *Tuoluoni jijing*, 18:812–25. On this work see Shinohara, "All-Gathering" and *Spells*, 1–88.
39. It is found in other sutras as well, such as *Wenshushili wen jing* 14:508. On the *Tuoluoni zaji* see Ochiai Toshinori, "Darani zasshū shoshu no kyōten ni tsuite."
40. *Hōbōgirin*, s.v. *bussokuseki* 佛足石; Karunaratne, "Significance"; Bizot, "La figuration": Lorrillard, "Aux origines"; Cicuzza, *Mirror*; Strong, *Relics of the Buddha*, 87; Skilling, "Symbols"; Anālayo, *Buddhapala*.
41. See *Miaojixiang pusa suo wen dasheng faluo jing*, 14:517–18, where the lists appear in a metrical laud 頌 (this text is attributed in the Taishō canon to Faxian 法賢 of the Song period [not to be confused with the noted pilgrim Faxian 法顯, 317–420] but this remains to be researched); *Dasheng baifuxiang jing* 16:329–30; and *Dasheng baifu zhuangyan xiang jing* 16:331–32. Both of these latter texts also give lists of thirty-two and eighty marks, and both are said to have been translated by Divākara 地婆訶羅 in 683, but their wording differs. All three of these sutras, then, seem to postdate *Explication of Dreams*. According to Skilling, the earliest list of signs (comprising about forty items) appears in a text by Buddhaghosa (fifth century; see Skilling, "Symbols," 67). But the notion that Buddhas' and bodhisattvas' bodies have special marks is widely distributed in earlier texts that don't provide complete lists of them. For examples see Zürcher, *Buddhist Conquest*, 224–25, 227, 421n143, 429n25; and Campany, *Signs from the Unseen Realm*, 65–67.
42. This is based on a comparison of the list given in Skilling, "Symbols," 73–74, which reflects Sanskrit and Tibetan versions of a *Mañjuśrī-paripṛcchā sutra* and the Chinese *Dasheng baifuxiang jing* (16:329–30) and *Dasheng baifu zhuangyan xiang jing* (16:331–32) with *Explication*'s initial list of 108 dream signs.

Appendix B

1. Compare this passage in Plutarch, *How One May Know One Is Making Progress in Virtue*: "It was Zeno's belief that everyone could, thanks to his dreams, have knowledge of what progress he was making. One has made real progress if he no longer dreams that he is giving in to some shameful passion, or giving his consent to something evil or unjust—or even committing it—and if, instead, the soul's faculties of representation and affectivity, relaxed by reason, shine as if in an ocean of diaphanous serenity, untroubled by waves.'" Quoted in Hadot, *Philosophy as a Way of Life*, 113n46.
2. On the role of dreaming in these lists of similes see Hattori, "Dream Simile."
3. See for example Nattier, "Realm of Akṣobhya."
4. Lokakṣema writes 見畜生相噉, 人民疾疫; Zhi Qian simply changes Lokakṣema's 噉 to 食; and *Mohe banruo chao jing* is identical at this point to Lokakṣema's version. Kumārajīva's smaller sutra mentions only 見畜生 as what's seen in the dream but

then has the bodhisattva vowing: 其世界中, 一切皆無三惡道名. His larger sutra lists the three rebirth paths as 地獄, 畜生, 餓鬼, while Mokṣala lists them as 泥犁, 薜荔, 禽獸三惡趣中.

5. Conze, *Eight Thousand Lines*, 228.
6. Karashima (*Critical Edition*, 356n49) understands this as "(The *bodhisattva-mahāsattva*) whom I saw in my dream had such aspects and images, which did not make me scared," but I fear he has misunderstood the referent of 是, "this." I should note that unless I'm mistaken the quotation marks are placed erroneously in the CBETA editions of both this and Zhi Qian's text.
7. Here, as in many cases, *Mohe banruo poluomi jing* and *Da zhidu lun* are virtually identical, so I don't discuss them separately.

Appendix C

1. Strickmann, "Dreamwork."
2. See TTC, 980, but compare Steavu, *Writ of the Three Sovereigns*, 196–97, 325.
3. Strickmann, "Dreamwork," 36.
4. *Taishang chiwen dongshen sanlu* 6b1–9.
5. Goble, *Chinese Esoteric Buddhism*, 118.
6. Or perhaps "go wherever you like in a dream." *Taishang chiwen dongshen sanlu* 6b10–8a1.

Bibliography

Works Cited by Abbreviation (and Abbreviations Used in This Bibliography)

BEB *Brill's Encyclopedia of Buddhism*. Edited by Jonathan A. Silk et al. 2 vols. Leiden: Brill, 2015–2019.

BDL *A Biographical Dictionary of Later Han to the Three Kingdoms (23–220 AD)*. Edited by Rafe de Crespigny. Leiden: E. J. Brill, 2007.

BDQ *A Biographical Dictionary of the Qin, Former Han & Xin Periods (221 BC–AD 24)*. Edited by Michael Loewe. Leiden: E. J. Brill, 2000.

BTSC *Beitang shuchao* 北堂書鈔. Compiled by Yu Shinan 虞世南. Facsimile reprint in 2 vols. of 1888 ed. Taipei: Wenhai chubanshe, 1962. Cited by scroll and folio page number.

CBETA Chinese Buddhist Electronic Text Association (https://www.cbeta.org/)

CCT *Classical Chinese Tales of the Supernatural and the Fantastic: Selections from the Third to the Tenth Century*. Edited by Karl S. Y. Kao. Bloomington: Indiana University Press, 1985.

CL *Ancient and Early Medieval Chinese Literature: A Reference Guide*. Edited by David R. Knechtges and Taiping Chang. 4 vols. Leiden: E. J. Brill, 2010–14.

CXJ *Chuxue ji* 初學記. Compiled by Xu Jian 徐堅 et al. 3 vols. continuously paginated. Beijing: Zhonghua shuju, 1962. Cited by scroll and page number.

DB *Dictionnaire biographique du haut moyen âge chinois: Culture, politique et religion de la fin des Han à la veille des Tang (IIIe–VIe siècles)*. Edited by François Martin and Damien Chaussende. Paris: Les belles lettres, 2020.

DDB Digital Dictionary of Buddhism 電子佛教辭典. Edited by A. Charles Muller. www.buddhism-dict.net.

DZ *Zhengtong daozang* 正統道藏. Shanghai: Shangwu, 1923–26; reprint, Taipei: Xinwenfeng, 1977. Texts in this canon are cited first by the number assigned them in Schipper and Verellen, *The Taoist Canon*, then by scroll and folio page number.

ECR1 *Early Chinese Religion, Part One: Shang through Han (1250 BC–220 AD)*. Edited by John Lagerwey and Marc Kalinowski. 2 vols. continuously paginated. Leiden: Brill, 2009.

ECR2 *Early Chinese Religion, Part Two: The Period of Division (220–589 AD)*. Edited by John Lagerwey and Lü Pengzhi. 2 vols. continuously paginated. Leiden: Brill, 2010.

ECT *Early Chinese Texts: A Bibliographical Guide*. Edited by Michael Loewe. Berkeley: Society for the Study of Early China, 1993.

EMC *Early Medieval China: A Sourcebook*. Edited by Wendy Swartz, Robert Ford Campany, Yang Lu, and Jessey J. C. Choo. New York: Columbia University Press, 2014.

HDW Hanji dianzi wenxian ciliao ku 漢籍電子文獻資料庫 electronic database edition.

HWCS *Han Wei congshu* 漢魏叢書. Compiled by Cheng Rong 程榮. Printed in 1592. Place of publication and printing house unknown; copy held at the Joseph Regenstein Library (East Asia Collection), University of Chicago.

HYD *Hanyu dacidian* 漢語大辭典. Edited by Luo Zhufeng 罗竹风. Shanghai: Shanghai cishu chubanshe, 1986.

LX *Gu xiaoshuo gouchen* 古小說鉤沈. Compiled by Lu Xun 魯迅. Beijing: Renmin wenxue chubanshe, 1954.

SSHY *Shih-shuo Hsin-yü: A New Account of Tales of the World*. Translated and edited by Richard B. Mather. 2nd edition. Ann Arbor: Center for Chinese Studies, University of Michigan, 2002.

SSMT *Shūshi meitsūki kenkyū (yakuchū hen)* 周氏冥通記研究（譯注篇）. Edited by Mugitani Kunio 麥谷邦夫 and Yoshikawa Tadao 吉川忠夫. Kyoto: Kyōto daigaku Jinbun kagaku kenkyūjo, 2003.

T *Taishō shinshū daizōkyō* 大正新脩大藏經. Edited by Takakusu Junjirō 高楠順次郎, Watanabe Kaigyōku 渡辺海旭, and Ono Gemmyō 小野玄妙. 100 vols. Tokyo: Taishō Issaikyō Kankōkai, 1924–1935; reprint, Taipei: Xinwen feng, 1983. In this bibliography, works cited from this canon are identified by the number assigned to them in it. In the body of the book, texts are cited by title followed (for citations of specific passages) by the volume, page, register, and (in most cases) line numbers.

TPGJ *Taiping guangji* 太平廣記. Compiled by Li Fang 李昉 et al. 4 vols. Shanghai: Shanghai guji chubanshe, 1990. Cited by scroll and serial position of the cited item in the scroll (e.g., "387.1" indicates the first passage anthologized in scroll 387).

TPYL *Taiping yulan* 太平御覽. Compiled by Li Fang 李昉 et al. Facsimile reprint of Shangwu yinshuguan 1935 printing from a Song copy. 4 vols. Beijing: Zhonghua shuju, 1992. Cited by scroll and folio page number.

TTC *The Taoist Canon: A Historical Companion to the Daozang*. Edited by Kristofer Schipper and Franciscus Verellen. Chicago: University of Chicago Press, 2004.

XSSJ *Xinji Soushen ji, xinji Soushen houji* 新輯搜神記, 新輯搜神後記. Edited by Li Jianguo 李劍國. 2 vols. continuously paginated. Beijing: Zhonghua shuju, 2007.

YWLJ *Yiwen leiju* 藝文類聚. Compiled by Ouyang Xun 歐陽詢 et al. Modern edition by Wang Shaoying 王紹楹. 2 vols. continuously paginated. Beijing: Zhonghua shuju, 1965. Cited by scroll and page number.

ZH *Zhonghua daozang* 中華道藏. Edited by Zhang Jiyu 張繼禹. 48 vols. Beijing: Huaxia chubanshe, 2004.

ZHDZ *Zhonghua dazangjing* 中華大藏經 (Hanwen bufen 漢文部分). 106 vols. Beijing: Zhonghua shuju chuban, 1984–1996. Passages are cited by the volume, page, register, and (in most cases) line numbers.

ZSMT *Zhoushi mingtong ji jiaoshi* 周氏冥通記校釋. Edited by Wang Jiakui 王家葵. Beijing: Zhonghua shuju, 2020.

ZT *Zuo Tradition: Zuozhuan* 左傳. Translated and edited by Stephen Durrant, Wai-yee Li, and David Schaberg. 3 vols. continuously paginated. Seattle: University of Washington Press, 2016.

Manuscripts

Pelliot 2682. *Baize jingguai tu* 白澤精怪圖
https://gallica.bnf.fr/ark:/12148/btv1b83033424/f1.image.r=Pelliot 2682
Pelliot 2751. *Ziwen xingshi jue* 紫文行事訣
https://gallica.bnf.fr/ark:/12148/btv1b83021869/f21.image.r=Pelliot 2751
Pelliot 3908. *Xinji Zhougong jiemeng shu* 新集周公解夢書
https://gallica.bnf.fr/ark:/12148/btv1b8300230n.r=P 3908?rk=128756;0
Pelliot 3017. *Jinzi dabao [ji]jing neilue chu jiaocuo ji shangsun zishu* 金字大寶「積」經內略出交錯及傷損字數
https://gallica.bnf.fr/ark:/12148/btv1b83007111.r=Pelliot 3017?rk=64378;0
Stein 351. *Dabao jijing* 大寶積經
http://idp.bl.uk/database/oo_scroll_h.a4d?uid=93037408;recnum=351;index=9

Works Cited by Title

The dynastic histories consulted are all in the widely available editions published by Zhonghua shuju in Beijing. I do not separately list their places or dates of publication.

Apidamo da piposha lun 阿毘達磨大毘婆沙論. T 1545.
Ayuwang zhuan 阿育王傳. T 2042.
Azhapoju guishen dajiangshang fo tuoluoni jing 阿吒婆拘鬼神大將上佛陀羅尼經. T 1238.

Baihutong 白虎通. References are to *Baihutong shuzheng* 白虎通疏證. Edited by Chen Li 陳立 and Wu Zeyu 吳則虞. Beijing: Zhonghua shuju, 1994.
Banzhou sanmei jing 般舟三昧經. T 418.
Baopuzi neipian 抱朴子內篇 by Ge Hong 葛洪. References are to *Baopuzi neipian jiaoshi* 抱朴子內篇校釋. Edited by Wang Ming 王明. 2nd edition. Beijing: Zhonghua shuju, 1985.
Beidou qixing huma fa 北斗七星護摩法. T 1310.
Bukong juansuo shenbian zhenyan jing 不空羂索神變真言經. T 1092.

Chaoriming sanmei jing 超日明三昧經. T 638.
Chengshi lun 成實論. T 1646.
Chengju guangming sanmeijing 成具光明三昧經. T 630.
Chisongzi zhangli 赤松子章曆. DZ 615.
Chu sanzang jiji 出三藏記集. T 2145.

Da baoji jing 大寶積經. T310.
Da fangbian fo bao'en jing 大方便佛報恩經. T 156.
Da fangdeng daji jing 大方等大集經. T 397.
Da fangdeng tuoluoni jing 大方等陀羅尼經. T 1339.
Da kongque zhou wang jing 大孔雀呪王經. T 985.
Da mingdu jing 大明度經. T 225.
Da xue 大學. References are to *Liji zhengyi* 禮記正義. Shisan jing zhushu 十三經注疏 edition. Shanghai: Shanghai guji chubanshe, 1990.

Da zhidu lun 大智度論. T 1509.
Daodian lun 道典論. DZ 1130.
Daodi jing 道地經. T 607.
Daojiao lingyan ji 道教靈驗記. DZ 590.
Daoxing banruo jing 道行般若經. T 224.
Dasheng baifuxiang jing 大乘百福相經. T 661.
Dasheng baifu zhuangyan xiang jing 大乘百福莊嚴相經. T 662.
Dashu jinnaluowang suowen jing 大樹緊那羅王所問經. T 625.
Dengzhen yinjue 登真隱訣. DZ 421.
Dili sanmeiye budong zunshengzhe niansong bimi fa 底哩三昧耶不動尊聖者念誦祕密法. T 1201.
Dongshen badi miaojing jing 洞神八帝妙精經. DZ 640.
Dongxuan lingbao daoxue keyi 洞玄靈寶道學科儀. DZ 1126.
Dongxuan lingbao qianzhen ke 洞玄靈寶千真科. DZ 1410.
Dongxuan lingbao sandong fengdao kejie yingshi 洞玄靈寶三洞奉道科戒營始. DZ 1125.
Dongxuan lingbao zhenling weiye tu 洞玄靈寶真靈位業圖. DZ 167.
Dongxuan lingbao ziran jiutian shengshen zhang jing 洞玄靈寶自然九天生神章經. DZ 318.
Dongzhen shangqing qingyao zishu jin'gen zhongjing 洞真上清青腰紫書金根衆經. DZ 1315.
Dongzhen taishang sanjiu suyu yujing zhenjue 洞真太上三九素語玉精真訣. DZ 1327.
Dongzhen taishang taixiao langshu 洞真太上太霄琅書. DZ 1352.
Dongzhen taishang zidu yanguang shenyuan bian jing 洞真太上紫度炎光神元變經. DZ 1332.
Dousha jing 兜沙經. T 280.

Faju biyu jing 法句譬喻經. T 211.
Faju jing 法句經. T 210.
Fangguang banruo jing 放光般若經. T 221.
Fanwang jing 梵網經. T 1484.
Fayan 法言 by Yang Xiong 揚雄. References are to *Fayan yishu* 法言義疏. Edited by Wang Rongbao 汪榮寶 and Chen Zhongtian 陳仲夭. Beijing: Zhonghua shuju, 2012.
Fayuan zhulin 法苑珠林 by Daoshi 道世. T 2122.

Gaoseng zhuan 高僧傳. T 2059.
Guan Xukongzang pusa jing 觀虛空藏菩薩經. T 409.
Guanding jing 灌頂經. T 1331.
Guanfo sanmei hai jing 觀佛三昧海經. T 643.
Guannian Amituofo xiang haisanmei gongde famen 觀念阿彌陀佛相海三昧功德法門. T 1959.
Guang hongming ji 廣弘明集. T 2103.
Guangzan jing 光讚經. T 222.

Hailongwang jing 海龍王經. T 598.
Han shu 漢書 by Ban Gu 班固, Ban Biao 班彪, et al.
Hebu jinguangming jing 合部金光明經. T 664.
Hōbōgirin 法寶義林: *Dictionnaire encyclopédique du Bouddhisme d'après les sources chinoises et japonaises*. Edited by Sylvain Lévi, J. Takakusu, and Paul Demiéville. Volumes are continuously paginated. Paris: Adrien Maisonneuve, 1981–.
Hou Han shu 後漢書 by Fan Ye 范曄.

Huainanzi 淮南子. References are to *Huainanzi jishi* 淮南子集釋. Edited by He Ning 何寧. Beijing: Zhonghua shuju, 1998.
Huangdi jiuding shendan jingjue 黄帝九鼎神丹經訣. DZ 885.
Huangtian shangqing jinque dijun lingshu ziwen shangjing 皇天上清金闕帝君靈書紫文上經. DZ 639.
Huangting neijing yujing zhu 黄庭內景玉經註. DZ 401.
Huayang Tao yinju neizhuan 華陽陶隱居內傳. DZ 300.

Jianbei yiqie zhide jing 漸備一切智德經. T 285.
Jietuo daolun 解脫道論. T 1648.
Jin shu 晉書 by Fang Xuanling 房玄齡 et al.
Jinguangming jing 金光明經. T 663.
Jinguangming zuishengwang jingshu 金光明最勝王經疏. T 1788.

Kaiyuan shijiao lu 開元釋教錄. T 2154.

Laozi Xiang'er zhu 老子想爾注. References are to *Laozi Xiang'er zhu jiaozheng* 老子想爾注校證. Edited by Rao Zongyi 饒宗頤. Shanghai: Shanghai guji chubanshe, 1991.
Liang shu 梁書 by Yao Silian 姚思廉.
Lidai sanbao ji 歷代三寶紀. T 2034.
Liexian zhuan 列仙傳. References are to *Liexian zhuan jiaojian* 列仙傳校箋. Edited by Wang Shumin 王叔岷. Beijing: Zhonghua shuju, 2007.
Liezi 列子. References are to *Liezi jishi* 列子集釋. Edited by Yang Bojun 楊伯峻. Beijing: Zhonghua shuju, 1979.
Liji 禮記. References are to *Liji jijie* 禮記集解. Compiled by Sun Xidan 孫希旦. Taipei: Wenshizhe chubanshe, 1990.
Lunheng 論衡 by Wang Chong 王充. References are to *Lunheng jiaoshi* 論衡校釋. Edited by Huang Hui 黄暉. Beijing: Zhonghua shuju, 1990.
Lunyu 論語. References are to *Lunyu jijie yishu* 論語集解義疏. Compiled by Huang Kan 皇侃. Edition: *Zhi buzu zhai congshu* 知不足齋叢書 compiled by Bao Tingbo 鮑廷博 (1728–1814), accessed via HDW.
Lüshi chunqiu 呂氏春秋. See Knoblock and Riegel, *Annals of Lü Buwei*.

Mengzi 孟子. *Duanju shisanjing* 斷句十三經 edition accessed via HDW.
Miaofa lianhua jing 妙法蓮華經. T 262.
Miaojixiang pusa suo wen dasheng faluo jing 妙吉祥菩薩所問大乘法螺經. T 473.
Mice huihan 秘冊匯函 compiled by Shen Shilong 沈士龍 and Hu Zhenheng 胡震亨, accessed via HDW.
Mingxiang ji 冥祥記 by Wang Yan 王琰. See Campany, *Signs from the Unseen Realm*.
Mohe banruo chao jing 摩訶般若鈔經. T 226.
Mohe banruo poluomi jing 摩訶般若波羅蜜經. T 223.
Mohe zhiguan 摩訶止觀. T 1911.

Nan Qi shu 南齊書 by Xiao Zixian 蕭子顯.
Nan shi 南史 by Li Yanshou 李延壽 and Li Dashi 李大師.

Oxford English Dictionary. Oxford: Oxford University Press, 1971.

Pusa benye jing 菩薩本業經. T 281.

Pusa nianfo sanmei jing 菩薩念佛三昧經. T 414.
Pusa shanjie jing 菩薩善戒經. 1583.
Pusa shizhu xingdao pin 菩薩十住行道品. T 283.

Sanguo zhi 三國志 by Chen Shou 陳壽.
Shangqing housheng daojun lieji 上清後聖道君列紀. DZ 442.
Shangqing jiudan shanghua taijing zhongji jing 上清九丹上化胎精中記經. DZ 1382.
Shangqing taiji zhenren shenxian jing 上清太極真人神仙經. DZ 1404.
Shangqing taishang huangsu sishisi fang jing 上清太上黄素四十四方經. DZ 1380.
Shangqing wozhong jue 上清握中訣. DZ 140.
Shangqing xiuxing jingjue 上清修行經訣. DZ 427.
Shangqing xiuxing yaoshi jing 上清修行要事經. DZ 1269.
Shangqing zhongjing zhu zhensheng bi 上清衆經諸真聖祕. DZ 446.
Shennong bencao jing 神農本草經. HDW; see also Wilms, *Divine Farmer's Classic*.
Shenxian zhuan 神仙傳 by Ge Hong 葛洪. See Campany, *To Live as Long as Heaven and Earth*.
Shichan boluomi cidi famen 釋禪波羅蜜次第法門. T 1916.
Shiyi mian shenzhou xinjing yishu 十一面神呪心經義疏. T 1802.
Shiyi xiangsinian rulai jing 十一想思念如來經. T 138.
Shuihudi Qin mu zhujian 睡虎地秦墓竹簡. Edited by Yu Haoliang 于豪亮 et al. Beijing: Wenwu chubanshe, 1990.
Si tianwang jing 四天王經. T 590.
Song shu 宋書 by Shen Yue 沈約.
Sun zhenren beiji qianjin yaofang 孫真人備急千金要方 by Sun Simo 孫思邈. DZ 1163.

Taiji zhenren jiuzhuan huandan jing yaojue 太極真人九轉還丹經要訣. DZ 889.
Taiping jing 太平經. References are to *Taiping jing hejiao* 太平經合校. Edited by Wang Ming 王明. Beijing: Zhonghua shuju, 1960.
Taiqing Daolin shesheng lun 太清道林攝生論. DZ 1427.
Taishang chiwen dongshen sanlu 太上赤文洞神三籙. DZ 589.
Taishang chu sanshi jiuchong baosheng jing 太上除三尸九蟲保生經. DZ 871.
Taishang huangting neijing yujing 太上黄庭內景玉經. DZ 331.
Taishang huangting waijing yujing 太上黄庭外景玉經. DZ 332.
Taishang lingbao wufu xu 太上靈寶五符序. DZ 388.
Taishang yupei jindang taiji jinshu shangjing 太上玉佩金璫太極金書上經. DZ 56.
Taiwei lingshu ziwen xianji zhenji shangjing 太微靈書紫文仙忌真記上經. DZ 179.
Tuoluoni jijing 陀羅尼集經. T 901.
Tuoluoni zaji 陀羅尼雜集. T 1336.

Wei shu 魏書 by Wei Shou 魏收.
Wenshushili banniepan jing 文殊師利般涅槃經. T 463.
Wenshushili wen jing 文殊師利問經. T 468.
Wushang biyao 無上祕要. DZ 1138.

Xiaopin banruo poluomi jing 小品般若波羅蜜經. T 227.
Xiulian dadan yaozhi 修鍊大丹要旨. DZ 912.
Xiuxi zhiguan zuochan fayao 修習止觀坐禪法要. T 1915.
Xiuxing daodi jing 修行道地經. T 606.
Xuandu lüwen 玄都律文. DZ 188.

Xukongzang pusa wen qi fo tuoluoni zhou jing 虛空藏菩薩問七佛陀羅尼呪經. T 1333.
Xunzi jijie 荀子. References are to *Xunzi jijie* 荀子集解. Compiled by Wang Xianqian 王先謙. 2 vols. continuously paginated. Beijing: Zhonghua shuju, 1987.

Yangxing yanming lu 養性延命錄. DZ 838.
Yanshi jiaxun 顏氏家訓 by Yan Zhitui 顏之推. References are to *Yanshi jiaxun jijie* 顏氏家訓集結. Edited by Wang Liqi 王利器. 2nd edition. Beijing: Zhonghua shuju, 1996.
Yi yuan 異苑 by Liu Jingshu 劉敬叔. In *Xuejin taoyuan* 學津討原, compiled by Zhang Pengyi 張鵬一. Facsimile reprint in *Baibu congshu jicheng* 百部叢書集成, edited by Yan Yiping 嚴一萍. Taipei: Yiwen yinshuguan, 1966.
Yiqiejing yinyi 一切經音義. T 2128.
Yongcheng jixian lu 墉城集仙錄. DZ 783.
Youming lu 幽明錄. LX.
Yunji qiqian 雲笈七籤. DZ 1032.

Zengyi ahan jing 增一阿含經. T 125.
Zhancha shan'e yebao jing 占察善惡業報經. T 839.
Zhen'gao 真誥. DZ 1016.
Zheng fahua jing 正法華經. T 263.
Zhengyi fawen xiuzhen zhiyao 正一法文修真旨要. DZ 1270.
Zhong benqi jing 中本起經. T196.
Zhongguan lun shu 中觀論疏. T 1824.
Zhoushi mingtong ji 周氏冥通記. DZ 302.
Zhu pusa qiufo benye jing 諸菩薩求佛本業經. T 282.
Zhuangzi 莊子. References are to *Zhuangzi jijie*/*Zhuangzi jijie neipian buzheng* 莊子集解／莊子集解內篇補正. Edited by Wang Xianqian 王先謙 and Liu Wu 劉武. Beijing: Zhonghua shuju, 1987.
Zhubing yuanhou lun jiaozhu 諸病源候論校注 by Chao Yuanfang 巢元方. HDW.
Ziting neibi jue xiuxing fa 紫庭內祕訣修行法. DZ 874.
Ziyang zhenren neizhuan 紫陽真人內傳. DZ 303.
Zunsheng pusa suo wen yiqie zhufa ru wuliangmen tuoluoni jing 尊勝菩薩所問一切諸法入無量門陀羅尼經. T1343.
Zuo zhuan 左傳. See Durrant, Li, and Schaberg, *Zuo Tradition*.
Zuochan sanmei jing 坐禪三昧經. T 614.

Works Cited by Author

Abramson, Marc S. "Deep Eyes and High Noses: Constructing Ethnicity in Tang China (618–907)." PhD dissertation, Princeton University, 2001.
Adamek, Wendi L. "Addressing the Mind: Developments in the Culture of Confession in Sui-Tang China." *Journal of Chinese Buddhist Studies* 28 (2015): 117–52.
———. *The Mystique of Transmission: On an Early Chan History and Its Contexts*. New York: Columbia University Press, 2007.
Adler, Shelley R. *Sleep Paralysis: Night-mares, Nocebos, and the Mind-Body Connection*. New Brunswick, NJ: Rutgers University Press, 2011.
Ahrens, Kathleen. "Conceptual Metaphors of the 'Self.'" *Hong Kong Baptist University Papers in Applied Language Studies* 12 (2008): 47–67.

Allan, Sarah. *Buried Ideas: Legends of Abdication and Ideal Government in Early Chinese Bamboo-Slip Manuscripts*. Albany: State University of New York Press, 2015.

———. "Not the *Lun yu*: The Chu Script Bamboo Slip Manuscript, *Zigao*, and the Nature of Early Confucianism." *Bulletin of the School of Oriental and African Studies* 72, no. 1 (2009): 115–51.

———. *The Way of Water and Sprouts of Virtue*. Albany: State University of New York Press, 1997.

Allen, Sarah M. *Shifting Stories: History, Gossip, and Lore in Narratives from Tang Dynasty China*. Cambridge, MA: Harvard University Asia Center, 2014.

Anālyo, Bhikkhu. *Buddhapala and the Bodhisattva Path*. Hamburg Buddhist Studies 8. Bochum/Freiburg: Projekt Verlag, 2017.

Anderl, Christoph. "Metaphors of 'Sickness and Remedy' in Early Chan Texts from Dunhuang." In *Reading Slowly: A Festschrift for Jens E. Braarvig*, edited by Lutz Edzard, Jens W. Borgland, and Ute Hüsken, 27–46. Wiesbaden: Harrassowitz, 2018.

Andersen, Poul. "Talking to the Gods: Visionary Divination in Early Taoism (the Sanhuang Tradition)." *Taoist Resources* 5, no. 1 (August 1994): 1–24.

Asad, Talal. "Remarks on the Anthropology of the Body." In *Religion and the Body*, edited by Sarah Coakley, 42–52. Cambridge: Cambridge University Press, 1997.

Ashmore, Robert. "The Art of Discourse: Xi Kang's 'Sound Is Without Sadness or Joy.'" In EMC, 201–29.

———. *The Transport of Reading: Text and Understanding in the World of Tao Qian (365–427)*. Cambridge, MA: Harvard University Press, 2010.

Atone, Joji. "Shan-tao: His Life and Thought." PhD dissertation, University of Michigan, 1988.

Austin, J. L. *How To Do Things with Words*. 2nd edition. Cambridge, MA: Harvard University Press, 1975.

———. "Performative-Constative." In *The Philosophy of Language*, edited by J. R. Searle, 1–12. Oxford: Oxford University Press, 1971.

Baldrian-Hussein, Farzeen. "The Book of the Yellow Court: A Lost Song Commentary of the 12th Century." *Cahiers d'Extrême-Asie* 14 (2004): 187–226.

Barbieri-Low, Anthony J. "Craftsman's Literacy: Uses of Writing by Male and Female Artisans in Qin and Han China." In *Writing and Literacy in Early China: Studies from the Columbia Early China Seminar*, edited by Li Feng and David Prager Branner, 370–99. Seattle: University of Washington Press, 2011.

Bareau, André. "L'allégorie de la mort dans le bouddhisme ancien." *Corps écrit* 18 (1986): 39–45.

Barrett, T. H. "Images of Printing in Seventh Century Chinese Religious Literature." *Chinese Science* 15 (1998): 81–93.

———. "Reading the *Liezi:* The First Thousand Years." In *Riding the Wind with Liezi: New Perspectives on the Daoist Classic*, edited by Ronnie Littlejohn and Jeffrey Dippmann, 15–30. Albany: State University of New York Press, 2011.

Baumann, Brian G. *Divine Knowledge: Buddhist Mathematics according to the Anonymous Manual of Mongolian Astrology and Divination*. Leiden: Brill, 2008.

Beal, Samuel. *Si-Yu-Ki: Buddhist Records of the Western World Translated from the Chinese of Hiuen Tsiang (A.D. 629)*. 2 vols. bound as one. London, 1884; reprint Delhi: Motilal, 1981.

Beecroft, Alexander. *Authorship and Cultural Identity in Early Greece and China: Patterns of Literary Circulation*. Cambridge: Cambridge University Press, 2010.

Behr, Wolfgang, and Bernhard Fuehrer. "Einführende Notizen zum Lesen in China mit besonderer Berücksichtigung der Frühzeit." In *Aspekte des Lesens in China in Vergangenheit und Gegenwart*, edited by Bernard Fuehrer, 1–44. Bochum: Projekt Verlag, 2005.

Behuniak, James, Jr. "Hitting the Mark: Archery and Ethics in Early Confucianism." *Journal of Chinese Philosophy* 37, no. 4 (2010): 588–604.

Bell, Catherine. *Ritual: Perspectives and Dimensions*. New York: Oxford University Press, 1997.

———. *Ritual Theory, Ritual Practice*. New York: Oxford University Press, 1992.

Benn, James A. "Another Look at the Pseudo-Śūraṃgama sūtra." *Harvard Journal of Asiatic Studies* 68, no. 1 (2008): 57–89.

Bennett, Tony. "Texts in History: The Determination of Readings and Their Texts." In *Reception Study: From Literary Theory to Cultural Studies*, edited by James L. Machor and Philip Goldstein, 61–74. New York: Routledge, 2001.

Bielefeldt, Carl. "Expedient Devices, the One Vehicle, and the Life Span of the Buddha." In *Readings of the Lotus Sūtra*, edited by Stephen F. Teiser and Jacqueline I. Stone, 62–82. New York: Columbia University Press, 2009.

Bizot, François. "La figuration des pieds du Bouddha au Cambodge." *Asiatische Studien / Études Asiatiques* 25, no. 4 (1971): 407–39.

Blackburn, Anne M. "The Text and the World." In *The Cambridge Companion to Religious Studies*, edited by Robert A. Orsi, 151–67. Cambridge: Cambridge University Press, 2012.

Bloom, Irene. "The Meaning of Sacrifices ('Jiyi')." In *Sources of Chinese Tradition*, edited by Wm. Theodore de Bary and Irene Bloom, 1: 339–42. 2nd edition. New York: Columbia University Press, 1999.

Bo Juncai 柏俊才. *Liang Wudi Xiao Yan kaolue* 梁武帝蕭衍考略. Shanghai: Shanghai guji chubanshe, 2008.

Bodde, Derk. "The Chinese Cosmic Magic Known as Watching for the Ethers." In *Studia Serica Bernard Karlgren Dedicata*, edited by Søren Egerod and Else Glahn, 14–35. Copenhagen: Ejnar Munksgaard, 1959.

———. *Festivals in Classical China: New Year and Other Annual Observances during the Han Dynasty, 206 B.C.–A.D. 220*. Princeton: Princeton University Press, 1975.

Bodiford, William M. "Keizan's Dream History." In *Religions of Japan in Practice*, edited by George J. Tanabe, Jr., 501–22. Princeton: Princeton University Press, 1999.

———. "Matara: A Dream King between Insight and Imagination." *Cahiers d'Extrême-Asie* 16 (2006–2007): 233–62.

Bokenkamp, Stephen R. *Ancestors and Anxiety: Daoism and the Birth of Rebirth in China*. Berkeley: University of California Press, 2007.

———. "Answering a Summons." In *Religions of China in Practice*, edited by Donald S. Lopez, Jr., 188–202. Princeton: Princeton University Press, 1996.

———. "Buddhism in the Writings of Tao Hongjing." *Daoism: Religion, History & Society*, no. 6 (2014): 247–68.

———. "Daoist Pantheons." In ECR2, 1169–1203.

———. *Early Daoist Scriptures*. Berkeley: University of California Press, 1997.

———. "The Early Lingbao Scriptures and the Origins of Daoist Monasticism." *Cahiers d'Extrême-Asie* 20 (2011): 95–124.

———. *A Fourth-Century Daoist Family: The Zhen'gao, or Declarations of the Perfected*. Vol. 1. Berkeley: University of California Press, 2021.

———. "Image Work: Dream Interpretation in a Late Fourth Century Daoist Text."

Paper presented at the workshop Visions of the Night: Dreams, Dreamers, and Religion in Medieval Societies, University of Southern California, April 2009.

———. "Sackcloth and Ashes: Self and Family in the *Tutan zhai*." In *Scriptures, Schools and Forms of Practice in Daoism: A Berlin Symposium*, edited by Poul Andersen and Florian C. Reiter, 33–48. Wiesbaden: Harrassowitz, 2005.

———. "Simple Twists of Fate: The Daoist Body and Its *Ming*." In *The Magnitude of "Ming": Command, Allotment, and Fate in Chinese Culture*, edited by Christopher Lupke, 151–68. Honolulu: University of Hawai'i Press, 2005.

———. "Sources of the Ling-pao Scriptures." In *Tantric and Taoist Studies in Honour of R. A. Stein*, edited by Michel Strickmann, 2: 434–86. Brussels: Institut Belge des Hautes Études Chinoises, 1983.

———. "Stages of Transcendence: The *Bhūmi* Concept in Taoist Scripture." In *Chinese Buddhist Apocrypha*, edited by Robert E. Buswell, Jr., 119-48. Honolulu: University of Hawai'i Press, 1990.

———. "Time After Time: Taoist Apocalyptic History and the Founding of the T'ang Dynasty." *Asia Major*, 3rd series, 7, no. 1 (1994): 59–88.

———. "What Daoist Body?" In *Purposes, Means and Conviction in Daoism: A Berlin Symposium*, edited by Florian C. Reiter, 131–50. Wiesbaden: Harrassowitz, 2007.

Bollée, W. B. "A Note on Evil and Its Conquest from Indra to Buddha." In *Prajñāpāramitā and Related Systems: Studies in Honor of Edward Conze*, edited by Lewis Lancaster, 371–82. Berkeley Buddhist Studies Series 1. Berkeley: University of California Press,, 1977.

Boltz, William G. "The Composite Nature of Early Chinese Texts." In *Text and Ritual in Early China*, edited by Martin Kern, 50–78. Seattle: University of Washington Press, 2005.

Boucher, Daniel. *Bodhisattvas of the Forest and the Formation of the Mahāyāna: A Study and Translation of the "Rāṣṭrapālaparipṛcchā-sūtra."* Honolulu: University of Hawai'i Press, 2008.

———. "Buddhist Translation Procedures in Third-Century China: A Study of Dharmarakṣa and His Translation Idiom." PhD dissertation, University of Pennsylvania, 2006.

———. "Dharmarakṣa and the Transmission of Buddhism to China." In "China at the Crossroads: A Festschrift in Honor of Victor H. Mair." Special issue of *Asia Major*, 3rd series, 19, nos. 1/2 (2006): 13–37.

———. "What Is a 'Hīnayāna Zealot' Doing in Fifth-Century China?" In *Buddhism Across Asia: Networks of Material, Intellectual and Cultural Exchange*, vol. 1, edited by Tansen Sen, 85–99. Singapore: Institute of Southeast Asian Studies, 2014.

Bourdieu, Pierre. *The Logic of Practice*. Translated by Richard Nice. Cambridge: Polity, 1990.

———. *In Other Words: Essays Towards a Reflexive Sociology*. Stanford: Stanford University Press, 1990.

———. *Outline of a Theory of Practice*. Translated by Richard Nice. Cambridge: Cambridge University Press, 1977.

Boyd, James W. *Satan and Māra: Christian and Buddhist Symbols of Evil*. Leiden: Brill, 1975.

Bray, Francesca, Vera Dorofeeva-Lichtmann, and Georges Métailié, eds. *Graphics and Text in the Production of Technical Knowledge in China: The Warp and the Weft*. Leiden: Brill, 2007.

Brindley, Erica Fox. "Capturing the World in Words: Later Mohist Hermeneutic Theories on Language and Disputation." *Early China* 43 (2020): 93–121.

———. "The Cosmic Power of Sound in the Late Warring States and Han Periods." *Journal of Chinese Religions* 35 (2007): 1–35.

———. *Individualism in Early China: Human Agency and the Self in Thought and Politics*. Honolulu: University of Hawai'i Press, 2010.

———. "Music, Cosmos, and the Development of Psychology in Early China." *T'oung Pao* 92, no. 1 (2006): 1–49.

Brokaw, Cynthia J. *The Ledgers of Merit and Demerit: Social Change and Moral Order in Late Imperial China*. Princeton: Princeton University Press, 1991.

Bronkhorst, Johannes. "The Buddha and the Jainas Reconsidered." *Asiatische Studien* 49, no. 2 (1995): 333–50.

———. "Did the Buddha Believe in Karma and Rebirth?" *Journal of the International Association of Buddhist Studies* 21, no. 1 (1998): 1–20.

Brown, Miranda. *The Politics of Mourning in Early China*. Albany: State University of New York Press, 2007.

Brown, Peter. *The Body and Society: Men, Women and Sexual Renunciation in Early Christianity*. New York: Columbia University Press, 1988.

Brown, Robert L. "The Nature and Use of the Bodily Relics of the Buddha in Gandhāra." In *Gandhāran Buddhism: Archaeology, Art, Texts*, edited by Pia Brancaccio and Kurt Behrendt, 183–209. Vancouver: University of British Columbia Press, 2006.

Brown, W. Norman. "Duty as Truth in Ancient India." *Proceedings of the American Philosophical Society* 116, no. 3 (1972): 252–68.

———. "Rg Veda 10.34 as an Act of Truth." In *Munshi Indological Felicitation Volume*, 8–10. N.p.: Bharatiya Vidya Bhavan, 1963.

Buckelew, Kevin. "Pregnant Metaphor: Embryology, Embodiment, and the Ends of Figurative Imagery in Chinese Buddhism." *Harvard Journal of Asiatic Studies* 78, no. 2 (2018): 371–411.

Bullock, Jeffrey S. *Yang Xiong: Philosophy of the Fa yan*. Highlands, NC: Mountain Mind Press, 2011.

Bumbacher, Stephan Peter. *Empowered Writing: Exorcistic and Apotropaic Rituals in Medieval China*. St. Petersburg, FL: Three Pines Press, 2012.

Burke, Peter. *The Historical Anthropology of Early Modern Italy: Essays on Perception and Communication*. Cambridge: Cambridge University Press, 1987.

Burlingame, E. W. "The Act of Truth (*Saccakiriya*): A Hindu Spell and Its Employment as Psychic Motif in Hindu Fiction." *Journal of the Royal Asiatic Society of Great Britain and Ireland* 49 (July 1917): 429–67.

Buswell, Robert E., Jr. "The Path to Perdition: The Wholesome Roots and Their Eradication." In *Paths to Liberation: The Mārga and Its Transformations in Buddhist Thought*, edited by Robert E. Buswell, Jr., and Robert M. Gimello, 107–34. Honolulu: University of Hawai'i Press, 1992.

Buswell, Robert E., Jr., and Robert M. Gimello. "Introduction." In *Paths to Liberation: The Mārga and Its Transformations in Buddhist Thought*, edited by Robert E. Buswell, Jr., and Robert M. Gimello, 1–36. Honolulu: University of Hawai'i Press, 1992.

Butler, Judith. *Bodies That Matter: On the Discursive Limits of Sex*. London: Routledge, 2011.

Bynum, Caroline Walker. *Metamorphosis and Identity*. New York: Zone, 2001.

Campany, Robert Ford. "Abstinence Halls (*zhaitang* 齋堂) in Lay Households in Early Medieval China." *Studies in Chinese Religions* 1, no. 4 (2016): 1–21.

———. "'Buddhism Enters China' in Early Medieval China." In *Old Society, New Belief: Religious Transformation of China and Rome, ca. 1st–6th Centuries*, edited by Poo Mu-chou, Harold Drake, and Lisa Raphals, 13–34. Oxford University Press, 2017.

———. "Buddhist Revelation and Taoist Translation in Early Medieval China." *Taoist Resources* 4, no. 1 (February 1993): 1–29.

———. *The Chinese Dreamscape, 300 BCE – 800 CE*. Cambridge, MA: Harvard University Asia Center, 2020.

———. "Chinese History and Writing about 'Religion(s)': Reflections at a Crossroad." In *Dynamics in the History of Religions between Asia and Europe: Encounters, Notions, and Comparative Perspectives*, edited by Volkhard Krech and Marion Steinicke, 273–94. Leiden: Brill, 2012.

———. "The Earliest Tales of the Bodhisattva Guanshiyin." In *Religions of China in Practice*, edited by Donald S. Lopez, Jr., 82–96. Princeton: Princeton University Press, 1996.

———. *A Garden of Marvels: Tales of Wonder from Early Medieval China*. Honolulu: University of Hawai'i Press, 2015.

———. "Ghosts Matter: The Culture of Ghosts in Six Dynasties *Zhiguai*." *Chinese Literature: Essays, Articles, Reviews* 13 (1991): 15–34.

———. "Living Off the Books: Fifty Ways to Dodge *Ming* 命 in Early Medieval China." In *The Magnitude of "Ming": Command, Allotment, and Fate in Chinese Culture*, edited by Christopher Lupke, 129–50. Honolulu: University of Hawai'i Press, 2005.

———. "Long-Distance Specialists in Early Medieval China." In *Literature, Religion, and East-West Comparison: Essays in Honor of Anthony C. Yu*, edited by Eric Ziolkowski, 109–24. Newark: University of Delaware Press, 2005.

———. *Making Transcendents: Ascetics and Social Memory in Early Medieval China*. Honolulu: University of Hawai'i Press, 2009.

———. "The Meanings of Cuisines of Transcendence in Late Classical and Early Medieval China." *T'oung Pao* 91, no. 1 (2005): 126–82.

———. "Miracle Tales as Scripture Reception: A Case Study involving the *Lotus Sutra* in China, 370–750 CE." *Early Medieval China* 24 (2018): 24–52.

———. "Notes on the Devotional Uses and Symbolic Functions of Sutra Texts as Depicted in Early Chinese Buddhist Miracle Tales and Hagiographies." *Journal of the International Association of Buddhist Studies* 14, no. 1 (1991): 28–72.

———. "On the Very Idea of Religions (in the Modern West and in Early Medieval China)." *History of Religions* 42, no. 4 (May 2003): 287–319.

———. "The Real Presence." *History of Religions* 32, no. 3 (February 1993): 233–72.

———. "'Religious' as a Category: A Comparative Case Study." *Numen* 65, no. 4 (May 2018): 333–76.

———. "Religious Repertoires and Contestation: A Case Study Based on Buddhist Miracle Tales." *History of Religions* 52, no. 2 (November 2012): 99–141.

———. "Secrecy and Display in the Quest for Transcendence in China, ca. 220 B.C.E.–350 C.E." *History of Religions* 45, no. 4 (May 2006): 291–336.

———. "Shangqing jing de biaoyan xingzhi" 上清經的表演性質. Translated by Qi Xuanming 戚軒銘, edited by Chen Weiqiang 陳偉強 [Timothy Wai Keung Chan]. In *Daojiao xiulian yu keyi de wenxue tiyan* 道教修煉與科儀的文學體驗, edited by Chen Weiqiang 陳偉強, 25–53. Nanjing: Fenghuang chubanshe, 2018.

———. *Signs from the Unseen Realm: Buddhist Miracle Tales from Early Medieval China*. Honolulu: University of Hawai'i Press, 2012.

———. *Strange Writing: Anomaly Accounts in Early Medieval China*. Albany: State University of New York Press, 1996.

———. "'Survival' as an Interpretive Strategy: A Sino-Western Comparative Case Study." *Method and Theory in the Study of Religion* 2, no. 1 (1990): 1–26.

———. "The *Sword Scripture*: Recovering and Interpreting a Lost 4th-Century Daoist Method for Cheating Death." *Daoism: Religion, History and Society* 道教研究學報, no. 6 (2014): 33–84.

———. "Taoist Bioethics in the Final Age: Therapy and Salvation in the *Book of Divine Incantations for Penetrating the Abyss*." In *Religious Methods and Resources in Bioethics*, edited by Paul Camenisch, 67–91. Dordrecht: Kluwer Academic Publishers, 1994.

———. *To Live as Long as Heaven and Earth: A Translation and Study of Ge Hong's Traditions of Divine Transcendents*. Berkeley: University of California Press, 2002.

———. "Two Religious Thinkers of the Early Eastern Jin: Gan Bao 干寶 and Ge Hong 葛洪 in Multiple Contexts." *Asia Major*, 3rd series, 18, no. 1 (2005): 175–224.

Capitanio, Joshua. "Dragon Kings and Thunder Gods: Rainmaking, Magic, and Ritual in Medieval Chinese Religion." PhD dissertation, University of Pennsylvania, 2008.

———. "Sanskrit and Pseudo-Sanskrit Incantations in Daoist Ritual Texts." *History of Religions* 57, no. 4 (May 2018): 348–405.

Carré, Patrick. *Le livre de la cour jaune: Classique taoïste des IV–Ve siècles*. Paris: Éditions du Seuil, 1999.

Carruthers, Mary. *The Craft of Thought: Meditation, Rhetoric, and the Making of Images, 400–1200*. Cambridge: Cambridge University Press, 1998.

Carter, Warren. "Narrative Readings, Contextualized Readers, and Matthew's Gospel." In *The Oxford Handbook of Biblical Narrative*, edited by Danna Nolan Fewell. Oxford: Oxford University Press, 2016. https://doi.org/10.1093/oxfordhb/9780199967728.013.26.

Cedzich, Angelika. "Ghosts and Demons, Law and Order: Grave Quelling Texts and Early Taoist Liturgy." *Taoist Resources* 4, no. 2 (December 1993): 23–35.

———. "The Organon of the Twelve Hundred Officials and Its Gods." *Daoism: Religion, History, and Society*, no. 1 (2009): 1–93.

Chang Chaoran [Zhang Chaoran] 張超然. "Killing Spirits from the Dead: The Object of Exorcism in Medieval Daoist Funeral Rites." In *Exorcism in Daoism: A Berlin Symposium*, edited by Florian C. Reiter, 11–30. Wiesbaden: Harrassowitz, 2011.

———. "Laizi sizhe de yangsha: Zhonggu tianshidao sangzang yishizhong de quxie duixiang" 來自死者的殃殺：中古天師道喪葬儀式中的驅邪對象. *Furen zongjiao yanjiu*, no. 25 (2012): 169–94.

Chang, Garma C. C., ed. *A Treasury of Mahāyāna Sūtras: Selections from the Mahāratnakūta Sūtra*. University Park: Pennsylvania State University Press, 1983.

Chapman, Jesse. "The Rhetoric and Ritual of Celestial Signs in Early Imperial China." PhD dissertation, University of California at Berkeley, 2015.

———. "Unwholesome Bodies: Reading the Sign of the Amputated Foot in Early China." *Asia Major*, 3rd series, 30, no. 2 (2017): 1–26.

Chappell, David W. "Chinese Buddhist Interpretations of the Pure Lands." In *Buddhist and Taoist Studies I*, edited by Michael Saso and David W. Chappell, 23–54. Honolulu: University Press of Hawai'i, 1977.

———. "The Formation of the Pure Land Movement in China: Tao-ch'o and Shan-tao." In *The Pure Land Tradition: History and Development*, edited by James Foard, Michael Solomon, and Richard K. Payne, 173–232. Berkeley: Institute of Buddhist Studies, 1996.

Chen, Jack W. *Anecdote, Network, Gossip, Performance: Essays on the "Shishuo xinyu."* Cambridge, MA: Harvard University Asia Center, 2021.

———. "On Mourning and Sincerity in the *Li ji* and the *Shishuo xinyu*." In *Memory in Medieval China: Text, Ritual, and Community*, edited by Wendy Swartz and Robert Ford Campany, 63–81. Leiden: Brill, 2018.

Chen, Jinhua. "The Indian Buddhist Missionary Dharmakṣema (385–433): A New Dating of His Arrival in Guzang and of His Translations." *T'oung Pao* 90, no. 4 (2004): 215–63.

———. "Meditation Traditions in Fifth-Century Northern China: With a Special Note on a Forgotten 'Kaśmīri' Meditation Tradition Brought to China by Buddhabhadra (359–429)." In *Buddhism Across Asia: Networks of Material, Intellectual and Cultural Exchange*, vol. 1, edited by Tansen Sen, 101–30. Singapore: Institute of Southeast Asian Studies, 2014.

———. "*Pañcavārṣika* Assemblies in Liang Wudi's Buddhist Palace Chapel." *Harvard Journal of Asiatic Studies* 66, no. 1 (2006): 43–103.

Ch'en, Kenneth K. S. *Buddhism in China: A Historical Survey*. Princeton: Princeton University Press, 1964.

Chen, Ruifeng. "The Relationship between Three Short Indigenous Chinese Buddhist Scriptures and the Textual Practices Found in their Dunhuang Manuscript Colophons." *T'oung Pao* 106, nos. 5–6 (2020): 552–601.

Cheng, Anne. *Histoire de la pensée chinoise*. Paris: Éditions du Seuil, 1997.

———. "What Did It Mean To Be a *Ru* in Han Times?" *Asia Major*, 3rd series, 14, no. 2 (2001): 101–18.

Cheung, Tak Ching Neky. "A Comparative Study of the Pure Land Teachings of Shandao (613–681) and Shinran (1173–1262)." Master's thesis, University of Hong Kong, 2001.

Childs-Johnson, Elizabeth, ed. *The Oxford Handbook of Early China*. New York: Oxford University Press, 2021.

Chittick, Andrew. *The Jiankang Empire in Chinese and World History*. Oxford: Oxford University Press, 2020.

———. *Patronage and Community in Medieval China: The Xiangyang Garrison, 400–600 CE*. Albany: State University of New York Press, 2009.

Choo, Jessey J. C. "That 'Fatty Lump': Discourses on the Fetus, Fetal Development, and Filial Piety in China before the Eleventh Century CE." *Nan Nü* 14, no. 2 (January 2012): 177–221.

Cicuzza, Claudio. *A Mirror Reflecting the Entire World: The Pāli Buddhapādamaṅgala or Auspicious Signs on the Buddha's Feet*. Bangkok: Fragile Palm Leaves Foundation and Lumbini: Lumbini International Research Institute, 2011.

Coakley, Sarah. "Introduction: Religion and the Body." In *Religion and the Body*, edited by Sarah Coakley, 1–14. Cambridge, MA: Harvard University Press, 1997.

Cole, Alan. *Text as Father: Paternal Seductions in Early Mahāyāna Buddhist Literature*. Berkeley: University of California Press, 2005.

Conze, Edward. *The Large Sutra on Perfect Wisdom*. Berkeley: University of California Press, 1975.

———. *The Perfection of Wisdom in Eight Thousand Lines and Its Verse Summary*. 2nd edition. Bolinas, CA: Four Seasons Foundation, 1975.

Cook, Constance A. *Ancestors, Kings, and the Dao*. Cambridge, MA: Harvard University Asia Center, 2017.

———. "Education and the Way of the Former Kings." In *Writing and Literacy in Early China: Studies from the Columbia Early China Seminar*, edited by Li Feng and David Prager Branner, 302–36. Seattle: University of Washington Press, 2011.

———. "Moonshine and Millet: Feasting and Purification Rituals in Ancient China." In *Of Tripod and Palate: Food, Politics, and Religion in Traditional China*, edited by Roel Sterckx, 9–33. New York: Palgrave Macmillan, 2005.

Cook, Scott. *The Bamboo Texts of Guodian: A Study and Complete Translation*. Ithaca: East Asia Program, Cornell University, 2012.

———. "The *Lüshi Chunqiu* and the Resolution of Philosophical Dissonance." *Harvard Journal of Asiatic Studies* 62, no. 2 (2002): 307–45.

Copp, Paul. *The Body Incantatory: Spells and the Ritual Imagination in Medieval Chinese Buddhism*. New York: Columbia University Press, 2014.

———. "*Dhāraṇī* Scriptures." In *Esoteric Buddhism and the Tantras in East Asia*, edited by Charles D. Orzech, Henrik H. Sørensen, and Richard K. Payne, 176–80. Leiden: Brill, 2011.

———. "Manuscript Culture as Ritual Culture in Late Medieval Dunhuang: Buddhist Talisman-Seals and Their Manuals." *Cahiers d'Extrême-Asie* 20 (2011): 193–226.

———. "Notes on the Term *Dhāraṇī* in Medieval Chinese Buddhist Thought." *Bulletin of the School of Oriental and African Studies* 71, no. 3 (2008): 493–508.

Cox, Collett. "Attainment through Abandonment: The Sarvāstivādin Path of Removing Defilements." In *Paths to Liberation: The Mārga and Its Transformations in Buddhist Thought*, edited by Robert E. Buswell, Jr., and Robert M. Gimello, 63–105. Honolulu: University of Hawai'i Press, 1992.

Crippen, Matthew, and Jay Schulkin. *Mind Ecologies: Body, Brain, and World*. New York: Columbia University Press, 2020.

Csikszentmihalyi, Mark. "Ethics and Self-Cultivation Practice in Early China." In ECR1, 519–42.

———. *Material Virtue: Ethics and the Body in Early China*. Leiden: Brill, 2004.

Csikszentmihalyi, Mark, and Michael Nylan. "Constructing Lineages and Inventing Traditions through Exemplary Figures in Early China." *T'oung Pao* 89, no. 1 (2003): 59–99.

Culler, Jonathan. "Literary Competence." In *Reader-Response Criticism: From Formalism to Post-Structuralism*, edited by Jane P. Tompkins, 101–17. Baltimore: Johns Hopkins University Press, 1980.

Cutter, Robert Joe. "Shen Who Couldn't Write: Literary Relationships at the Court of Liu Jun." In *Reading Medieval Chinese Poetry: Text, Context, and Culture*, edited by Paul W. Kroll, 36–54. Leiden: Brill, 2015.

Dachille, Rae. "Inscribing the Corpus: Scribal and Ritual Practice in the Material Culture of Dunhuang." *Numen* 67, nos. 2–3 (2020): 113–37.

Darnton, Robert. "First Steps toward a History of Reading." In *Reception Study: From Literary Theory to Cultural Studies*, edited by James L. Machor and Philip Goldstein, 160–79. New York: Routledge, 2001.

Davis, Winston. *Dojo: Magic and Exorcism in Modern Japan*. Stanford: Stanford University Press, 1980.

Dayal, Har. *The Bodhisattva Doctrine in Buddhist Sanskrit Literature*. London: Routledge & Kegan Paul, 1932; reprint Delhi: Motilal Banarsidass, 1978.

De Groot, J. J. M. *The Religious System of China*. 6 vols. continuously paginated. Leiden: Brill, 1892–1910.

De la Vallée Poussin, Louis. "Le Bouddha et les abhijñās." *Le Muséon* 44 (1931): 335–42.

DeCaroli, Robert. *Haunting the Buddha: Indian Popular Religions and the Formation of Buddhism*. Oxford: Oxford University Press, 2004.

Deleanu, Florin. "A Preliminary Study on An Shigao's Translation of the *Yogācārabhūmi*." *Journal of the Department of Liberal Arts—Kansai Medical University* 17 (1997): 33–52.

———. "A Preliminary Study on Meditation and the Beginnings of Mahāyāna." *Annual Report of the International Research Institute for Advanced Buddhology at Soka University* 2 (1999): 65–113.

———. "The Transmission of Xuanzang's Translation of the *Yogācārabhūmi* in East Asia." In *Kongōji Issaikyō no sōgōteki kenkyū to Kongōji shōgyō no kisokuteki kenkyū* 金剛寺一切経の総合的研究と金剛寺聖教の基礎的研究, edited by Ochiai Toshinori 落合俊典, 589–632 (1–44). Koyama: Kabushiki kaisha, 2008.

Demiéville, Paul. "Sur la mémoire des existences antérieures." *Bulletin de l'École Française d'Extrême-Orient* 27 (1927): 283–98.

Denecke, Wiebke. *The Dynamics of Masters Literature: Early Chinese Thought from Confucius to Han Feizi*. Cambridge, MA: Harvard University Asia Center, 2010.

Des Jardins, Marc. *Le sūtra de la Mahāmāyūrī: Rituel et politique dans la Chine des Tang (618–907)*. Québec City: Presses de l'Université Laval, 2011.

Despeux, Catherine. "Buddhist Healing Practices at Dunhuang in the Medieval Period." In *Buddhist Healing in Medieval China and Japan*, edited by C. Pierce Salguero and Andrew Macomber, 118–59. Honolulu: University of Hawai'i Press, 2020.

———. "Symbolic Pregnancy and the Sexual Identity of Taoist Adepts." In *Transforming the Void: Embryological Discourse and Reproductive Imagery in East Asian Religions*, edited by Anna Andreeva and Dominic Steavu, 147–85. Leiden: Brill, 2016.

———, ed. *Médecine, religion et société dans la Chine médiévale: Étude de manuscrits chinois de Dunhuang et de Turfan*. 3 vols. continuously paginated. Paris: Collège de France, Institut des Hautes Études Chinoises, 2010.

Dessein, Bart. "Abhidharma in China: Reflections on 'Matching Meanings' and *Xuanxue*." In *Text, History, and Philosophy: Abhidharma across Buddhist Scholastic Traditions*, edited by Bart Dessein and Weijen Teng, 279–95. Leiden: Brill, 2016.

———. "Contaminants and the Path to Salvation: A Study of the Sarvāstivāda *Hṛdaya* Treatises." *Asian Philosophy* 19, no. 1 (2009): 63–84.

———. "Of Seeds and Sprouts: Defilement and Its Attachment to the Life-Stream in the Sarvāstivāda *Hṛdaya* Treatises." *Asian Philosophy* 18, no. 1 (2008): 17–33.

Di Lu and Vivienne Lo. "Scent and Synaesthesia: The Medical Use of Spice Bags in Early China." *Journal of Ethnopharmacology* 167 (2015): 38–46.

Dien, Albert E. *Six Dynasties Civilization*. New Haven, CT: Yale University Press, 2007.

Dien, Albert E., and Keith N. Knapp, eds. *The Cambridge History of China*. Vol. 2, *The Six Dynasties, 220–589*. Cambridge: Cambridge University Press, 2019.

Diény, Jean-Pierre. "Le fenghuang 鳳凰 et le phénix." *Cahiers d'Extrême-Asie* 5 (1990): 1–13.

———. "Le saint ne rêve pas: de Zhuangzi à Michel Jouvet." Études chinoises 20 (2001): 127–99.

Ding Changyun 丁常雲. "Daojiao de siling chongbai ji qi shehui sixiang neirong" 道教的四靈崇拜及其社會思想內容. *Daojiaoxue tansuo,* no. 10 (1997): 113–31.

Ding Huang 丁煌. "Daojiao de muyu tanjiu" 道教的沐浴探究. In *Lisu yu zongjiao* 禮俗與宗教, edited by Lin Fushi, 117–27. Beijing: Zhongguo dabaike quanshu chubanshe, 2005.

Donner, Neal. "Chih-i's Meditation on Evil." In *Buddhist and Taoist Practice in Medieval Chinese Society: Buddhist and Taoist Studies II*, edited by David W. Chappell, 49–64. Honolulu: University of Hawai'i Press, 1987.

———. "The Great Calming and Contemplation of Chih-i—chapter 1: The Synopsis." PhD dissertation, University of British Columbia, 1976.

Donner, Neal, and Daniel B. Stevenson. *The Great Calming and Contemplation: A Study and Annotated Translation of the First Chapter of Chih-I's Mo-ho chih-kuan*. Honolulu: University of Hawai'i Press, 1993.

Douglas, Mary. *Implicit Meanings: Essays in Anthropology*. London: Routledge & Kegan Paul, 1975.

———. *Purity and Danger: An Analysis of the Concepts of Pollution and Taboo*. 2nd edition. London: Routledge & Kegan Paul, 1969.

Drège, Jean-Pierre. *Les bibliothèques en Chine au temps des manuscrits (jusqu'au Xe siècle)*. Paris: École Française d'Extrême-Orient, 1991.

———. *Le papier dans la Chine impériale: Origine, fabrication, usages*. Paris: Les Belles Lettres, 2017.

Drège, Jean-Pierre, and Dimitri Drettas. "Oniromancie." In *Divination et société dans la Chine médiévale*, edited by Marc Kalinowski, 369–404. Paris: Bibliothèque nationale de France, 2003.

Drettas, Dimitri. "Le rêve mis en ordre: Les traités onirologiques des Ming à l'épreuve des traditions divinatoire, médicale et religieuse du rêve en Chine." PhD dissertation, École Pratique des Hautes Études, 2007.

Drewes, David. "The Forest Hypothesis." In *Setting Out on the Great Way: Essays on Early Mahāyāna Buddhism*, edited by Paul Harrison, 73–93. Sheffield: Equinox, 2018.

———. "Revisiting the Phrase '*sa pṛthivīpradeśaś caityabhūto bhavet*' and the Mahāyāna Cult of the Book." *Indo-Iranian Journal* 50, no 2 (June 2007): 101–43.

Ducor, Jérôme. "Les sources de la Sukhāvatī, autour d'une étude récente de G. Fussman." *Journal of the International Association of Buddhist Studies* 27, no. 2 (2004): 357–410.

Dudbridge, Glen. *Books, Tales and Vernacular Culture: Selected Papers on China*. Leiden: Brill, 2005.

———. *A Portrait of Five Dynasties China from the Memoirs of Wang Renyu (880–956)*. Oxford: Oxford University Press, 2013.

———. *Religious Experience and Lay Society in T'ang China: A Reading of Tai Fu's "Kuang-i chi."* Cambridge: Cambridge University Press, 1995.

Durrant, Stephen, Wai-yee Li, and David Schaberg. *Zuo Tradition: Zuozhuan*. 3 vols. continuously paginated. Seattle: University of Washington Press, 2016.

Ebrey, Patricia Buckley. *Confucianism and Family Rituals in Imperial China: A Social History of Writing about Rites*. Princeton: Princeton University Press 1991.

Eidinow, Esther. "The (Ancient Greek) Subject Supposed to Believe." *Numen* 66, no. 1 (December 2019): 56–88.

Elvin, Mark. "Between the Earth and Heaven: Conceptions of the Self in China." In *The Category of the Person: Anthropology, Philosophy, History*, edited by Michael Carrithers, Steven Collins, and Steven Lukes, 156–89. Cambridge: Cambridge University Press, 1985.

Esler, Dylan. "Note d'oniromancie tibétaine: Réflexions sur le chapitre 4 du *Bsam-gtan mig-sgron* de Gnubs-chen sangs-rgyas ye-shes." *Acta Orientalia Belgica* 25 (2012): 317–28.

Eyl, Jennifer. *Signs, Wonders, and Gifts: Divination in the Letters of Paul*. New York: Oxford University Press, 2019.

Falk, Harry, and Karashima Seishi. "A First-Century *Prajñāpāramitā* Manuscript from Gandhāra: *parivarta 1*." *Annual Report of the International Research Institute for Advanced Buddhology at Soka University* 15 (2012): 19–61.

———. "A First-Century *Prajñāpāramitā* Manuscript from Gandhāra: *parivarta 5*." *Annual Report of the International Research Institute for Advanced Buddhology at Soka University* 16 (2013): 97–170.

Faure, Bernard. *Visions of Power: Imagining Medieval Japanese Buddhism*. Translated by Phyllis Brooks. Princeton: Princeton University Press, 1996.

Fish, Stanley E. "Literature in the Reader: Affective Stylistics." In *Reader-Response Criticism: From Formalism to Post-Structuralism*, edited by Jane P. Tompkins, 70–100. Baltimore: Johns Hopkins University Press, 1980.

———. "Yet Once More." In *Reception Study: From Literary Theory to Cultural Studies*, edited by James L. Machor and Philip Goldstein, 29–38. New York: Routledge, 2001.

Fitzgerald, Timothy. "Experience." In *Guide to the Study of Religion*, edited by Willi Braun and Russell T. McCutcheon, 125–39. London: Cassell, 2000.

Forte, Antonino. "The South Indian Monk Bodhiruci (d. 727): Biographical Evidence." In *A Life Journey to the East: Sinological Studies in Memory of Giuliano Bertuccioli (1923–2001)*, edited by Antonino Forte and Federico Masini, 77–116. Kyoto: Scuola Italiana di Studi sull' Asia Orientale, 2002.

Foucault, Michel. *The Hermeneutics of the Subject: Lectures at the Collège de France, 1981–1982*. Edited by Frédéric Gros. Translated by Graham Burchell. New York: Picador, 2001.

———. *Technologies of the Self: A Seminar with Michel Foucault*. Edited by Luther H. Martin, Huck Gutman, and Patrick H. Hutton. Amherst: University of Massachusetts Press, 1988.

Fukatsu Tanefusa 深津胤房. "Kodai chūgokujin no shisō to seikatsu: yume ni tsuite" 古代中國人の思想と生活：夢について. In *Uno Testuto sensei hakuju shukuga kinen Tōyōgaku ronsō* 宇野哲人先生白壽祝賀記念東洋學論叢, 939–61. Tokyo: Uno Testuto sensei hakuju shukuga kinen kai, 1974.

Funayama Tōru 船山 徹. "Buddhist Theories of Bodhisattva Practice as Adopted by Daoists." *Cahiers d'Extrême-Asie* 20 (2011): 15–33.

———. "Guṇavarman and Some of the Earliest Examples of Ordination Platforms (*jietan*) in China." In *Images, Relics and Legends: The Formation and Transformation of Buddhist Sacred Sites, Essays in Honour of Professor Koichi Shinohara*, edited by James A. Benn, Jinhua Chen, and James Robson, 21–45. Oakville, ON: Mosaic Press, 2012.

———. "Rikuchō jidai ni okeru bosatsukai no juyō katei" 六朝時代における菩薩戒の受容過程. *Tōhō gakuhō* 67 (1995): 1–135.

Furth, Charlotte. "From Birth to Birth: The Growing Body in Chinese Medicine." In *Chinese Views of Childhood*, edited by Anne Behnke Kinney, 157–91. Honolulu: University of Hawai'I Press, 1995.

Galambos, Imre. *Orthography of Early Chinese Writing: Evidence from Newly Excavated Manuscripts (490–221 BC)*. Budapest: Eötvös Loránd University, 2006.

———. "Punctuation Marks in Medieval Chinese Manuscripts." In *Manuscript Cultures: Mapping the Field*, edited by Jörg Quenzer, Dmitry Bondarev, and Jan-Ulrich Sobisch, 341–58. Berlin: De Gruyter, 2014.

Gao Yang 高陽. "The Idea of the Anavatapta Lake in India and Its Adoption in East Asia." *Religions* 11, no. 3 (2020): 1–16. https://doi.org/10.3390/rel11030134.

Geaney, Jane. *On the Epistemology of the Senses in Early Chinese Thought*. Honolulu: University of Hawai'i Press, 2002.

———. "Guarding Moral Boundaries: Shame in Early Confucianism." *Philosophy East and West* 54, no. 2 (2004): 113–42.

Gentz, Joachim. "Defining Boundaries and Relations of Textual Units: Examples from the Literary Tool-Kit of Early Chinese Argumentation." In *Literary Forms of Argument in Early China*, edited by Joachim Gentz and Dirk Meyer, 112–57. Leiden: Brill, 2015.

———. "The Past as a Messianic Vision: Historical Thought and Strategies of Sacralization in the Early Gongyang Tradition." In *Historical Truth, Historical Criticism, and Ideology: Chinese Historiography and Historical Culture from a New Comparative Perspective*, edited by Helwig Schmidt-Glintzer, Achim Mittag, and Jörn Rüsen, 227–54. Leiden: Brill, 2005.

Gethin, Rupert M. L. "The Mātikās: Memorization, Mindfulness and the List." In *In the Mirror of Memory: Reflections on Mindfulness and Remembrance in Indian and*

Tibetan Buddhism, edited by Janet Gyatso, 149–72. Albany: State University of New York Press, 1992.

Gibas, Piotr. "Mozi and the Ghosts: The Concept of *Ming* 明 in Mozi's 'Ming gui' 明鬼." *Early China* 40 (2017): 89–123.

Giddings, William J. "A Structuralist Examination of the Origins of the Māra Mytheme and Its Function in the Narrative of the *Daoxing Bore Jing*, the Earliest Complete Recension of the *Aṣṭasāhasrikā-prajñā-pāramitā-sūtra*." PhD dissertation, King's College London, 2014.

Gilks, Peter James. "No Turning Back: The Concept of Irreversibility in Indian Mahāyāna Literature." PhD dissertation, Australian National University, 2010.

Gimello, Robert M. "Mārga and Culture: Learning, Letters, and Liberation in Northern Sung Ch'an." In *Paths to Liberation: The Mārga and Its Transformations in Buddhist Thought*, edited by Robert E. Buswell, Jr., and Robert M. Gimello, 371–437. Honolulu: University of Hawai'i Press, 1992.

Ginzburg, Carlo. *The Cheese and the Worms: The Cosmos of a Sixteenth-Century Miller*. Translated by Anne and John Tedeschi. Baltimore: Johns Hopkins University Press, 1980.

Girard, Frédéric. "Le journal des rêves de Myōe, moine japonais de l'école Kegon." *Journal Asiatique* 278 (1990): 167–93.

———. *Un moine de la secte Kegon à l'époque de Kamakura: Myōe (1173–1232) et le journal de ses rêves*. Paris: École Française d'Extrême-Orient, 1990.

Girardot, Norman. *Myth and Meaning in Early Taoism*. Berkeley: University of California Press, 1983.

Giuffrida, Noelle. "Representing the Daoist God Zhenwu, the Perfected Warrior, in Late Imperial China." PhD dissertation, University of Wisconsin, 1999.

Gjertson, Donald E. *Miraculous Retribution: A Study and Translation of T'ang Lin's "Ming-pao chi."* Berkeley: Centers for South and Southeast Asia Studies, University of California, and Institute of Buddhist Studies, 1989.

Glass, Andrew. "Guṇabhadra, Baoyun, and the Saṃyuktāgama." *Journal of the International Association of Buddhist Studies* 31, nos. 1–2 (2008): 185–203.

Goble, Geoffrey C. *Chinese Esoteric Buddhism: Amoghavajra, the Ruling Elite, and the Emergence of a Tradition*. New York: Columbia University Press, 2019.

Goldin, Paul R. "Confucius and His Disciples in the *Lunyu*: The Basis for the Traditional View." In *Confucius and the Analects Revisited: New Perspectives on Composition, Dating, and Authorship*, edited by Michael Hunter and Martin Kern, 92–115. Leiden: Brill, 2018.

———. "Han Law and the Regulation of Interpersonal Relations: 'The Confucianization of the Law' Revisited." *Asia Major*, 3rd series, 25, no. 1 (2012): 1–31.

Goldin, Paul R., ed. *A Concise Companion to Confucius*. Oxford: Wiley, 2017.

Graham, A. C. *The Book of Lieh-tzu: A Classic of the Tao*. 2nd edition. New York: Columbia University Press, 1990.

———. *Chuang-tzu: The Inner Chapters*. London: George Allen & Unwin, 1981.

———. "The Date and Composition of *Lieh-tzu*." In *Studies in Chinese Philosophy and Philosophical Literature*, 216–82. Albany: State University of New York Press, 1990.

Graziani, Romain. "The Subject and the Sovereign: Exploring the Self in Early Chinese Self-Cultivation." In ECR1, 459–517.

———. *Fictions philosophiques du "Tchouang-tseu."* Paris: Gallimard, 2006.

Greene, Eric M. *Chan Before Chan: Meditation, Repentance, and Visionary Experience in Chinese Buddhism*. Honolulu: University of Hawai'i Press, 2021.

———. "*Pratītyasamutpāda* in the Translations of An Shigao and the Writings of His Chinese Followers." In *Text, History, and Philosophy: Abhidharma across Buddhist Scholastic Traditions*, edited by Bart Dessein and Weijen Teng, 248–78. Leiden: Brill, 2016.

———. *The Secrets of Buddhist Meditation: Visionary Meditation Texts from Early Medieval China*. Honolulu: University of Hawai'i Press, 2021.

———. "Visions and Visualizations: In Fifth-Century Chinese Buddhism and 19th-Century Experimental Psychology." *History of Religions* 55, no. 3 (February 2016): 289–328.

Gregory, Peter N., ed. *Sudden and Gradual: Approaches to Enlightenment in Chinese Thought*. Honolulu: University of Hawai'i Press, 1987.

Griffiths, Richard J. *Religious Reading: The Place of Reading in the Practice of Religion*. Oxford: Oxford University Press, 1999.

Groner, Paul. "The Ordination Ritual in the *Platform Sūtra* within the Context of the East Asian Buddhist Vinaya Tradition." In *Fo Kuang Shan Report of International Conference on Ch'an Buddhism*, 220–50. Kaohsiung, Taiwan: Fa Kuang, 1990.

Guggenmos, Esther-Maria. "A List of Magic and Mantic Practices in the Buddhist Canon." In *Coping with the Future: Theories and Practices of Divination in East Asia*, edited by Michael Lackner, 151–95. Leiden: Brill, 2018.

———. "*Qian* Divination and its Ritual Adaptations in Chinese Buddhism." *Journal of Chinese Religions* 46, no. 1 (May 2018): 43–70.

Gundersen, Guttorm Norberg. "Attacked by Māra: Tiantai Zhiyi (538–597) and the Birth of Chinese Buddhist Meditative Demonology." Master's thesis, University of Oslo, 2017.

Hadot, Pierre. *Philosophy as a Way of Life*. Edited with an introduction by Arnold I. Davidson. Translated by Michael Chase. Oxford: Blackwell, 1995.

———. *What Is Ancient Philosophy?* Translated by Michael Chase. Cambridge, MA: Harvard University Press, 2002.

Hall, Alaric. "The Evidence for *Maran*, the Anglo-Saxon 'Nightmares.'" *Neophilologus* 91, no. 2 (April 2007): 299–317.

Hamar, Imre, and Takami Inoue, eds. *Faith in Buddhism*. Budapest: Institute for East Asian Studies, Eötvös Loránd University, 2016.

Hao Chunwen 郝春文. *Dunhuang Manuscripts: An Introduction to Texts from the Silk Road*. Translated by Stephen F. Teiser. Diamond Bar, CA: Portico, 2020.

Harbsmeier, Christoph. "The Authenticity and Nature of the *Analects* of Confucius." *Journal of Chinese Studies [Hong Kong]* no. 68 (January 2019): 171–234.

Harper, Donald. "A Chinese Demonography of the Third Century B.C." *Harvard Journal of Asiatic Studies* 45, no. 2 (December 1985): 459–98.

———. *Early Chinese Medical Literature*. London: Kegan Paul, 1998.

———. "A Note on Nightmare Magic in Ancient and Medieval China." *T'ang Studies* 6 (1988): 69–76.

———. "The Seat of Taiyi 太一 (Grand One) and New Light on an Old Problem: How Did Daoist Religion Happen?" In *Zhongguo zaoqi shushu, yishu yu wenhua jiaoliu: Li Ling xiansheng qizhi huadan qingshou lunwen ji* 中國早期數術, 藝術與文化交流: 李零先生七秩華誕慶壽論文集, edited by Yin Yao et al., 309–52. Hangzhou: Zhejiang daxue chubanshe, 2021.

———. "Spellbinding." In *Religions of China in Practice*, edited by Donald S. Lopez, Jr., 241–50. Princeton: Princeton University Press, 1996.

———. "The Textual Form of Knowledge: Occult Miscellanies in Ancient and Medieval Chinese Manuscripts, Fourth Century B.C. to Tenth Century A.D." In *Looking at It from Asia: The Processes that Shaped the Sources of History of Science*, edited by Florence Bretelle-Establet, 37–80. Paris: Springer, 2010.

———. "Wang Yen-shou's Nightmare Poem." *Harvard Journal of Asiatic Studies* 47, no. 1 (June 1987): 239–83.

Harper, Donald, and Marc Kalinowski. "Introduction." In *Books of Fate and Popular Culture in Early China: The Daybook Manuscripts of the Warring States, Qin, and Han*, 1–10. Leiden: Brill, 2017.

Harper, Donald, and Marc Kalinowski, eds. *Books of Fate and Popular Culture in Early China: The Daybook Manuscripts of the Warring States, Qin, and Han*. Leiden: Brill, 2017.

Harris-McCoy, Daniel E. *Artemidorus' Oneirocritica: Text, Translation, and Commentary*. Oxford: Oxford University Press, 2012.

Harrison, Paul M. "*Buddhānusmṛti* in the *Pratyutpanna-buddha-saṃmukhāvasthita-samādhi-sūtra*." *Journal of Indian Philosophy* 6, no. 1 (1978): 35–57.

———. "Commemoration and Identification in *Buddhānusmṛti*." In *In the Mirror of Memory: Reflections on Mindfulness and Remembrance in Indian and Tibetan Buddhism*, edited by Janet Gyatso, 215–38. Albany: State University of New York Press, 1992.

———. "The Earliest Chinese Translations of Mahāyāna Buddhist Sutras: Some Notes on the Works of Lokakṣema." *Buddhist Studies Review* 10, no. 2 (1993): 135–77.

———. "Mediums and Messages: Reflections on the Production of Mahāyāna Sūtras." *Eastern Buddhist* 35, nos. 1/2 (2003): 116–51.

———, trans. *The Pratyutpanna Samādhi Sūtra Translated by Lokakṣema*. BDK English Tripiṭika. Berkeley: Numata Center for Buddhist Translation and Research, 1998.

Hattori, Masaaki. "The Dream Simile in Vijñānavāda Treatises." In *Indological and Buddhist Studies: Volume in Honour of Professor J.W. de Jong on His Sixtieth Birthday*, edited by L.A. Hercus et al., 235–41. Sidney: Australian National University, 1982.

Heirman, Ann. "Chinese Nuns and their Ordination in Fifth Century China." *Journal of the International Association of Buddhist Studies* 24, no. 2 (2001): 275–304.

Hendrischke, Barbara. *The Scripture on Great Peace: The "Taiping jing" and the Beginnings of Daoism*. Berkeley: University of California Press, 2006.

Hilgert, Markus. "'Text-Anthropologie': Die Erforschung von Materialität und Präsenz des Geschriebenen als hermeneutische Strategie." *Mitteilungen der Deutschen Orient-Gesellschaft zu Berlin* 142 (2010): 87–126.

Hirakawa Akira 平川彰. "The Rise of Mahāyāna Buddhism and its Relationship to the Worship of Stūpas." Translated by Taitetsu Unno. *Memoirs of the Research Department of the Tōyō Bunko*, no. 22 (1963): 57–106.

Holt, John. *Discipline: The Canonical Buddhism of the Vinayapiṭaka*. Delhi: Motilal Banarsidass, 1983.

Horton, Sarah Johanna. "*Mukaekō*: Practice for the Deathbed." In *Death and the Afterlife in Japanese Buddhism*, edited by Jacqueline I. Stone and Mariko Namba Walter, 27–60. Honolulu: University of Hawai'i Press, 2008.

Hou Xudong. "The Buddhist Pantheon." In ECR2, 1095–1168.

Hsu, Alexander Ong. "Practices of Scriptural Economy: Compiling and Copying a Seventh-Century Chinese Buddhist Anthology." PhD dissertation, University of Chicago, 2018.

Hu Baozhu. *Believing in Ghosts and Spirits: The Concept of Gui in Ancient China*. Sankt Augustin: Institut Monumenta Serica, 2021.

Huang, Shih-shan Susan 黃士珊. "Daoist Imagery of Body and Cosmos, Part 1: Body Gods and Starry Travel." *Journal of Daoist Studies* 3 (2010): 57–90.

———. "Daoist Imagery of Body and Cosmos, Part 2: Body Worms and Internal Alchemy." *Journal of Daoist Studies* 4 (2011): 33–64.

———. "Daoist Seals, Part 1: Activation and Fashioning." *Journal of Daoist Studies* 10 (2017): 70–101.

———. "Media Transfer and Modular Construction: The Printing of *Lotus Sutra* Frontispieces in Song China." *Ars Orientalis* 41 (2011): 135–64.

Huang Yi-Long and Chang Chih-ch'eng. "The Evolution and Decline of the Ancient Chinese Practice of Watching for the Ethers." *Chinese Science*, no. 13 (1996): 82–106.

Hubbard, Jamie. *Absolute Delusion, Perfect Buddhahood: The Rise and Fall of a Chinese Heresy*. Honolulu: University of Hawai'i Press, 2001.

Humphrey, Caroline, and James Laidlaw. *The Archetypal Actions of Ritual: A Theory of Ritual Illustrated by the Jain Rite of Worship*. Oxford: Clarendon, 1994.

Hunter, Michael. *Confucius beyond the Analects*. Leiden: Brill, 2017.

———. "To Leave or Not To Leave: The *Chu ci* 楚辭 (Verses of Chu) as Response to the *Shi jing* 詩經 (Classic of Odes)." *Early China* 42 (2019): 111–46.

———. *The Poetics of Early Chinese Thought: How the Shijing Shaped the Chinese Philosophical Tradition*. New York: Columbia University Press, 2021.

Hunter, Michael, and Martin Kern, eds. *Confucius and the Analects Revisited: New Perspectives on Composition, Dating, and Authorship*. Leiden: Brill, 2018.

Hureau, Sylvie. "Buddhist Rituals." In *Early Chinese Religion, Part Two: The Period of Division (220–589 AD)*, edited by John Lagerwey and Lü Pengzhi, 1207–44. Leiden: Brill, 2010.

———. "Translations, Apocrypha, and the Emergence of the Buddhist Canon." In ECR2, 741–74.

Hurvitz, Leon. *Scripture of the Lotus Blossom of the Fine Dharma (The Lotus Sutra)*. Revised edition. New York: Columbia University Press, 2009.

Hutton, Eric. *Xunzi: The Complete Text*. Princeton: Princeton University Press, 2014.

Iser, Wolfgang. *The Implied Reader: Patterns of Communication in Prose Fiction from Bunyan to Beckett*. Baltimore: Johns Hopkins University Press, 1974.

———. "The Reading Process: A Phenomenological Approach." In *Reader-Response Criticism: From Formalism to Post-Structuralism*, edited by Jane P. Tompkins, 50–69. Baltimore: Johns Hopkins University Press, 1980.

Jackson, Michael. "Knowledge of the Body." *Man*, new series, 18, no. 2 (1983): 327–45.

James, William. *The Varieties of Religious Experience: A Study in Human Nature*. New York: Modern Library, 1902.

Jan Yün-hua. "The Power of Recitation: An Unstudied Aspect of Chinese Buddhism." *Studi storico religiosi* 1, no. 2 (1977): 289–99.

Janousch, Andreas. "The Emperor as Bodhisattva: The Bodhisattva Ordination and Ritual Assemblies of Emperor Wu of the Liang Dynasty." In *State and Court Ritual in China*, edited by Joseph P. McDermott, 112–49. Cambridge: Cambridge University Press, 1999.

Jansen, Thomas. *Höfische Öffentlichkeit im frühmittelalterlichen China: Debatten im Salon des Prinzen Xiao Ziliang*. Freiburg im Breisgau: Rombach, 2000.

Jay, Martin. *Songs of Experience: Modern American and European Variations on a Universal Theme*. Berkeley: University of California Press, 2005.

Jensen, Christopher Jon. "Dreaming Betwixt and Between: Oneiric Narratives in Huijiao and Daoxuan's *Biographies of Eminent Monks*." PhD dissertation, McMaster University, 2018.

Jian Boxian 簡博賢. *Jincun nanbeichao jingxue yiji kao* 今存南北朝經學遺籍考. Taipei: Liming, 1975.

Jiang Boqin 姜伯勤. "'Xuandu lü' niandai ji suo jian daoguan zhidu" 玄都律年代及所見道官制度. *Wei Jin nanbeichao Sui Tang shi ziliao*, no. 11 (1991): 50–58.

Jiang Shaoyuan 江紹源. *Zhongguo gudai lüxing zhi yanjiu* 中國古代旅行之研究. Shanghai: Shangwu, 1935.

Johnson, Mark. *The Meaning of the Body: Aesthetics of Human Understanding*. Chicago: University of Chicago Press, 2007.

Johnston, Ian. *The Mozi: A Complete Translation*. New York: Columbia University Press, 2010.

Johnston, Ian, and Wang Ping. *The Mingjia and Related Texts: Bilingual Edition*. Hong Kong: Chinese University of Hong Kong Press, 2019.

Jung, Ghichul. "'Natural Land is Too Weak to Sustain the Great Dharma': Daoxuan's Commentary on the *Sīmā* and Medieval Chinese Monasticism." *Journal of the International Association of Buddhist Studies* 42 (2019): 265–314.

Kakiuchi Tomoyuki 垣内智之. "Tōbu kukū no zaishi to Tai'itsu" 頭部九宮の存思と太一. *Tōhō shūkyō* 東方宗教 91 (1998): 22–40.

Kalinowski, Marc, ed. *Divination et société dans la Chine médiévale*. Paris: Bibliothèque nationale de France, 2003.

Kaltenmark, Max. "The Ideology of the *T'ai-p'ing ching*." In *Facets of Taoism*, edited by Holmes Welch and Anna Seidel, 19–52. New Haven, CT: Yale University Press, 1979.

———. *Le Lie-sien tchouan: Biographies légendaires des immortels taoïstes de l'antiquité*. Beijing: Université de Paris, Publications du Centre d'études sinologiques de Pékin, 1953.

Kalupahana, David. *A History of Buddhist Philosophy: Continuities and Discontinuities*. Honolulu: University of Hawai'i Press, 1992.

Kamitsuka Yoshiko 神塚淑子. "The Concept of Māra and the Idea of Expelling Demons." Translated by Amy Lynn Miller and Thomas H. Peterson. *Taoist Resources* 6, no. 2 (1996): 30–50.

———. "Ma no kannen to shōma no shisō" 魔の觀念と消摩の思想. In *Chūgoku kodōkyō shi kenkyū* 中國古道教史研究, edited by Yoshikawa Tadao 吉川忠夫, 80–144. Tokyo: Dōhō, 1993.

Karashima Seishi 辛島靜志. *A Critical Edition of Lokakṣema's Translation of the Aṣṭasāhasrikā Prajñāpāramitā*. Tokyo: International Research Institute for Advanced Buddhology, Soka University, 2011.

———. *A Glossary of Lokakṣema's Translation of the Aṣṭasāhasrikā Prajñāpāramitā*. Tokyo: International Research Institute for Advanced Buddhology, Soka University, 2010.

———. "Was the *Aṣṭasāhasrikā Prajñāpāramitā* Compiled in Gandhāra in Gandhārī?" *Annual Report of the International Research Institute for Advanced Buddhology at Soka University* 18 (2015): 113–62.

———. "Who Composed the Mahāyāna Scriptures? The Mahāsāṃgikas and *Vaitulya* Scriptures." *Annual Report of the International Research Institute for Advanced Buddhology at Soka University* 16 (2013): 171–88.

Karetzky, Patricia Eichenbaum. "Māra, Buddhist Deity of Death and Desire." *East and West* 32 (1982): 75–92.

Karunaratne, T. B. "The Significance of the Signs and Symbols on the Footprints of the Buddha." *Journal of the Sri Lanka Branch of the Royal Asiatic Society*, new series, 20 (1976): 47–60.

Keane, Webb. "On the Materiality of Religion." *Material Religion* 4, no. 2 (2008): 230–31.

Kern, Martin. "Creating a Book and Performing It: The 'Yao lüe' Chapter of the *Huainanzi* as a Western Han *Fu*." In *The Huainanzi and Textual Production in Early China*, edited by Sarah A. Queen and Michael Puett, 124–50. Leiden: Brill, 2014.

———. "The Formation of the *Classic of Poetry*." In *The Homeric Epics and the Chinese "Book of Songs": Foundational Texts Compared*, edited by Fritz-Heiner Mutschler, 39–72. Newcastle upon Tyne : Cambridge Scholars Publishing, 2018.

———. "Ritual, Text, and the Formation of the Canon: Historical Transitions of *Wen* in Early China." *T'oung Pao* 87, nos. 1–3 (2001): 43–91.

———. "'Xi shuai' 蟋蟀 ('Cricket') and Its Consequences: Issues in Early Chinese Poetry and Textual Studies." *Early China* 42 (2019): 39–74.

Khoroche, Peter. *Once the Buddha Was a Monkey: Ārya Śūra's "Jātakamālā."* Chicago: University of Chicago Press, 1989.

Kieschnick, John. *The Eminent Monk: Buddhist Ideals in Medieval Chinese Hagiography*. Honolulu: University of Hawai'i Press, 1997.

———. *The Impact of Buddhism on Chinese Material Culture*. Princeton: Princeton University Press, 2003.

Kim, Jayne Sun. "A History of Filth: Defilement Discourse in Medieval Japan." PhD dissertation, Columbia University, 2004.

Kimbrough, R. Keller. "Reading the Miraculous Powers of Japanese Poetry: Spells, Truth Acts, and a Medieval Buddhist Poetics of the Supernatural." *Japanese Journal of Religious Studies* 32, no. 1 (2005): 1–33.

Kinney, Anne Behnke. "Dyed Silk: Han Notions of the Moral Development of Children." In *Chinese Views of Childhood*, edited by Anne Behnke Kinney, 17–56. Honolulu: University of Hawai'i Press, 1995.

———. *Representations of Childhood and Youth in Early China*. Stanford: Stanford University Press, 2004.

Kleeman, Terry F. *Celestial Masters: History and Ritual in Early Daoist Communities*. Cambridge, MA: Harvard University Asia Center, 2016.

Klein, Esther S. "Were There 'Inner Chapters' in the Warring States? A New Examination of Evidence about the *Zhuangzi*." *T'oung Pao* 96, nos. 4–5 (2010): 299–369.

Kloetzli, Randy. *Buddhist Cosmology: From Single World System to Pure Land*. Delhi: Motilal, 1983.

Knapp, Keith N. "Accounts of Filial Sons: *Ru* Ideology in Early Medieval China." PhD dissertation, University of California at Berkeley, 1996.

———. "Borrowing Legitimacy from the Dead: The Confucianization of Ancestral Worship." In ECR2, 143–92.

———. "The *Ru* Reinterpretation of *xiao*." *Early China* 20 (1995): 195–222.

———. *Selfless Offspring: Filial Children and Social Order in Medieval China*. Honolulu: University of Hawai'i Press, 2005.

Knechtges, David R. *Wen xuan or Selections of Refined Literature, Volume One: Rhapsodies on Metropolises and Capitals*. Princeton: Princeton University Press, 1983.

Knoblock, John, and Jeffrey Riegel. *The Annals of Lü Buwei*. Stanford: Stanford University Press, 2000.

Kobayashi Masayoshi 小林正美. *Rikuchō dōkyōshi kenkyū* 六朝道教史研究. Tokyo: Sōbunsha, 1990.

Kohn, Livia. "Counting Good Deeds and Days of Life: The Quantification of Fate in Medieval China." *Asiatische Studien/Études Asiatiques* 52, no. 3 (1998): 833–70.

———. "Daoist Monastic Discipline: Hygiene, Meals, and Etiquette." *T'oung Pao* 87, nos. 1–3 (2001): 153–93.

———. "Kōshin: A Taoist Cult in Japan, Part 1: Contemporary Practices." *Japanese Religions* 18, no. 2 (1993): 113–19.

———. "Kōshin: A Taoist Cult in Japan, Part 2: Historical Development." *Japanese Religions* 20, no. 1 (1995): 34–55.

———. "Kōshin: A Taoist Cult in Japan, Part 3: The Scripture—A Translation of the Kōshinkyō." *Japanese Religions* 20, no. 2 (1995): 123–42.

———. "Mirror of Auras: Chen Tuan on Physiognomy." *Asian Folklore Studies* 47, no. 2 (1988): 215–56.

———. "Taoism in Japan: Positions and Evaluations." *Cahiers d'Extrême-Asie* 8 (1995): 389–412.

———. "A Textbook of Physiognomy: The Tradition of the *Shenxiang quanbian*." *Asian Folklore Studies* 45, no. 2 (1986): 227–58.

Komjathy, Louis. "Mapping the Daoist Body, Part I: The *Neijing tu* in History." *Journal of Daoist Studies* 1 (2008): 67–92.

Kong, Choy Fah. *Saccakiriyā: The Belief in the Power of True Speech in Theravada Buddhism*. Singapore: n.p., 2012.

Kornicki, Peter Francis. *Languages, Scripts, and Chinese Texts in East Asia*. Oxford: Oxford University Press, 2018.

Kósa, Gábor. "'Trusting Words' in Pre-Buddhist Chinese Texts." In *Faith in Buddhism*, edited by Imre Hamar and Takami Inoue, 67–91. Budapest: Institute for East Asian Studies, Eötvös Lorand University, 2016.

Kotyk, Jeffrey. "Early Tantric Hemerology in Chinese Buddhism: Timing of Rituals according to Śubhakarasiṃsha and Yixing." *Canadian Journal of Buddhist Studies*, no. 13 (2018): 1–29.

———. "The Sinicization of Indo-Iranian Astrology in Medieval China." *Sino-Platonic Papers* 282 (September 2018).

Krais, Beate. "Gender and Symbolic Violence: Female Oppression in the Light of Pierre Bourdieu's Theory of Social Practice." In *Bourdieu: Critical Perspectives*, edited by Craig Calhoun, Edward LiPuma, and Moishe Postone, 156–77. Chicago: University of Chicago Press, 1993.

Krijgsman, Rens. "An Inquiry into the Formation of Readership in Early China: Using and Producing the **Yong yue* 用曰 and *Yinshu* 引書 Manuscripts." *T'oung Pao* 104, nos. 1–2 (2018): 2–65.

———. "The Rise of a Manuscript Culture and the Textualization of Discourse in Early China." DPhil dissertation, Pembroke College, University of Oxford, 2016.

———. "A Self-Reflexive Praxis: Changing Attitudes towards Manuscript and Text in Early China." *Early China* 42 (2019): 75–110.

———. "Traveling Sayings as Carriers of Philosophical Debate: From the Intertextuality of the **Yucong* 語叢 to the Dynamics of Cultural Memory and Authorship in Early China." *Asiatische Studien / Études Asiatiques* 68, no. 1 (2014): 83–116.

Kristeva, Julia. *Powers of Horror: An Essay on Abjection*. Translated by Leon S. Roudiez. New York: Columbia University Press, 1982.

Kroll, Paul W. "Between Something and Nothing." *Journal of the American Oriental Society* 127, no. 4 (2007): 403–13.

———. "Body Gods and Inner Vision: The Scripture of the Yellow Court." In *Religions of China in Practice*, edited by Donald S. Lopez, Jr., 149–55. Princeton: Princeton University Press, 1996.

———. "In the Halls of the Azure Lad." *Journal of the American Oriental Society* 105, no. 1 (1985): 75–94.

———. *A Student's Dictionary of Classical and Medieval Chinese*. Leiden: Brill, 2015.

Kuo Li-ying. *Confession et contrition dans le bouddhisme chinois du Ve au Xe siècle*. Paris: Publications de l'Ecole Française d'Extrême-Orient, 1994.

———. "The *Da fangdeng tuoluoni jing* (*Vaipulya-dhāraṇī-sūtra*) and Dunhuang Evidence." *Bulletin de l'École française d'Extrême-Orient* 105 (2019): 179–228.

———. "Divination, jeux de hazard et purification dans le bouddhisme chinois: Autour d'un *sūtra* apocryphe chinois, le *Zhancha jing*." In *Bouddhisme et cultures locales: Quelques cas de réciproques adaptations*, edited by Fukui Fumimasa and Gérard Fussman, 145–67. Paris: École française d'Extrême-Orient, 1994.

———. "La récitation des noms de Buddha en Chine et au Japon." *T'oung Pao* 81, nos. 4-5 (1995): 230–68.

Kuramoto Shōtoku 倉本尚德. "Hokuchō jidai ni okeru hōdōzan to kōsōgyō" 北朝時代における方等懺と好相行. *Bukkyō bunka kenkyū ronshū* 仏教文化研究論集 12 (2008): 50–80.

Lackner, Michael. *Der chinesische Traumwald: Traditionelle Theorien des Traumes und seiner Deutung im Spiegel der ming-zeitlichen Anthologie Meng-lin hsüan-chieh*. Frankfurt: Peter Lang, 1985.

Lai, Whalen. "The *Chan-ch'a ching*: Religion and Magic in Medieval China." In *Chinese Buddhist Apocrypha*, edited by Robert E. Buswell, Jr., 175–206. Honolulu: University of Hawai'i Press, 1990.

———. "Legends of Births and the Pure Land Tradition in China." In *The Pure Land Tradition: History and Development*, edited by James Foard, Michael Solomon, and Richard K. Payne, 173–232. Berkeley: Center for South and Southeast Asian Studies, University of California at Berkeley, and Institute of Buddhist Studies, 1996.

Lakoff, George, and Mark Johnson. *Metaphors We Live By*. Chicago: University of Chicago Press, 1980.

———. *Philosophy in the Flesh: The Embodied Mind and Its Challenge to Western Thought*. New York: Basic Books, 1999.

Lamotte, Étienne. "Passions and Impregnations of the Passions in Buddhism." In *Buddhist Studies in Honour of I. B. Horner*, edited by L. Cousins, A. Kunst, and K. R. Norman, 91–104. Dordrecht: D. Reidel, 1974.

———. "Un sūtra composite de l'*Ekottarāgama*." *Bulletin of the School of Oriental and African Studies* 30 (1967): 105–16.

———. *Le Traité de la grande vertu de sagesse de Nāgārjuna (Mahāprajñāpāramitāśāstra)*. Tome I: chapitres I–XV. Louvain: Bureaux du Muséon, 1944.

———. *Le Traité de la grande vertu de sagesse de Nāgārjuna (Mahāprajñāpāramitāśāstra)*. Tome II: chapitres XV–XXX. Louvain: Institut Orientaliste, 1949, reprint 1981.

Langenberg, Amy Paris. *Birth in Buddhism: The Suffering Fetus and Female Freedom*. London and New York: Routledge, 2017.

Ledderose, Lothar. *Ten Thousand Things: Module and Mass Production in Chinese Art*. Princeton: Princeton University Press, 2001.

Legge, James. *The Sacred Books of China: The Texts of Confucianism. Part 3: The Lî Kî, I–X*. London: Oxford University Press, [1885] 1926.

———. *The Sacred Books of China: The Texts of Confucianism. Part 4: The Lî Kî, XI–XLVI*. London: Oxford University Press, [1885] 1926.

Lettere, Laura. "The *Guoqu xianzai yinguo jing* as an Adaptation of the Chinese Translation of the *Buddhacarita*." *Journal of Chinese Religions* 47, no. 2 (November 2019): 117–51.

Lévi, Jean. *Les entretiens de Confucius*. Vol. 2 of *Les deux arbres de la voie*. Paris: Les Belles Lettres, 2018.

Lévi-Strauss, Claude. *Tristes tropiques*. Paris: Librairie Plon, [1955] 1993.

Lewis, Mark Edward. *The Construction of Space in Early China*. Albany: State University of New York Press, 2006.

———. *Writing and Authority in Early China*. Albany: State University of New York Press, 1999.

Li Feng and David Prager Branner, eds. *Writing and Literacy in Early China: Studies from the Columbia Early China Seminar*. Seattle: University of Washington Press, 2011.

Li Fengmao [Lee Feng-mao] 李豐楙. "Liuchao daojiao de zhongmo lun: moshi, yangjiu bailiu yu qiyun shuo" 六朝道教的終末論: 末世, 陽九百六與劫運說. In *Daojia wenhua yanjiu* 道家文化研究 9, edited by Chen Guying 陳鼓應, 82–99. Shanghai: Shanghai guji chubanshe, 1992.

Li Jianmin 李建民. "Contagion and Its Consequences: The Problem of Death Pollution in Ancient China." In *Medicine and the History of the Body: Proceedings of the 20th, 21st and 22nd International Symposium on the Comparative History of Medicine, East and West*, edited by Yasuo Otsuka, Shizu Sakai, and Shigehisa Kuriyama, 201–22. Tokyo: Ishiyaku EuroAmerica, 1999.

———. "Suibing yu changsuo: Chuantong yixue dui chongbing de yi Zhong jieshi" 祟病與場所: 傳統醫學對祟病的一種解釋. *Hanxue yanjiu* 12, no. 1 (1994): 101–48.

———. "They Shall Expel Demons: Etiology, the Medical Canon and the Transformation of Medical Techniques before the Tang." In ECR1, 1103–50.

Lin Fushi 林富士 [Lin Fu-shih]. "Medical Knowledge and Uses of Hair in Traditional China." In *Medicine and the History of the Body: Proceedings of the 20th, 21st and 22nd International Symposia on the Comparative History of Medicine East and West*, edited by Kawakita Yoshio, 365–77. Chicago: Medico Dental Media, 1995.

———. "Religious Taoism and Dreams: An Analysis of the Dream-data Collected in the *Yün-chi ch'i-ch'ien*." *Cahiers d'Extrême-Asie* 8 (1995): 95–112.

———. "Renjian zhi mei: Han Tang zhi jian jingmei gushi xilun" 人間之魅: 漢唐之間精魅故事析論. *Zhongyang yanjiuyuan lishi yuyan yanjiusuo jikan* 78, no. 1 (2007): 107–79.

———. "Shi mei" 釋魅. In *Guimei shenmo: Zhongguo tongsu wenhua cexie* 鬼魅神魔: 中國通俗文化側寫, edited by Poo Mu-chou, 109–34. Taipei: Maitian chubanshe, 2005.

Lipiello, Tiziana. *Auspicious Omens and Miracles in Ancient China: Han, Three Kingdoms, and Six Dynasties*. Monumenta Serica Monographs 39. Sankt Augustin: Monumenta Serica Institute, 2001.

Liszka, James Jakób. *A General Introduction to the Semeiotic of Charles Sanders Peirce*. Bloomington: Indiana University Press, 1996.

Liu Shu-fen 劉淑芬. "Zhonggu sengren de famo wenshu" 中古僧人的伐魔文書. In *Guimei shenmo: Zhongguo tongsu wenhua cexie* 鬼魅神魔: 中國通俗文化側寫, edited by Poo Mu-chou, 135–74. Taipei: Maitian chubanshe, 2005.

Liu, Yan. *Healing with Poisons: Potent Medicines in Medieval China*. Seattle: University of Washington Press, 2021.

Liu Yi 劉屹. "Early Medieval Concepts of Demon Troops, Discussed with the Focus on Wang Ningzhi's Request for Demon Troops to Provide Support" 中古早期的鬼兵觀念: 以王凝之所請鬼兵為中心. In *Exorcism in Daoism: A Berlin Symposium*, edited by Florian C. Reiter, 51–67. Wiesbaden: Harrassowitz, 2011.

Liu Zhao 劉釗. *Chutu jianbo wenzi congkao* 出土簡帛文字叢考. Taipei: Taiwan guji, 2004.

Loewe, Michael. *Divination, Mythology and Monarchy in Han China*. Cambridge: Cambridge University Press, 1994.

———. *Dong Zhongshu, a "Confucian" Heritage and the Chunqiu fanlu*. Leiden: Brill, 2011.

———. "The Organs of Han Imperial Government: *Zhongdu guan*, *duguan*, *xianguan* and *xiandao guan*." *Bulletin of the School of Oriental and African Studies* 71, no. 3 (2008): 509–28.

Lopez, Donald S., Jr. *Hyecho's Journey: The World of Buddhism*. Chicago: University of Chicago Press, 2017.

Lorrillard, Michel. "Aux origins du bouddhisme siamois: Le cas des *buddhapāda*." *Bulletin de l'École Française d'Extrême-Orient* 87, no. 1 (2000): 23–55.

Lowe, Bryan D. "The Discipline of Writing: Scribes and Purity in Eighth-Century Japan." *Japanese Journal of Religious Studies* 39, no. 2 (2012): 201–39.

———. *Ritualized Writing: Buddhist Practice and Scriptural Cultures in Ancient Japan*. Honolulu: University of Hawai'i Press, 2017.

Lu Di 蘆笛. "Ancient Chinese People's Knowledge of Macrofungi during the Period from 220 to 589." *East Asian Science, Technology, and Medicine*, no. 37 (2013–14): 36–68.

———. "Ping daojiao dianji 'Zhong zhicao fa' de ziranshi jiazhi" 评道教典籍'种芝草法'的自然史价值. *Zhejiang shiyong jun* 浙江食用菌 18, no. 1 (2010): 56–59.

Lu, Lu. "An Analogy of Pots in the *Daodi jing* 道地經 and Its Sanskrit Parallel." *Annual Report of the International Research Institute for Advanced Buddhology at Soka University* 22 (2019): 209–12.

Mageo, Jeannette Marie. "Theorizing Dreaming and the Self." In *Dreaming and the Self: New Perspectives on Subjectivity, Identity, and Emotion*, edited by Jeannette Marie Mageo, 3–22. Albany: State University of New York Press, 2003.

Mai, Cuong T. "Visualization Apocrypha and the Making of Buddhist Deity Cults in Early Medieval China: With Special Reference to the Cults of Amitābha, Maitreya, and Samantabhadra." PhD dissertation, Indiana University, 2009.

Mailloux, Steven. "Interpretation and Rhetorical Hermeneutics." In *Reception Study: From Literary Theory to Cultural Studies*, edited by James L. Machor and Philip Goldstein, 39–60. New York: Routledge, 2001.

Major, John S. "New Light on the Dark Warrior." *Journal of Chinese Religions* 13 (1985): 65–86.

Major, John S., Sarah A. Queen, Andrew Seth Meyer, and Harold D. Roth. *The Huainanzi: A Guide to the Theory and Practice of Government in Early Han China*. New York: Columbia University Press, 2010.

Makeham, John. *Name and Actuality in Early Chinese Thought*. Albany: State University of New York Press, 1994.

———. *Transmitters and Creators: Chinese Commentators and Commentaries on the Analects*. Cambridge, MA: Harvard University Asia Center, 2003.

Makita Tairyō 牧田諦亮. *Gikyō kenkyū* 疑經研究. Kyoto: Kyoto University Jinbun kagaku kenkyūsho, 1976.

———. *Rikuchō kōitsu Kanzeon ōkenki no kenkyū* 六朝古逸觀世音應驗記の研究. Kyoto: Hyōrakuji shoten, 1970.

Maspero, Henri. *Taoism and Chinese Religion*. Translated by Frank A. Kierman, Jr. Amherst: University of Massachusetts Press, 1981.

Mather, Richard B. *Shih-shuo Hsin-yü, A New Account of Tales of the World*. 2nd edition. Ann Arbor: Center for Chinese Studies, University of Michigan, 2002.

Mattingly, Cheryl. *Healing Dramas and Clinical Plots: The Narrative Structure of Experience*. Cambridge: Cambridge University Press, 1998.

Mauss, Marcel. *Techniques, technologie et civilisation*. Edited by Nathan Schlanger. Paris: Presses Universitaires de France, 2012.

McBride, Richard D, II. "Dhāraṇī and Spells in Medieval Sinitic Buddhism." *Journal of the International Association of Buddhist Studies* 28, no. 1 (2005): 85–114.

———. "Esoteric Buddhism and Its Relation to Healing and Demonology." In *Esoteric Buddhism and the Tantras in East Asia*, edited by Charles D. Orzech, Henrik H. Sørensen, and Richard K. Payne, 208–14. Leiden: Brill, 2011.

———. "Practical Buddhist Thaumaturgy: The 'Great Dhāraṇī on Immaculately Pure Light' in Medieval Sinitic Buddhism." *Journal of Korean Religions* 2, no. 1 (2011): 33–73.

McDaniel, Justin Thomas. "Philosophical Embryology: Buddhist Texts and the Ritual Construction of a Fetus." In *Imagining the Fetus: The Unborn in Myth, Religion, and Culture*, edited by Vanessa R. Sasson and Jane Marie Law, 91–106. Oxford: Oxford University Press, 2009.

McGovern, Nathan. "Protestant Presuppositions and the Study of the Early Buddhist Oral Tradition." *Journal of the International Association of Buddhist Studies* 42 (2019): 449–91.

McGuire, Beverley. "Seeing Suchness: Emotional and Material Means of Perceiving Reality in Chinese Buddhist Divination Rituals." In *Historicizing Emotions: Practices and Objects in India, China, and Japan*, edited by Barbara Schuler, 261–94. Leiden: Brill, 2018.

McMahan, David L. *Empty Vision: Metaphor and Visionary Imagery in Mahāyāna Buddhism*. London: RoutledgeCurzon, 2002.

McNicholl, Adeana. "The Generative Power of Disgust: Somaesthetics and the Abject *Preta*." *Journal of the International Association of Buddhist Studies* 43 (2020): 129–65.

McRae, John R. "Daoxuan's Vision of Jetavana: The Ordination Platform Movement in Medieval Chinese Buddhism." In *Going Forth: Visions of Buddhist Vinaya*, edited by William M. Bodiford, 68–100. Honolulu: University of Hawai'i Press, 2005.

Meyer, Dirk. "A Device for Conveying Meaning: The Structure of the Guodian Tomb One Manuscript 'Zhong xin zhi dao.'" *Bochumer Jahrbuch zur Ostasienforschung* 29 (2005): 57–78.

———. *Documentation and Argument in Early China: The Shangshu 尚書 (Venerated Documents) and the Shu Traditions*. Berlin: De Gruyter, 2021.

———. *Philosophy on Bamboo: Text and the Production of Meaning in Early China*. Leiden: Brill, 2012.

Milburn, Olivia. "Marked Out for Greatness? Perceptions of Deformity and Physical Impairment in Ancient China." *Monumenta Serica* 55, no. 1 (2007): 1–22.

Miller, James. *The Way of Highest Clarity: Nature, Vision and Revelation in Medieval China*. Magdalena, NM: Three Pines Press, 2008.

Miyakawa Hisayuki 宮川尚志. "Dōkyōteki shintairon ni okeru shichu to konpaku" 道教的身体論における尸蟲と魂魄. In *Chūgokuteki jinseikan, sekaikan* 中国的人生観, 世界観, edited by Naitō Motoharu 內藤幹治, 259–71. Tokyo: Tōhō shoten, 1994.

Miyazawa Masayori 宮沢 正順. "Dōkyō reigen ki ni tsuite" 道教霊験記について. *Sankō bunka kenkyūjo nenpō* 18 (1985): 1–38.

Mochizuki Shinkō 望月信享. *Bukkyō daijiten*. 10 vols. continuously paginated. Tokyo: Sekai seiten kankō kyōkai, 1933–36.

———. *Bukkyō kyōten seiritsu ron 仏教経典成立史論*. Kyoto: Hōzōkan, 1946.

Mollier, Christine. *Une apocalypse taoïste du début du Ve siècle: Le Livre des Incantations Divines des Grottes Abyssales*. Paris: Collège de France, 1990.

———. *Buddhism and Taoism Face to Face: Scripture, Ritual, and Iconographic Exchange in Medieval China*. Honolulu: University of Hawai'i Press, 2008.

———. "Talismans." In *Divination et société dans la Chine médiévale: Études des manuscrits de Dunhuang de la Bibliothèque nationale de France et de la British Library*, edited by Marc Kalinowski, 403–29. Paris: Bibliothèque nationale de France, 2003.

———. "Visions of Evil: Demonology and Orthodoxy in Early Taoism." In *Daoism in History: Essays in Honour of Liu Ts'un-yan*, edited by Benjamin Penny, 74–100. London: Routledge, 2006.

Mugitani Kunio 麥谷邦夫 and Yoshikawa Tadao 吉川忠夫, eds. *Shūshi meitsūki kenkyū (yakuchū hen)* 周氏冥通記研究（譯注篇）. Kyoto: Kyōto daigaku Jinbun kagaku kenkyūjo, 2003.

Moro Shigeki 師 茂樹. "*Senzatsukyō* no seiritsu to juyō: naze uranai hitsuyō to sareta no ka" 占察経の成立と受容 ：なぜ占いが必要とされたのか. *Nippon bukkyō gakkai nenpō* 77 (2011): 135–57.

Mrozik, Susanne. "Materializations of Virtue: Buddhist Discourses on Bodies." In *Bodily Citations: Religion and Judith Butler*, edited by Ellen T. Armour and Susan M. St. Ville, 15–47. New York: Columbia University Press, 2006.

Nattier, Jan. *A Few Good Men: The Bodhisattva Path according to The Inquiry of Ugra (Ugraparipṛcchā)*. Honolulu: University of Hawai'i Press, 2003.

———. *A Guide to the Earliest Chinese Buddhist Translations: Texts from the Eastern Han and Three Kingdoms Periods*. Bibliotheca Philologica et Philosophica Buddhica X. Tokyo: International Research Institute for Advanced Buddhology, Soka University, 2008.

———. "The Indian Roots of Pure Land Buddhism: Insights from the Oldest Chinese Versions of the *Larger Sukhāvatīvyūha*." *Pacific World: Journal of the Institute of Buddhist Studies* 5 (2003): 179–201.

———. "The Proto-History of the *Buddhāvataṁsaka*: The *Pusa benye jing* 菩薩本業經 and the *Dousha jing* 兜沙經." *Annual Report of the International Research Institute for Advanced Buddhology at Soka University* 8 (2005): 323–60.

———. "The Realm of Akṣobhya: A Missing Piece in the History of Pure Land Buddhism." *Journal of the International Association of Buddhist Studies* 23, no. 1 (2000): 71–102.

———. "Re-Evaluating Zhu Fonian's *Shizhu duanjie jing* (T309): Translation or Forgery?" *Annual Report of the International Research Institute for Advanced Buddhology at Soka University* 13 (2010): 231–58.

———. "Who Produced the *Da mingdu jing* (T225)? A Reassessment of the Evidence." *Journal of the International Association of Buddhist Studies* 31, nos. 1–2 (2008): 295–338.

Needham, Rodney. *Belief, Language and Experience*. Oxford: Blackwell, 1972.

Nichols, Michael D. *Malleable Māra: Transformations of a Buddhist Symbol of Evil*. Albany: State University of New York Press, 2019.

Nichols, Stephen G. "Introduction: Philology in a Manuscript Culture." *Speculum* 65, no. 1 (1990): 1–10.

Nickerson, Peter. "The Great Petition for Sepulchral Plaints." In *Early Daoist Scriptures* by Stephen R. Bokenkamp, 230–74. Berkeley: University of California Press, 1997.

Nishioka Hiromu 西岡弘. "Akumu no zō" 惡夢の贈. *Ikeda Suetoshi hakushi koki kinen Tōyōgaku ronshū* 池田末利博士古稀記念東洋學論集, 313–28. Hiroshima: Ikeda Suetoshi hakushi koki kinen gikyōkai, 1980.

Nugent, Christopher M. B. *Manifest in Words, Written on Paper: Producing and Circulating Poetry in Tang Dynasty China*. Cambridge, MA: Harvard University Asia Center, 2010.

———. "Structured Gaps: The *Qianzi wen* and Its Paratexts as Mnemotechnics." In *Memory in Medieval China: Text, Ritual, and Community*, edited by Wendy Swartz and Robert Ford Campany, 158–92. Leiden: Brill, 2018.

Nylan, Michael. *The Five "Confucian" Classics*. New Haven, CT: Yale University Press, 2001.

———. "Living Without Sin: Reflections on the Pre-Buddhist World in Early China." In *Sins and Sinners: Perspectives from Asian Religions*, edited by Phyllis Granoff and Koichi Shinohara, 57–72. Leiden: Brill, 2012.

———. "Toward an Archaeology of Writing: Text, Ritual, and the Culture of Public Display in the Classical Period (475 BCE–220 CE)." In *Text and Ritual in Early China*, edited by Martin Kern, 3–49. Seattle: University of Washington Press, 2005.

Nylan, Michael, and Michael Loewe, eds. *China's Early Empires: A Re-appraisal*. Cambridge: Cambridge University Press, 2010.

Nylan, Michael, and Thomas Wilson. *Lives of Confucius: Civilization's Greatest Sage through the Ages*. New York: Doubleday, 2010.

Obringer, Frédéric. *L'aconit et l'orpiment: Drogues et poisons en Chine ancienne et médiévale*. Paris: Fayard, 1997.

Ochiai Toshinori 落合俊典. "Darani zasshū shoshu no kyōten ni tsuite" 陀羅尼雜集所收の經典について. *Journal of the International College for Advanced Buddhist Studies* 6 (2003): 59–85.

Olivelle, Patrick. *Saṃnyāsa Upaniṣads: Hindu Scriptures on Asceticism and Renunciation*. New York: Oxford University Press, 1992.

Ong, Roberto Keh. *The Interpretation of Dreams in Ancient China*. Bochum: Studienverlag Brockmeyer, 1985.

Onions, C. T., ed. *The Oxford Dictionary of English Etymology*. Oxford: Clarendon, 1966.

Orsborn, Matthew. *See* Shi Huifeng.

Orsi, Robert A. *History and Presence*. Cambridge, MA: Harvard University Press, 2016.

Ortner, Sherry B. "Patterns of History: Cultural Schemas in the Foundings of Sherpa Religious Institutions." In *Culture Through Time: Anthropological Approaches*, edited by Emiko Ohnuki-Tierney, 57–93. Stanford: Stanford University Press, 1990.

Orzech, Charles D. "Tantric Subjects: Liturgy and Vision in Chinese Esoteric Ritual Manuals." In *Chinese and Tibetan Esoteric Buddhism*, edited by Yael Bentor and Meir Shahar, 17–40. Leiden: Brill, 2017.

Orzech, Charles D., and Henrik H. Sørensen. "*Mudrā*, Mantra, Mandala." In *Esoteric Buddhism and the Tantras in East Asia*, edited by Charles D. Orzech, Henrik H. Sørensen, and Richard K. Payne, 76–88. Leiden: Brill, 2011.

Orzech, Charles D., Henrik H. Sørensen, and Richard K. Payne, eds. *Esoteric Buddhism and the Tantras in East Asia*. Leiden: Brill, 2011.

Ōtsuka Nobuo 大塚伸夫. *Indo shoki mikkyō seiritsu katei no kenkyū* インド初期密教成立過程の研究. Tokyo: Shunjusha, 2013.

Overby, Ryan. "Why Don't We Translate Spells in the Scriptures? Medieval Chinese Exegesis on the Meaning and Function of Dhāraṇī Language." *Journal of the International Association of Buddhist Studies* 42 (2019): 493–514.

Pagel, Ulrich. *The Bodhisattvapiṭaka: Its Doctrines, Practices and their Position in Mahāyāna Literature*. Tring: Institute of Buddhist Studies, 1995.

Palumbo, Antonello. *An Early Chinese Commentary on the Ekottarika-āgama: The Fenbie gongde lun 分別功德論 and the History of the Translation of the Zengyi ahan jing 增一阿含經*. Taipei: Dharma Drum, 2013.

Pankenier, David W. "Weaving Metaphors and Cosmo-Political Thought in Early China." *T'oung Pao* 101, nos. 1–3 (2015): 1–34.

Pas, Julian. "Shan-tao's Interpretation of the Meditative Vision of Buddha Amitayus." *History of Religions* 14, no. 2 (November 1974): 96–116.

———. *Visions of Sukhāvatī: Shan-Tao's Commentary on the Kuan Wu-liang-shou-Fo jing*. Albany: State University of New York Press, 1995.

Patton, Kimberley C. "'A Great and Strange Correction': Intentionality, Locality, and Epiphany in the Category of Dream Incubation." *History of Religions* 43, no. 3 (February 2004): 194–223.

Pedersen, K. Priscilla. "Notes on the *Ratnakūṭa* Collection." *Journal of the International Association of Buddhist Studies* 3, no. 2 (1980): 60–66.

Peirce, Charles Sanders. *The Collected Papers of Charles Sanders Peirce. Volume 2: Elements of Logic*. Cambridge, MA: Harvard University Press, 1932.

———. *The Essential Peirce: Selected Philosophical Writings, Volume 2 (1893–1913)*. Bloomington: Indiana University Press, 1998.

Pettit, Jonathan E., and Chao-jan Chang. *A Library of Clouds: The Scripture of the Immaculate Numen and the Rewriting of Daoist Texts*. Honolulu: University of Hawai'i Press, 2020.

Pettit, Jonathan E., and Matthew Wells. "Revelation in Early Daoist Hagiography: A Study of *The Traditions of Lord Pei*." *Asia Major*, 3rd series, 33, no. 2 (2020): 1–24.

Poirier, Sylvie. "'This is Good Country. We Are Good Dreamers': Dreams and Dreaming in the Australian Western Desert." In *Dream Travelers: Sleep Experiences and Culture in the Western Pacific*, edited by Roger Ivar Lohmann, 107–25. New York: Palgrave Macmillan, 2003.

Pollock, Sheldon. *The Language of the Gods in the World of Men: Sanskrit, Culture, and Power in Premodern India*. Berkeley: University of California Press, 2006.

Poo Mu-chou [Pu Muzhou] 蒲慕州. "The Culture of Ghosts in the Six Dynasties Period (c. 220–589 CE)." In *Rethinking Ghosts in World Religions*, edited by Poo Mu-chou, 237–68. Leiden: Brill, 2009.

———. "Ritual and Ritual Texts in Early China." In ECR1, 281–314.

———. "The Taming of Ghosts in Early Chinese Buddhism." In *Old Society, New Belief: Religious Transformation of China and Rome, ca. 1st–6th Centuries*, edited by Poo Mu-chou, H. A. Drake, and Lisa Raphals, 165–82. New York: Oxford University Press, 2017.

———. "Zhongguo gudai gui lunshu de xingcheng" 中國古代鬼論述的形成. In *Guimei shenmo: Zhongguo tongsu wenhua cexie* 鬼魅神魔：中國通俗文化側寫, edited by Pu Muzhou, 19–40. Taipei: Maitian chubanshe, 2005.

Poo Mu-chou, ed. *Guimei shenmo: Zhongguo tongsu wenhua cexie* 鬼魅神魔：中國通俗文化側寫. Taipei: Maitian chubanshe, 2005.

Porkert, Manfred. *Biographie d'un taoïste légendaire: Tcheou Tseu-yang*. Paris: Collège de France, Institut des Hautes Études Chinoises, 1979.

Postone, Moishe, Edward LiPuma, and Craig Calhoun. "Introduction: Bourdieu and Social Theory." In *Bourdieu: Critical Perspectives*, edited by Craig Calhoun, Edward LiPuma, and Moishe Postone, 1–13. Chicago: University of Chicago Press, 1993.

Poulet, Georges. "Criticism and the Experience of Interiority." In *Reader-Response Criticism: From Formalism to Post-Structuralism*, edited by Jane P. Tompkins, 41–49. Baltimore: Johns Hopkins University Press, 1980.

Pregadio, Fabrizio. *Great Clarity: Daoism and Alchemy in Early Medieval China*. Stanford: Stanford University Press, 2006.

———, ed. *The Encyclopedia of Taoism*. London: Routledge, 2008.

Proudfoot, Wayne. *Religious Experience*. Berkeley: University of California Press, 1985.

Pu Chengzhong. "Notes on the *Chengju guangming jing*, 'Sutra of Achieving the Bright Light Concentration.'" *Buddhist Studies Review* 25, no. 1 (2008): 27–53.

Puett, Michael. "Innovation as Ritualization: The Fractured Cosmology of Early China." *Cardozo Law Review* 28 (2006): 23–36.

———. "Theodicies of Discontinuity: Domesticating Energies and Dispositions in Early China." *Journal of Chinese Philosophy* 37, supplement 1 (2010): 51–66.

Quinter, David. "Visualizing the *Mañjuśrī Parinirvāṇa Sutra* as a Contemplation Sutra." *Asia Major*, 3rd series 23, no. 2 (2010): 97–128.

Radice, Thomas. "Method Mourning: Xunzi on Ritual Performance." *Philosophy East & West* 67, no. 2 (2017): 466–93.

Radich, Michael. "Fei Changfang's Treatment of Sengyou's Anonymous Texts." *Journal of the American Oriental Society* 139, no. 4 (2019): 819–41.

———. *The Mahāparinirvāṇa-mahāsūtra and the Emergence of Tathāgatagarbha Doctrine*. Hamburg: Hamburg University Press, 2015.

———. "A 'Prehistory' to Chinese Debates on the Survival of Death by the Spirit, with a Focus on the Term *shishen* 識神/ *shenshi* 神識." *Journal of Chinese Religions* 44, no. 2 (November 2016): 105–26.

———. "A Triad of Texts from Fifth-Century Southern China: The **Mahāmāyā-sūtra*, the *Guoqu xianzai yinguo jing*, and a *Mahāparinirvāṇa-sūtra* Ascribed to Faxian." *Journal of Chinese Religions* 46, no. 1 (May 2018): 1–41.

Raphals, Lisa. "Body, Mind, and Spirit in Early Chinese Medicine." *T'oung Pao* 106, nos. 5–6 (2020): 525–51.

———. *Divination and Prediction in Early China and Ancient Greece*. Cambridge: Cambridge University Press, 2013.

Raz, Gil. "Birthing the Self: Metaphor and Transformation in Medieval Daoism." In *Gendering Chinese Religion: Subject, Identity, and Body*, edited by Jinhua Jia, Xiaofei Kang, and Ping Yao, 183–200. Albany: State University of New York Press, 2014.

———. "Creation of Tradition: The Five Talismans of the Numinous Treasure and the Formation of Early Daoism." PhD dissertation, Indiana University, 2004.

———. *The Emergence of Daoism: Creation of Tradition*. London: Routledge, 2012.

Renberg, Gil H. *Where Dreams May Come: Incubation Sanctuaries in the Greco-Roman World*. 2 vols. continuously paginated. Leiden: Brill, 2017.

Richter, Antje. *Letters and Epistolary Culture in Early Medieval China*. Seattle: University of Washington Press, 2013.

Richter, Matthias L. *The Embodied Text: Establishing Textual Identity in Early Chinese Manuscripts*. Leiden: Brill, 2013.

———. "Textual Identity and the Role of Literacy in the Transmission of Early Chinese Literature." In *Writing and Literacy in Early China: Studies from the Columbia Early China Seminar*, edited by Li Feng and David Prager Branner, 206–38. Seattle: University of Washington Press, 2011.

Rickett, W. Allyn. *Guanzi: Political, Economic, and Philosophical Essays from Early China*. Vol. 1, revised edition. Boston: Cheng and Tsui, 2001.

———. *Guanzi: Political, Economic, and Philosophical Essays from Early China*. Vol. 2. Princeton: Princeton University Press, 1998.

Robert, Jean-Noël. *Le sûtra du Lotus*. Paris: Fayard, 1997.

Robinet, Isabelle. *Méditation taoïste*. Paris: Dervy Livres, 1979.

———. *La révélation du Shangqing dans l'histoire du Taoïsme*. 2 vols. Paris: École Française d'Extrême-Orient, 1984.

Robson, James. *Power of Place: The Religious Landscape of the Southern Sacred Peak (Nanyue 南嶽) in Medieval China*. Cambridge, MA: Harvard University Asia Center, 2009.

———. "Signs of Power: Talismanic Writing in Chinese Buddhism." *History of Religions* 48, no. 2 (November 2008): 130–69.

———. "Sin, Sinification, Sinology: On the Notion of Sin in Buddhism and Chinese Religions." In *Sins and Sinners: Perspectives from Asian Religions*, edited by Phyllis Granoff and Koichi Shinohara, 73–92. Leiden: Brill, 2012.

Rom, Avital Hedva. "Polyphonic Thinking: Music and Authority in Early China." PhD dissertation, University of Cambridge, 2019.

Rong Xinjiang 荣新江. *Eighteen Lectures on Dunhuang*. Translated by Imre Galambos. Leiden: Brill, 2013.

Ronkin, Noa. *Early Buddhist Metaphysics: The Making of a Philosophical Tradition*. London: RoutledgeCurzon, 2005.

Roth, Harold D. *Original Tao: Inward Training and the Foundations of Taoist Mysticism*. New York: Columbia University Press, 2004.

Rothschild, N. Harry. *Emperor Wu Zhao and Her Pantheon of Devis, Divinities, and Dynastic Mothers*. New York: Columbia University Press, 2015.

Rotman, Andy. *Thus Have I Seen: Visualizing Faith in Early Indian Buddhism*. Oxford: Oxford University Press, 2009.

Rulu. *Teachings of the Buddha: Selected Mahāyāna Sūtras*. Bloomington, IN: AuthorHouse, 2012.

Russell, T. C. "Revelation and Narrative in the *Zhoushi mingtongji*." *Early Medieval China* 1 (1994): 34–59.

Sahlins, Marshall. "Goodbye to *Tristes Tropes*: Ethnography in the Context of Modern World History." *Journal of Modern History* 65, no. 1 (1993): 1–25.

———. *The Western Illusion of Human Nature*. Chicago: Prickly Paradigm Press, 2008.

Salguero, C. Pierce. "Fields of Merit, Harvests of Health: Some Notes on the Role of Medical Karma in the Popularization of Buddhism in Early Medieval China." *Asian Philosophy* 23, no.4 (2013): 341–49.

———. "'A Flock of Ghosts Bursting Forth and Scattering': Healing Narratives in a Sixth-Century Chinese Buddhist Hagiography." *East Asian Science, Technology, and Medicine*, no. 32 (2010): 89–120.

Salomon, Richard. *The Buddhist Literature of Ancient Gandhāra: An Introduction with Selected Translations*. Somerville, MA: Wisdom Publications, 2018.

———, with contributions by Andrew Glass. *Two Gāndhārī Manuscripts of the "Songs of Lake Anavatpta" (Anavatapta-gāthā)*. Seattle: University of Washington Press, 2008.

Sanft, Charles. *Communication and Cooperation in Early Imperial China: Publicizing the Qin Dynasty*. Albany: State University of New York Press, 2014.

———. *Literate Community in Early Imperial China: The Northwestern Frontier in Han Times*. Albany: State University of New York Press, 2019.

Sasaki Shizuka. "The Concept of 'Remodelling the World.'" In *Setting Out on the Great Way: Essays on Early Mahāyāna Buddhism*, edited by Paul Harrison, 141–76. Sheffield: Equinox, 2018.

Satlow, Michael L. "Tradition: The Power of Constraint." In *The Cambridge Companion to Religious Studies*, edited by Robert A. Orsi, 130–50. Cambridge: Cambridge University Press, 2012.

Saussy, Haun. "Reading From, Reading Into: The Challenge of the Bamboo Odes." *Bamboo and Silk* 4, no. 1 (2021): 200–213.

Schaberg, David. "The Logic of Signs in Early Chinese Rhetoric." In *Early China/Ancient Greece: Thinking Through Comparisons*, edited by Stephen Durrant and Steven Shankman, 155–86. Albany: State University of New York Press, 2002.

Schafer, Edward H. "The Development of Bathing Customs in Ancient and Medieval China and the History of the Floriate Clear Palace." *Journal of the American Oriental Society* 76, no. 2 (1956): 57–82.

———. *Mao Shan in T'ang Times*. 2nd edition. Boulder, CO: Society for the Study of Chinese Religions Monograph 1, 1989.

———. *Mirages on the Sea of Time: The Taoist Poetry of Ts'ao T'ang*. Berkeley: University of California Press, 1985.

Schipper, Kristofer. *Concordance du Houang-t'ing king*. Paris: École Française d'Extrême-Orient, 1975.

———. *Le corps taoïste: Corps physique, corps social*. Paris: Fayard, 1982.

———. "Purity and Strangers: Shifting Boundaries in Medieval Taoism." *T'oung Pao* 80, nos. 1–3 (1994): 61–81.

———. "The Taoist Body." *History of Religions* 17, nos. 3–4 (February–May 1978): 355–86.

Schmid, David Neil. "Revisioning the Buddhist Cosmos: Shifting Paths of Rebirth in Medieval Chinese Buddhism." *Cahiers d'Extrême-Asie* 17 (2008): 293–325.

Schopen, Gregory. *Figments and Fragments of Mahāyāna Buddhism in India: More Collected Papers*. Honolulu: University of Hawai'i Press, 2005.

Schwermann, Christian. "Collage-Technik als Kompositionsprinzip klassischer chinesischer Prosa: Der Aufbau des Kapitels 'Tang wen' (Die Frage des Tang) im *Lie zi*." *Bochumer Jahrbuch zur Ostasienforschung* 29 (2005): 125–57.

———. "The Fragrance of the Buddha, the Scent of Monuments, and the Odor of Images in Early India." *Bulletin de l'École Française d'Extrême-Orient* 101 (2015): 11–30.

———. "Relic." In *Critical Terms for Religious Studies*, edited by Mark C. Taylor, 256–68. Chicago: University of Chicago Press, 1998.

Seaman, Gary. *Journey to the North: An Ethnohistorical and Annotated Translation of the Chinese Folk Novel "Pei-yu chi."* Berkeley: University of California Press, 1987.

Searle, J. R. "What Is a Speech Act?" In *The Philosophy of Language*, edited by J. R. Searle, 39–53. Oxford: Oxford University Press, 1971.

Sen, Tansen. "Yijing and the Buddhist Cosmopolis of the Seventh Century." In *Texts and Transformations: Essays in Honor of the 75th Birthday of Victor H. Mair*, edited by Haun Saussy, 345–68. Amherst, NY: Cambria Press, 2018.

Seymour, Kelsey. "The Buddha's Voice: Ritual Sound and Sensory Experience in Medieval Chinese Religious Practice." PhD dissertation, University of Pennsylvania, 2018.

Sharf, Robert H. "Buddhist Modernism and the Rhetoric of Meditative Experience." *Numen* 42, no. 3 (January 1995): 228–83.

———. *Coming to Terms with Chinese Buddhism: A Reading of the Treasure Store Treatise*. Honolulu: University of Hawai'i Press, 2002.

———. "Experience." In *Critical Terms for Religious Studies*, edited by Mark C. Taylor, 94–116. Chicago: University of Chicago Press, 1998.

———. "On Pure Land Buddhism and Ch'an/Pure Land Syncretism in Medieval China." *T'oung Pao* 88, nos. 4–5 (2002): 282–331.

Shaughnessy, Edward L. "Of Trees, a Son, and Kingship: Recovering an Ancient Chinese Dream." *Journal of Asian Studies* 77, no. 3 (2018): 593–609.

———. "The Tsinghua Manuscript **Zheng Wen Gong wen Tai Bo* and the Question of the Production of Manuscripts in Early China." *Bamboo and Silk* 3 (2020): 54–73.

Shi Huifeng [Matthew Orsborn]. "Annotated English Translation of Kumārajīva's *Xiaopin Prajñāpāramitā Sūtra*." *Asian Literature and Translation* 4, no. 1 (2017): 187–238.

Shih, Robert. *Biographies des moines éminents (Kao seng tchouan) de Houei-kiao*. Louvain: Institut orientaliste de l'Université de Louvain, 1968.

Shinohara, Koichi. "The All-Gathering Maṇḍala Initiation Ceremony in Atikūṭa's Collected Dhāraṇī Scriptures: Reconstructing the Evolution of Esoteric Buddhist Ritual." *Journal Asiatique* 298, no. 2 (2010): 389–420.

———. "Removal of Sins in Esoteric Buddhist Rituals: A Study of the *Dafangdeng Dhāraṇī Scripture*." In *Sins and Sinners: Perspectives from Asian Religions*, edited by Phyllis Granoff and Koichi Shinohara, 243–75. Leiden: Brill, 2012.

———. *Spells, Images, and Maṇḍalas: Tracing the Evolution of Esoteric Buddhist Rituals*. New York: Columbia University Press, 2014.

Shryock, J. K. *The Study of Human Abilities: The Jen wu chih of Liu Shao*. American Oriental Series 11. New Haven, CT: American Oriental Society, 1937.

Shulman, David, and Guy G. Stroumsa, eds. *Self and Self-Transformation in the History of Religions*. Oxford: Oxford University Press, 2002.

Silk, Jonathan A. "Good and Evil in Indian Buddhism." *Journal of Indian Philosophy* 35, no. 3 (2007): 253–86.

———. "The Origins and Early History of the *Mahāratnakūṭa* Tradition of Mahāyāna Buddhism with a Study of the *Ratnarāśisūtra* and Related Materials." PhD dissertation, University of Michigan, 1994.

Sivin, Nathan. *Chinese Alchemy: Preliminary Studies*. Cambridge, MA: Harvard University Press, 1968.

———. "State, Cosmos, and Body in the Last Three Centuries B.C." *Harvard Journal of Asiatic Studies* 55, no. 1 (1995): 5–37.

Skeat, Walter W. *An Etymological Dictionary of the English Language*. Revised edition. Oxford: Clarendon, 1910.

Skilling, Peter. "Symbols on the Body, Feet, and Hands of a Buddha. Part I: Lists." *Journal of the Siam Society* 80, no. 2 (1992): 67–79.

———. "Vaidalya, Mahāyāna, and Bodhisattva in India: An Essay Towards Historical Understanding." In *The Bodhisattva Ideal: Essays on the Emergence of Mahāyāna*, edited by Bhikkhu Nyanatusita himi, 69–162. Kandy: Buddhist Publication Society, 2013.

Slingerland, Edward. "Conceptions of the Self in the *Zhuangzi*: Conceptual Metaphor Analysis and Comparative Thought." *Philosophy East & West* 54, no. 3 (2004): 322–42.

———. *Confucius: Analects, with Selections from Traditional Commentaries*. Indianapolis: Hackett, 2003.

———. *Effortless Action: Wu-wei as Conceptual Metaphor and Spiritual Ideal in Early China*. Oxford: Oxford University Press, 2003.

———. "Metaphor and Meaning in Early China." *Dao* 10, no. 1 (2011): 1–30.

———. *Mind and Body in Early China: Beyond Orientalism and the Myth of Holism*. New York: Oxford University Press, 2019.

Smith, Jonathan Z. *Drudgery Divine: On the Comparison of Early Christianities and the Religions of Late Antiquity*. Chicago: University of Chicago Press, 1990.

———. *Imagining Religion: From Babylon to Jonestown*. Chicago: University of Chicago Press, 1982.

———. *Relating Religion: Essays in the Study of Religion*. Chicago: University of Chicago Press, 2004.

———. "Tillich['s] Remains." *Journal of the American Academy of Religion* 78, no. 4 (2010): 1139–70.

———. *To Take Place: Toward Theory in Ritual*. Chicago: University of Chicago Press, 1987.

———. "Towards Interpreting Demonic Powers in Hellenistic and Roman Antiquity." *Aufstieg und Niedergang der römischen Welt* 16, no. 1 (1978): 425–39.

Smith, Thomas E. "Ritual and the Shaping of Narrative: The Legend of Han Emperor Wu." PhD dissertation, University of Michigan, 1992.

Smith, Wilfred Cantwell. *Believing: An Historical Perspective*. Oxford: Oneworld, 1998.

Sørensen, Henrik H. "Central Divinities in the Esoteric Buddhist Pantheon in China." In *Esoteric Buddhism and the Tantras in East Asia*, edited by Charles D. Orzech, Henrik H. Sørensen, and Richard K. Payne, 90–132. Leiden: Brill, 2011.

———. "Divine Scrutiny of Human Morals in an Early Chinese Buddhist Sutra: A Study of the *Si tianwang jing* (T 590)." *Studies in Central and East Asian Religions* 8 (1995): 44–83.

———. "The Spell of the Great, Golden Peacock Queen: The Origin, Practices, and Lore of an Early Esoteric Buddhist Tradition in China." *Pacific World: Journal of the Institute of Buddhist Studies* 8 (2006): 89–123.

———. "Spells and Magical Practices as Reflected in the Early Chinese Buddhist Sources (c. 300–600 CE) and Their Implications for the Rise and Development of Esoteric Buddhism." In *Chinese and Tibetan Esoteric Buddhism*, edited by Yael Bentor and Meir Shahar, 41–71. Leiden: Brill, 2017.

Soymié, Michel. "Le Lo-feou chan: Étude de géographie religieuse." *Bulletin de l'École Française d'Extrême-Orient* 48, no. 1 (1956): 1–139.

Stanley-Baker, Michael. "Cultivating Body, Cultivating Self: A Critical Translation and History of the Tang Dynasty *Yangxing yanming lu* 養性延命錄 (Records of Cultivating Nature and Extending Life)." Master's thesis, Indiana University, 2006.

———. "Drugs, Destiny, and Disease in Medieval China: Situating Knowledge in Context." *Daoism: Religion, History and Society*, no. 6 (2014): 113–56.

———. "Palpable Access to the Divine: Daoist Medieval Massage, Visualisation and Internal Sensation." *Asian Medicine* 7 (2012): 101–27.

Steavu, Dominic. "The Marvelous Fungus and *The Secret of Divine Immortals*." *Micrologus: Nature, Sciences and Medieval Societies* 26 (2018): 353–84.

———. *The Writ of the Three Sovereigns: From Local Lore to Institutional Daoism*. Hong Kong: Chinese University of Hong Kong Press, 2019.

Stein, Rolf A. "Religious Taoism and Popular Religion from the Second to Seventh Centuries." In *Facets of Taoism: Essays in Chinese Religion*, edited by Holmes H. Welch and Anna Seidel, 53–81. New Haven, CT: Yale University Press, 1979.

Sterckx, Roel. *Food, Sacrifice, and Sagehood in Early China*. Cambridge: Cambridge University Press, 2011.

———. "Sages, Cooks, and Flavours in Warring States and Han China." *Monumenta Serica* 54 (2006): 1–46.

Stevenson, Daniel B. "Buddhist Practice and the *Lotus Sūtra* in China." In *Readings of the Lotus Sūtra*, edited by Stephen F. Teiser and Jacqueline I. Stone, 132–50. New York: Columbia University Press, 2009.

———. "Four Kinds of Samādhi in Early T'ien-t'ai Buddhism." In *Traditions of Meditation in Chinese Buddhism*, edited by Peter N. Gregory, 45–98. Honolulu: University of Hawai'i Press, 1986.

———. "Pure Land Buddhist Worship and Meditation in China." In *Buddhism in Practice*, edited by Donald S. Lopez, Jr., 359–79. Princeton: Princeton University Press, 1995.

Stone, Jacqueline I. *Right Thoughts at the Last Moment: Buddhism and Deathbed Practices in Early Medieval Japan*. Honolulu: University of Hawai'i Press, 2016.

———. "With the Help of 'Good Friends': Deathbed Ritual Practices in Early Medieval Japan." In *Death and the Afterlife in Japanese Buddhism*, edited by Jacqueline I. Stone and Mariko Namba Walter, 61–101. Honolulu: University of Hawai'i Press, 2008.

Storch, Tanya. "Fei Changfang's *Records of the Three Treasures throughout the Successive Dynasties* (*Lidai sanbao ji*) and Its Role in the Formation of the Chinese Buddhist Canon." In *Spreading Buddha's Word in East Asia: The Formation and Transformation of the Chinese Buddhist Canon*, edited by Wu Jiang and Lucille Chia, 109–42. New York: Columbia University Press, 2016.

Strassberg, Richard E. *Wandering Spirits: Chen Shiyuan's Encyclopedia of Dreams*. Stanford: Stanford University Press, 2008.

Strauch, Ingo. "Early Mahāyāna in Gandhāra: New Evidence from the Bajaur Mahāyāna Sūtra." In *Setting Out on the Great Way: Essays on Early Mahāyāna Buddhism*, edited by Paul Harrison, 207–42. Sheffield: Equinox, 2018.

Strickmann, Michel. *Chinese Magical Medicine*. Edited by Bernard Faure. Stanford: Stanford University Press, 2002.

———. *Chinese Poetry and Prophecy: The Written Oracle in East Asia*. Edited by Bernard Faure. Stanford: Stanford University Press, 2005.

———. "The *Consecration Sūtra*: A Buddhist Book of Spells." In *Chinese Buddhist Apocrypha*, edited by Robert E. Buswell, Jr., 75–118. Honolulu: University of Hawai'i Press, 1990.

———. "Dreamwork of Psycho-Sinologists: Doctors, Taoists, Monks." In *Psycho-Sinology: The Universe of Dreams in Chinese Culture*, edited by Carolyn T. Brown, 25–46. Washington, DC: Woodrow Wilson International Center for Scholars, 1988.

———. *Mantras et mandarins: Le bouddhisme tantrique en Chine*. Paris: Gallimard, 1996.

———. "Notes on Mushroom Cults in Ancient China." Gent: East Asian History of Science Library, Rijksuniversiteit Gent, 1966.

———. "On the Alchemy of T'ao Hung-ching." In *Facets of Taoism*, edited by Holmes H. Welch and Anna Seidel, 123–92. New Haven, CT: Yale University Press, 1979.

———. "The Seal of the Law: A Ritual Implement and the Origins of Printing." *Asia Major*, 3rd series, 6, no. 2 (1993): 1–83.

———. *Le taoïsme du Mao chan: Chronique d'une révélation*. Paris: Collège de France, Institut des Hautes Études Chinoises, 1981.

———. "A Taoist Confirmation of Liang Wu Ti's Suppression of Taoism." *Journal of the American Oriental Society* 98, no. 4 (1978): 467–75.

Strong, John S. *Relics of the Buddha*. Princeton: Princeton University Press, 2004.

Struve, Lynn A. *The Dreaming Mind and the End of the Ming World*. Honolulu: University of Hawai'i Press, 2019.

Suit, Natalia K. *Qur'anic Matters: Material Mediations and Religious Practice in Egypt*. London: Bloomsbury, 2020.

Sun Xidan 孫希旦, ed. *Liji jijie* 禮記集解. 2 vols. continuously paginated. Taipei: Wenshizhe, 1990.

Swanson, Paul L. *Clear Serenity, Quiet Insight: T'ien-t'ai Chih-i's Mo-ho chih-kuan*. 3 vols. continuously paginated. Honolulu: University of Hawai'i Press, 2018.

———. "Dandala, Dhāraṇī, and Denarii: A T'ien-t'ai Perspective on *The Great Vaipulya Dhāraṇī Sūtra*." *Buddhist Literature* 2 (2001): 197–233.

Tanabe, George J., Jr. *Myōe the Dreamkeeper: Fantasy and Knowledge in Early Kamakura Buddhism*. Cambridge, MA: Harvard University Press, 1992.

———. "Telling Beads: The Forms and Functions of the Buddhist Rosary in Japan." *Beiträge des Arbeitskreises Japanische Religionen*, 2012. http://tobias-lib.uni-tuebingen.de/portal/bajr/.

Taves, Ann. *Fits, Trances, and Visions: Experiencing Religion and Explaining Experience from Wesley to James*. Princeton: Princeton University Press, 1999.

———. *Religious Experience Reconsidered: A Building-Block Approach to the Study of Religion and Other Special Things*. Princeton: Princeton University Press, 2009.

Taylor, Charles. "To Follow a Rule." In *Bourdieu: Critical Perspectives*, edited by Craig Calhoun, Edward LiPuma, and Moishe Postone, 45–60. Chicago: University of Chicago Press, 1993.

Teiser, Stephen F. "The Literary Style of Dunhuang Healing Liturgies." *Dunhuang Tulufan yanjiu* 14 (2014): 355–77.

———. "Ornamenting the Departed: Notes on the Language of Chinese Buddhist Ritual Texts." *Asia Major*, 3rd series, 22, no. 1 (2009): 201–37.

———. *Reinventing the Wheel: Paintings of Rebirth in Medieval Buddhist Temples*. Seattle: University of Washington Press, 2006.

———. *The Scripture on the Ten Kings and the Making of Purgatory in Medieval Chinese Buddhism*. Honolulu: University of Hawai'i Press, 1994.

Teiser, Stephen F., and Jacqueline I. Stone. "Interpreting the *Lotus Sūtra*." In *Readings of the Lotus Sūtra*, edited by Stephen F. Teiser and Jacqueline I. Stone, 1–61. New York: Columbia University Press, 2009.

Thompson, George. "On Truth-Acts in Vedic." *Indo-Iranian Journal* 41, no. 2 (1998): 125–53.

Thote, Alain. "Daybooks in Archaeological Context." In *Books of Fate and Popular Culture in Early China: The Daybook Manuscripts of the Warring States, Qin, and Han*, 11–56. Leiden: Brill, 2017.

Tian, Xiaofei. *Beacon Fire and Shooting Star: The Literary Culture of the Liang (502–557)*. Cambridge, MA: Harvard University Press, 2007.

———. *Family Instructions for the Yan Clan and Other Works by Yan Zhitui (531–590s)*. Edited by Paul W. Kroll. Boston and Berlin: De Gruyter, 2021.

———. *Tao Yuanming and Manuscript Culture: The Record of a Dusty Table*. Seattle: University of Washington Press, 2005.

———. "Yu Xin's 'Memory Palace': Writing Trauma and Violence in Early Medieval Chinese Aulic Poetry." In *Memory in Medieval China: Text, Ritual, and Community*, edited by Wendy Swartz and Robert Ford Campany, 124–57. Leiden: Brill, 2018.

Tokiwa Daijō 常盤大定. *Gokan yori Sōsei ni itaru yakkyō sōroku 後漢より宋齊に至る訳経總録*. Reprint. Tokyo: Kokusho kankōkai, 1973.

Tokuno, Kyoko. "The Evaluation of Indigenous Scriptures in Chinese Buddhist Bibliographical Catalogues." In *Chinese Buddhist Apocrypha*, edited by Robert E. Buswell, Jr., 31–74. Honolulu: University of Hawai'i Press, 1990.

Tompkins, Jane P. "An Introduction to Reader-Response Criticism." In *Reader-Response Criticism: From Formalism to Post-Structuralism*, edited by Jane P. Tompkins, ix–xxvi. Baltimore: Johns Hopkins University Press, 1980.

Tsai, Julius N. "Opening Up the Ritual Casket: Patterns of Concealment and Disclosure in Early and Medieval Chinese Religion." *Material Religion* 2, no. 1 (2006): 38–67.

Tsien, Tsuen-hsuin. *Written on Bamboo and Silk: The Beginnings of Chinese Books and Inscriptions*. 2nd edition. Chicago: University of Chicago Press, 2004.

Tsukamoto Zenryū 塚本善隆. *A History of Early Chinese Buddhism*. Translated by Leon Hurvitz. 2 vols. Tokyo: Kodansha, 1985.

Udemmadu, Thecla Ngozi, and Patrick Ik. Umezi. "The Language of the Sacraments of the Catholic Church: Austin and Searle's Model." *International Journal of Religion and Human Relations* 9, no. 1 (2017): 107–30.

Urban, Hugh. "The Torment of Secrecy: Ethical and Epistemological Problems in the Study of Esoteric Traditions." *History of Religions* 37, no. 3 (February 1998): 209–48.

Van Norden, Bryan W., ed. *Confucius and the Analects: New Essays*. New York: Oxford University Press 2002.

Vance, Brigid E. "Exorcising Dreams and Nightmares in Late Ming China." In *Psychiatry and Chinese History*, edited by Howard Chiang, 17–36. London: Pickering & Chatto, 2014.

———. "Textualizing Dreams in a Late Ming Dream Encyclopedia." PhD dissertation, Princeton University, 2012.

Verellen, Franciscus. "The Beyond Within: Grotto-heavens in Taoist Ritual and Cosmology." *Cahiers d'Extrême-Asie* 8 (1995): 265–90.

———. *Du Guangting (850–933): Taoïste de cour à la fin de la Chine médiévale*. Paris: Collège de France, 1989.

———. "Encounter as Revelation: A Taoist Hagiographic Theme in Medieval China." *Bulletin de l'École française d'Extrême-Orient* 85 (1998): 363–84.

———. "Evidential Miracles in Support of Taoism: The Inversion of a Buddhist Apologetic Tradition in Late T'ang China." *T'oung Pao* 78, nos. 4–5 (1992): 217–63.

———. *Imperiled Destinies: The Daoist Quest for Deliverance in Medieval China*. Cambridge, MA: Harvard University Asia Center, 2019.

Wang, Eugene Y. "Of the True Body: The Famen Monastery Relics and Corporeal Transformation in Tang Imperial Culture." In *Body and Face in Chinese Visual Culture*, edited by Wu Hung and Katherine R. Tsiang, 79–118. Cambridge, MA: Harvard University Asia Center, 2005.

———. *Shaping the Lotus Sutra: Buddhist Visual Culture in Medieval China*. Seattle: University of Washington Press, 2005.

Wang Li 王力. *Wang Li gu Hanyu zidian* 王力古漢語字典. Beijing: Zhonghua shuju, 2000.

Waring, Luke. "What the Single Bamboo Slip Found in Mawangdui Tomb M2 Tells Us about Text and Ritual in Early China." *T'oung Pao* 106, nos. 1–2 (2020): 56–86.

Watson, Burton. *The Complete Works of Chuang Tzu*. New York: Columbia University Press, 1968.

———. *Hsün Tzu: Basic Writings*. New York: Columbia University Press, 1963.

Wayman, Alex. "The Hindu-Buddhist Rite of Truth: An Interpretation." In *Buddhist Insight: Essays by Alex Wayman*, edited by George R. Elder, 391–98. New Delhi: Motilal, 2002.

Weingarten, Oliver. "'Self-Cultivation' (*xiushen* 修身) in the Early Edited Literature: Uses and Contexts." *Oriens Extremus* 54 (2015): 163–208.

Weinstein, Stanley. *Buddhism Under the T'ang*. Cambridge: Cambridge University Press, 1987.

Willemen, Charles, Bart Dessein, and Collett Cox. *Sarvāstivāda Buddhist Scholasticism*. Leiden: Brill, 1998.

Williams, Paul. *Mahāyāna Buddhism: The Doctrinal Foundations*. 2nd edition. London: Routledge, 2009.

Wilms, Sabine. *The Divine Farmer's Classic of Materia Medica*. 3rd edition. Corbett, OR: Happy Goat, 2017.

Wilson, Liz. *Charming Cadavers: Horrific Figurations of the Feminine in Indian Buddhist Hagiographic Literature*. Chicago: University of Chicago Press, 1996.

Wilson, Thomas. "Sacrifice and the Imperial Cult of Confucius." *History of Religions* 41, no. 3 (February 2002): 251–87.

———. "Spirits and the Soul in Confucian Ritual Discourse." *Journal of Chinese Religions* 42, no. 2 (November 2014): 185–212.

Wittgenstein, Ludwig. *Tractatus Logico-Philosophicus*. 2nd edition. London: Routledge & Kegan Paul, 1972.

Wolf, Lucas. "Ritual Refashioned: Buddhism, Lingbao and the Adaptation of Vows (*yuan* 願)." *Studies in Chinese Religions* 6, no. 2 (2020): 182–200.

Wong, Dorothy C. [王靜芬]. "Bukong Juansuo Guanyin xintan" 不空羂索觀音新探. *Dunhuang Tulufan yanjiu* 15 (2015): 17–52.

———. "The Case of Amoghapāśa." *Journal of Inner Asian Art and Archaeology* 2 (2007): 151–58.

———. *Chinese Steles: Pre-Buddhist and Buddhist Use of a Symbolic Form*. Honolulu: University of Hawai'i Press, 2004.

Wright, Arthur F. *Studies in Chinese Buddhism*. Edited by Robert M. Somers. New Haven, CT: Yale University Press, 1990.

Wu Jiang. "The Chinese Buddhist Canon through the Ages: Essential Categories and Critical Issues in the Study of a Textual Tradition." In *Spreading Buddha's Word in East Asia: The Formation and Transformation of the Chinese Buddhist Canon*, edited by Wu Jiang and Lucille Chia, 15–45. New York: Columbia University Press, 2016.

Wu Kang 吳康. *Zhongguo guishen jingguai* 中國鬼神精怪. Changsha: Hunan wenyi chubanshe, 1992.

Wu, Pei-Yi. "Self-Examination and Confession of Sins in Traditional China." *Harvard Journal of Asiatic Studies* 39, no. 1 (1979): 5–38.

Xiao Dengfu 蕭登福. "Daojiao shouyi xiuchifa zhi yuanqi ji qi yanbian" 道教守一修持法之源起及其演變. *Daojiao yanjiu*, no. 1 (2006): 1–12.

Yamabe Nobuyoshi. "Bonmōkyō ni okeru kōsōgyō no kenkyū: toku ni zenkan kyōten to no kanrensei ni chakumoku shite" 梵網経における好相行の研究：特に禅觀経典との關連性に着目して. In *Hokuchō Zui Tō Chūgoku bukkyō shisōshi* 北朝隋唐中国仏教思想史, edited by Aramaki Noritoshi 荒牧典俊, 205–69. Kyoto: Hōzōkan, 2000.

———. "The Sūtra on the Ocean-Like Samādhi of the Visualization of the Buddha: The Interfusion of the Chinese and Indian Cultures in Central Asia as Reflected in a Fifth Century Apocryphal Sūtra." PhD dissertation, Yale University, 1999.

———. "Visionary Repentance and Visionary Ordination in the *Brahmā Net Sūtra*." In *Going Forth: Visions of Buddhist Vinaya*, edited by William M. Bodiford, 17–39. Honolulu: University of Hawai'i Press, 2005.

Yamabe Nobuyoshi and Fumihiko Sueki. *The Sutra on the Concentration of Sitting Meditation*. BDK English Tripiṭika. Berkeley: Numata Center for Buddhist Translation and Research, 2009.

Yamada Toshiaki 山田利明. "Deigan kyūkyū setsu kō" 泥丸九宮說考. *Tōyō gaku ronsō* 東洋學論叢 41 (1988): 103–18.

Yan Changgui 晏昌貴. "Daybooks and the Spirit World." In *Books of Fate and Popular Culture in Early China: The Daybook Manuscripts of the Warring States, Qin, and Han*, 207–47. Leiden: Brill, 2017.

Yang Bojun 楊伯峻. *Lunyu yizhu* 論語譯注. Beijing: Guji chubanshe, 1958.

Yang Gang and Christoph Anderl. "Prognostication in Chinese Buddhist Historical Texts:

The *Gaoseng zhuan* and the *Xu gaoseng zhuan*." *Acta Orientalia Academiae Scientiarum Hungaricae* 73, no. 1 (2020): 1–45.

Yates, Robin D. S. "Medicine for Women in Early China: A Preliminary Survey." *Nan Nü* 7, no. 2 (January 2005): 127–81.

———. "Purity and Pollution in Early China." *Zhongguo kaoguxue yu lishixue zhi zhenghe yanjiu* 4 (1997): 479–536.

———. "Slavery in Early China: A Socio-Cultural Approach." *Journal of East Asian Archaeology* 3, nos. 1–2 (2002): 283–331.

———. "Soldiers, Scribes, and Women: Literacy among the Lower Orders in Early China." In *Writing and Literacy in Early China: Studies from the Columbia Early China Seminar*, edited by Li Feng and David Prager Branner, 339–69. Seattle: University of Washington Press, 2011.

Yifa. "From the Chinese Vinaya Tradition to Chan Regulations: Continuity and Adaptation." In *Going Forth: Visions of Buddhist Vinaya*, edited by William M. Bodiford, 124–35. Honolulu: University of Hawai'i Press, 2005.

Yoshikawa Tadao 吉川忠夫 and Funayama Toru 船山徹, trans. *Kōsōden* 高僧傳. Tokyo: Iwanami shoten, 2009.

Yoshikawa Tadao 吉川忠夫 and Mugitani Kunio 麥谷邦夫, eds. *Zhen'gao jiaozhu* 真誥校註. Translated from the Japanese by Zhu Yueli 朱越利. Beijing: Zhongguo shehui kexue chubanshe, 2006.

Young, Serinity. *Dreaming in the Lotus: Buddhist Dream Narrative, Imagery, and Practice*. Boston: Wisdom, 1999.

Young, Stuart. *Conceiving the Indian Buddhist Patriarchs in China*. Honolulu: University of Hawai'i Press, 2015.

Yü, Chün-fang. *Kuan-yin: The Chinese Transformation of Avalokiteśvara*. New York: Columbia University Press, 2001.

Yusa Noboru 遊佐 昇. "Tōdai ni mirareru Kyūku tenson Shinko ni tsuite" 唐代に見られる救苦天尊信仰について. *Tōhō shūkyō* 73 (1989): 19–40.

Zacchetti, Stefano. *The Da zhidu lun* 大智度論 *(*Mahāprajñāpāramitopadeśa) and the History of the Larger Prajñāpāramitā: Patterns of Textual Variation in Mahāyāna Sūtra Literature.* Edited by Michael Radich and Jonathan Silk. Bochum/Freiburg: Projekt Verlag, 2021.

———. *In Praise of the Light: A Critical Synoptic Edition with an Annotated Translation of Chapters 1–3 of Dharmarakṣa's Guan zan jing* 光讚經, *Being the Earliest Translation of the Larger Prajñāpāramitā*. Tokyo: International Research Institute for Advanced Buddhology, Soka University, 2005.

———. "Notions and Visions of the Canon in Early Chinese Buddhism." In *Spreading Buddha's Word in East Asia: The Formation and Transformation of the Chinese Buddhist Canon*, edited by Wu Jiang and Lucille Chia, 81–108. New York: Columbia University Press 2016.

———. "Prajñāpāramitā Sūtras." In BEB, 171–209.

Zhang Hanmo. *Authorship and Text-Making in Early China*. Boston and Berlin: Walter de Gruyter, 2018.

Zhang Shaoying. "Incubating Prognostic Dreams: An Initial Study of the *Secret Book of Praying for Dreams*." *Dreaming* 31, no. 4 (2021): 342–54.

Zhang Zhenjun. *Hidden and Visible Realms: Early Medieval Chinese Tales of the Supernatural and the Fantastic*. New York: Columbia University Press, 2018.

Zhao Chengpu 赵成甫, ed. *Nanyang Handai huaxiang zhuan* 南陽漢代畫像磚. Beijing: Wenwu chubanshe, 1990.

Zheng Binglin 鄭炳林. *Dunhuang xieben jiemeng shu jiaolu yanjiu* 敦煌寫本解夢書校錄研究. Beijing: Minzu chubanshe, 2005.

Zheng Binglin 鄭炳林 and Yang Ping 羊萍. *Dunhuang ben mengshu* 敦煌本夢書. Lanzhou: Gansu wenhua chubanshe, 1995.

Zhiru. *The Making of a Savior Bodhisattva: Dizang in Medieval China*. Honolulu: University of Hawai'i Press, 2007.

Zhou Boqun 周博群. "Subtle and Dangerous: The Crossbow Trigger Metaphor in Early China." *Early China* 44 (2021): 1–28.

Zito, Angela. "Silk and Skin: Significant Boundaries." In *Body, Subject, and Power in China*, edited by Angela Zito and Tani E. Barlow, 103–30. Chicago: University of Chicago Press, 1994.

Zürcher, Erik. *Buddhism in China: Collected Papers of Erik Zürcher*. Edited by Jonathan A. Silk. Leiden: Brill, 2013.

———. *The Buddhist Conquest of China: The Spread and Adaptation of Buddhism in Early Medieval China*. 3rd edition. Leiden: Brill, 2007.

Index

Italic page numbers refer to tables.

affordances of dreams, 22, 149, 166–67
Allan, Sarah, 237n3
Amoghavajra, *Dili sanmeiye budong zunshengzhe niansong bimi fa*, 63
An Shigao, *Daodi jing*, 86–87
Analects (*Lunyu*), 33, 122–23, 125, 174
Annals of Master Lü (*Lüshi chunqiu*), 39, 51, 123, 125, 136
Array of the Five Talismans (*Taishang lingbao wufu xu*), 53–54
Artemidorus, *Oneirocritica*, 89, 228n38, 228n45
Asad, Talal, 20
Atikūṭa, *Compendium of Dhāraṇīs* (*Tuoluoni jijing*), 48–49, 108
auspicious dreams, 57, 60, 63, 110, 137, 220n147
Austin, J. L., 233n113
awakening: as metaphor for self-cultivational attainment, 175–78; recalling dreams and, 103

Bell, Catherine, 159
Bhadrapāla, 133–34
Bodhiruci, 85, 137
bodhisattva path: difficulty, 240n45; irreversibility, 87, 105, 137; obstacles, 92, 100–102, 231nn81–82; practitioners, 90; signs of progress, 113–17; stages, 87, 92–93, 105; texts on, 86–87. *See also* Perfection of Wisdom texts; *Sutra on the Explication of Dreams for Bodhisattvas*
bodhisattva precepts, 114–15
bodhisattvas: dreaming and *samādhi*, 229n59; reciting names of, 128; Sound Observer (Guanshiyin), 62, 126–27, 128, 137
bodies: Dao and, 69; flowing *qi*, 26, 60–61; illnesses caused by contact with pollution, 34–35, 69; inner structure (three primes), 57, 60–61, 65–66, 220n148; metaphors, 26; polluting agents within, 70–73, 74; somatic signs, 113, 115–16; three barriers, 59–60, 221n159. *See also* corpses
Bokenkamp, Stephen R., 210n13, 210n22, 222n181, 222n186, 223n195, 244n109
Boqi, 44, 45, 47, 48
Bourdieu, Pierre, 20
Brahmā Net Sutra (*Fanwang jing*), 114–15
Brown, Peter, 79–80
Buddhism: lists in, 89–90; meditation, 55, 119, 133–37; monks, 78, 236n164; sensation in, 63, 211–12n35, 214n68. *See also* bodhisattva path
bureaucratic metaphor, 26, 27, 45–46, 74, 77–78, 215n74
Burke, Peter, 206n45
Buswell, Robert E., Jr., 230n72
Butler, Judith, 71, 224n208

Carruthers, Mary, 19, 79
Chao Yuanfang, *Origins and Symptoms of Medical Disorders* (*Zhubing yuanhou lun*), 35–36, 107–8
Chart of Auspicious Responses (*Ruiying tu*), 160
Cheang, Alice, 214n65
Chen Shiyuan, *Mengzhan yizhi*, 89
Christianity: medieval monasteries, 79–80, 119–20; Protestantism, 17, 20, 52, 78–79, 205–6n34
cloudsouls (*hun*), 40, 41, 54, 56, 58, 65–66, 71, 74
Cloudy Bookcase with Seven Labels (*Yunji qiqian*), 54, 81–83, 110
Coakley, Sarah, 20
Compendium of Dhāraṇīs (*Tuoluoni jijing*), 48–49, 108, 110–11
Confucius, 28, 122–23, 125, 169, 174–75, 180–81, 237n3
Consecration Sutra (*Guanding jing*), 64
Conze, Edward, 230n77, 232n105
Copp, Paul, 37

corpses (*shi*): as abjects, 71, 224n208; depredations, 52–54, 59, 64; expelling, 27, 52–54, 71–73, 81, 82; sins reported by, 27, 53, 67; three (*san shi*), 52–54, 70–73, 74, 81–82, 222n189
Csikszentmihalyi, Mark, 213n54

Da baoji jing. See *Ratnakūṭa*
Da mingdu jing, 104
Dao'an, 86
Daode jing commentaries, 69–70
Daodi jing, 86–87
Daoism: deities, 148, 149, 150, 156, 157; rituals, 115; secret transmissions of knowledge in lineages, 158–59, 161, 162. *See also* Shangqing (Upper Purity) Daoism
Daoxing banruo jing, 104
Dayal, Har, 212n39
death: awakening analogy, 177–78; pollution related to, 35–36, 38, 39, 58–59, 71
deathbed practice, signs in, 114
Declarations of the Perfected (*Zhen'gao*), 36–37, 58, 144, 146, 148, 211nn31–32
deer-musk incense (*shexiang*), 34, 76, 210n16
defilement. *See* foul dreams; pollution
Deleanu, Florin, 230n77
demons: cultural context, 40; dreams of, 108; exorcisms, 47, 49, 51–52, 75–76; foul dreams caused by, 9, 31, 34, 54–56, 65, 70, 74–75; interference with progress on bodhisattva path, 102; *mo*, 73; names, 47, 52, 67; ordinary, 225n219; pollution from, 35, 39, 40; protection from, 34, 36–37, 54–56, 60, 64; *qi*, 36–37, 68; texts on, 44–48; unbound hair, 46. *See also* Māra
Deneke, Wiebke, 21
Dhāraṇī Sutra in Which the Bodhisattva Akāśagarbha Questions Seven Buddhas (*Xukongzang pusa wen qi fo tuoluoni zhou jing*), 48
Dharmakṣema, 115
Dharmapriya, 104
Dharmarakṣa, 86, 87
diagnostic paradigm: access to inner state of dreamer, 82–84; defined, 9; differences from prospective paradigm, 83–84; interpreting dreams, 112–17, 118–19, 120–21, 184; medical diagnoses based on dreams, 107–8; practical logic, 24; seeking diagnostic dreams, 109–12, 199–201; texts in, 81–83, 84, 118–21. *See also* signs; *Sutra on the Explication of Dreams for Bodhisattvas*
Diény, Jean-Pierre, 170, 248n23
Dili sanmeiye budong zunshengzhe niansong bimi fa, 63
"Discourse on a Dream of the Three Corpses" ("Meng sanshi shuo"), 71
Discussions at the White Tiger Hall (*Baihu tong*), 213n51
divination, 82, 120
Divine Farmer's Classic of Materia Medica (*Shennong bencao jing*), 34, 35
Donner, Neal, 231n80
Douglas, Mary, 39–40
Dousha jing, 87
dream accounts, 50. See also *Records of Master Zhou's Communications with the Unseen World*
dream agents: appearances in dreams, 71, 224n211; within dreamer's body, 65–67, 70–73; infusions or miasmas, 34–36, 43, 70; moral nature, 32; non-personified, 68–70; personified, 70–73, 74–75; *qi* as, 68; *xie*, 68–70. *See also* demons
dream signs. *See* signs
dreambooks, 84, 89, 118, 120, 236n164. See also *Sutra on the Explication of Dreams for Bodhisattvas*
dreams: affordances, 22, 149, 166–67; anomalousness, 1; auspicious, 57, 60, 63, 110, 137, 220n147; cognitive models, 10, 22–24, 23, 58–59, 78; as direct encounters or contacts, 17, 40–42, 124, 127, 145, 146–49, 167, 169; eliciting, 109–12, 199–201; functions for humans, 185–86; karmic effects of deeds done in, 240n50; nightmares, 31–33; not seen as psychological phenomenon, 17, 83, 118, 167; not speaking of, 49–51; practical logic, 5–7, 10, 18, 21–24, 23, 207n51; as private experiences, 17, 18, 79; purifying, 62; sexual, 79–80; similarities to waking visions, 145; underlying logics, 227n27. *See also* foul dreams; interpretation of dreams; self-cultivation, dreaming and
dreamscape, 7–10. *See also* paradigms
Drège, Jean-Pierre, 217n118
Drettas, Dimitri, 217n118
Du Guangting, *Records of Numinous Verifications of Daoism* (*Daojiao lingyan ji*), 129–30, 131–33

Du Yu, *Zuo Tradition* (*Zuo zhuan*) commentary, 32

e, meanings of term, 32–33, 209n1, 223n196
e meng. *See* foul dreams
Ebrey, Patricia Buckley, 213n57
emptiness, 135
esotericizing dynamic, 34, 158–66
esoteric scriptures, 115–16
Essential Prescriptions for Urgent Ills (*Beiji qianjin yaofang*), 38
Essentials of the Practice of Perfection: Protocols of Right Unity (*Zhengyi fawen xiuzhen zhiyao*), 54–55
evil dreams. *See* foul dreams
exorcisms, 44, 45, 47, 48, 49, 51–52, 56, 75–76. *See also* demons; oneiric pollution, expunging
exorcistic paradigm. *See* purification paradigm
Explication of Dreams for Bodhisattvas. See *Sutra on the Explication of Dreams for Bodhisattvas*
Exposition of the Meaning of the Analects (*Lunyu yishu*), 174–75
Eyl, Jennifer, 216n101

Fangguang banruo jing, 104
Fazhong, 42
Fei Changfang, *Record of the Three Treasures through the Generations* (*Lidai sanbao ji*), 86
Foucault, Michel, 21
foul dreams (*e meng*): causes, 9, 34–35, 53–54, 58–59, 65–67; effects on communities, 79–80; effects on self-cultivation, 31, 78; meanings of term, 31–33; pollution from, 40–43, 79–80; preventing, 34, 44, 63–67, 76–77, 221–22n177; purification rituals and, 31, 63–67; remaining silent about, 50; responses, 44, 75–76, 183, 184. *See also* dream agents; oneiric pollution, expunging; purification paradigm

Ge Hong, *Master Who Embraces the Unhewn* (*Baopuzi neipian*), 34, 44, 55–56, 210n16, 246n142
Geaney, Jane, 38
Gethin, Rupert M. L., 89–90
ghosts: as dream agents, 34, 70; dreams of, 108; effects of contacts with, 39, 68–69, 70; protection from, 60; vengeful, 172
Gimello, Robert M., 208n64
Greene, Eric M., 115, 119, 229n60, 231n82, 236n161
Guanzi, 55
gui. *See* demons; ghosts; spirits
Guṇabhadra, 61–62
Guṇavarman, *Upāli Asks about the Method of Bodhisattva Ordination* (*Youboli wen pusa shoujie fa*), 115

habitus, 20, 28
Hadot, Pierre, 21
hair, unbound, 46
Han Zhong, 116
Harbsmeier, Christoph, 33
Harper, Donald, 33, 45, 47–48, 215n78
Harrison, Paul M., 226n19, 240n45
He Dongru, *Menglin xuanjie*, 89
He Wenxing, 142
hearing: in dreams, 90, 96; as source of pollution, 38, 50. *See also* sensation
hermeneutics, 112–17
Huainanzi, 55, 172–73, 175–76, 177, 223n194
Huang Kan, *Exposition of the Meaning of the Analects* (*Lunyu yishu*), 174–75
Huang Tang, *Menglin xuanjie*, 89
"Human Nature Comes via Mandate" ("Xing zi ming chu"), 37
Humphrey, Caroline, 20

illnesses. *See* medicine
incubation, 109–12
incubatory spells, 110–12, 199–201
interpretation of dreams: authorities, 119–20; by communities, 17–19; hermeneutics, 112–17; prospective paradigm, 9, 83–84, 120. *See also* diagnostic paradigm; dreambooks; *Sutra on the Explication of Dreams for Bodhisattvas*

James, William, 17
Japan, pollution concerns in, 77
jataka narratives, 117
Jensen, Christopher Jon, 119–20, 214n71, 227n27, 236n164
Ji Zang, 178
Jianbei yiqie zhide jing, 87
Jianwen, emperor of Jin (Sima Yu), 34, 59, 210n13
Johnson, Mark, 25, 207n51

Kang Mengxiang, 32–33
Karashima Seishi, 233n108

karma, 92, 96, 100–101, 102, 231nn81–82, 240n50
Keizan, 241–42n68
Kim, Jayne Sun, 77
Kristeva, Julia, 71
Kroll, Paul W., 219n141
Kumārajīva, 33, 104, 116, 128, 140, 195

Lady Right Blossom of the Cloudy Copse Palace, 34, 210n12
Laidlaw, James, 20
Lakoff, George, 25, 207n51
Laozi, 129–30, 152, 154, 167
Legge, James, 217–18n120
Lévi, Jean, 33
Lévi-Strauss, Claude, 226n15
Li Chong, 175, 247n16
Liezi, 179–80, 185, 203n8
Listenwissenschaft, 89
lists, in Buddhism, 89–90
Liu Shao, *Treatise on Human Character* (*Renwu zhi*), 116
Lokakṣema, 87, 104, 133, 241n66
long-distance specialists, 151
Lotus Sutra (*Miaofa lianhua jing*): "Chapter on Comfortable Conduct" ("Anle xing pin"), 128, 137–40; reciting, 62, 140, 241n63
Lu Hanzhen, 131
Lu Xiujing, 221n159

Mañjuśrī, 111, 136
Mañjuśrī Parinirvāṇa Sutra (*Wenshushili banniepan jing*), 136
manuscript culture, 11–16
Mao Gu (Lord Certifier of Registers), 146–47, 153, 156, 165, 214n66
Mao Ying (Supervisor of Lifespans), 147–48, 150, 155, 214n66
Mao Zhong (Lord Protector of Lifespans), 41–42, 148, 149, 152, 214n66, 245n122
Māra: distinction from ordinary demons, 225n219; interference with progress on bodhisattva path, 73, 99, 101–2, 231n86; visions caused by, 49; warnings about, 91, 93
Master Who Embraces the Unhewn (*Baopuzi neipian*), 34, 44, 55–56, 210n16, 246n142
Mauss, Marcel, 20
medicine: diagnostic use of dreams, 107–8; illnesses caused by contact with pollution, 34–35, 69. *See also* diagnostic paradigm
meditation: effects on dreams, 133–37; protective goals, 55–56; visions in, 119, 133–36
Mencius, 40
Menglin xuanjie, 89
"Method for Expelling the Three Corpses and Nine Worms, including a Medicinal Formula" ("Chuqu sanshi jiuchong fa bing yaoshu"), 72–73
"Method for Ridding Oneself of the Three Corpses Using Talismans" ("Qu sanshi fufa"), 52–53
mo, 73. *See also* demons
Mohe banruo chao jing, 104
Mohe banruo poluomi jing, 104
Mokṣala, *Fangguang banruo jing*, 104
monks: Buddhist, 78, 236n164; Christian, 79–80, 119–20
music, 38, 50, 213n51
Myōe, 233–34n127, 241–42n68

narrative communities, 128–29
Nattier, Jan, 230n72
New Collection of the Duke of Zhou's Book for Interpreting Dreams (*Xinji Zhougong jiemeng shu*), 50–52
Nie Daozhen: *Mañjuśrī Parinirvāṇa Sutra* (*Wenshushili banniepan jing*), 136; *Zhu pusa qiufo benye jing*, 87
nightmares, 31–33. *See also* foul dreams
non-dreaming of sages, 170–75
Nylan, Michael, 209n10

Oceanic Samādhi Sutra on Visualizing the Buddha (*Guanfo sanmei hai jing*), 95
Oceanic Scripture on the Samādhi of the Contemplation of the Buddha (*Guanfo sanmei hai jing*), 137
oneiric pollution, expunging: combinatory methods, 54–61; on one's own authority, 49–54, 217n110; for others, 61–62; summoning divine aid, 44–49; through dreams, 62. *See also* foul dreams; pollution; purification paradigm
oneiric touching, 40–41
Origins and Symptoms of Medical Disorders (*Zhubing yuanhou lun*), 35–36, 107–8
Orsi, Robert A., 18
Ortner, Sherry B., 124

Palumbo, Antonello, 10–11
paradigms: common features, 169–70, 184; comparisons, 183–85; prospective, 9, 83–84, 120; questions answered, 7–8; visitation, 9, 120, 124. *See also* diagnostic paradigm; purification paradigm; spillover paradigm
Peirce, Charles Sanders, 83
Perfection of Wisdom in 8,000 *Lines* (*Aṣṭasāhasrikā prajñāpāramitā*), 103–4, 240n50, 241n66
Perfection of Wisdom texts (Prajñāpāramitā sutras): comparison of versions, 194–98; diagnostic use of dreams, 103–5; dream signs, 105–7; foul dreams prevented by, 63–64; goals, 232n103; Māra in, 102; spillover paradigm and, 106, 137, 240n50
pollution: agents within bodies, 70–73, 74; avoiding for self-cultivation, 38–39; from blood, 39, 222n180; from childbirth, 39; cultural importance, 39–40, 43, 77–78; from death, 35–36, 38, 39, 58–59, 71; forms, 39–40; of hybrid beings, 70–71; from menstrual blood, 39; metaphorical, 43, 77–78; physical spread, 33–38; preventing transmission, 77–78; through dream contacts, 33, 40–43, 64; through sensory contacts, 33, 37–38, 50, 77–78; through transgressions, 74, 77–78. *See also* foul dreams; oneiric pollution, expunging
practical logic: of diagnostic paradigm, 24; of dreams, 5–7, 10, 18, 21–24, 23, 207n51; of purification paradigm, 23–24, 23, 75–76; of spillover paradigm, 24
Prajñāpāramitā sutras. *See* Perfection of Wisdom texts
Precious Scripture of the Interior Landscape of the Yellow Court (*Huangting neijing yujing*), 60
predictions. *See* prospective paradigm
Prohibitions for Transcendents Recorded by the Perfected, from the Purple Texts Inscribed by Spirits (*Taiwei lingshu ziwen xianji zhenji shangqing*), 73–75
prospective paradigm, 9, 83–84, 120
Protestantism, 17, 20, 52, 78–79, 205–6n34. *See also* Christianity
Protocols of the Twelve Hundred Officers (*Qian er bai guan yi*), 55
purification paradigm: compared to other paradigms, 184; defined, 9, 40; dream models, 58–59, 78; practical logic, 23–24, 23, 75–76; role in self-cultivation, 31, 75, 183, 184; social contexts, 78–80. *See also* foul dreams; pollution
purification rituals, 31, 37, 63–67. *See also* oneiric pollution, expunging
purity, 38–39, 75, 78, 211n32. *See also* pollution
Pusa benye jing, 87
Pusa shizhu xingdao pin, 87

qi: befouling, 34, 35, 77–78; body and self and, 26, 60–61; of demons, 36–37, 68; relationship to foul dreams, 35, 59, 60, 68, 108; *xie qi*, 68–70

Rao Zongyi, 223n195
Ratnakūṭa (*Heap of Jewels; Da baoji jing*), 85–86, 90, 226n19
Record of Buddhist Teachings from the Kaiyuan Era (*Kaiyuan shijiao lu*), 85–86
Record of the Three Treasures through the Generations (*Lidai sanbao ji*), 86
Records concerning Cultivating One's Nature and Lengthening Life (*Yangxing yanming lu*), 50
Records of Master Zhou's Communications with the Unseen World (*Zhoushi mingtong ji*): dream accounts, 141, 142, 143–45, 146–53, 162–65, 184, 243n96, 246–47n144; dreams as training ground, 154–58, 184–85; esotericizing dynamic, 160–66; Liang emperor Wu's response, 160; making of text, 142–45; overview, 140–42; ritual treatment of text, 145–46; Tao's comments, 162, 246–47n144; use of ellipses, 146, 147, 158, 164; waking visions, 144, 145. *See also* Zhou Ziliang
Records of Rites (*Li ji*), 39, 50, 123
Records of Rites of the Elder Dai (*Da Dai liji*), 39
relics, 90, 91, 99, 230n75
religion, experience-based model, 17–18
religious communities, 17–18, 79–80, 119–20
religious experiences, 18, 206n37
repentance and confession rituals, 114–15
Rites of Zhou (*Zhou li*), 209n1
ritualization, 159

rituals: actualizing the three barriers, 34, 59–60; auspicious signs and, 108–9, 114–15; in dreams, 90; dreams following performances, 109, 111; exorcisms, 44, 45, 47, 48, 49, 51–52, 56, 75–76; performances, 28, 52; petitioning Celestial Master, 220n154; preparations, 52, 217–18n120; purification, 31, 37, 63–67
role performances, 27–28
Ruizong, emperor of Tang, 85

sages, sleep without dreaming, 170–75
Sahlins, Marshall, 46–47, 52, 207n51
Saussy, Haun, 14
Schleiermacher, Friedrich, 17
Schmid, David Neil, 22
Schopen, Gregory, 229n63
Script Explained and Graphs Explicated (*Shuowen jiezi*), 32, 51–52
Scripture of the Forty-Four Methods on Yellow Silk (*Shangqing taishang huangsu sishisi fang jing*), 110
Scripture of the Wondrous Essence of the Eight Thearchs (*Dongshen badi miaojing jing*), 109–10
Scripture of the Yellow Court (*Huangting jing*), 60
Scripture on Divining Requital for Good and Evil Deeds (*Zhancha shan'e yebao jing*), 116–17
Scripture on Great Peace (*Taiping jing*), 36, 55, 68–69, 219n137
Scripture on the Contemplation of the Bodhisattva Ākāśagarbha (*Guan Xukongzang pusa jing*), 137
Searle, J. R., 233n113
secrecy. *See* esotericizing dynamic
self-cultivation: canons of practice, 19–21, 28, 29, 183, 184–85; common experiences, 118–19; by Confucius, 122–23; defined, 16–17; discipline in, 1–4, 11–12, 19–21; emic analogues, 24–25; metaphors, 24–27, 175–78; obstacles, 117; as path or road (*dao*), 25; practitioners, 1, 13, 15–16, 28–29, 118–19; purity/pollution rules, 38–40; ritual performances, 28; role performances, 27–28; soteriological goals, 11, 16–17. *See also* bodhisattva path; texts
self-cultivation, dreaming and: connections to waking life, 169–70; contradictions, 5; contrast between dreaming and waking, 170, 175–78, 179–82; dream signs related to self-cultivation, 83–84; effects of foul dreams, 31, 78; importance, 183; not dreaming as sign of attainment, 170–75; signs of soteriological status, 112–14, 115–18. *See also* diagnostic paradigm; dreams; paradigms; purification paradigm; spillover paradigm
self-ordination rituals, 114–15
semiotics, 83
sensation: in Buddhism, 63, 211–12n35, 214n68; in dreams, 90, 96; entry to body through, 26; hearing, 38, 50, 90, 96; smell, 211–12n35, 212n41, 214n68; transmission of substances by, 37–38; vision, 90
sexual dreams, in medieval Christian monasteries, 79–80
Shandao, 36
Shangqing (Upper Purity) Daoism: deities, 34, 36, 41–42, 141, 147–48, 210n12, 214n66; heavens, 61, 147, 148–49; rules for practitioners, 73–74, 220n153; scriptures, 64–67, 73–75, 110, 145, 146; secrets, 34, 159, 161, 162; view of human body, 60–61. *See also* Daoism; *Records of Master Zhou's Communications with the Unseen World*
Sharf, Robert H., 18, 206n35, 206n37
Shen Yue, 117
Shuihudi daybooks, 44, 45, 46–48
sight. *See* sensation; vision
signs, in semiotics, 83
signs (*xiang*): dream, 83–84, 88, 107–9, 118–20; of progress on bodhisattva path, 113–17; somatic, 113, 115–16; standardization, 118–19. See also *Sutra on the Explication of Dreams for Bodhisattvas*
Sima Yu (Jin emperor Jianwen), 34, 59, 210n13
Slingerland, Edward, 122–23, 205n34
Smith, Jonathan Z., 6, 7, 40
Song Yanhua, 71
soteriological goals, 11, 16–17
sound: hearing in dreams, 90, 96; polluting, 38, 50. *See also* sensation
Sound Observer (Guanshiyin), 62, 126–27, 128, 137
speech, pollution through, 50
spillover paradigm: attractiveness, 166–68; compared to other paradigms, 184–85; components, 124; defined, 9–10; dreams as events, 124, 127, 132,

148, 167–68, 238n10; dreams as portals, 123, 124, 166–67; dreams as training ground, 154–58, 167; dreams related to waking concerns, 153, 158; effects of dreams in real life, 127, 128, 132, 184–85; encounters in dreams, 124, 127, 145, 146–49, 167; esotericizing dynamic and, 158–66; narratives preserved in texts, 128–33; in Perfection of Wisdom texts, 106, 137; performances in dreams, 167–68; practical logic, 24; relations between waking self-cultivation pursuits and dreams, 124, 125–28, 133–40, 148, 166–68, 183–85; stimulus and response and, 125–33. See also *Records of Master Zhou's Communications with the Unseen World*

spirits (*jing*): amorous encounters with, 76; Boqi, 44, 45, 47, 48; effects of contacts with, 35, 68–69, 70. *See also* dream agents; ghosts

Stevenson, Daniel B., 231n80

stimulus and response (*ganying*), 124–33

Strickmann, Michel, 141, 199–200, 203n9

Sun Simo, *Essential Prescriptions for Urgent Ills* (*Beiji qianjin yaofang*), 38

Supreme Scripture of Purple Texts Inscribed by the Spirits (*Huangtian shangqing jingque dijun lingshu ziwen*), 64–67

Sutra of Spells of the Great Peacock Queen (*Da kongque zhou wang jing*), 111

Sutra of the Divinely Transforming Mantras of [the Bodhisattva] Sound Observer of the Unfailing Net (*Bukong juansuo shenbian zhenyan jing*), 137

Sutra on Achieving the Bright Light Concentration (*Chengju guangming sanmeijing*), 33

Sutra on Meditation on the Buddhas of the Present (*Banzhou sanmei jing / Pratyutpanna samādhi sutra*), 133–36

Sutra on the Explication of Dreams for Bodhisattvas (*Pusa shuomeng jing*): bodhisattva path stages, 87, 92–93; conclusion (part 4), 88–89; diagnoses and prescriptions (part 3), 86, 90, 91–96, 97–98, 99–100, 103, 107; as dreambook, 83–84, 89, 118; etiologies of obstacles, 99–102; initial dream signs list (part 2), 86, 87, 88, 89–91, 184, 187–93; problems with text, 87–88, 227–28nn34–35; setting of scene (part 1), 88; structure, 86, 88; textual history, 85–86

Sutra on the Four Celestial Kings (*Si tianwang jing*), 64

Svapnanirdeśa, 85

Taishō shinshu daizōkyō, 87

Tao Hongjing: *Declarations of the Perfected* (*Zhen'gao*), 36–37, 58, 144, 146, 148, 211nn31–32; Emperor Wu and, 141, 160–61; life of, 246n130; Zhou Ziliang as disciple, 141–42. See also *Records of Master Zhou's Communications with the Unseen World*

Tao Kedou, 58, 172

texts: audiences, 15–16; authorship, 12–13, 143; buried in tombs, 215–16n87; canonical, 14; factors in preservation, 14–16, 128–29; manuscripts, 11–16; prescriptive, 11–12, 72; production and transmission, 12–16; readers' engagement with, 14; rhetorical reading, 15; on self-cultivation, 1–4, 12–16; social embeddedness, 12–16, 128–29; use as sources, 10–11, 16, 21

Thote, Alain, 215–16n87

Three Dongshen Registers of Red Writs of the Most High (*Taishang chiwen dongshen sanlu*), 199–201

travel: in dreams, 149–51, 243n96; long-distance specialists, 151

Treatise on the Great Perfection of Wisdom (*Da zhidu lun*), 33, 104, 195

truth acts, 107

Upāli Asks about the Method of Bodhisattva Ordination (*Youboli wen pusa shoujie fa*), 115

Upper Purity Daoism. *See* Shangqing Daoism

Urban, Hugh, 159

Vaipulya Dhāraṇī Sutra (*Da fangdeng tuoluoni jing*), 42–43, 111–12

Verellen, Franciscus, 69

vision, in dreams, 90. *See also* sensation

visions, 49, 119, 133–36, 144, 145

visitation paradigm, 9, 120, 124, 132

waking experiences: truth acts, 107; visions, 49, 119, 133–36, 144, 145. *See also* awakening; self-cultivation; spillover paradigm

Wang Jiakui, 143, 244nn101–2, 244n111
Wang Sengqian, 154
Wang Yan, *Records of Signs from the Unseen Realm* (*Mingxiang ji*), 125–29
Wang Yanshou, "Rhapsody on Dreams" ("Meng fu"), 49
Wen, emperor of Song, 61
White Marsh Diagrams of Spectral Prodigies (*Baize jingguai tu*), 44–48
whitesouls (*po*), 40, 41, 54, 56, 58, 65–67, 71, 74, 75
women: childbirth, 38, 39; menstrual blood, 39; pregnant, 38
worms: as abjects, 71, 224n208; Buddhist view of, 224n214; corpses and, 67, 81–82; expelling, 72; nine, 52–53, 70–71; three (*san chong*), 34, 60, 70–71
Wu, emperor of Liang, 141, 143, 160–61, 244n111

Xiang'er zhu, 69–70
Xiao Yan. *See* Wu, emperor of Liang
Xiaopin banruo poluomi jing, 104
xie, meanings of, 68–70. *See also* dream agents
Xiuxing daoji jing, 87
Xu Hui, 41–42
Xu Lian, 41–42
Xu Mi, 41, 58–59
Xu Shen, *Script Explained and Graphs Explicated* (*Shuowen jiezi*), 32, 51–52
Xuanzang, 85, 112–13, 211–12n35
Xunzi, 38, 39, 40, 50, 173–74

Yang Bojun, 33
Yang Xi, 34, 41, 56, 58, 59–60, 141, 147, 148
Yates, Robin D. S., 212n47, 213–14n57
Yellow Thearch's Classic on the Numinous Pivot, The (*Huangdi neijing lingshu*), 107
Yijing, *Sutra of Spells of the Great Peacock Queen* (*Da kongque zhou wang jing*), 111, 233–34n127
Yu Fakai, 178

Zhang Fengyi, *Mengzhan leikao*, 89
Zhang Junfang, *Cloudy Bookcase with Seven Labels* (*Yunji qiqian*), 54, 81–83, 110
Zhang Renbiao, 131–32
Zhang Rong, 131, 132
Zhao Weibo, 245n122
Zheng Binglin, 217n118
Zheng Xuan, 209n1
Zhi Qian: *Da mingdu jing*, 104; *Pusa benye jing*, 87
Zhisheng, *Record of Buddhist Teachings from the Kaiyuan Era* (*Kaiyuan shijiao lu*), 85–86
Zhiyi, 102, 108, 115, 225n219
Zhonghua dazang jing, 87
Zhongzong, emperor of Tang, 85
Zhou Ziliang: death, 141, 142, 153, 161, 165–66, 242n72; family, 141–42, 151–52, 158, 161–62; life of, 141–42, 160; records of visions and dreams, 141, 142, 143–45, 146–49, 162–65, 184, 246–47n144. See also *Records of Master Zhou's Communications with the Unseen World*
Zhou Ziyang, 154
Zhu Fayi, 62
Zhu Fonian, 104
Zhuangzi: butterfly dream, 181–82; on death, 177–78; on differences between dreaming and waking, 180–82; on dreams, 185; on fish traps and rabbit snares, 186; on meditation, 55; metaphors, 25, 177–78; on non-dreaming of sages, 171–72, 173; perfected persons, 28; *Qiwu lun* chapter, 40; on transformation, 176; on wandering, 185

Harvard-Yenching Institute Monograph Series (titles now in print)

24. *Population, Disease, and Land in Early Japan, 645–900*, by William Wayne Farris
25. *Shikitei Sanba and the Comic Tradition in Edo Fiction*, by Robert W. Leutner
26. *Washing Silk: The Life and Selected Poetry of Wei Chuang (834?–910)*, by Robin D. S. Yates
28. *Tang Transformation Texts: A Study of the Buddhist Contribution to the Rise of Vernacular Fiction and Drama in China*, by Victor H. Mair
30. *Readings in Chinese Literary Thought*, by Stephen Owen
31. *Remembering Paradise: Nativism and Nostalgia in Eighteenth-Century Japan*, by Peter Nosco
33. *Escape from the Wasteland: Romanticism and Realism in the Fiction of Mishima Yukio and Oe Kenzaburo*, by Susan Jolliffe Napier
34. *Inside a Service Trade: Studies in Contemporary Chinese Prose*, by Rudolf G. Wagner
35. *The Willow in Autumn: Ryutei Tanehiko, 1783–1842*, by Andrew Lawrence Markus
36. *The Confucian Transformation of Korea: A Study of Society and Ideology*, by Martina Deuchler
37. *The Korean Singer of Tales*, by Marshall R. Pihl
38. *Praying for Power: Buddhism and the Formation of Gentry Society in Late-Ming China*, by Timothy Brook
39. *Word, Image, and Deed in the Life of Su Shi*, by Ronald C. Egan
41. *Studies in the Comic Spirit in Modern Japanese Fiction*, by Joel R. Cohn
42. *Wind Against the Mountain: The Crisis of Politics and Culture in Thirteenth-Century China*, by Richard L. Davis
43. *Powerful Relations: Kinship, Status, and the State in Sung China (960–1279)*, by Beverly Bossler
44. *Limited Views: Essays on Ideas and Letters*, by Qian Zhongshu; selected and translated by Ronald Egan
45. *Sugar and Society in China: Peasants, Technology, and the World Market*, by Sucheta Mazumdar
49. *Precious Volumes: An Introduction to Chinese Sectarian Scriptures from the Sixteenth and Seventeenth Centuries*, by Daniel L. Overmyer
50. *Poetry and Painting in Song China: The Subtle Art of Dissent*, by Alfreda Murck
51. *Evil and/or/as the Good: Omnicentrism, Intersubjectivity, and Value Paradox in Tiantai Buddhist Thought*, by Brook Ziporyn

53. *Articulated Ladies: Gender and the Male Community in Early Chinese Texts*, by Paul Rouzer
55. *Allegories of Desire: Esoteric Literary Commentaries of Medieval Japan*, by Susan Blakeley Klein
56. *Printing for Profit: The Commercial Publishers of Jianyang, Fujian (11th –17th Centuries)*, by Lucille Chia
57. *To Become a God: Cosmology, Sacrifice, and Self-Divinization in Early China*, by Michael J. Puett
58. *Writing and Materiality in China: Essays in Honor of Patrick Hanan*, edited by Judith T. Zeitlin and Lydia H. Liu
59. Rulin waishi *and Cultural Transformation in Late Imperial China*, by Shang Wei
60. *Words Well Put: Visions of Poetic Competence in the Chinese Tradition*, by Graham Sanders
61. *Householders: The Reizei Family in Japanese History*, by Steven D. Carter
62. *The Divine Nature of Power: Chinese Ritual Architecture at the Sacred Site of Jinci*, by Tracy Miller
63. *Beacon Fire and Shooting Star: The Literary Culture of the Liang (502–557)*, by Xiaofei Tian
64. *Lost Soul: "Confucianism" in Contemporary Chinese Academic Discourse*, by John Makeham
65. *The Sage Learning of Liu Zhi: Islamic Thought in Confucian Terms*, by Sachiko Murata, William C. Chittick, and Tu Weiming
66. *Through a Forest of Chancellors: Fugitive Histories in Liu Yuan's* Lingyan ge, *an Illustrated Book from Seventeenth-Century Suzhou*, by Anne Burkus-Chasson
67. *Empire of Texts in Motion: Chinese, Korean, and Taiwanese Transculturations of Japanese Literature*, by Karen Laura Thornber
68. *Empire's Twilight: Northeast Asia Under the Mongols*, by David M. Robinson
69. *Ancestors, Virgins, and Friars: Christianity as a Local Religion in Late Imperial China*, by Eugenio Menegon
70. *Manifest in Words, Written on Paper: Producing and Circulating Poetry in Tang Dynasty China*, by Christopher M. B. Nugent
71. *The Poetics of Sovereignty: On Emperor Taizong of the Tang Dynasty*, by Jack W. Chen
72. *Ancestral Memory in Early China*, by K. E. Brashier
73. *'Dividing the Realm in Order to Govern': The Spatial Organization of the Song State*, by Ruth Mostern
74. *The Dynamics of Masters Literature: Early Chinese Thought from Confucius to Han Feizi*, by Wiebke Denecke
75. *Songs of Contentment and Transgression: Discharged Officials and Literati Communities in Sixteenth-Century North China*, by Tian Yuan Tan
76. *Ten Thousand Scrolls: Reading and Writing in the Poetics of Huang Tingjian and the Late Northern Song*, by Yugen Wang
77. *A Northern Alternative: Xue Xuan (1389–1464) and the Hedong School*, by Khee Heong Koh
78. *Visionary Journeys: Travel Writings from Early Medieval and Nineteenth-Century China*, by Xiaofei Tian

79. *Making Personas: Transnational Film Stardom in Modern Japan*, by Hideaki Fujiki
80. *Strange Eventful Histories: Identity, Performance, and Xu Wei's* Four Cries of a Gibbon, by Shiamin Kwa
81. *Critics and Commentators: The* Book of Poems *as Classic and Literature*, by Bruce Rusk
82. *Home and the World: Editing the Glorious Ming in Woodblock-Printed Books of the Sixteenth and Seventeenth Centuries*, by Yuming He
83. *Courtesans, Concubines, and the Cult of Female Fidelity*, by Beverly Bossler
84. *Chinese History: A New Manual, Third Edition*, by Endymion Wilkinson
85. *A Comprehensive Manchu-English Dictionary*, by Jerry Norman
86. *Drifting among Rivers and Lakes: Southern Song Dynasty Poetry and the Problem of Literary History*, by Michael Fuller
87. *Martial Spectacles of the Ming Court*, by David M. Robinson
88. *Modern Archaics: Continuity and Innovation in the Chinese Lyric Tradition, 1900–1937*, by Shengqing Wu
89. *Cherishing Antiquity: The Cultural Construction of an Ancient Chinese Kingdom*, by Olivia Milburn
90. *The Burden of Female Talent: The Poet Li Qingzhao and Her History in China*, by Ronald Egan
91. *Public Memory in Early China*, by K. E. Brashier
92. *Women and National Trauma in Late Imperial Chinese Literature*, by Wai-yee Li
93. *The Destruction of the Medieval Chinese Aristocracy*, by Nicolas Tackett
94. *Savage Exchange: Han Imperialism, Chinese Literary Style, and the Economic Imagination*, by Tamara T. Chin
95. *Shifting Stories: History, Gossip, and Lore in Narratives from Tang Dynasty China*, by Sarah M. Allen
96. *One Who Knows Me: Friendship and Literary Culture in Mid-Tang China*, by Anna Shields
97. *Materializing Magic Power: Chinese Popular Religion in Villages and Cities*, by Wei-Ping Lin
98. *Traces of Grand Peace: Classics and State Activism in Imperial China*, by Jaeyoon Song
99. *Fiction's Family: Zhan Xi, Zhan Kai, and the Business of Women in Late-Qing China*, by Ellen Widmer
100. *Chinese History: A New Manual, Fourth Edition*, by Endymion Wilkinson
101. *After the Prosperous Age: State and Elites in Early Nineteenth-Century Suzhou*, by Seunghyun Han
102. *Celestial Masters: History and Ritual in Early Daoist Communities*, by Terry F. Kleeman
103. *Transgressive Typologies: Constructions of Gender and Power in Early Tang China*, by Rebecca Doran
104. *Li Mengyang, the North-South Divide, and Literati Learning in Ming China*, by Chang Woei Ong
105. *Bannermen Tales (Zidishu): Manchu Storytelling and Cultural Hybridity in the Qing Dynasty*, by Elena Suet-Ying Chiu

106. *Upriver Journeys: Diaspora and Empire in Southern China, 1570–1850*, by Steven B. Miles
107. *Ancestors, Kings, and the Dao*, by Constance A. Cook
108. *The Halberd at Red Cliff: Jian'an and the Three Kingdoms*, by Xiaofei Tian
109. *Speaking of Profit: Bao Shichen and Reform in Nineteenth-Century China*, by William T. Rowe
110. *Building for Oil: Daqing and the Formation of the Chinese Socialist State*, by Hou Li
111. *Reading Philosophy, Writing Poetry: Intertextual Modes of Making Meaning in Early Medieval China*, by Wendy Swartz
112. *Writing for Print: Publishing and the Making of Textual Authority in Late Imperial China*, by Suyoung Son
113. *Shen Gua's Empiricism*, by Ya Zuo
114. *Just a Song: Chinese Lyrics from the Eleventh and Early Twelfth Centuries*, by Stephen Owen
115. *Shrines to Living Men in the Ming Political Cosmos*, by Sarah Schneewind
116. *In the Wake of the Mongols: The Making of a New Social Order in North China, 1200–1600*, by Jinping Wang
117. *Opera, Society, and Politics in Modern China*, by Hsiao-t'i Li
118. *Imperiled Destinies: The Daoist Quest for Deliverance in Medieval China*, by Franciscus Verellen
119. *Ethnic Chrysalis: China's Orochen People and the Legacy of Qing Borderland Administration*, by Loretta Kim
120. *The Paradox of Being: Truth, Identity, and Images in Daoism*, by Poul Andersen
121. *Feeling the Past in Seventeenth-Century China*, by Xiaoqiao Ling
122. *The Chinese Dreamscape, 300 BCE–800 CE*, by Robert Ford Campany
123. *Structures of the Earth: Metageographies of Early Medieval China*, by D. Jonathan Felt
124. *Anecdote, Network, Gossip, Performance: Essays on the* Shishuo xinyu, by Jack W. Chen
125. *Testing the Literary: Prose and the Aesthetic in Early Modern China*, by Alexander Des Forges
126. *Du Fu Transforms: Tradition and Ethics amid Societal Collapse*, by Lucas Rambo Bender
127. *Chinese History: A New Manual (Enlarged Sixth Edition)*, Vol. 1, by Endymion Wilkinson
128. *Chinese History: A New Manual (Enlarged Sixth Edition)*, Vol. 2, by Endymion Wilkinson
129. *Wang Anshi and Song Poetic Culture*, by Xiaoshan Yang
130. *Localizing Learning: The Literati Enterprise in Wuzhou, 1100–1600*, by Peter K. Bol
131. *Making the Gods Speak: The Ritual Production of Revelation in Chinese Religious History*, by Vincent Goossaert
132. *Lineages Embedded in Temple Networks: Daoism and Local Society in Ming China*, by Richard G. Wang
133. *Rival Partners: How Taiwanese Entrepreneurs and Guangdong Officials Forged the China Development Model*, by Wu Jieh-min; translated by Stacy Mosher

134. *Saying All That Can Be Said: The Art of Describing Sex in* Jin Ping Mei, by Keith McMahon
135. *Genealogy and Status: Hereditary Office Holding and Kinship in North China under Mongol Rule*, by Tomoyasu Iiyama
136. *The Threshold: The Rhetoric of Historiography in Early Medieval China*, by Zeb Raft
137. *Literary History in and beyond China: Reading Text and World*, edited by Sarah M. Allen, Jack W. Chen, and Xiaofei Tian
138. *Dreaming and Self-Cultivation in China, 300 BCE–800 CE*, by Robert Ford Campany